Sociology and Health Care

AN INTRODUCTION FOR NURSES AND OTHER HEALTH CARE PROFESSIONALS

John Bond BA
Lecturer in Sociology, Health Care Research Unit,
The University of Newcastle upon Tyne

Senga Bond BA MSc PhD RGN FRCN
Lecturer in Nursing Research, Health Care Research Unit,
The University of Newcastle upon Tyne

CHURCHILL LIVINGSTONE
EDINBURGH LONDON MELBOURNE AND NEW YORK 1986

CHURCHILL LIVINGSTONE
Medical Division of Longman Group UK Limited

Distributed in the United States of America by
Churchill Livingstone Inc., 1560 Broadway, New York,
N.Y. 10036, and by associated companies, branches and
representatives throughout the world.

First published 1986
    Reprinted 1988
    Reprinted 1989

ISBN 0 443 02592 4

British Library Cataloguing in Publication Data
Bond, John
    Sociology and health care: an introduction for nurses
    and other health care professionals.
    1. Social medicine
    I. Title   II. Bond, Senga
    362.1'042   RA418

Library of Congress Cataloging in Publication Data
Bond, John.
    Sociology and health care.
    Includes index.
    1. Nursing — Social aspects. 2. Social medicine.
3. Sociology. I. Bond, Senga. II. Title. |DNLM:
1. Delivery of Health Care — nurses' instruction.
2. Sociology — nurses' instruction. 3. Sociology,
Medical — nurses' instruction. W 84.1 B711s|
RT86.5.B66   1986   610.73   85–7726

Produced by Longman Singapore Publishers (PTE) Ltd.
Printed in Singapore

Acknowledgements

We are grateful to the following for permission to reproduce copyright material: the author W. Wallace and Aldine Publishing Co. for Figure 12.1; the authors E. C. Cuff and G. C. F. Payne and George Allen and Unwin Ltd for Figure 2.1; the author R. Dingwall and Basil Blackwell for Figure 8.4; the authors G. W. Brown, J. L. T. Birley and J. K. Wing and *The British Journal of Psychiatry* for Figure 6.1; the Controller of Her Majesty's Stationery Office for Table 3.6; the author J. M. Atkinson and Macmillan Ltd for Table 12.1; the author P. Armitage and *Nursing Times* for Table 7.1; the author W. Worsley and Penguin Books Ltd for Figure 5.1; the authors R. Dingwall and T. Murray and *The Sociology of Health and Illness* for Figure 9.1; the authors E. J. Miller and G. V. Gwynne and Tavistock Publications for Figure 7.3.

We are also grateful to the following for permission to reproduce photographic material: Derek Bayes and Dame Cicely Saunders; BBC Hulton Picture Library; Calderstones Hospital; City and Hackney Community Health Council; Department of Occupational Health, University of Newcastle upon Tyne; Hexham Courant; Nursing Mirror; Nursing Standard; Nursing Times; University of Chicago Library.

Contents

Introduction

We have written this book to provide an introduction to sociology, particularly sociology relevant to health and illness, for members of the health care professions. Its intention is to develop a sociological awareness which will assist health professionals to understand the social basis of much of their work and to use sociology to ask appropriate questions, consider relevant factors and provide workable solutions to some of their problems. Because a number of texts already exist which are devoted to medical sociology or written with a bias towards doctors we have written for a readership we regard as principally nurses, midwives, health visitors and remedial therapists, although some of the material has been used to teach doctors.

The approach we have taken differs from that of texts which already exist to serve this readership, and we have tried to go beyond them to provide a grounding in the mainstream of sociological theory, albeit still at an introductory level.

Sociology is included in the curriculum of most health professionals. As long ago as 1968 the Royal Commission on Medical Education recommended that all medical students should pursue studies of sociology. Since then it has been included in the curriculum of other health professionals, though with varying degrees of explicitness. This has allowed sociology to be taught as just 'common sense'. One of the purposes of this book is to demonstrate that sociology is more than just 'common sense' and provide some ideas about how the subject matter may be taught.

While meeting curriculum requirements is important, we feel that there are more fundamental reasons for health professionals acquiring some knowledge of sociology. Of particular importance is gaining an understanding of the social changes taking place — for example in the age structure, marriage patterns, the types of illness being treated, patient expectations, the organisation and structure of professions — all of which have implications for the work of health professionals. We recognise the relevance of broad social changes and changes more directly relevant to health and illness but it is also important to consider why other social features, such as the structure of British society, are relatively enduring, and to consider their implications for health.

Because the delivery of health care is essentially a social activity, gaining an understanding of the social processes involved should prove useful in caring for patients and their families. This is equally relevant for social interaction with colleagues, supervisors and subordinates, and all of those with whom health professionals deal in the course of their work. A sociological understanding should help us to appreciate why people indulge in particular behaviour or take particular decisions, and why differences exist between individuals and groups in relation to health and illness.

In writing this book we have tried to avoid an over-simplistic approach while recognising that some readers will be coming to sociology for the first time. We assume that readers will be critical, generally interested in society and in examining it from a number of perspectives. We have therefore introduced a range of sociological perspectives which necessitate asking different questions about the social world and include some of the debates which exist between those favouring one approach or another. We have tried to be eclectic but inevitably personal biases are evident.

We have also attempted to take account of readers' likely knowledge and interests, using examples which will be familiar to some and giving them less explicit definition than would be required by a lay readership. British sources are drawn on heavily since this is the system of state health provision with which the majority of readers are likely to be familiar. Many issues, however, are of international significance; sometimes no British work is available to illustrate a point and, because American theorists are currently so influential in medical and mainstream sociology, we have referred to many of their studies.

We have selected issues which we consider are of concern to health professionals generally. Inevitably personal interests also influence selection and emphasis. The authors are: a sociologist working in health care research with a bias toward structuralist sociology (JB); and a nurse with a background in psychology but with leanings toward interactionist sociology (SB). This may help explain the emphasis given to social structure and the heavy use of nursing sources with a whole chapter devoted to death, dying and bereavement. We have taken account of comments from other sociologists and health professionals and we have attempted to provide a balanced set of chapters while introducing such topical issues as unemployment and health, and managerialism in nursing.

The book is divided into 13 chapters, the first of which constitutes an introduction to the subject and points out some of the distinctive features of sociology as an autonomous and vital discipline within the social sciences, and how it is relevant to health care.

The idea of different perspectives in sociology is taken up in Chapter 2. We identify some major theories and concepts used in different interpretations of society. The idea that there exist a variety of sociological perspectives is carried forward throughout the book and we demonstrate how they have contributed in relevant ways to identifying problems in the health field, adding to our understanding of them and offering solutions for them.

Chapter 3 focuses on a major aspect of social structure, namely social stratification and the concepts of class, status and power. The chapter reviews briefly inequalities in the health status of different social groups and presents some of the competing explanations of inequalities in health.

Chapter 4 expands on some of the themes introduced in Chapter 3 by exploring social influences on health and the role of prevention. It examines broad structural influences in society on health and illness, using the example of the production and consumption of food, and describes a social model of the causes of illness.

Chapter 5 introduces the concept of the life career and focuses on the nature of the family in different cultures and sub-cultures. It discusses the functions of the family in modern Britain. In Chapter 6 the role of the family in the maintenance of health and at times of illness is discussed. A review of family care and community care is provided.

Chapter 7 focuses on the concepts of institution and organisation by examining the structure of and behaviour in health care organisations. It explores competing approaches to the study of organisations, highlighting the strengths and weaknesses of each for the study of health care organisations.

Chapter 8 is concerned with the patient career and introduces the concepts of deviance and labelling. The processes experienced by people when becoming patients are discussed. The medical model of disease and the social model of illness are described and two models of illness behaviour are explored.

Chapter 9 focuses on interaction between health professionals and their clients. It draws on some ideas introduced in Chapter 7 on role and negotiation and in Chapter 8 on the patient career. The important idea that professionals respond to patients as a limited number of types is developed and the chapter concludes by considering interaction in relation to the management of pain.

This is followed, in Chapter 10, by sociological aspects of death, dying and bereavement. This topic has only recently achieved prominence in the education of health professionals and the sociological literature remains relatively sparse. We give attention to definitions of dying and to social processes which surround death, particularly in institutions. As a case example we focus on miscarriage, stillbirth, and perinatal death.

In Chapter 11 we turn our attention to the professional career, with an emphasis on how lay persons are socialised through their formal and informal education to become professionals. How different sociological perspectives deal with the theme of professional socialisation is discussed. We conclude the chapter with an examination of the relationship between gender and profession.

Our penultimate chapter revives the theme of sociological perspectives. Chapter 12 is devoted to an examination of methods of sociological research and presents this in relation to perspectives and the knowledge base of sociology. Research on suicide is used as a means of demonstrating that different perspectives raise different kinds of sociological questions and finding answers to these questions is done in different ways. We advocate a position of methodological pluralism.

Finally we provide an overview of the contribution we think that sociology can make to health professionals as they go about their work and, more generally, to society. To this end we appeal to ways of using and producing sociological knowledge in the field of health care.

Every chapter stands on its own but it is important to grasp the major ideas of different sociological perspectives outlined in Chapter 2 in order to appreciate fully subsequent chapters. Major concepts are introduced at the first most appropriate place throughout the book. It is logical therefore to read from the beginning. A glossary is provided to assist the understanding of unfamiliar sociological concepts.

We are aware of the offence caused to some people by the sexist nature of the English language. When the book was first drafted we attempted to use male and female pronouns in alternate chapters when the gender of the referent was not relevant. This proved too confusing and so we have had to revert to using, where possible, plurals and non-gender words. We have, however, tended to refer to female health professionals since he/she, or worse (s)he, is cumbersome.

The preparation of this book was greatly assisted by the help we received from a number of people, in particular the painstaking comments made on an early draft by Malcolm Colledge, Helen Evers, Eileen Fairhurst, Marion Ferguson, David O'Brien, Rex Taylor and Jean Walker. We have drawn extensively on the work of some authors; notably Berger & Berger whose approach to writing an introductory text influenced our style, Cuff & Payne whose work influenced Chapter 2 and Dingwall & Lewis whose reader on the sociology of the professions made a timely arrival when Chapter 11 was being rewritten.

Rik Walton of Newcastle Polytechnic took many of the photographs for us and Margaret Derby, Malcolm Sellers and Graham Walton proved to be effective librarians. We would particularly like to thank Eva Brown who typed and retyped the manuscript and Joyce Crawley who assisted in preparing the references.

We have found writing this book an arduous task but we, and our students, have gained enormously from the labour. Its eventual appearance is in no small way due to the patience of our publishers.

Newcastle upon Tyne, 1986 J.B.
S.B.

A sociological understanding
Sociology on offer
A sociological alternative

1

Sociology and health care

Sociology is a relatively recent addition to the syllabuses of health care professionals; yet the interrelationship between sociology and health is not new. Indeed the very early social surveys by Rowntree (1901) and Booth (1892, 1894) showed that ill-health was related to poverty and one of the early classic works in sociology took suicide as its subject (Durkheim, 1897). As our views about the nature of health and health care evolve, so the range of subjects regarded as relevant increases. This expansion means that more and more subjects are included in professional education, each competing for time in the curriculum. Sociology is one such subject.

To some the inclusion of sociology is regarded as unnecessary because it is nothing more than 'common sense'. That some people view sociology in this way is not surprising given that sociology is the study of society and all of us know a great deal about the society in which we live and work. It is by virtue of our being social animals that we give particular meanings to everything and everyone we experience. Long before we understand the word 'sociology' we are already taking for granted much of what are the central concerns of sociology. It is this early introduction to some of the subject matter which makes sociology appear to be nothing more than 'common sense'. In writing this book we believe and will try to

1

show that sociology is more than common sense. It is a particular way of interpreting the world. We also believe that an understanding of sociology is fundamental to a deeper understanding of the society in which we live and this is an important feature of professional knowledge. What, then, is sociology?

A SOCIOLOGICAL UNDERSTANDING

Often introductory text books in sociology begin by posing the question 'What is sociology?'. This can be answered in a number of different ways. One is to say what sociology is not.

Sometimes it is confused with social work. But social work is not sociology although, like other caring professionals, social workers may use the findings of sociological studies to help them understand aspects of their work. Social work offers a practical approach to the solution of social problems. This is not to say that social problems do not interest sociologists, for they do. However, sociology is *not only* about social problems.

It is our view that sociology is about *understanding* the social world by examining it from *particular perspectives*. By focusing on the social world we distinguish it from the personal or private world of each of us; between what C. Wright Mills calls society's *public issues* and individuals' *private troubles*. Private troubles occur within an individual's experience, resulting from his own personal characteristics or from his relationships with others. Public issues, on the other hand, transcend the experiences of a single individual. They are concerned with the ways in which individuals' experiences overlap to form some wider fabric of social organisation (Mills, 1970).

Let us consider a female student nurse on these terms. During her initial education a student nurse will experience a number of troubles. Examples of such troubles, which are sufficiently important to prompt individual nurses to leave nursing, may be poor staff relations, late notification of offduty, absence of ward teaching, lack of someone to talk to, being physically tired out, having to do night duty (Birch, 1975). By attending to the problems of an individual nurse some successful solution may be found for her. However, in a school where one in three learners do not complete their training this represents a public issue where solutions are found not so much in the characteristics of the individual student nurses but in the structure and functioning of the organisation, be it the school or the clinical setting where students receive their education. Effective actions to remedy the situation are likely to be oriented toward the institution and its organisation rather than individual student nurses. It is to public issues or social issues that sociologists turn their attention.

Sociology and other social sciences

If sociology is about social issues how then does a *sociological* understanding differ from that provided by the other social sciences? All social sciences—sociology, psychology, anthropology, economics, politics, history—are concerned with human action or behaviour, but they differ in the particular attributes of behaviour they study. Consider the Stock Exchange as an example. In everyday life the Stock Exchange may not be particularly important to you. Yet, like events in Parliament and Prime Minister's Question Time, the daily financial report on Radio 4 is a British institution. Whereas journalists are interested in reporting the daily events of the Stock Exchange and quoting the Financial Times Index, our social science colleagues would have a broader perspective. Historians would be interested in the influences on its development, and economists would study the process of economic transactions through share dealing. Psychologists might study risk-taking behaviour among brokers while sociologists would be concerned with the nature and variety of human relationships and interactions. They might want to describe the power and prestige of the different kinds of participant, and this can be done with only marginal reference to economics, history or psychology.

The above example illustrates the different interests of the social sciences, yet in one sense all social sciences are alike because they rely on providing knowledge about the world in a scientific way. That is, the statement they make about the world can be tested and verified empirically. While this basic scientific rationale provides a common grounding, the social sciences differ in the concepts they use, the kinds of questions they pose about the world, the methods they use to answer the questions and the kinds of solutions or explanations they provide. They differ also in the kinds of assumptions they hold about the world and this influences the problems they select for study. For example, a major field of interest in psychology is individual differences—examining whether these are related to difference in genetic make-up, personality, intelligence or environment. Psychologists spend a great deal of effort in trying to tease out the genetic as compared with the environmental influences on human behaviour. Sociologists, on the other hand, generally assume that human action is culturally and socially shaped rather than genetically determined. While appreciating a genetic influence, they would be unlikely to explore individual differences from this perspective. Their interest lies in exploring how social life and the organisation of society influences individuals and groups, be it the society of which they are themselves members or a different one.

The kinds of questions social scientists ask about the world depends on the concepts and the theories they use. It is the way that concepts and theories are used that gives each social science, and indeed other sciences, their distinctive approach to the subject matter they study. As you read this book you will come across many of the major concepts and theories of sociology. Indeed, it is only through grasping and working with these concepts and theories as they are used in sociology that you will begin to develop a sociological understanding.

In order to achieve a sociological understanding we must suspend our taken-for-granted assumptions and take account of the variety of meanings of actions and events, which can be interpreted or explained in different ways by people who hold different perspectives. For example, one health education campaign was mounted on the assumption that the reason for women not attending for antenatal care was that they were unaware of the risks of postponing medical care. Yet studies which have asked women for *their* views report that women attend for antenatal care later than advised by obstetricians for a whole host of reasons. These reasons range from covering up the pregnancy because of the stigma of illegitimacy to the inconvenience of clinic appointments (Garcia,

1982). However, the official explanation blames the ignorance of patients.

Consider also the issue of wearing cheap disposable paper face masks to carry out aseptic techniques. This practice continues in many hospitals. The official explanation is that it reduces the chance of hospital staff passing on potentially harmful micro-organisms from their noses and mouths to patients and of inhaling micro-organisms from patients. There is a mass of evidence, however, which shows that these particular masks provide a totally ineffective barrier; and when no such infection is present there is no point in wearing them anyway (Rogers, 1981). Why then do some hospital workers, despite the evidence, continue to dress up in this ritualistic way? Other rituals exist, such as nurses continuing to wear caps. Why do they want to, and why do hospitals want to hold on to their own distinctive caps when mergers occur? Why do some groups continue to wear a specific uniform rather than the ubiquitous white coat worn by many other health professionals?

Despite the recognition of the importance of parents staying overnight with young children who must be in hospital (Central Health Services Council, 1959), why do some places still not readily offer accommodation? What makes some parents feel uncomfortable about staying with their child?

Posing questions like these to different kinds of people is likely to yield different answers and the *official* response as given by the organisation is not necessarily the only or the most helpful *explanation* of what is happening.

It is by addressing questions about social issues like those just mentioned that a sociological understanding of them emerges. An explanation of how this is done is given by Peter Berger in his book *Invitation to Sociology*. He uses the analogy of the puppet theatre to represent the actions of individuals in society (Berger, 1966, p. 199). In a puppet theatre we can see the puppets dancing on their stage. We can see and know that they dance because the strings control their actions. In a similar way individuals in any society also obey a variety of rules. Some of these are practical, like driving on the left-hand side of the road, which has become law. Others have less obvious practical implications but have always existed, for example the fact that in Britain men and women marry only one spouse at a time. We know that this is not a universal form of social organisation for in some societies men may have more than one wife, while in others women may have more than one husband. Yet in our society we rarely challenge such a basic rule as 'one spouse at a time'. To do so creates news. Even the increasing numbers of cohabiting couples do not appear to challenge this rule. By responding to social rules, all of us are very much akin to the puppets. However, unlike puppets, we have the possibility of stopping, standing outside our stage and becoming a member of the audience. In the audience we begin to see how our society works—how rules develop and are maintained or change. Of course, as with the puppet theatre, different members of the audience will perceive different explanations of *why* things are as they are. Yet to be able to ask questions and provide answers about the forms of social organisations around us, such as the family, the political system or our working environment, we require a sociological understanding. It must be clear that such an understanding of our own society is not the monopoly of sociologists; we would recommend it to anyone who is concerned about the society of which they are a part. That, of course, includes all health care professionals.

SOCIOLOGY ON OFFER

What specifically does sociology have to offer the health professions? There are two kinds of sociological data which are relevant. First there are data collected through *sociology in health care* and second, there are data collected through a *sociology of health care*.

Sociology in health care. These data reflect the use of sociological ideas related to practice, client groups or professionals in ways that can be used by planners. For example, sociological concepts and methods were used in research commissioned by the Briggs Committee on Nursing (1972), and included a survey of the social characteristics of practising and non-practising nurses. Similarly one of us (JB) was involved in the Edinburgh University's Nursing Research Unit's study of Women in Nursing (Hockey, 1976) which was concerned with manpower shortage, student wastage and nursing organisation. These studies, using sociological concepts and methods, reflect the concern of management with problems of manpower and wastage and provide information as a basis for managing the service.

Health planners also make use of sociological knowledge in health care. Sociologists (Goffman, 1961; Townsend, 1962) have studied what happens to people who live in large groups in hospitals or asylums. For many years the mentally ill, the mentally handicapped and the elderly were cared for in such institutions (Fig. 1.1); indeed many continue to be housed in such environments. It was discovered that, in time, they learn particular ways of behaving, a process which has come to be known as *institutionalisation*. Most people do not live in large groups, nor are they confined to spending most of their days and nights within the institution (prisoners and closed religious orders being exceptions). We usually live in small groups—in families or with flatmates—and, as well as carrying out many activities with them, we go out to work and leisure in a range of different environments and meet different groups of people. Health planners have used their knowledge in planning services for the mentally ill, the mentally handicapped and, more recently, the elderly (Walker, 1982).

To help these groups to live as 'normal' lives as possible they are now increasingly being cared for in small groups, living in ordinary housing in towns and villages and being encouraged to participate in local activities (Fig. 1.2).

Sociology of health care. In contrast, a sociology of health care has been concerned with analysis of providers of health care and what they have provided. A good example of this is Eliot Freidson's extended analysis of the medical profession (Freidson, 1975). Both David Towell and Robert Dingwall provide similar analyses of the nursing profession. Towell (1976) studied the way in which psychiatric nursing students became psychiatric nurses in a hospital which used different types of treatment in different wards. Dingwall (1977) studied the everyday world of health visiting in order to provide insights into how nurses learn to do health visiting. The insights which such studies provide frequently challenge the assumptions that health care professionals themselves hold about their own occupations.

Fig. 1.1 Mentally-handicapped men confined in an institution with their days filled doing repetitive activities. (courtesy of Calderstones Hospital).

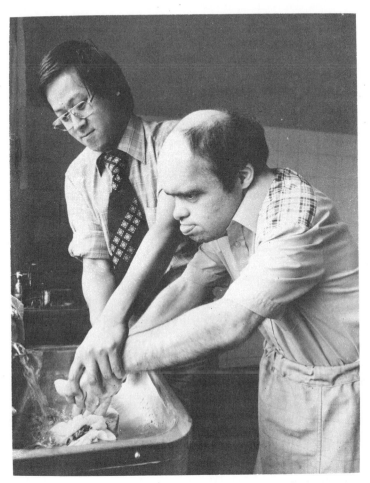

Fig. 1.2 Learning self-care skills to prepare for discharge from an institution (courtesy of Nursing Mirror).

The sociology of health care has also considered the practice of health care as social action. One of us (SB) undertook a study to examine communication processes in a radiotherapy department. This study examined the processes by which patients came to interpret their illness, going beyond what they were told or not told about it by hospital staff. It also examined what nurses believed and assumed to be true about patients and how this influenced their communication practices (Bond, 1978).

Charlotte Kratz, in her study of the care of the long-term sick in the community, also added to our knowledge of the different ways that district nurses manage stroke patients by identifying how they implicitly categorise them (Kratz, 1978). It is by using sociological theory and methods that a fresh perspective is obtained which aids our understanding of the way that health care is practised in a whole variety of settings.

Sociology in health care refers to those concerned with policy and planning using sociological concepts and methods to collect data to assist them in their work. *Sociology of health care* is about developing a sociological understanding of health providers and their practices. This is typically the work of professional sociologists and is embedded in sociological theory.

A SOCIOLOGICAL ALTERNATIVE

As well as providing sociological data which has relevance for the organisation of the health professions and their practices, *sociology also offers an alternative way of viewing and explaining health care and health problems.*

The medical model

The traditional and generally accepted view of the health field is that improvements in health and the quality of health care are attributable to the art and science of medicine. This has become known as the *medical model* of health. The link between health and the medical care system was created and is maintained by the powerful image of the role of medicine in the eradication of infections and parasitic diseases, advances in surgery, the application of technology and new drugs, and lowered infant mortality rates. The result of this orientation is an emphasis on the *treatment of illness* by medical means rather than on *health* or *normality*.

This emphasis is reflected in the education of health care workers, where curricula tend to be based on diseases according to medical specialties, and allocations for clinical experience are organised around medical specialties. Such teaching often takes disease or ill-health, rather than health or normality, as its starting point.

Historically it is easy to see why this is so. The history of medicine is full of examples of abnormality being presented to physicians, whose main endeavours have been in developing methods of treatment and in seeking causes within biological functioning.

The social model

The emphases of sociological perspectives of health and illness are on such aspects of health care as rehabilitation, prevention of illness and the social management of illness, rather than on biological and medical aspects of health care. This approach has become known as the *social model* of health. It contributes an understanding of illness and disease by pointing up the social rather than the biological contexts. A useful sociological model would illuminate how social processes work in defining illness, in understanding the causes of illness and promotion of health or in interpreting the organisational structures within the health care system. By 'model' we mean here a theoretical representation of reality.

An important distinction between medical and social models lies in the very definition of illness. The medical model defines patients as ill when they have certain biological and physiological signs. For example, when haemoglobin reaches a certain low level the patient is judged as anaemic and treatment advised. One very elderly women, who still managed and enjoyed going out for rides in her son's car, was thought very pale by her district nurse. A blood sample was taken and the resulting haemoglobin level was 6 g/dl—less than half the desirable level. Her general practitioner urged her to have a blood transfusion. The old woman did not feel ill or incapacitated, and her lifestyle was not being interfered with by her poor blood chemistry. By her definition she was not ill and so she wanted nothing to do with blood transfusions. Her interpretation, unlike that of her doctor and nurse, was based not on medical criteria but on social criteria.

This description of medical and social models emphasises different aspects of health and illness. However, they provide complementary explanations, rather than alternative explanations. A good example of the value of both models is Thomas McKeown's historical analysis of improvements in health in

England and Wales. McKeown (1979) concluded that the major contributions to improvements in health since the eighteenth century were, in order of importance, limitation in family size, an increase in food supplies, a healthier physical environment and specific preventive and therapeutic measures. He predicts that:

> 'improvement in health is likely to come in future, as in the past, from modification of the conditions which lead to disease, rather than from intervention in the mechanism of disease after it has occurred' (McKeown, 1979, p. 198).

The health field concept

Marc Lalonde, as Canada's Minister of Health and Welfare, explicitly incorporated McKeown's ideas in his health field concept, which draws on medical and social models of health and illness. In this, health is attributed to four main elements: *Human Biology, Environment, Lifestyle* and *Health Care Organisation* (Lalonde, 1974).

Human Biology. The human biology element includes those aspects of mental and physical health which are a direct consequence of the basic biology of the individual. These include genetic inheritance, processes of maturation and ageing, and the complex biological systems of the human organism. The health implications of our complex biology are enormous and include malfunctions, chronic and degenerative diseases and genetic disorders.

Environment. In the environmental element Lalonde includes all those matters related to health which are external to the human body and over which the *individual* has little or no personal control. These include ensuring that food, drugs, cosmetics and the water supply are safe and uncontaminated, that the health hazards of all forms of pollution are controlled, that the spread of communicable diseases is prevented, that effective sewage disposal is carried out and that the social environment, including rapid social change, does not have harmful effects on health.

Lifestyle. The lifestyle category in the health field concept includes those decisions made by individuals themselves, which have implications for their health. These include what we choose to eat, whether and how we exercise, our use of additive substances and how we get about. Many habits and decisions create self-imposed risks to health, and when illness or death results it is attributable to the victim's own lifestyle.

Health Care Organisation. Health care organisation consists of 'the quantity, quality, arrangement, nature and relationships of people and resources in the provision of health care' (Lalonde, 1974, p. 32). This is usually referred to as the health care system and includes medical practice, nursing, paramedical pactice, hospitals, nursing homes, prescribed drugs, community health care, ambulance and dental services, as well as other health services such as chiropody, homeopathy and osteopathy.

Lalonde contends that most of society's efforts to improve health and the bulk of direct health expenditure have been focused on this fourth element of the health field concept, health care organisation. Yet when the *causes* of ill health are examined they are rooted in the other three elements. In effect we continue to promote an illness service rather than a health service. The health field concept, with its emphasis on four analytically separate yet complementary components, radically changes a perspective on health away from both health care organisation and the dominant medical model to one which is far more comprehensive as well as analytic.

There is sometimes a tendency to regard the medical and social models as alternatives, presenting an either/or viewpoint regarding the appropriate way to conceptualise health concerns. By incorporating the social dimension into Lalonde's health field concept we can see more clearly that elements make differential contributions and will interact in different ways for different problems. For example, an examination of the underlying causes of death from road traffic accidents can be found in risks taken by individuals, with lesser importance given to the design and composition of cars and roads, and less again to the availability of emergency treatment. Human biology makes little contribution to causation in this area. When lifestyle factors are identified the risks taken by individuals can be considered under such headings as impaired driving, carelessness, failure to wear seat belts, or speeding. Impaired driving would include the effects of alcohol or drug abuse, sleepiness or distractions. In each of these there are social considerations.

Health professionals may find it helpful to consider illness and patients' responses to their predicament from viewpoints other than medical ones, by attending to the contributions of different disciplines and different perspectives. In Chapter 2 we describe a number of sociological perspectives.

REFERENCES

Berger P L 1966 Invitation to sociology: a humanistic perspective. Penguin Books, Harmondsworth

Birch J 1975 To nurse or not to nurse: an investigation into the causes of withdrawal during nurse training. Royal College of Nursing, London

Bond S 1978 Processes of communication about cancer in a radiotherapy department. Unpublished PhD thesis, University of Edinburgh

Booth C 1892 Pauperism: a picture and the endowment of old age, an argument. MacMillan, London

Booth C 1894 The aged poor in England and Wales. Condition. MacMillan, London

Central Health Services Council 1959 The welfare of children in hospital. Report of the Committee. HMSO, London

Dingwall R 1977 The social organisation of health visitor training. Croom Helm, London

Durkheim E 1897 Suicide. A study in sociology. Routledge & Kegan Paul, London, 1952

Freidson E 1975 Profession of medicine. A study of the sociology of applied knowledge. Dodd, Mead & Co, New York

Garcia J 1982 Women's views of antenatal care. In: Enkin M, Chalmers I (eds) Effectiveness and satisfaction in antenatal care. Heinemann, London, ch 5, p 81–91

Goffman E 1961 Asylums. Essays on the social situation of mental patients and other inmates. Anchor Books, New York

Hockey L 1976 Women in nursing. Hodder & Stoughton, London

Kratz C R 1978 Care of the long-term sick in the community: particularly patients with stroke. Churchill Livingstone, Edinburgh

Lalonde M 1974 A new perspective on the health of Canadians. A working document. Information Canada, Ottawa

McKeown T 1979 The role of medicine. Dream, mirage or nemesis? Basil Blackwell, Oxford

Mills C W 1970 The sociological imagination. Penguin Books, Harmondsworth

Report of the Committee on Nursing 1972 (The Briggs Report), Cmnd 5115. HMSO, London

Rogers K B 1981 Face masks: which, when, where and why? Journal of Hospital Infection 2: 1–4

Rowntree B S 1901 Poverty :a study of town life. MacMillan, London

Towell D 1976 Understanding psychiatric nursing—a sociological study of modern psychiatric nursing practice. Royal College of Nursing, London

Townsend P 1962 The last refuge. A survey of residential institutions and homes for the aged in England and Wales. Routledge & Kegan Paul, London

Walker A (ed) 1982 Community care: the family, the state and social policy. Basil Blackwell & Martin Robertson, Oxford

FURTHER READING

Berger P L 1966 Invitation to sociology: a humanistic perspective. Penguin Books, Harmondsworth
Mills C W 1970 The sociological imagination. Penguin Books, Harmondsworth

2

Perspectives in sociology

INTRODUCTION

In Chapter 1 we spent some time identifying the distinctiveness of sociology—that social phenomena could be regarded
sociologically rather than from the perspective of one of the
other social sciences. It would be incorrect, however, to say
that there is a single sociological perspective or one correct
sociological approach. Indeed sociology, like all other social
sciences, is characterised by a variety of perspectives. In this
chapter we introduce the three major sociological perspectives—structuralism, interactionism and ethnomethodology.
We show that they make different assumptions, use concepts
in different ways, pose different questions and arrive at different explanations. Perspectives are not right or wrong; simply different, and often complementary.

An appreciation of these different sociological approaches
provides some organising principles for understanding why
sociologists, interested in similar social problems, ask different questions about them and study them in different ways.
We shall highlight this difference briefly in relation to mental
illness. Furthermore, if studies are not interpreted within the
broad perspective in which they have their origins, their findings risk becoming nothing more than a series of disjointed

facts which convey a sense of arbitrariness as to their scope and methods.

This chapter is intended to provide an understanding of the main features of the different perspectives from which sociological studies of health topics, and the social world more generally, are conceptualised and hence assist in their interpretation throughout the remaining chapters. In order to grasp these differences it is important to appreciate the contribution that theory makes to characterising sociological perspectives. We deal with this issue first.

THEORY IN SOCIOLOGY

The word theory often gives rise to difficulties because it is used to describe everything, in education particularly, which is not practical. When theory is used, as in sociological theory or economic theory, then this refers to a set of conjectures or tentative explanations of social reality.

Each one of us uses theory constantly. We carry in our heads our personal theories or models which represent the world about us. To do this we use selected concepts and the relationships between them. It is because we do not all share the same theories that we see the world differently. In other words facts do not speak for themselves; rather facts are interpreted in the light of some particular theory. It is because we have particular ideas about the nature of the 'family' and 'government' that we have difficulties in conceptualising kinship networks and political structures in other cultures and why members of our own society place different interpretations on concepts like delinquency, and questions of human origins.

Some facts are more generally accepted than others, and this may involve a process of accumulating particular knowledge which produces convergent theory. For example, we now take for granted the fact that the world is spherical. Yet at the time of Columbus' famous voyage it was certainly not taken for granted and the world was believed to be flat by many. It is by testing our hypothetical explanations that we accumulate knowledge and what may begin as scientific facts gradually become accepted into common sense knowledge.

Today we are in a position of uncertainty with some of the theories which are evolving about the origins and antecedents of child abuse and mental illness. It is accepted theory which will influence the kind of interventions produced, those holding different theories will produce different ideas about what is appropriate.

It is not only facts which are disputed, but also their explanations. If we return to the example of the use of antenatal care, a fact observed by many midwives and obstetricians is that more women from the lower social classes are late bookers for antenatal care. The figures or facts are that in 1981 18% of women with husbands in Social Class V occupations booked for maternity care later than 20 weeks after conception while for Social Class I the figure was 11% (see Ch. 3). Competing theoretical explanations of why this should be the case are that it is due to the different amounts of knowledge available to women in different class positions, or that women regard antenatal care as of variable significance and their individual viewpoints influence their attendance. It happens that a higher percentage in Social Class V do not regard antenatal care as sufficiently worthwhile to attend. These two theoretical explanations of the nature of social behaviour, one emphasising class based divisions and the other taking a perspective which emphasises the relevance of how individuals view their world, are typical of different sociological perspectives.

Sociological theories are made explicit or can be inferred from the research question asked, the facts collected and the methods used to carry out an investigation. In every day life and in professional life we tend not to make our theories explicit. When a patient is admitted to care some form of assessment is generally carried out. Depending on who does the assessment, be it members of different professional groups or different individuals within a profession, given freedom they are likely to assess different patient features. That is, different facts will be collected about the patient. In some cases facts will also be collected about his family. The information collected will depend on the theory being used by the professional which determines his interpretation of the nature of patients, their rights, the recovery process and so on. In the last few years we have become aware of the value of supportive relationships to prevent psychiatric problems among those facing particular kinds of stress such as bereavement, amputation, mastectomy and myocardial infarction. Whether information about such relationships is collected and *used* will depend on whether the professional incorporates this fact into his theoretical ideas about his responsibilities for patient recovery and the nature of rehabilitation itself. Patient assessment, as an exmaple of social behaviour, is guided by theory and accumulated knowledge of the kind mentioned above operates within the confines of theory. The same rationale operates for sociological theory.

We cannot therefore ignore theory, we can only choose among alternatives. In sociology, theory is made sufficiently explicit to be able to do so. However theory is not static, and theory itself is *socially constructed* according to the time in which it is developed and the prevalent belief systems operating in society. Theory development therefore is best understood in a historical context, and fashions in the acceptability of different theories can be interpreted equally within a broader social picture. The acceptability of different theoretical explanations of the influence of race on intelligence is a recent example of the fit between theories and the acceptability of broader ideas about the nature of man and society. Later in the chapter it will become obvious that sociological theories, and more generally perspectives, have evolved as products of their time.

The role of theory

It would be a mistake to regard theories as right or wrong. There are, rather, theories which are more or less useful or profitable. No one theory is a completely accurate representation of reality but some provide better insight into a particular phenomenon than do others. The usefulness of any theory depends on how it functions:
1. to explain past events,
2. to predict future events, and
3. to generate new theory.

One function of theory is to provide explanations of what facts already exist about some phenomenon. Often facts appear trivial and disjointed yet they may be linked by some theoretical explanation. One example of this is the similar responses observed (facts) to bereavement, to being made redundant at work and to amputation. In all cases they may be explained by response to the loss of something valued. This kind of theorising is possible because of an existing system of relationships connecting different facts. When they are linked theoretically this adds to our understanding of otherwise disparate phenomena. By using theory we are able to summarise social actions which are generalisable beyond the immediate field of study, i.e. empirical generalisation. By the same token, theory should be able to *predict* future social action. Using the above example, if a valued object is lost then similar responses would be anticipated to those already observed. In many areas of sociological concern theory is too embryonic for accurate prediction, and awaits refinement and empirical testing.

Finally good theory should lend itself to generating new theory capable of more parsimonious explanation and prediction. One aspect of this is that good theory should generate testable hypotheses which give rise to empirical studies. Theory therefore should point to areas yet to be explored and indicate which facts to observe while defining them clearly. In this way new findings and empirical generalisations emerge which are then used to amend existing theory if this is warranted. We will return to this aspect of theory again in Chapter 12 when we deal with sociological methods.

PERSPECTIVES ON MENTAL ILLNESS

Let us begin to consider some different sociological perspectives by examining mental illness (after Cuff & Payne, 1979). This topic has been of interest to scientists for a considerable period of time; but explanations of mental illness may also be religious or supernatural—for example, it may be thought to be due to possession by spirits. Scientific approaches to explaining odd behaviour may be biological, psychological and sociological (among others). Even definitions of what constitutes mental illness differ. Ever since Durkheim in the middle of the last century attributed suicide to social causes, other aspects of health and illness have been regarded as the appropriate subject matter of sociology. According to Durkheim, the behaviour of individuals depends on their social environment and what their society influences them into doing. Therefore, while *individuals* are mentally ill, some sociologists look for reasons not in these individuals themselves but in particular aspects of the social structure in which mentally ill people live.

One such approach was demonstrated by Hollingshead and Redlich (1958), who sought to show that the incidence and type of mental illness varied as a consequence of position in the social class structure. Thus, while the highest social class contained 3.1% of the population, only 1% of the mentally ill came from this class. Conversely, they showed that the lowest social class included 17.8% of the population but contributed 36.8% of mentally ill people. Illness designated as 'neurotic' was concentrated in the higher levels of social class while 'psychotic' types of illness predominated in the lower social classes. Without going into further detail, this analysis reveals a particular sociological perspective which makes certain assumptions about the nature of society and the causes of mental illness. This perspective can be broadly labelled *structuralist* because it views society as being structured in certain ways, social class being one of them. People belonging to the same social class are assumed to be similar in certain ways—similar roles in the economic order of society, similar lifestyles, attitudes and educational backgrounds. It is therefore considered appropriate to examine whether variations in mental illness coincide with these divisions. In this case mental illness does appear to differ by incidence and type in different social classes. Another example of a structuralist approach to mental illness would be to relate it to different areas of residence—in a city compared with suburbs and rural areas. Here the scientist tests a hypothesis that there is a correlation between different areas of residence (and, arguably, different lifestyles and organisation) and rates and types of mental illness. Indeed Dunham and Faris (1965) showed that, in Chicago, the incidence of schizophrenia varied in different parts of the city with the highest rates in areas close to the city centre with many lodging houses, foreign-born communities and 'down and outs'. They suggest that it is the social disorganisation of these areas which predisposes to schizophrenia.

The researchers identify a link between the spatial pattern of the city and each area's distinctive ecology with different kinds and levels of social organisation. This in turn results in producing schizophrenic illness at specific levels of incidence. In other words, the *structural* organisation of urban, social and economic life influences the condition of individuals who live there.

In contrast with structuralists, sociologists who take an *interactionist perspective* provide a rather different view of mental illness. They begin with no taken-for-granted definition of what mental illness is; they do not see it as something lying within the individual himself. Rather it is a *social status* conferred on an individual by other members of society. For interactionists, mental illness is not like some disese within the person which can be universally observed and defined. Being regarded as mentally ill depends on individuals making that definition of others, labelling them and acting towards them as if they were mentally ill. The definition of mental illness occurs in the process of social interaction.

This is in contrast to an understanding of mental illness founded on assumptions about society with a structure which exerts strong influences on individual members and how they behave. Interactionists stress individual actions and perceptions, each person taking account of the actions of others on the basis of the meanings and interpretations they give to them. It is not a case of individuals being governed by and reflecting the structure of their society. Rather, individuals, through social actions, *create* their society. Individuals have to interpret their world, make sense of it and give meaning to it. Thus 'mental illness' and 'mental patient' are not absolute conditions or objects which exist 'out there'. Interactionists concern themselves in studying the processes by which people go about classifying others as 'mentally ill'.

In social life some people occupying particular roles have more power than others when it comes to labelling people as mentally ill. Szasz (1971) has taken this approach in examining the process of a person's becoming so labelled. While most of us would say that we could recognise someone who was mentally ill, it is psychiatrists who are generally accepted as experts in doing so. Psychiatrists have considerable power to declare that someone is sick, requires treatment and may be

placed in an institution. Such is that power th
likely to accept their categorisation that someon
ill and to act towards that individual accordingly
the individual becomes one who is 'mentally ill' i
the basis of his behaviour but because he now has a particular
label attached to him. If others apply the label it is less likely
to stick if it is not also supported by a psychiatrist's opinion.
What psychiatrists label as mental illness may change over
time. For example, in 1974 the American Psychiatric Association voted to decide whether homosexuality was a mental
illness. Since 1974 it has not been considered an illness.

However, not everyone agrees with such categorisation.
Studies based on interactionist assumptions have shown that
disagreements occur over the interpretation and meanings
given to the behaviour observed. The differentiation of the
'mentally ill' from 'normal' members of society can be contingent upon the particular circumstances of the social situation
in which people find themselves. Scheff (1964) examined the
psychiatric screening procedures used in a mid-western state
in America to decide whether patients should be released.
Scheff found that this decision is influenced more by the financial, ideological and political position of the examining
psychiatrist than patient factors. The study demonstrated that
court appointed psychiatrists with particular ideological and
political views were predisposed to assume that the person
was ill from the outset. Within this frame of reference which
pre-classifies the patient, psychiatrists then go on to interpret
the patients' behaviour and records. Scheff argues that without this prior definition of the person as mentally ill, the patient's records, behaviour and responses to the psychiatrist's
tests can be interpreted differently.

On the other side of the coin, interactionists are also concerned with the individual's conception of himself. This follows from the assumption that individuals have to interpret
and give meaning to their own actions as well as making sense
of those of others with whom they interact. How individuals
act depend on their own self-image and this is constructed
largely from our interpretation of how other people react to
what we say and do. This has led to studies of the effects of
labelling people as mentally ill and how these individuals see
themselves. Conferring the label subsequently produces ab-

normal behaviour because of the way others act towards the person so labelled, which in turn produces actions by him which he recognises that others expect of him.

These examples demonstrate the very different kinds of sociological analysis produced by sociologists who rely on the assumptions of the interactionist perspective, and the structuralists who take as their starting point a very different conception of the social world. As a result they use different conceptual frameworks, carry out different kinds of studies and use different methods to collect and analyse the data which provides the basis for their explanations. Neither is more correct than the other; they simply represent different ways of viewing the social world.

A third and more recent perspective in sociology is represented by an approach known as *ethnomethodology*, again choosing questions and investigating the social world on the basis of a different set of assumptions and choosing a different conceptual framework from the perspectives described above.

The ethnomethodological approach assumes that the social world is constantly being created by members of society which for them is unproblematic because it is regarded as the result of society's members using their own common sense. Society is created by its members using their taken-for-granted common sense knowledge about how the world works and how they can deal with it in acceptable ways. The concern of ethnomethodologists is to study and explain how it is that society's members actually accomplish the social world which they create through commonly accepted, albeit sophisticated methods. Of major importance is language; we accomplish social encounters largely through conversation. Individuals have learned methods for doing so and ethnomethodologists are interested in how they have achieved such methods.

Ethnomethodologists would be unlikely to study mental illness as such; they would be more likely to have as their concern the society-building methods that people use which may have relevance to mental illness. Turner (1968) has suggested that former mental patients can be faced with particular problems when taking up conversations with acquaintances.

The focus of his study was how former mental patients 're-sumed contact' after being discharged from a mental hospital. Cuff and Payne (1979) write:

'His focus of study is in the way persons 'resume contact' after having been discharged from the mental institution. Turner suggests that in *any* subsequent encounter between *any* two persons, it may be the case that the parties to the conversation do some work of recognition. He argues that when persons engage in this 'resuming' work they offer identifications of themselves and the persons they are talking to, and in so doing they are suggesting a relationship between them. These identifications can be, and usually are, offered without explicitly announcing that one is a friend, or a long lost acquaintance. For example, by saying 'Hi Chuck, how did it go last night? I sure wish I could've made it,' as the opening utterance in an encounter the speaker is, without spelling it out word for word, probably identifying himself and the person he is talking to as 'friends'. Turner adds that part of this resuming work may involve bringing the parties to the conversation up to date, i.e. filling each other in on newsworthy items which have happened to them individually since they last met. In the case of an encounter involving a 'former mental patient', however, Turner illustrates how troubles in everyday resuming work can be generated. For example, it may require the 'former mental patient' to accept unwanted identification. After all, it is likely that such an individual wants to forget that he has been mentally ill; he may consider his 'former state' is irrelevant to his current life, as a broken leg. But when resuming involves bringing the parties up to date, it is often difficult to avoid the topic of his recent experiences. Turner appeals to his materials and to our common-sense knowledge of the social world to suggest that the identity, 'former mental patient' is one which persons who have not been mentally ill are most likely to use, in preference to any other, when they are doing resuming work with someone they know to have been mentally ill. Thus, the ethnomethodologist, by analysing conversational materials, can show us how interactional troubles can be generated and managed in everyday encounters. In particular, Turner's work illustrates how such analysis can illuminate some interactional problems involving persons who have been 'mentally ill'. (p. 19–20).

The example of mental illness, which will be elaborated in Chapter 4, serves as a means to illustrate that within sociology there are different ways of conceptualising and studying any topic. As we will show in subsequent chapters, there is no single sociological approach to health and illness, the family, old age, professional careers or indeed any subject of interest to sociologists. Sociologists recognise themselves and are rec-ognised by others as adhering to a particular perspective. It is reflected in the way that they carry out sociological studies. Let us now begin to elaborate further some of the basic fea-tures of these sociological approaches.

STRUCTURALISM AS A PERSPECTIVE

Structuralism as a broad approach is based on the assumption that all of our social behaviour, out attitudes and values, are the result of the organisation and structure of the society in which we live. A major refinement of this, however, is to view the components of social structure as in consensus with each other or, alternatively to view them as in conflict.

Structural functionalism—a consensus perspective

All sociological perspectives have in common a focus on the ordered nature of society—that is, a belief that in most situations the range of possible actions is fairly limited and we have a fair idea of how we would behave as well as being able to predict, within limits, the behaviour of others. The notion of order is relevant to situations as diverse as a couple out on their first date or the stability of whole societies. It is at the societal extreme that the consensus perspective is situated, based on the assumption that, in the main, societies can be regarded as stable and generally integrated wholes which differ by their cultural and social structural arrangements. This perspective in sociology owes a great deal to an analogy with natural and biological sciences. At the time sociology was emerging as a new discipline, there was also a thrust towards scientific methods in the natural sciences. Comte (1798–1857), a French philosopher who coined the word sociology, believed that sociology was about adapting and applying methods of physical sciences to social life, to make 'law-like' statements about the determinants of human behaviour and to reshape society by being able to predict and hence control its workings. Sociology, which attempts to adhere to the canons of physical science, is sometimes referred to as 'scientistic'. Comte's emphasis was on the structures of whole societies and the change of whole societies.

A second step in the notion of societies as integrated wholes was based in part upon a crude analogy between society and biological organisms. The analogy arises from the fact that both societies and biological organisms have, on the one hand, a propensity to survive against all odds and, on the other hand, a propensity to decay. Most, if not all, biological organisms are systems made up of a number of distinguishable interrelated parts. Each of these parts affects and responds to changes in other parts of the organism. This analogy does not mean that the social system mirrors the biological system in terms of structure, but that the different parts of the social system are also affected by and respond to changes in other parts of the system. Different parts of the biological system fulfil different functions and roles; hence the sociological analogy of functionalism. Some functions are more essential for the organism's survival than others; so, too, individuals and institutions fulfil a variety of functions and roles. When the human organism loses an eye it adapts to change in circumstances; in the event of heart failure the body eventually dies. The human organism is therefore an open and adaptive system which, however, is not immortal. Likewise in its simplest form structural functionalism describes society as an adaptive and open system whose different parts function to keep it unified and relatively unchanging.

Durkheim and functionalism

A major and long-lasting contribution to functionalism was made by Emile Durkheim (1858–1917). One feature of this was to regard the interrelated components of society as being *moral* entities. Furthermore, through their associations with each other, members of society develop what Durkheim (1964a) called a 'collective consciousness' which constrains how they behave and which also gives rise to expectations and restraints in how others behave. The nature of these social constraints on our behaviour was what Durkheim meant by 'the moral reality' of society—that society, over and above individuals, had its own moral order which also included the collective values of its members. In order that individuals can operate in a society there has to be some framework of order which is rooted in members holding certain values in common. Consensus in society is achieved through this sharing and cohesiveness. For Durkheim this basic agreement is synonymous with an understanding of the concept of society itself.

Durkheim's emphasis on the moral nature of social relationships permeates his work. His analysis of the division of labour in society is a moral rather than an economic one. It is based on common values and expectations about what is appropriate for society at that time. Durkheim assumes a high degree of cohesiveness, with different components of the social structure adapting to maintain society in equilibrium. Stability does not mean that societies are static, but that the systems within society are able to adjust and adapt in an orderly and evolutionary way to achieve a new state of equilibrium.

One repercussion of the functionalism of Durkheim is a tendency to regard society as an independently existing entity, existing in its own right over and above its members. This is reflected in Durkheim's views of the appropriate subject matter for sociological research—that is, to study 'social facts' and in a scientific way (Durkheim, 1964b). 'Social facts' are different from other kinds of facts because they are the very fabric of society, evolving out of human relationships and association. An example of a social fact is the *rate* of suicide in a population, which cannot be reduced to single cases of suicide without losing sight of the *rate*. Thus the suicide rate per 1000 of population is an example of a social fact. Similarly other collective phenomena like 'crime', 'fashion' and 'mental illness' which transcend the behaviour of individual people are social facts. Durkheim regarded some social facts as 'normal' in that they are appropriate to and necessary for the operation of a 'healthy' and well ordered society. Social facts which were harmful to society were categorised as 'pathological', thus reinforcing the organic analogy.

Durkheim's scientific leanings were further expressed in his views that sociologists explain social facts by finding out not only their causes but also their *functions*, i.e. the part social facts play in helping to maintain an orderly society. In trying to identify functions, the sociologist has to examine the 'general needs' of the social organism. Social facts will be explained by antecedent social facts—but the sociologist works back only as far as the social organisation of groups. Thereafter he enters the realms of psychological and biological explanation and so would no longer be thinking sociologically.

The importance of Durkheim's contribution to sociology lies not only in his theory of society but also in his major work on the methods to be used in studying society. In sociology, as in all disciplines, it can be said that theory guides method.

We will demonstrate in Chapter 12 Durkheim's enduring influence on research methods from a functionalist perspective.

Developments in structural-functionalism

It would be misleading to characterise a universal functionalist approach but there is a limited number of variants. We can only touch on two of these here—the contributions of Talcott Parsons (1902–1979) and Robert Merton (b.1910).

Parsons—the social system

Talcott Parsons' most significant contribution has been his attempt to construct a model of the working of all parts of the social system (Parsons, 1951). In his vast output of work certain central and recurrent features emerge.

In explaining the concept of function, Parsons' view of the social system is of a network of interlocking systems and subsystems functioning together in order to meet the needs of each other. Order is achieved by integrating disparate motivations into a coherent and ordered society or, to use Parsons' terminology, by integrating the *personality system* and the *cultural system* with the *social system*. These systems cohere with each other by a *central value system* or shared orientation towards action which Parsons, like Durkheim, claims as the basis of society. Stable expectations and behaviours are developed through the *role* relationships which arise; in turn these expecations enable others to meet them and to carry out role obligations in return for the rights which adhere to their respective roles. Thus behaviour is made predictable and society persists even though its members change. We will encounter the importance of this analysis when we deal with socialisation in Chapter 5, and with the sick role in Chapter 8.

Before functions can be attributed to parts of systems, their value systems must first be defined. Value systems legitimise the *norms* upon which social processes are based, and so in order to understand the components of social systems a first concern is to define their prevailing goals and values. Parsons

devotes attention to four major sub-systems which are themselves structural features of society. These are:

1. The economy, which provides and distributes the material
   resources needed by members of society.
2. The political sub-system, which serves the function of
   selecting the collective goals of society and motivating society's members to achieve them.
3. Kinship institutions, whose functions are to maintain accepted and expected forms of social interaction and control
   interpersonal tensions through the process of socialising
   individuals into competent role-players.
4. Community and cultural institutions, such as religion, education and mass communication, which function to integrate the various elements of the social system. They may
   be reinforced by formal agencies of social control like the
   judiciary, police and military forces.

From this approach the problem emerges of explaining how
these sub-systems maintain their integration, and that of the
whole social system, given the necessary diversity of roles and
norms in modern society.

The key for Parsons is the continual striving towards an ideal
state of equilibrium which is attained through the process of
socialisation and *social control*, so that individuals are motivated towards the fulfilment of role expectations. In so doing
the *personality system* is related to the social structure in
which the individual is situated. Socialisation and the internalisation of norms are key processes but they are related to the
functions of the social structure. Individuals must be adequately socialised into roles appropriate to attain the goals
of the particular institutions or sub-systems, and goals are related to the functions of the institution. We shall show how
this analysis applies to the family in Chapter 5.

Individual components of society are tied to the larger society by shared value systems and by their specific functional
requirements, which they can only meet through the society
and which must be met for them to 'survive'. Thus the continued existence of a system depends on its ability to *adapt*,
to attain its goals, to integrate constituent parts and to permit
maintenance of the dominant value system and the pattern of
interaction it lays down.

While there is an emphasis on integration and the persistence of social systems, Parsons does attend to social change. Change can arise in two ways: from pressures exerted by environmental transitions or from within the institution itself. Institutional pressure derives from *strain* within one of the sub-systems, creating disequilibrium. Ultimately, however, the crucial focus for change is the cultural value system of society which expresses its moral sentiments and normative expectations. Any changes in society, according to Parsonian theory, must be to adjust and adapt towards a new type of stability or towards meeting more effectively the goals and functions of the system. This is expressed as the 'dynamic equilibrium' of social systems, with an emphasis on the functional consequences of change or conflict rather than on the sources or causes of conflict. In this sense it is emphatically a consensus perspective.

Merton's functionalism

Not all functionalists use the organic analogy, nor do they all attempt to consider the inter-relatedness of the component parts of social systems. This has been the position of Robert Merton (1967) who regards the Parsonian scheme as altogether too grand in its attempt to include all of society, at all levels, within its social structure. He argues that the tendency to dwell on the functions of social systems, as Parsons does, should be limited to the observed consequences of social events. He also considers that the functionalist view that particular social beliefs or practices are functional in the same way for the *entire* social or cultural system is too simplistic. His view is that a particular arrangement, activity or belief may be functional for only a part of the total society. This has led Merton to develop a theory which can be said to be *middle-range*. Rather than try to consider total societal functions, he focuses on the consequences of one institutional area for another.

To help in the development of middle-range theories, Merton introduced three new concepts to functionalism.

1. Functions may be *latent*, i.e. unintended or unrecognised as well as *manifest*, i.e. intended and recognised.

2. Because not all items necessarily fulfil positive functions, or not for the whole society, they can be *dysfunctional*—leading to instability and disruption rather than to the stable maintenance of the system.
3. Rather than the conservative assumption that there are re-cognisable activities which are indispensable to a society because they fulfil functional pre-requisites, e.g. the pro-duction and distribution of scarce resources in particular ways, Merton argues that there are *functional alternatives*, i.e. different and equally successful ways of providing for functions. This gets away from the functionalist conserva-tive tendency to argue that something is indispensable for the wellbeing of society—that is society could not survive without marriage, for example, to produce families and progeny.

Merton's brand of functionalism yields more for empirical sociologists than do the more grandiose theoretical schemata of Parsons. It offers insights which suggest that behaviour is not always what it seems, that the consequences of actions are not always what they are intended to be, that what may be regarded as 'bad' for a community could, in fact, turn out to perform vital functions. A structure which has existed un-questioned for generations could turn out to have *dysfunc-tional* consequences and *functional alternatives* may be available which could do the job more effectively.

Merton also deals with conflict, but his analysis points out that conflict can be functional as well as dysfunctional for so-cial systems, in a number of ways. However, like other struc-turalists, Merton's analysis does not apply to individuals or groups; like them he operates at the level of the needs of systems—whether of societies or their sub-systems. Like the other structural-functionalists, Merton does not deal with con-sequences but with functions, i.e. whether or not actions meet needs which are held to prevail within a system. As such there is no satisfactory explanation of social change or the causes, as distinct from the consequences, of action.

Structuralism—a conflict approach

Conflict theorists tend to regard themselves as radical critics of the consensus theorists, with their emphasis on maintaining the status quo. As such they are sometimes regarded as political rather than sociological, most strongly exemplified in the writings of Karl Marx (1818–1883).

Marx as a sociological theorist

The Marxist sociologist who attempts to understand social phenomena within a Marxist perspective is not necessarily supportive of Marxist political theory or ideology, or only in as much as these provide meaningful explanations of society.

Marxism is essentially a historical interpretation of the evolution of societies or social systems. It explains social change historically by examining the evolution of modern industrial society from ancient economies based on slavery, through the medieval economy based on serfdom, to the capitalist economy based on wage labour. Marxism is also deterministic in that it predicts the evolution of capitalist society to the socialist economy. Like some other forms of structuralism it is synthetic in its approach to social change, being concerned with the whole of society rather than with specific aspects (Lefebvre, 1968).

Some aspects of Marx's social philosophy are central to his sociological theory (Bottomore & Rubel, 1965). For Marx all societies are *stratified* into distinct *groups* and *classes*. In Chapter 3 we focus on the concept of *social stratification* and indicate how Marxism has influenced sociological thinking, and in Chapter 4 we demonstrate its implications for the social causes of illness. Underlying Marxist theory is the notion that power and authority are linked closely to the economic organisation of society. In capitalistic societies the power of relationships is exemplified by the conflict between the owners of capital (*the bourgeoisie*) and the working class (*the proletariat*). The relationship between these two social groups is characterised by exploitation.

Marxism sees society as a product of the *conflict* between these two groups or social classes, and predicts that the struggle will be resolved through revolutionary rather than evolutionary social change. Societies pass through definite stages of development, with each stage containing contradictions and conflicts that lead to social change. But society and history are not seen as solely external to man. It is through man's own activity as a member of a social class with his distinctive class consciousness that the social and historical world is created and changed.

Like most structuralist theories, Marxism perceives society as a totality, a structure of interrelated levels. This is depicted in Figure 2.1. The economic substructure is closely bound up with the *superstructure*—that is, those institutions such as the mass media, the church, the family and the educational system, which produce knowledge—and with the relationship between the social classes.

Social change must begin with the forces of production. When they develop in such a way that they cease to fit with the relations of production, that is the relations between the owners and non-owners of the means of production, they create contradictions within the substructure of society. These

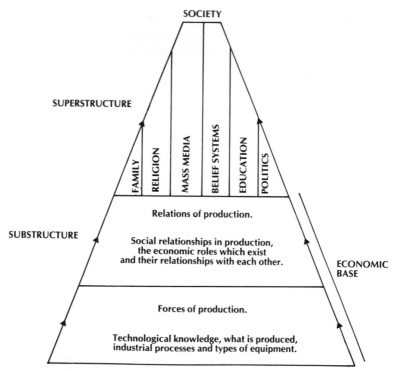

Fig. 2.1 Relationship between the different levels in Marx's social structure (Cuff & Payne, 1979).

contradictions, for example between increasing industrial production by skilled artisans in social relationships with the characteristics of feudal societies, are perceived by the proletariat who must act in a concerted and vigorous way to overcome them. Thus a Marxist theory is more than economic determinism, because it emphasises that society's members must take positive action to bring about changes in production and hence to other parts of society.

This is expressed in Marx's theory of social change applied to capitalism. Social change would not happen until the bulk of the population, the free labourers, developed a consciousness of what was happening in their society and acted together in a social group, i.e. as a social class. Only through involvement in various forms of action could members of the proleteriat develop their own ideology and begin to create a society which meets their own interest.

Marx's theory is, of course, much wider-ranging than that presented here, but all of it draws on a basic conflict between different classes based on different economic groups.

Max Weber

The major attack on Marxist theory has been on his position that only changes in the economic base can change society. Max Weber's (1864–1920) basic position is that many factors must come together to produce social change. His major thesis *The Protestant Ethic and the Spirit of Capitalism* (1930, first published in German in 1904–5) argued that it was the religious ideals of Calvinism which transformed people's behaviour and produced capitalism, by turning their religious zeal into economic production through hard work rather than by detaching themselves from work to pursue their religious interests. Work on earth to gain God's favour of a place in heaven created the impetus for maximisation of efficiency and for finding the best means of doing the work. In his analysis of world religions Weber attempted to show that religious ideas—a component in Marx's superstructure—could affect economic behaviour.

Weber's other challenge to Marx was over the derivation of the power available to social groups. He did not agree that power derived solely from economic relations, the relations to private property and the means of production. For Weber there are different dimensions to power relationships. We take up these dimensions in Chapter 3 when we deal with social stratification and consider the competing interests of class and status groups to establish the right to wield power. This is further discussed in relation to bureaucracy in health organisation in Chapter 7. The conflict between different class groups is a core assumption of Weberian sociology which, despite its challenge to Marxism, owes its central ideas and concepts to Marxist theory.

Since Marx and Weber, other sociologists have continued to examine the structure of society along class lines as well as expanding ideas about the basis of class and class consciousness. Furthermore, as capitalist societies have been superseded by other forms of economic organisation, there is a continued analysis and refinement of Marx's concepts to accommodate these new types of social structure.

The structuralist contribution

We have compared some major ideas in consenses and conflict styles of structuralism, and, have pointed out their basic difference in viewing groups in society. On the one hand consensus theory views the social system as essentially cohesive, with individuals and groups reciprocating and cooperating with each other by adhering to an integrating system of norms and values. Social life is therefore characterised by its continuity and stability rather than by change. On the other hand, conflict theorists point up the divisiveness, conflict and hostility that is inevitably generated by social structures, creating groups with different and antagonistic interests. Social change comes about by groups attempting to preserve, extend or realise their own interests at the cost of other groups.

Despite these divergent views, both groups of structuralists are concerned with finding out how the whole of society works, identifying the interrelationships between its key parts and discovering how the social structure influences individuals. Inevitably this leads to making assumptions that social structures are systems of some kind, comprising some kind of parts which are related in some way, and when there is sufficient change in the nature of these parts, then this will bring about a change in the social structure as a whole. How the theorists differ in how they approach an understanding of the social world is in their respective views of the nature of the system, the parts, the relationships between parts and therefore the differential importance of certain parts. Nevertheless, the emphasis on the social world as a structured system allows them to be classified as structuralists.

SYMBOLIC INTERACTIONALISM AS A PERSPECTIVE

In some ways symbolic interactionism is an embracing term given to a number of characteristics which identify a broad sociological perspective. Many of the core ideas in symbolic interactionism characterise a rather different frame of reference known as *action theory*, which evolved from Max Weber's simple idea that sociologists should proceed to *understand* those they study. This is achieved by attempting to look upon the world as they do; by appreciating how the world looks to them. To this is added learning the ideas, motives and goals which make people act. By learning these things about individuals, the sociologist should gain an understanding of why they act in certain ways in order to achieve particular ends in the face of their individual circumstances as they see them.

This approach, emphasising understanding the individual, is very different from that of functionalism with its emphasis on social structures and facts which exist independently of individual members of society. Though Parsons sought to build his structural functionalist theories from the elements of individuals' social action, he set them within the broader social systems which governed individual action. His emphasis therefore was on the understanding of social action by reference to social systems rather than of social action as generated through individuals in their particular circumstances. Thus, *social action* is attractive to a broad range of social theories but is difficult to study empirically while linked to broad social structures rather than to small groups. It has been left to those within the broad perspective of social interactionism to translate their theoretical position into empirical studies.

The bases of symbolic interactionism

The main ideas of symbolic interactionism were provided by George H. Mead (1863–1931, Fig. 2.2) in Chicago earlier this century, and the major contributions to this perspective have continued to be American. At the heart of Mead's approach is the assumption that there is a difference between animal *reaction* and human *conduct*. Conduct requires the possession of *mind* which is distinctive to the human species. To this is added the concept of *self*. Individuals both undergo experiences and are aware of doing so.

Mead (1934) regards human action as very different from human behaviour. Behaviour is limited to a stimulus-response relationship. The concept of action depends on individuals' ability to plan their actions, reflect on past experience and reflect on themselves in the same way as they look upon other

Fig. 2.2 The father of symbolic interactionism: George Herbert Mead (1863–1931) (courtesy of University of Chicago Library).

kinds of objects in the environment. It is the capacity for self-consciousness which makes human beings different from animals, and central to this is the ability of the individual to take the same attitude towards himself as others take towards him. In this sense he becomes an object like any other object; to look upon oneself as an object is to see oneself as others do.

For different individuals the same object, be it a pine tree or antenatal care, will have very different meanings which will depend on such factors as previous experience and current purposes. The social significance of the pine tree will differ as a result of individuals' experiences. The post office engineer, through social interaction with fellow workers, may find himself classifying a pine tree as suitable or not suitable for a telegraph pole. He will have learnt from colleagues early on in his career that elms and oaks are not suitable for the job. The country boy will learn from his peers that pine trees burn well but too quickly and are therefore not as suitable for fuel as oak or beech. When out on an expedition a naturalist will refer to different pine trees by their various Latin names since this will have more significance to his colleagues. Similarly, for a pregnant woman the value of antenatal care is determined by the individual's knowledge of pregnancy, her experience of pregnancy and the experience of her peers. To health professionals the value of antenatal care will be determined by the kinds of information they receive during their professional training.

An individual will also experience the many different meanings he himself holds for others, reflected back to him. In order to handle this complexity, the individual constructs a picture of himself according to the general, typical and predominant views of himself as shown by others. This is carried out largely through the medium of language—'only human beings share language'—which Mead refers to as the *significant symbol*. Through such exchanges the individual learns the ways of acting which others expect of him and the self-consciousness necessary to engage in social life. The meanings of all objects are similarly derived from social interaction of the individual with other members of society. Such meanings are handled in and modified through an interpretation process used by people in dealing with the things they encounter.

It is explaining such processes that is the hallmark of symbolic interactionist approaches—providing an understanding of how and why things are as they are, by finding out about the circumstances of people's lives. As Blumer (1969) contends, these circumstances do not exist *in themselves* as stimuli to which the individual reacts. Rather, what constitutes circumstances depends on the purposes, plans and knowledge that the individual has *in mind*. Social action therefore has to be interpreted as the mindful action of individuals iniated to bring about certain purposes.

Blumer provides a major critique of those sociological approaches which attempt to ape the natural sciences by linking dependent and independent variables without any real understanding of either the variables themselves or what processes actually link them. This is because sociological abstractions used as variables, such as *authority* or *group morale*, have different indicators depending on the circumstances in which they are being studied. It would be inappropriate to use the same indicators, for example of social integration, when applied to cities and to a class of students. What Bulmer is saying is that social life is extremely complex because of the elaborate and various processes which exist and about which we have only the most limited findings, and because the *inner* workings of social life which give rise to them are equally complex.

Blumer, therefore, advocates an approach to sociological enquiry which is distinctly sociological in that it examines in detail particular instances of social life as they occur in their natural settings. In advocating a *naturalistic* approach the researcher is aiming to put himself in the position of seeing the world in the same way as those he is studying. In carrying out studies which have been intensively concerned with topics limited to particular occasions or a narrow set of circumstances, symbolic interactionists have made a distinctive contribution to knowledge. One such contribution attempts to show how variable settings, which may differ by way of the content of their subject matter, display similar characteristics in terms of formal properties or structural arrangements. For example, much work has been done by symbolic interactionists on the concept of *career*. This is linked not only to occupational life; the career concept, as one of progression with differentiated stages, can be applied to prisoners, patients and indeed the life cycle itself. Career can be said to have *formal* properties in that there is a chronological ordering of steps which are relatively predictable, each one bringing its typical experiences, tasks and problems. *Career* is therefore a formal generalisation, typical of the kind of formal approach used by symbolic interactionists; we pick it up in Chapter 5 in relation to the life career, Chapter 8 when we discuss the patient career and in Chapter 11 for the professional career.

A similar idea is that social contexts influence interaction and, in Chapter 10, we discuss how *uncertainty* influences the care of dying patients. Uncertainty as a social context would be equally relevant to playing bridge, arms and wage negotiations, managing information about a diagnosis or buying a house.

Symbolic interactionists have also shown how behaviour which from one perspective would be interpreted as totally irrational, from another perspective is a rational response to circumstances. We take up this idea in Chapter 8 when we discusss some ideas about illness behaviour and particularly the work of Erving Goffman. This is associated with an interest in the processes by which members of society define their own circumstances and respective identities. This is encapsulated in a dictum attributed to W.I. Thomas: 'if men define situations as real, they are real in their consequences' (Merton, 1968, p. 475). This definitional approach has had particular applications in what has come to be known as *the labelling theory of deviance*, that is, how members of the community come to define and label some of its members as deviant in certain respects and interact with them in such a way that the person takes on the characteristics related to the label. We shall deal with labelling in Chapter 8 as it applies to patients.

The individual and society

For symbolic interactionists the organisation of social life arises from within society itself and out of the processes of interaction between its members. They do not accept that external factors, such as economic ones, determine the form that society takes, although such factors do exert influence. Such influences will vary, however, depending on how they are perceived and dealt with. While the organisation of social life arises from within, it does not take on any autonomous features like those attributed by structuralist sociologists. To assume that society imposes or determines the action of society's members is incompatible with an interactionist perspective. Neither do the symbolic interactionists regard the structure of society as rigidly adhering to some *basic*, almost universal structure, as Marxist theory does. Rather, society consists of a relatively loosely articulated array of heterogeneous and overlapping social groups. While the relationships between groups or sub-groups may be characterised as competitive, there is no basic theoretical reason why one group should predominate. Relevant concepts and the processes of gaining or maintaining social dominance or control have been articulated by Anselm Strauss in relation to the division of labour in psychiatric hospitals. We will develop this idea of the *negotiated order* of society as groups continuously organising in Chapter 7 when we look at health care organisations.

Typically, symbolic interactionists are concerned not with an embracing concept of *society* but with the way in which individual members of society are engaged in indicating to others who and what they take themselves to be. This draws heavily on Mead's view of the self as something created in and through social interaction. This self is portrayed in the conventional ways in which people communicate their social status, social role and sense of self. Erving Goffman sought to understand how people come to decide, through social interaction, who they are. He employs the metaphor of life being just like life on the stage. We develop this idea in Chapter 3 when we discuss how individuals engage in *impression management* in order to portray a particular identity and have this identity reaffirmed by others.

How do we come to achieve our sense of self? Particularly, what role does adult life play in modifying the sense of self achieved in childhood? Interactionists emphasise the continuous nature of socialisation extending throughout adulthood. This we we shall elaborate when we discuss ageing in Chapter 5 and professional socialisation in Chapter 11.

Some criticisms of symbolic interactionism

Just as symbolic interactionists criticise sociological theory which conforms to natural science, which attempts an excessively deterministic view of the relationship between the individual and society, and which takes the macro-structure of society as its base, so reciprocal criticisms are levelled at symbolic interactionism. These include an indifference to problems of evidence, proof and systematic theory; an avoidance of regard for the structural constraints which foreclose available choices open to individuals; and an absence of any attempt to gain an overview of social organisation, with an accompanying neglect of social stratification. Much of this criticism is directed not only at the basic theoretical assumptions of symbolic interactionism but also at the *naturalistic* qualitative methods which it employs, and which are at odds with the *quantitative* methods employed by some structuralists.

PHENOMENOLOGY AND ETHNOMETHODOLOGY AS A PERSPECTIVE

Here we give far less attention to ethnomethodology as a perspective than its current importance in sociology merits. This is because, to-date, ethnomethodology has contributed relatively little to our sociological knowledge about health and illness. Its basic assumptions, deriving largely from the phenomenological philosophy of Edmund Husserl (1859–1938) are very different from those of other sociological theories.

Husserl attempts to describe the ultimate foundations of human experience by 'seeing beyond' the particulars of every day experiences to describe the 'essences' which underpin them. Only by grasping such essences do we have a foundation for all experience which enables us to recognise and classify it in an intelligible form. In order to grasp these essences it is necessary for the philosopher to disengage from our usual ideas about the world, to examine the stream of experiences available to us—past, present and future. Phenomenology is about perceiving phenomena in the world as objects or events which are, in essential respects, *common—*

the same for others as they are for ourselves. Therefore, the foundations of social life are not within the mind and experience of an individual, but in a commonly lived world of experience. This is a social world known in common with others.

It was Alfred Schutz (1899–1959) who developed this phenomenological approach into a sociological scientific study of social life which has subsequently come to be known as ethnomethodology (ethno = people, ethnomethodology = the study of people's methods). This is especially though not solely concerned with the language used in and to describe everyday life. The approach is concerned with the basis of the common assumptions we all make in order to render comprehensible the routines and activities of our everyday lives. Such order is achieved through what Alfred Schutz has termed our *taken-for-granted assumptions*, in other words our expectations of what should happen in a normal day and how we expect others to act. For example, we expect shops to close on Sunday, we expect the accident and emergency department to be busy on Saturday evenings, we know how to behave in the presence of our peers, teachers and parents. This social fabric is maintained by what Schutz (1972) has called *typifications*—common ways of classifying objects such as tree or woman, events such as visit to the doctor or getting breakfast, and experiences such as pain or love, but in ways which are capable of being redefined or adapted. One taken-for-granted assumption is that others, by and large, see the world as we do, something which clearly is not always borne out. These elements of everyday life are not only learned through the process of socialisation but are also identified as 'mental tools' which we carry around with us in order that we can adapt our own actions according to the situations in which we find ourselves. Thus, like the interactionists, phenomenologists and ethnomethodologists (e.g. Garfinkel, 1967) are concerned with how members of a social group perceive, define and classify the ways in which they actually perform their activities, and what meanings they assign to acts occurring in the context of their everyday lives.

We shall examine some ideas on professionals' typifications of patients, and their effects, in Chapter 9 when we deal with social interaction.

GARFINKEL'S CONCEPTUAL FRAMEWORK

In order to grasp the distinctiveness of ethnomethodology it is important to understand some rather basic though complex concepts. Their difficulty is partly due to the radical differences in perspective of ethnomethodologists, as well as to the language used by writers like Garfinkel (1967).

Rather than use the term actors or participants, ethnomethodologists talk about *members*. They prefer this term because it covers belief of a shared social life with others. Members recognise and produce social activities using methods which make them unproblematically available to other members. In order to produce routine and unproblematic features of our everyday lives we engage in sense-making work. In other words it is by *members' methods* of engaging in sense-making work that we actually accomplish the social world—be it telling a joke, carrying out a clinic or giving a lecture. Not only do we make it clear to others that this is what we are doing, but others also engage in sense-making work to comprehend and let us know that they comprehend what is going on—or that, in fact, they do not understand and would like us to make things clearer. This means that the social world is not something imposed from 'out there' or inherited by virtue of an assigned role. Rather, Garfinkel proposes that we must accomplish our social world and that we do so in ways which we ordinarily take for granted and do not stop to analyse. Ethnomethodologists regard it as their task to provide such an analysis in order to explain how we achieve the social world we inhabit.

Members' actions and speech are features of the organised social settings in which they are used and which they in turn produce. In this sense they are *indexical* to social settings. Garfinkel uses the term *indexicality* to stress the occasioned nature of everyday happenings—the particulars of social occasions and events. For instance, there is no standardised use of words. How the words 'he's had it' are interpreted will depend on the particular occasion and the taken-for-granted analytic work of members. Similarly, the nature of the occasion, what it is, and what it means—be it a social chat or a disciplinary hearing—is not unambiguous. What it is has to be achieved by the members involved in it.

This work is what ethnomethodologists refer to as 'repairing indexical particulars'—how members go about arriving at a limited definition of what they are engaged in. Not only members, but also ethnomethodologists studying members, must go through the same process to review and document what is of significance and arrive at a shorthand description of particular occasions. In every new situation the same processes have to be engaged in to produce the members' sense of it.

Garfinkel's analysis of the repair of indexical expression emphasises this as a member's practical problem and the means whereby he accomplishes the social world. This whole enterprise is characterised by *reflexivity*. Reflexivity refers to the essential interdependence of the circumstances members attribute to social events and their descriptions or accounts of what the events themselves are. In other words, circumstances are embedded in descriptions or accounts of events and accounts or descriptions of events are embedded in their particular circumstances. Thus, members who are taking part in some social occasion use its features both to make visible to others what is happening and to make the features themselves come about. They do so by using members' commonsense methods to make this world describable to themselves and to others. Ethnomethodologists, in attempting to explicate these methods, are themselves confronted with making sense of what is happening and must examine their own reflexivity, something members take for granted.

In some respects, ethnomethodology is like symbolic interactionism in that it is concerned with studying social interactions as a process of meaningful communicative activity. There the similarity ends however. Jack Douglas (1976) argues that while interactionists focus their attention on ongoing social interactions between individuals, they interpret these interactions in a *scientistic* fashion. They, like the functionalists, are concerned with hypothesis testing and identifying cause and effect. To arrive at this level of explanation requires the translation of observations and statements about everyday happenings into more abstract theoretical statements. The phenomenological and ethnomethodological position is that this level of theorising and the methods used to achieve it are basically inappropriate for achieving a real understanding of everyday life. 'There is no way of getting at the social meanings from which one implicitly or explicitly infers the larger patterns except through some form of communication with the members of that society or group; and, to be valid and reliable, any such communication with the members presupposes an understanding of their language, their use of language, their own understanding of what the people doing the observations are up to, and so on almost endlessly.' (Douglas, 1976, p. 9). Thus the phenomena to be studied must be the phenomena *as experienced* in everyday life and not the phenomena observed and interpreted by the scientist with his own particular taken-for-granted assumptions, which will differ from those of the subject being studied. Similarly, the methods used for such empirical studies must be those which facilitate gaining this kind of understanding. Of course this position is open to the criticism that while ethnomethodologists study members' methods they simultaneously employ these methods themselves. Ethnomethodologists would reply that it is necessary to construct methods of data collection and analysis appropriate to the empirical settings in which the search is conducted rather than producing a set of generalised methodological directives appropriate to particular settings. They will be judged therefore on the basis of the detailed arguments in reported empirical studies.

SUMMARY

This chapter has introduced the major perspectives in sociology. In doing so we have commented on the central position of theory in our everyday lives as well as its formal role in sociology. Our actions and how we interpret the world are guided by personal and often implicit theories. So too are the interpretations of the social world and the studies carried out by sociologists, but their theories are made explicit and are open to public scrutiny. One aspect of becoming familiar with sociology is to recognise the different major theories before making a decision about which you should subscribe to as most useful for explaining particular social phenomena. Sociologists themselves have to make such decisions.

Structuralism, interactionism and ethnomethodology have

each been characterised as expounding their particular theories of society, its composition, how it changes and what are the central concepts and processes. A very broad and introductory approach to this has been necessary and, while we have touched on some of the major divisions in their broad perspectives, there are many other variations which students of sociology will encounter.

As a component of sociological perspectives, different questions are asked about social phenomena and they are investigated in different ways. The example of mental illness was used to demonstrate the kinds of research questions and approaches that evolve from different perspectives. This is typical of the diversity to be found in the way that health topics are conceptualised and in the approaches used to study the social world more generally. There are ongoing debates around major sociological, theoretical and research methodological issues and these will surface in some of the ensuing chapters, especially Chapter 12 which deals with research methods.

It is important to grasp that sociological thoery is not something distinct from the sociological research which provides us with a sociology of health. Without sociological theory providing particular sociological perspectives it would be well-nigh impossible to comprehend the basis of research and the assumptions on which it is based. We have attempted to show that there is no one perspective in sociology nor indeed could a sociology be constructed by taking the 'best' bits from each theory. Sociological theorists take up far too strongly held positions within their own camps to permit this to happen and tend to adhere to one perspective which they regard as *the* approach to sociology. We have tried to present a description of major perspectives without advocating that overall one has more relevance or more to offer than another. Different perspectives generate research on different topics and choose different methods in doing so. As you read on you will encounter studies which adhere to one perspective or another. In this way we amass knowledge, not in any absolute sense of final truths, but by shedding some light on different aspects of our social world. However, it remains your judgement, as to whether sociology does help in seeing your own social world and the world of health more sensitively, more comprehensively or more clearly. For this to happen, a sociological understanding must be acquired.

It may be helpful to return to this chapter again once you have encountered some sociological concepts and empirical studies, thereby enhancing your understanding of both perspectives and findings.

REFERENCES

Blumer H 1969 Symbolic interactionism: perspective and method. Prentice Hall, Englewood Cliffs, NJ

Bottomore T B, Rubel M (eds) 1965 Karl Marx: selected writings in sociology and social philosophy. Penguin Books, Harmondsworth

Cuff E C, Payne G C F 1979 Perspectives in sociology. Allen & Unwin, London

Douglas J D 1976 Understanding everyday life. In: Douglas J D (ed) Understanding everyday life. Toward the reconstruction of sociological knowledge. Routledge & Kegan Paul, London, ch 1, p 3–44

Dunham H W, Faris R E C 1965 Mental disorders in urban areas. University of Chicago Press, Chicago

Durkheim E 1964a The division of labour in society. Free Press, New York

Durkheim E 1964b Rules of sociological method. Free Press, New York

Garfinkel H 1967 Studies in ethnomethodology. Prentice Hall, Englewood Cliffs, NJ

Hollingshead A B, Redlich F C 1958 Social class and mental illness: a community study. Wiley, New York

Lefebvre H 1968 The sociology of Marx. Pantheon Books, New York

Mead G H 1934 Mind, self and society. The University of Chicago Press, Chicago

Mead G H 1964 On social psychology: selected papers. Strauss A (ed) The University of Chicago Press, Chicago

Merton R 1967 On theoretical sociology. Free Press, New York

Merton R 1968 Social theory and social structure. Free Press, New York

Parsons T 1951 The social system. Routledge & Kegan Paul, London

Scheff T J 1964 The societal reaction to deviance: ascriptive elements in the psychiatric screening of mental patients in a Midwestern State. Social Problems 11: 401–413

Schutz A 1972 The phenomenology of the social world. Heinemann, London

Szasz T S 1971 The manufacture of madness. Routledge & Kegan Paul, London

Turner R 1968 Talk and troubles: contact problems of former mental patients. Unpublished Ph.D dissertation, University of California, Berkeley

Weber M 1948 The protestant ethic and the spirit of capitalism. Unwin University Books, London

FURTHER READING

Cuff E C, Payne G C F 1984 Perspectives in sociology, 2nd edn. Allen & Unwin, London

3

Social stratification

INTRODUCTION

In the last chapter we introduced you to a number of different sociological perspectives. Common to all these is a concern with social order. We shall explore this topic in a number of places throughout the book. In this chapter we look at social order from the structuralist perspective by describing the many forms of social stratification and show how the concept of social stratification relates to people's experiences and to their use of health services.

We shall examine the major structural concepts—class, status and power—and discuss how people move upwards or downwards within a stratification system. The difficulties of measuring social class are discussed as a preliminary to understanding data which link indicators of health like mortality and morbidity rates to social structural indices. Inequalities in health are explored.

We are all familiar with the notion of the geological stratification of rocks which are ordered according to their age. In societies there are also criteria by which social groups are stratified. In many societies occupation is the main criterion upon which stratification is based, but different cultures also use caste, as in India; race, as in South Africa; or ethnicity, as was used in Nazi Germany.

Our analogy between geological stratification and social stratification could be misleading. Worsley (1977) notes a number of ways in which the analogy is wrong. Since the principle of rock stratification is based on the age of the rocks it is a permanent system. In contrast, social systems are more flexible and can change over time because the principles of social stratification are *socially constructed*. In many social strata the different levels are defined in terms of inferiority or superiority in income, power and prestige. These criteria are socially constructed. For example, some occupations which were prestigious 30 years ago are less so today; a number of senior nurses make this claim about nursing. Another characteristic of social stratification not found in geological stratification is that *conflict* often exists between different social strata, for example between management and labour and between ethnic minorities and the major social group. Also the principles of social stratification allow individuals to *move* from one social stratum to another; for instance, the child of a labourer becomes a doctor, or a man from the ranks gains officer status. This is called *social mobility*. Geological strata are of course *static* (although rock formations may move).

A distinctive feature of all social stratification is *inequality* between the strata. There are two aspects of inequality that are particularly important. The first concerns the distribution of income, wealth, prestige, education, power and health. The second concerns the way in which individuals differentiated by such criteria relate to each other. 'Forelock tugging' is an obvious example of the way two individuals, from different social strata, relate to each other. Another common example is the differential use of first names and nicknames.

In sociology a number of different concepts are used to describe social stratification and inequality. It was Max Weber who made the initial and important distinctions between *class*, *status* and *power*.

CLASS

One of our most frequent uses of the concept social stratification is when we talk about *social class*. This is used not only by sociologists, to distinguish between different social groups, but also in government statistics, by politicians and in everyday language. However, because it is used in so many ways—to categorise people by income, power, wealth, prestige or occupation—it is an awkward concept.

Much of the attention given by sociologists to the concept of class comes from the writings of Karl Marx. Yet Marx himself never fully defined social class, although his general conceptions about social classes and their behaviour are fairly clear. Marx divided capitalist society into two classes: the bourgeoisie, who were the owners of the means of production, and the proletariat, who were not. His analysis of class struggles and conflict, which was central to his political ideology as opposed to his sociological insights, was based on this fundamental distinction between the two classes.

In contrast, Max Weber's use of the concept of class is somewhat wider in scope (Gerth & Mills, 1948). In Weber's sense a person's class position is the location which he shares with those who are similarly placed in the processes of production, distribution and exchange. It includes not only the specific relationship between the bourgeoisie and proletariat but all those situations where there is a market relationship. For example, Weber would include the ownership of domestic property as a criterion for locating a person's class. Significant inequalities between members of the proletariat arising from home ownership would not be recognised be Marx as locating individuals' different classes.

Weber also recognised a greater variety of relationships to the means of production. Marx's dichotomy between the bourgeoisie and proletariat meant that shopkeepers and wage earners could be a single economic and social group: the proletariat. Similarly there is no room in this classification for the non-manufacturing industries, ranging from the social service industries and the distribution industries to the financial service industries of banking and insurance. Weber, in contrast, recognised that individuals could be classified by class according to all of these different relationships with the processes of production, because they determined the lifestyle and life chances of different groups in society. Thus Weber argued that a person's class position differs because of the meaning he can and does give to the use of his property as well as because of its ownership.

The Weberian concept of class allows us to understand inequalities of class, not just in terms of the relationship between the owners and non-owners of the means of production. It allows us to understand inequalities in income, occupation and education. In this sense, class becomes a more complex social phenomenon which embraces all aspects of *economic* position in society. Inequalities of class refer to economic inequalities of income, wealth and education rather than to inequalities of power and prestige.

STATUS

The concept of *status*, as outlined by Weber, focuses on social estimation and prestige, and although closely related to the concept of class is *not* synonymous with it. Thus status implies not merely the apportionment of prestige for some specific occupational or other role, but involves the apportionment of generalised prestige which segregates one group from another. Both class and status are derived from different economic aspects of social behaviour. Weber placed the emphasis in status on styles of consumption; that is, the way income is used rather than income itself. Therefore status is determined not by income *per se* but by place of residence, type of speech, social origins, social habits and educational background.

Although there is often a strong relationship between economic class as defined by occupation and status as defined by styles of consumption, there are a number of familiar examples where high status is not matched by high occupational class. Compare the position of the poor aristocrat in a stately home with increasing debts arising from death duties, and the *nouveau riche* who may well be better placed in the economic hierarchy but are not admitted to the highest social gatherings. Many of the health professions are relatively high status occupations despite their relatively low incomes, as are the clergy.

Like class, status is a complex concept. For example, there is little theoretical discussion about the characteristics of status whose possession leads to high or low prestige. Indeed there has been little attempt to determine the characteristics empirically. Most empirical work undertaken has consisted of surveys of occupational prestige rather than other facets of prestige. These studies have shown remarkable unanimity (Goldthorpe & Hope, 1974; Runciman, 1966), which suggests that status is defined by common consent.

These empirical studies do not, however, explain *how* prestige is differentially assigned between occupational groups. A functionalist explanation is provided by Davis and Moore (1945):

> 'If the rights and perquisites of different positions in a society must be unequal, then the society must be stratified, because that is precisely what stratification means. Social inequality is thus an unconsciously evolved device by which societies ensure that the most important positions are conscientiously filled by the most qualified persons.' (p. 243).

Rex (1961) believes that the assignment of prestige is quite arbitrary and considers the only plausible explanation is that different social positions derive prestige because they are historically important. This, however, does not tell us why they were afforded such relative prestige in the first place.

POWER

The third aspect of social stratification is power. Weber is less explicit about his concept of power than he is about either class or status. Whereas he speaks of low class or low status, there is no comparable notion of low power. However, power is implicitly a third dimension in that Weber is concerned with the relative power of classes and status groups. Power is a commonly used word, but what do sociologists mean by it? The holders of power in a society need not necessarily be highly rewarded or have a high-prestige position. We hear regularly of the power of trade union officials and of ward domestics and nursing auxiliaries, who neither are highly paid nor hold significant prestige in the community.

In order to understand the implicit notion of power we must introduce the concepts of *authority* and *legitimacy*. Authority is the probability that a specific order, say given by senior nurses, will be obeyed by specific individuals or groups, say student nurses. The essential difference between power and authority is the continuity of the latter. Power is more often momentary: the ward sister gives an order and despite disagreement the student nurse obeys. The exercise of this power has little continuing effect but the authority of the ward sister persists.

By *legitimacy* Weber means that people accept the authority as just and that those endowed with authority are given it rightfully. In other words, the authority of the ward sister is accepted by the student nurse as just, and the ward sister's right to issue orders even though she might disagree. The student nurse would be less likely to regard the authority of a nursing auxiliary as legitimate, although at times they too can exert power in the organisation of a ward.

In the same way that power need not coincide with class or status, inequality of power need not parallel inequality of status or class, although there is usually a demonstratable connection between a person's class position and his or her power position. But to the extent that power is a separate dimension of social stratification, so power is a separate dimension of inequality. In order to understand the stratifications and inequalities in our society it is necessary to keep in mind that all three dimensions are relevant.

ASCRIBED CLASSES

Because of the emphasis on the economic aspects of class this has encouraged an emphasis on occupational class. We *acquire* our occupational class, whereas other strata within a system of social stratification can be identified on the basis of *ascribed* characteristics—characteristics with which we are born. Age, gender and race are ascribed characteristics which we implicitly or explicitly order hierarchically. This raises the question of the extent to which strata defined on the basis of ascribed characteristics also constitute a class or a status group. (Fig. 3.1)

Age, gender and race are natural attributes which are usually relatively easily identified. But inequalities between people in different age groups, between men and women, and between people of different races are more than biologically determined. They are all social constructions. For in-

Fig. 3.1 Some Community Health Councils provide positive support to members of disadvantaged ethnic minorities to assist them obtain health care (courtesy of City and Hackney Community Health Council).

stance, different societies construct old age in different ways: functionally, formally and temporally. In societies where old age is defined in *functional* terms, observed changes in a person's ability to undertake the normal activities of the adult status signifies the end of active participation as an adult. He becomes one of the aged. In societies where old age is defined in *formal* terms the change in status is normally linked to some external event such as becoming a grandparent or being awarded a pension. In some societies old age is related *temporally* and chronological age is used as an indicator of the status of old age. This happens in some hospitals in Britain where all 'medical' admissions aged 65 or over enter wards designated 'geriatric'.

Gender, age and race in modern Britain are all ascribed characteristics which have been used to determine the division of labour in society. From a Marxist perspective women are economically exploited by men, the elderly by the young, and black people by white people. From a Weberian perspective inequalities between men and women, people in different age groups and people of different races directly reflect the inequalities of the productive system and the hierarchy of the economic structure of society. Thus in both these senses men and women, the young and the old, and black people and white people can be regarded as distinct classes. Other features can equally be used as the basis for class divisions, for example occupational classes—professional and non-professionals; educational classes—graduates and non-graduates; and housing classes—owner-occupiers and tenants.

SOCIAL MOBILITY

Social mobility refers to the movement of people within a stratification system. Mobility may be upwards or downwards. A nurse whose parents are from the manual classes is said to be upwardly mobile while the teacher's son who sweeps the roads is said to be downwardly mobile. These are both forms of *vertical mobility*. The teacher who changes school or the occupational therapist who changes from working in a hospital to working in the community experience *horizontal mobility* and would not, generally, be referred to as socially mobile. In everyday language we often talk of geographical mobility. The family who move to another town or city or even country are geographically mobile. If the reason for the move is to take up a better job then they are probably socially mobile as well. However, social mobility and geographical mobility are not synonymous.

Influences on social mobility

Within any system of social stratification there are five mechanisms which a person can use to achieve upward social mobility. These mechanisms are related, so that one or more of them might be used by the person consciously or unconsciously seeking upward social mobility. Perhaps the most obvious means, obvious given the importance of the economic element in stratification systems, is through economic activity such as hard work, luck or crime. By raising his income a person has the means to afford the lifestyle of a higher class.

The second mechanism available in most societies is marriage. This is particularly the case for women, who are able to achieve upward mobility by marrying a man from a higher social class. Nowadays this mechanism is not restricted to women, however, since men also marry women in higher social classes and manage to maintain their new position by the economic activity of their spouses.

Education offers the third mechanism for social mobility. Social mobility is achieved as part of an educational process which often complements the efforts of economic activity. The manual labourer's child who attends university is an obvious example.

A fourth mechanism of social mobility is political. This occurs when the social mobility of individuals or whole groups is achieved through political pressures, negotiations or guarantees. This is a particularly important mechanism in terms of group mobility. The Suffragette Movement and the Women's Movement, through mechanisms of franchise and pressing for equal employment and other social opportunity, have through political action increased the chances for women of upward social mobility.

Finally Goffman (1971) coined the phrase *impression management* to describe social mobility achieved through the manipulation of status symbols and personal attraction. Used by itself impression management is unlikely to be a successful mechanism for upward mobility except for the small minority who have particularly attractive personalities and social skills. However, this mechanism is important in conjunction with one or more of the other four mechanisms. The *nouveaux riches*, for example, are only acceptable to the aristocracy when they present the 'right' status images of themselves, and the brilliant working-class lad who, against the odds, makes it to the law courts must also learn how to conduct himself socially.

Patterns of social mobility in Britain

It is widely argued that Britain nowadays is a more open society; that is, that there is greater opportunity for social mobility. Since the 1940s the favourable conditions necessary for increased social mobility have been encouraged by the social policies of successive goverments. Until recently, continuous economic growth has transformed the occupational structure of society by increasing the proportion of non-manual occupations, thus providing opportunities for upward mobility. At the same time largescale educational reforms were carried through which greatly increased educational provision and established a formal equality of educational opportunity. In conjunction with other social policies educational reforms were intended to encourage a more open society.

But how successful have postwar social policies been in facilitating increased social mobility? Goldthorpe (1980) concluded, in his analysis of data collected from the British mobility surveys, that there has been little increase in relative mobility rates; but because of the changes in the occupational structure, there has been a general shift upwards in absolute terms. To the average British person this is reflected in the better standard of living experienced by all strata of British society since 1940. However, the general conclusion from these data is that, while Britain is better off, it is not a more open society than it was 50 years ago, and there continues to be little relative social mobility between the various strata.

MEASUREMENT OF SOCIAL CLASS

It will be clear from the space devoted to the subject of social stratification that we consider it to be an essential ingredient to the understanding of our social structure. The concepts of social stratification, although complex, are crucial to any examination of the nature of our society. Historically, the concepts of class, status and power have played a central role in sociological theory. They have also been important concepts in public discussions of social and political change and policy.

In most empirical sociological research and in Government

statistics and analysis the complex theoretical niceties discussed above are displaced by the need for pragmatic measures of 'social class'. In British research almost the sole criterion of social class which has been used is occupation. This is probably because no better empirical method of stratifying people has been found. Moreover, occupation has been shown consistently to be highly related to most other factors associated with social class, particularly income and education and, as we show below, health.

Official measures of social class

Since the 1911 Census, official statistics and studies have incorporated a measure of social class. In 1911 the Registrar General graded occupations into eight classes according to the 'social position' of the occupation. The criteria used were arbitrary and have been frequently criticised. In the 1921 Census the number of classes was reduced to five. Arbitrary updating of the measures has continued to the present. At the time of the 1981 Census the Registrar General used two methods of defining social class; both were based on occupation and both deliberately combined the concepts of class and status.

Social class. The present Social Class groupings are as follows:

I   Professional, etc. occupations
II Intermediate occupations
III Skilled occupations
    (N) non-manual
    (M) manual
IV Partly skilled occupations
V   Unskilled occupations

Table 3.1 gives examples of occupations which fall into each of these six categories. The basis and rationale of the social Class categories is outlined in the *Classification of Occupations, 1980*:

The occupation groups included in each of these categories have been selected in such a way as to bring together, so far as possible, people with similar levels of occupational skill. In general each occupation group is assigned as a whole to one or another social class and no account is taken of differences between individuals in the same occupation group e.g. differences of education or level of remuneration. However persons of a particular employment status within occupation groups are allocated to the appropriate Social Classes as derived by the following rules:

(a) each occupation is given a basic Social Class
(b) persons of foreman status whose basic Social Class is IV or V are allotted to Social Class III
(c) persons of manager status are allocated to Social Class II except for the following:
Social Class I for group 007.1
Social Class III for groups 039.4 and 057.3 and if the basic class is IV or V.

(OPCS, 1980, p. xi)

In making comparisons between different years, particularly with years following a decennial Census, care should be taken in the interpretation of the trends because of changes in the allocation of occupations to the six Social Class categories. The most extensive changes occurred between the 1951 Census and the 1961 Census but significant changes have been made at other times.

Socio-economic groups. Since the 1951 Census occupations have also been classified into socio-economic groups. This classification similarly reflects, to some extent, the social standing of occupational groups in society. The classification aims to bring together people with jobs of similar social and economic status. The socio-economic groups are:

1. Employers and managers in central and local government, industry, commerce—large establishments.
2. Employers and managers in industry and commerce—small establishments.
3. Professional workers—self-employed.
4. Professional workers—employees.
5. Intermediate non-manual workers.
6. Junior non-manual workers.
7. Personal service workers.
8. Foreman and supervisors—non-manual.
9. Skilled manual workers.
10. Semi-skilled manual workers.
11. Unskilled manual workers.
12. Own account workers (other than professionals).
13. Farmers—employers and managers.
14. Farmers—own account.
15. Agricultural workers.
16. Members of Armed Forces.
17. Occupations inadequately described.

Table 3.1 Occupations in Registrar General's social class categories

I Professional	II Managerial	III (N) Skilled non-manual	III (M) Skilled manual	IV Partly skilled	V Unskilled
lawyer	farmer	cashier	machine tool setter	machine tool operator	builders labourer
university lecturer	nurse	secretary	fitter	postman	messenger
doctor	office manager		miner (face worker)	traffic warden	railway porter
					window cleaner

Table 3.2 Occupations in eight social classes used in British Social Mobility Study

Professionally qualified and high administrative	Managerial and executive	Inspectional, supervisory, and other non-manual higher grade	Inspectional, supervisory and other non-manual	Routine non-manual work	Skilled manual	Semi-skilled manual	Unskilled manual
lawyer	headmaster	colliery engineer	accountant's clerk	tax officer	taxi driver	bus conductor	builders labourer
doctor	missionary	social worker	shop manageress	receptionist	slater	farm labourer	railway porter
surveyor	nurse administrator	qualified nurse			miner (face worker)	postman	window cleaner

In both the classification of Social Class and the classification of Socio-economic Group married women are normally classified by their husband's occupation, and retired persons according to their main occupation or husband's main occupation. For this reason these classifications are less reliable for women and retired people.

Other measures of social class

Many sociologists were unhappy with the Registrar General's classification of social class and wanted a classification more firmly based on the social perceptions of occupational prestige. For the seminal study of social mobility (Glass, 1954) a seven-category scale was developed, and this was modified subsequently to include the following eight categories:

1. Professional qualified and high administrative.
2. Managerial and executive with some responsibility for directing and initiating policy.
3. Inspectional, supervisory and other non-manual higher grade.
4. Inspectional, supervisory and other non-manual.
5. Routine grades of non-manual work.
6. Skilled manual occupations.
7. Semi-skilled manual occupations.
8. Routine manual occupations.

Table 3.2 gives examples of occupations which fall into each of these eight categories.

Like the Registrar General's classification this categorisation of occupations is somewhat arbitrary, since it is impractical to invite samples of the population to rank 20 000 or more occupations. In the further development of this measure Goldthorpe and Hope (1974) used a basic 20 occupations and related these to the ranking of a further 860 by asking subsamples of people to rank two groups of twenty occupations: the basic 20 and a variable 20. In order to extend the concept they also asked each informant to rank both groups of occupations on four separate dimensions: (a) standard of living, (b) prestige in the community, (c) power and influence over other people, and (d) value to society. This approach does achieve more consistent grading of occupations but at the cost of distinguishing a large and cumbersome number of grades.

Emphasis on the status aspects of occupation has been criti-

cised for its *normative* emphasis on the measurement of social class. Writers like Peter Townsend have argued that,
because they emphasise status rather than economic class, the
classifications developed are more suitable for measuring the
inequalities of occupational prestige than inequalities of class.
He argues that this approach conditions society to interpret
and accept inequality as one involving differences in the absolute distribution of occupations. Thus some inequalities,
which are avoidable, are regarded as unavoidable and aspirations for social equality are interpreted only as aspirations for
upward occupational mobility and not equality (Townsend,
1979). Despite these criticisms Townsend himself is able to
show gross irregularities between occupational classes and it
is to some of these to which we now turn.

SOCIAL CLASS DIFFERENCES IN BRITAIN

Social class differences in Britain are well documented and
have been brought together in a useful source book by Ivan
Reid (1977). They occur in all walks of life: in the economic
sphere—income and resources, occupational pensions, expenditure, and employment; in health and use of health services; in the family and life-style; in education; and in politics,
religion, leisure and opinion. To reproduce here evidence of
these differences would be duplicating the work of other writers who have concentrated specifically on social class differences and inequality. We will, however, identify some of the
inequalities in health and the use of health services in Britain.

Inequality in health

The World Health Organisation has defined health as 'the
state of complete physical, mental and social well-being and
not merely the absence of disease and infirmity' (WHO, 1983,
p. 1). This perspective of health emphasises the necessity of
individuals to identify and define their own health. In Chapter
1 we used the example of the elderly lady who was found by
routine examination to have anaemia, but felt fine and was
therefore unwilling to receive a blood transfusion, to illustrate

the sometimes conflicting perspectives of the health professional and the patient.
  The art of measuring individuals' perceptions of their own health is as yet embryonic, although some fairly crude attempts have been made over the years (Maddox, 1964). At the same time, conceptions of health and illness vary among different groups of people within the same society (for example, between people in different social strata) and between different societies, as well as in any single society over time (Morris, 1975). As a result, in our analysis of inequalities we are forced to rely on the medical model of health which, in theory, can claim to have a number of standardised measures of health.

Infant mortality

A common set of indicators of a nation's health is those concerned with mortality. Particular attention is given to infant mortality, which has been given widespread media coverage. The infant mortality rate is the proportion of still-births and deaths of children under one year of age per 1000 live births. The national rate has fallen from as high as 150 per 1000 live births at the turn of the century to under 20 at the beginning of the present decade. Despite this decline, during the period mentioned the relative disparity between the social classes has remained: the higher the social class the lower the death rate. Table 3.3–3.5 show these data for England and Wales and for Scotland for the period 1939–1980. Data for England and Wales are only available for selected years, and are collected through *ad hoc* enquiry, whereas data are collected and published annually in Scotland. Table 3.3 shows that the still-birth rate declined in England and Wales and in Scotland, but inequality remained marked in 1975. However, recent data from Scotland suggests that the relative position of the lower social classes might be improving. Because of the small number of still-births nowadays confirmation of this trend must await the publication of data from the years 1981–1983.
  Table 3.4 shows that the neonatal death rate (deaths in the first four weeks of life) has also declined over the same period. Inequality persists between social classes I and V and in Scotland there has been no relative improvement for the lower social classes up to 1980. Table 3.5 shows that post-neo-

Table 3.3 Still-births by social class in England and Wales, and Scotland
(Rates per 1000 total births)

Social class	England and Wales 1939	1949–50[1]	1964–65[2]	1975–76[3]	1980
I Professional	—	15.9*	11.8	7.8	—
II Managerial	—	19.4*			—
III Skilled manual and non-manual	—	21.0*	15.6	9.8	—
IV Partly skilled	—	22.9*	17.2	12.0	—
V Unskilled	—	25.5*			—

Social class	Scotland[4] 1939	1949	1964	1975	1980
I Professional	33.9	17.3	9.3	7.8	5.1
II Managerial	37.8	21.4	12.3	7.7	5.5
III Skilled manual and non-manual	44.5	26.5	17.6	11.2	6.7
IV Partly skilled	38.0	28.7	19.9	12.9	7.9
V Unskilled	42.4	35.0	23.7	14.4	6.6

* Single legitimate births only
Sources
[1] Heady J A Heasman M A 1959 Social and biological factors in infant mortality. Studies on Medical and Population Subjects, No. 15. HMSO, London, Table 5A
[2] Spicer C C, Lipworth L 1966 Regional and social factors in infant mortality. Studies on Medical and Population Subjects, No. 19. HMSO, London, Table 13
[3] Office of Population, Censuses and Surveys, Medical Statistics Division 1978 Social and biological factors in infant mortality, 1975–76. Occasional Paper No. 12. OPCS, London, Table 6
[4] Registrar General for Scotland 1982 Annual Report, 1980. HMSO, Edinburgh, Table D1.3

natal death rates (deaths after the first four weeks but in the first year of life) have also declined in England and Wales and in Scotland. These data suggest that up to 1975 the mortality differences between classes I and V have been wider after, rather than during, the early weeks of life. Thus we can see that social class is related somewhat to infant death rates, but we need to go beyond these data to discover the specific factors which cause the inequality.

Table 3.4 Neonatal death rates by social class in England and Wales, and Scotland (Rates per 1000 live births)

Social class	England and Wales 1939	1949–50[1]	1964–65[2]	1975–76[3]	1980
I Professional	—	12.2*	9.2	7.9	—
II Managerial	—	14.2*			—
III Skilled manual and non-manual	—	15.9*	11.8	9.3	—
IV Partly skilled	—	17.9*	13.2	11.7	—
V Unskilled	—	19.1*			—

Social class	Scotland[4] 1939	1949	1964	1975	1980
I Professional	25.9	13.7	9.5	7.6	3.9
II Managerial	25.1	17.9	10.9	8.7	5.8
III Skilled manual and non-manual	38.6	22.6	15.8	11.2	7.7
IV Partly skilled	34.8	24.4	18.0	10.8	6.6
V Unskilled	39.9	31.3	21.9	14.6	8.6

* Single legitimate births only
Sources
[1] Heady J A, Heasman M A 1959 Social and biological factors in infant mortality. Studies on Medical and Population Subjects, No. 15. HMSO, London, Table 5B(i)
[2] Spicer C C, Lipworth L 1966 Regional and social factors in infant mortality. Studies on Medical and Population Subjects, No. 19. HMSO, London, Table 10
[3] Office of Population, Censuses and Surveys, Medical Statistics Division 1978 Social and biological factors in infant mortality, 1975–76. Occasional Paper No. 12. OPCS, London, Table 6
[4] Registrar General for Scotland 1982 Annual Report, 1980. HMSO, Edinburgh, Table F1.4

Adult mortality

Similar disparities between the social classes are evident if we look at the mortality of men aged 20–64. Table 3.6 shows the standard mortality ratios of men aged 20–64 for the period 1921–1972. The standard mortality ratio is the number of deaths, either total or cause-specific, in a given occupational group expressed as a percentage of the number of deaths that

Table 3.5 Post neonatal death rates by social class in England and Wales, and Scotland (Rates per 1000 live births)

Social class	England and Wales 1939	1949-50[1]	1964-65[2]	1975-76[3]	1980
I Professional	—	4.8*	3.5	3.0	—
II Managerial	—	5.7*			—
III Skilled manual and non-manual	—	10.3*	5.4	4.0	—
IV Partly skilled	—	13.7*	7.6	6.1	—
V Unskilled	—	17.0*			—

Social class	Scotland[4] 1939	1949	1964	1975	1980
I Professional	7.6	4.9	2.9	1.8	4.8
II Managerial	14.8	9.1	3.8	3.8	2.6
III Skilled manual and non-manual	30.2	16.2	6.8	4.7	3.8
IV Partly skilled	33.4	22.9	8.5	5.1	3.5
V Unskilled	44.9	30.8	13.5	10.8	7.5

* Single legitimate births only
Sources
[1] Heady J A, Heasman M A 1959 Social and biological factors in infant mortality. Studies on Medical and Population Subjects, No. 15. HMSO, London, Table 5B (ii)
[2] Spicer C C, Lipworth L 1966 Regional and social factors in infant mortality. Studies on Medical and Population Subjects, No. 19. HMSO, London, Table 11
[3] Office of Population, Censuses and Surveys, Medical Statistics Division 1978. Social and biological factors in infant mortality, 1975-76. Occasional Paper No. 12. OPCS, London, Table 6
[4] Registrar General for Scotland 1982 Annual Report, 1980. HMSO, Edinburgh, Table F1.4

would have been expected in that occupational group if the age-and-sex-specific rates in the general population had obtained. Table 3.6 suggests that between 1949-53 and 1959-63 the risk of premature death of adult men of different social classes appear to have become more unequal and, 10 years later, there was little sign of any narrowing of the gap. Townsend (1974, 1979) argues that, due to changes in the classification of occupations in 1960, the data shown in Table 3.6 mask an even greater inequality between adult men of different social class at risk of premature death from 1959 onwards.

Table 3.6 Mortality of men by social class in England and Wales (standardised mortality rates)

| Social class | Men aged 15–64 | | | | | |
| | 1930–32 | 1945–53* | 1959–63 | | 1970–72 | |
			unajusted	(adjusted)†	unajusted	(adjusted)†
I Professional	90	86	76	(75)	77	(75)
II Managerial	94	92	81	(–)	81	(–)
III Skilled manual and non-manual	97	101	100	(–)	104	(–)
IV Partly skilled	102	104	103	(–)	114	(–)
V Unskilled	111	118	143	(127)	137	(121)

* Corrected figures as published in Register General 1971 Decennial Supplement, England Wales, 1961: Occupational Mortality Tables. London, HMSO, p. 22
† Occupations in 1959–63 and 1970–72 have been reclassified according to the 1950 classification of occupations.
Source Townsend P, Davidson N 1982 Inequalities in Health. Penguin Books, Harmondsworth, p. 67

When individual occupational classes are considered these show even greater inequalities. The *Decennial Supplement 1970–72* on occupational mortality reports that the standard mortality ratios for men age 15–64 were: 49 for university teachers; 70 for sales managers; 99 bread, milk and laundry roundsmen; 112 for painters and decorators; 124 for process workers; 164 for steel erecters and riggers; 171 for fishermen; and 273 for bricklayers and builders' labourers (OPCS, 1978, Appendix 2, Table A).

Morbidity

Numbers of deaths can be accurately measured and therefore mortality statistics are reliable. In contrast morbidity data are far less reliable. The annual *General Household Survey* has provided regular information about morbidity since 1970. However, the types of morbidity data collected in the *General Household Survey* are difficult to interpret. Whether people report illness differs according to their customary expectations of their own state of health, and according to the degree of inconvenience and cost attached to being sick.

The *General Household Survey* data suggest that morbidity is greater amongst the socially and materially deprived, especially during middle and old age. Analysis of these data are reported in full in the Working Party Report, *Inequalities in Health* (DHSS, 1980; Townsend & Davidson, 1982), which says that inequality between classes, in general, is at least as wide according to the various morbidity indicators such as the rate of chronic sickness or rate of sickness absence as it is for mortality. For example, according to the *General Household Survey* in 1971 in England and Wales nearly two and a half times as many unskilled manual workers as professional workers reported absence from work due to illness or injury during a two week period, and they lost an average of four and a half times as many days from work in the year due to illness (OPCS, 1973, p. 304).

A recent article by Jon Stern has questioned the validity of this kind of analysis. He claims that the use of official definitions of social class, which are based on achieved social class, are likely to result in a biased estimate of the trends in health inequalities when the absolute rate of social mobility varies over time. A more realistic procedure would be to compare mortality and morbidity rates by the social class of origin, i.e. the parents' social class (Stern, 1983). Unfortunately Government statistics have not been collected on this basis and we suspect that such a change in how data are collected would be difficult to make.

Use of health services

Ever since Richard Titmuss first wrote: 'higher income groups know how to make better use of the service; they tend to receive more specialist attention; occupy more of the beds in better equipped and staffed hospitals . . .' (Titmuss, 1968, p. 196) there has been considerable interest in the subject of use of health services by people in different social classes.

Of course the problem, as always, is not straightforward. It is not simply a matter of analysing data about the use of services by different social classes, but because of *real* inequalities in health, the use of services must be related to the need for services. Both Brotherston (1976) and Forster (1976) have used *General Household Survey* data to look at the relationship between health, service use and social class. Brotherston calculated a 'use-need ratio' for general practitioner consultations and the number of days with restricted activity and found that the ratio declined from the highest to the lowest socio-economic group. A similar trend was found by the Research Working Group in *Inequalities and Health* (DHSS, 1980; Townsend & Davidson, 1982) using aggregated data for the years 1974–76. Forster used aggregated *General Household Survey* data for the years 1971 and 1972 and also found statistically significant trends with social class for a consultation rate/morbidity ratio where the morbidity measure took into account both chronic sickness rates and sickness absence rates. There are weaknesses in this method (see *Inequalities in Health* for a comprehensive review) and therefore the conclusions can only be accepted as tentative.

Qualitative data from two studies of general practice suggest that middle-class patients receive longer consultations than working-class patients (Buchan & Richardson, 1973; Cartwright & O'Brien, 1976) and that more problems were discussed at consultations with middle-class patients than with

Fig. 3.2 The poor quality of some inner-city general practitioner services could be reflected in the quality of surgeries? (courtesy of City and Hackney Community Health Council).

working-class ones. These data suggest that middle-class patients are receiving a better service when they consult their general practitioner (Fig. 3.2).

Social class differences in the use of hospital services have been reviewed by Carstairs and Patterson (1966). Using hospital admission rates and data about length of stay in hospital in Scotland for 1963 they found clear evidence of increased use from Social Class I to Social Class V. More recent data, reported in *Inequalities in Health* (DHSS, 1980; Townsend & Davidson, 1982) confirmed these trends.

Perhaps one of the most striking conclusions of the *Inequalities in Health* report was that social class differences appear to be greater in the use of preventive services. Routinely collected Scottish data about antenatal booking show that, although there has been an increase in the proportion of women in all social classes booking by 20 weeks of gestation, the proportion of married women making a later antenatal booking, that is after more than 20 weeks of gestation, increased for lower social classes (Table 3.7). We have some difficulty in interpreting the marked increase in the proportion of women booking by 20 weeks, and refer to this example again in Chapter 12 when discussing the use of official statistics in research.

Similar class differences have been found in presentation for postnatal examination, immunisation, antenatal and postnatal supervision and uptake of vitamin supplements (Gordon, 1951). Cartwright (1970) in her study of family planning services found a clear relationship with social class of the proportion of mothers having an antenatal examination, attending a family planning clinic and discussing birth control with their general practitioner. Finally, Sanson and colleagues (1972) found that women from Social Class IV and V were less likely to be screened for cervical cancer, though this disease is more prevalent among women of the lower social classes.

The data reported in this chapter, and other studies reported elsewhere (Townsend, 1974, 1979; Brotherston, 1976; DHSS, 1980; Townsend & Davidson, 1982), suggest quite convincingly that, despite the overall increased affluence of Britain, there remains a strong relationship between social stratification and health. Why do such inequalities persist? How can health professionals assist in reducing these inequalities to improve the health of those worst off? We need to understand clearly the reasons for inequality before we are in a position to do much about it.

UNDERSTANDING SOCIAL CLASS

In this chapter we have tried to emphasise the importance of the concept of social stratification for the understanding of

Table 3.7 Percentage of married women making a late antenatal booking (after more than 21 weeks gestation)

	Scotland	
Social class	1971[1]	1981[2]
I Professional	28	11
II Managerial	35	12
III Skilled manual and non-manual	36	12
IV Partly skilled	39	15
V Unskilled	47	18

Sources
[1] Brotherston Sir J 1976 Inequality: Is it inevitable? In: Carter C O, Peel J (eds) Equalities and Inequalities in Health. Academic Press, London, p. 85
[2] Information Services Division 1983 Unpublished Tables.

society as a whole and for the understanding of the health of society. To this end we have introduced the reader to the concepts of class, status and power, and have indicated how social class in particular is associated with inequalities in health. One of the obvious dangers of this strategy will be that the reader, like many other health professionals, will leap to the conclusion that social stratification is the cause of health problems and inequalities. The over-simplification of social class has led many notable analysts to reduce their statements to a trite comment that some human action is 'due to social class'. In Chapter 2 we used the example of late booking for antenatal care in our discussion of fact and theory. The example is relevant again here. One might be tempted to conclude that women are late attenders for antenatal care *because* of their social class. Such a conclusion is not only misleading but can also be positively harmful to individual mothers. What is important is not social class *per se*, but what lies behind the classification in terms of the social processes which link an individual's action to her occupational classification. Women are likely to attend late for antenatal care not because their occupational classification is Social Class V but because social class V women tend to live some distance away from clinics; to have heard too many unpleasant stories about antenatal clinics; or to be unable to find a baby-sitter while they attend. Sally MacIntyre (1980), in interviews with women having first babies found that few had ever given any thought to, or been given specific information about, the purpose of antenatal care, which was something that seemed to be taken for granted by health professionals. Reasons for late booking will depend on a number of social and environmental factors which relate to social class but do not themselves constitute social class.

Studies like that by Blaxter and Paterson (1982), described in Chapter 6, begin to explain something of why class differences exist. Blaxter and Paterson found that mothers and daughters in Social Class IV and V, who were the products of disadvantaged social and medical histories, lacked a concept of positive health and showed scepticism and even fatalism about the benefits of preventive medicine or dentistry. 'If your kids are healthy, they're healthy. If they're going to be ill, they'll be ill.' If such a belief system is widespread in social class V families, it is not surprising that differences exist between social classes in the use of preventive services. Differences in use of services of course is only one reason for differences in morbidity and mortality.

The higher mortality rates of the lower social classes could be explained by a number of social and environmental factors. We shall look at some of these in detail in the next chapter when we consider the social causes of illness. It is sufficient to say that there is evidence that the lower social classes experience more environmental and occupational hazards than the higher social classes. Dietary and social habits such as drinking and smoking probably also play some part in determining some of the social class differences in health.

Another explanation of inequalities in health has been provided by Raymond Illsley. In an investigation of women with one child at the time living in Aberdeen in 1951–4 he found that women who are upwardly socially mobile tend to have a high IQ (a measure of environment rather than a genetic predictor), higher education and occupational skills. These women also tend to be tall, to be in good health, and to have low rates of prematurity, infant and maternal mortality. Conversely, he found that the women who were downwardly socially mobile at marriage tended to have the opposite characteristics (Illsley, 1955). In his recent book (Illsley, 1980) he updated some of the data and showed that the same processes were operating 20 years later in Aberdeen.

Of course, one explanation of this selective mobility at marriage is to attribute it to post-marital social, economic and environmental conditions. However, Illsley found that even some of the women who were living in the poor housing of the 1950s, or living in their parents' home, or even those who conceived prenuptially, were upwardly mobile. These data suggest that the experiences of children in similar social classes, as measured by the social class of their father, was varied. Variations in diet and environmental factors are all positively correlated with such factors as education and intelligence. These predispose to occupational attainment. Thus it would appear that social mobility differentiates between the fit and not so fit. As one early sociologist put it: 'physical superiority has been the condition which has favoured the social promotion of individuals and has facilitated their social climbing, while physical inferiority has facilitated the social sinking of individuals and their location in the lower social strata' (Sorokin, 1959, p. 275).

It follows that the greatest contribution that health professionals can make toward the reduction of health inequalities is to have a positive approach to the problems facing the lower social classes. It is not a matter of attributing blame to the patient and using the excuse that poor health or unequal use of service is 'due to social class'. Attention needs to be given to finding out what factors, which happen to link with social class, lie behind observed differences. These are matters which require sociological investigation. Only in this way, by beginning to understand what *causes* inequalities in health, can we provide socially appropriate services and promote health.

The relevance of social stratification will be taken up again, particularly in relation to the social causes of illness (Ch. 4), professional-client interaction (Ch. 9) and in relation to death and dying (Ch. 10).

SUMMARY

In this chapter we have discussed social stratification from the structuralist perspective. In particular we have outlined differences between the Marxian and Weberian approaches to social class. Marx divided society into two social classes: the bourgeoisie and the proletariat, and emphasised that the inequality between them was based on the exploitation of the proletariat by the bourgeoisie. Weber identified a number of social classes which were based on the shared experiences of people who are similarly placed in the processes of production, distribution and exchange. It embraces all aspects of economic position in society.

We described the common method of categorising people according to social class as used by the Registrar General and Office of Population, Censuses and Surveys in Government publications. We saw that this method of classification related more closely to Weber's concept of status, which focuses on the social estimation and prestige of a particular social group. Thus we saw that the official definition of social class is based on the relative prestige of different occupational groups rather than on their economic position.

The third aspect of social stratification highlighted in this chapter is power. In order to understand this concept we introduced Weber's concepts of authority and legitimacy. We saw that authority was more enduring than power which is often momentary and not always legitimated. Legitimacy means that people accept the authority as just and those endowed with authority are given it rightfully.

The chapter also explored the mechanisms by which people move between different social strata and identified different influences on social mobility. We reported the findings of Goldthorpe's study of social mobility in Britain which suggests that there has been little increase in relative mobility rates; although because of the changes in the occupational structure, there has been a general movement upwards in absolute terms.

The chapter concludes with an extended summary of data presented in the report *Inequalities in Health* which highlighted the relative disadvantages of people in the Registrar General's Social Classes IV and V. Individuals in these social groups were shown on a variety of mortality and morbidity indicators to be less healthy and, relative to their need for health services, used these services less frequently than people in Social Classes I, II or III. Finally we suggest that health professionals should seek explanations for such inequalities beyond the simple observation that poor health or unequal use of service is 'due to social class'.

REFERENCES

Blaxter M, Paterson E 1982 Mothers and daughters: a three generational study of health attitudes and behaviour. Heinemann Educational Books, London
Brotherston Sir J 1976 The Galton lecture: 1975. Inequality: is it inevitable? In: Carter C O, Peel J (eds) Equalities and inequalities in health. Academic Press, London, p 73–104
Buchan I C, Richardson I M 1973 Time study of consultations in general practice, Scottish Health Service Study No. 27. Scottish Home and Health Department, Edinburgh
Carstairs V, Patterson P E 1966 Distribution of hospital patients by social class. Health Bulletin XXIV: 59–65
Cartwright A 1970 Parents and family planning services. Routledge & Kegan Paul, London
Cartwright A, O'Brien M 1976 Social class variations in health care and in the nature of general practitioner consultations. In: Stacey M (ed) The sociology of the National Health Service, Sociological Review Monograph No. 22. University of keele, p 77–98
Davis K, Moore W E 1945 Some principles of stratification. American Sociological Review X: 242–249
Department of Health and Social Security 1980 Inequalities in health. Report of a research working group. DHSS, London
Forster D P 1976 Social class differences in sickness and general practitioner consultations. Health Trends 8: 29–32
Gerth H H, Mills C W 1948 From Max Weber: essays in sociology. Routledge & Kegan Paul, London
Glass D V (ed) 1954 Social mobility in Britain. Routledge & Kegan Paul, London
Goffman E 1971 The presentation of self in every day life. Penguin Books, Harmondsworth
Goldthorpe J H 1980 Social mobility and class structure in modern Britain. Clarendon Press, Oxford
Goldthorpe J H, Hope K 1974 The social grading of occupations: a new approach and scale. Clarendon Press, Oxford
Gordon I 1951 Social status and active prevention of disease. Monthly Bulletin of the Ministry of Health 10: 59–61
Illsley R 1955 Social class selection and class differences in relation to stillbirths and infant deaths. British Medical Journal II: 1520–1524
Illsley R 1980 Professional or public health? Sociology in health and medicine. The Nuffield Provincial Hospitals Trust, London
MacIntyre S 1980 Needs and expectations in obstetrics. Health Bulletin 38: 113–118
Maddox G L 1964 Self-assessment of health status. A longitudinal study of selected elderly subjects. Journal of Chronic Diseases 17: 449–460
Morris J N 1975 Uses of epidemiology, 3rd edition. Churchill Livingstone, Edinburgh
Office of population, Censuses and Surveys 1973 The General Household Survey, Introductory Report, 1971. HMSO, London

Office of Population, Censuses and Surveys 1978 Occupational mortality: the Registrar General's decennial supplement for England and Wales, 1970–72. HMSO, London

Office of Population, Censuses and Surveys 1980 The classification of occupations and coding index, 1980. HMSO, London

Reid I 1977 Social class differences in Britain. Open Books, London

Rex J 1961 Key problems of sociological theory. Routledge & Kegan Paul, London

Runciman W G 1966 Relative deprivation and social justice. Routledge & Kegan Paul, London

Sanson C D, Wakefield J, Yule R 1972 Cervical cytology in the Manchester area: changing patterns of response. In: Wakefield J (ed) Seek wisely to prevent. HMSO, London, ch 13, p 151–159

Sorokin P A 1959 Social and cultural mobility. Free Press, Illinois

Stern J 1983 Social mobility and the interpretation of social class mortality differentials. Journal of Social Policy 12: 27–49

Titmuss R 1968 Commitment to welfare. Allen & Unwin, London

Townsend P 1974 Inequality and the health service. Lancet II: 1179–1190

Townsend P 1979 Poverty in the United Kingdom. A survey of household resources and standards of living. Penguin Books, Harmondsworth

Townsend P, Davidson N (eds) 1982 Inequalities in health. The Black Report. Penguin Books, Harmondsworth

World Health Organisation 1983 Basic documentation, 33rd edition. WHO, Geneva

Worsley P (ed) 1977 Introducing sociology, 2nd edition. Penguin Books, London

FURTHER READING

Runciman W G 1966 Relative deprivation and social justice. Routledge & Kegan Paul, London, P 36–52

Townsend P, Davidson N (eds) 1982 Inequalities in health. The Black Report. Penguin Books. Harmondsworth

Worsley P (ed) 1977 Introducing sociology, 2nd edition. Penguin Books, Harmondsworth, ch 8, p 395–476

Social causes
Illness and the individual
Health, stress and coping
Prevention

4

Social influences on health and the role of prevention

INTRODUCTION

Our discussion in the last chapter concerning inequality in health indicates a number of social influences on illness and health. In this chapter we develop this theme by outlining what sociologists mean by the social causes of illness. Then we will discuss what John McKinlay has called the 'manufacturers of illness', those aspects of the social, economic and political structure, the individuals, groups and organisations which, in addition to producing material goods and services also produce, as an inevitable by-product, widespread morbidity and mortality. We review some of the evidence which supports the general hypothesis that stressful life events, like bereavement or loss of a job, have a role in the aetiology of illness and that social conditions give rise to depression. We examine one model to explain the relationship between life events and health, and why it is that individuals have different experiences. Finally we raise the topic of prevention.

All of us will be aware of at least one of the following social influences on aetiology. Smoking increases the risk of a person acquiring lung cancer, bronchitis and heart disease. Excessive alcohol consumption in association with driving, cycling or walking increases the likelihood of a person sustaining injuries from road traffic accidents. Living in areas of the world where poor sanitation, overcrowding and inadequate nutrition is rife increases one's chances of contracting an infectious disease such as TB or cholera. Working as a coalminer increases the risk of many lung diseases, but particularly pneumoconiosis. These examples, and numerous others, indicate the ubiquity of social influences on the aetiology of illness and disease. There are few illnesses which have not been linked to some kind of human behaviour or another. Yet health professionals make limited use of this information.

A story of a doctor trying to explain the dilemmas of modern medical practice, related by the sociologist Irving Zola, suggests why this might be:

> 'You know', he said, 'sometimes it feels like this. There I am standing by the shore of a swiftly flowing river and I hear the cry of a drowning man. So I jump into the river, put my arms around him, pull him to the shore and apply artificial respiration. Just when he begins to breathe, there is another cry for help. So I jump into the river, reach him, pull him to shore, apply artificial respiration, and then just as he begins to breathe, another cry for help. So back in the river again, reaching, pulling, applying, breathing and then another yell. Again and again, without end, goes the sequence. You know, I am so busy jumping in, pulling them to shore, applying artificial respiration, that I have no time to see who the hell is upstream pushing them all in.' (Quoted in McKinlay, 1979, p. 9).

This simple story usefully sums up the theme of this chapter.

SOCIAL CAUSES

In Chapter 1 we described two different models of health— the medical model and the social model. We also introduced Lalonde's health field concept to show the complementary nature of the two approaches.

The medical model is a limited one, although it is also an effective one. We know that social factors—the environmental and life-style elements of Lalonde's model—influence our examples: smoking, alcohol consumption, poor sanitation and coal-mining as an occupation. Thereafter it is essentially physical means—the human biology element of the health field concept—which play a major role in the aetiology of lung cancer, road traffic accidents, TB and pneumoconiosis. Sociology is not only concerned with the link between smoking and cancer, alcohol consumption and road traffic accidents, sanitation and TB, and coal-mining (Fig. 4.1) and pneumoconiosis. It is also concerned with the question of *why* people smoke, drink, live in poor housing and engage in coal-mining. Sociological answers to these questions are complex and the answers we provide by way of illustration may be speculative and may not be based on a full reading of the sociological theory and empirical data concerning the examples we have cited.

Both smoking and alcohol consumption afford examples of social actions which have symbolic meaning to the individual and the social group in which he interacts. A school child will often take to smoking not because he enjoys the activity necessarily but because of its symbolic value in his social group. The symbolic value is reinforced by one 'manufacturer of illness': the tobacco industry. Some adolescents sniff glue

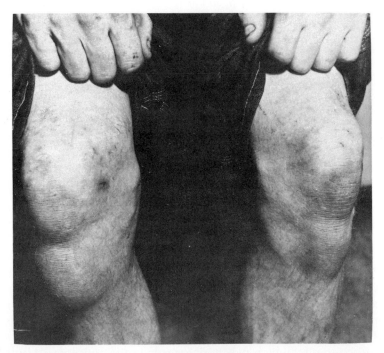

Fig. 4.1 'Beat Knee'—a form of housemaids knee in a coalminer. Results from kneeling in narrow seams with limited working height (courtesy of Department of Occupational Health, University of Newcastle upon Tyne).

because of its symbolic significance in certain deviant sub-cultures.

Inadequate sanitation, and coal-mining as an occupation, are not social actions and therefore have no symbolic significance. They are, however, important structural characteristics of a stratified society. People tend to get TB if they live in over-crowded housing with poor sanitation and contract pneumoconiosis if they work at the coal face. Whether or not one lives or works in these kinds of environment depends on one's position in society. As we saw in Chapter 3, inequalities in health are often explained in structural terms by sociologists.

A social model of the causes of illness and disease focuses on the individual and his relationship to the structure of society. It takes as its concern how an individual perceives and reacts emotionally to his structural position in society and why he perceives or reacts in the way he does. We will describe such a model of the social causes of illness and disease, which relates to physical and bio-chemical factors in its development. It will focus on the way the individual perceives and reacts to his way of life.

Illness and social structure

From the structuralist perspectives we can all identify those elements of the way society is organised which appear to be directly related to the aetiology of illness. At the broadest level the social, economic and political structure of capitalist society can be identified as a major contributor to illness in Britain. (Whether alternative social, political and economic structures exist or could exist which would make British society more healthy is not considered in this book because of the complexity of the issues involved. In the present chapter we are concerned with a description of social causes of illness. Prescriptions for a healthier Britain are left to more speculative and authoritative writers).

A major characteristic of modern industrial societies, both western capitalist and eastern state capitalist, is their preoccupation with economic growth. Social and economic policies practised in pursuit of the single goal of greater growth invariably neglect a variety of health hazards. By being critical of societies' pursuit of economic growth we are not arguing that consideration of health should be paramount in our quest for social progress. Yet it is important that these arguments are understood in order that the costs and benefits of such a policy can be balanced.

We do not have to look far to find examples of what McKinlay calls 'the manufacturers of illness'. From the economic perspective of growth, cigarette production is wealth-producing, both to the tobacco industry and to the central Governments who levy taxes on tobacco products. Yet we are all aware of the good scientific evidence about the relationship between smoking and ill health. The promotion of tobacco products is also a major wealth-producing activity for the advertising agencies, not to mention our flourishing tobacconist's shops. In order to expand their markets and increase their production of wealth 'the manufacturers of illness' promote their products in other countries and cultures. Thus a high proportion of the wealth in developing countries is being spent on tobacco products with the consequent cost to health (Doyal & Pennell, 1979).

The example of tobacco is not, however, the best illustration of the ubiquitous nature of the goal of growth. The production and consumption of food, in our view, better illustrates the extent to which the economic structure of society influences health.

Production

A number of disabling conditions have been related to the nature and organisation of the production of food. Occupational diseases related to farming are less often reported because there are often insufficient cases concentrated in one place for a connection to become clear. The effects of chemicals and pesticides used in modern farming on health are not clearly understood, yet the prophetic work of Rachel Carson (1963) on the relationship between pesticides and the natural food chain in lower order species indicates the likelihood of health hazards to both farm workers and consumers. The long-term effects of slight poisoning such as lead poisoning, like the long-term effects of smoking, are subtle and will probably only be noticed after many years of exposure. Some of the effects of the use of modern chemicals in farming have been discovered by chance. In 1967 five workers on a Derbyshire farm reported being impotent. The disability disappeared after they were taken off crop spraying (Smith, 1977). In 1977 over half of the male workers in a Californian pesticide factory were found to be sterile or had very low sperm counts (Whorton et al, 1977).

Agricultural chemicals are a potential danger not only to those who manufacture and use them, but also to the public at large. The presence of high levels of nitrates seeping from fertilisers into the water supply has been linked with stomach cancer (The Lancet, 1977). So far these conclusions have only been made from observational data and require further research before the full effects of nitrates in the water supply are known.

Like agricultural workers, many food processing workers are poorly paid. They also work in some of the worst conditions of the manufacturing industry. Many aspects of food handling and packing are probably hazardous to the workers' health. The dust from cardboard and paper, the dyes, plastics and resins on the boxes, the noise in bottling plants and the fumes from cutting and sealing film wrapping have all been identified as potential health hazards (Kinnersley, 1973).

Consumption

Whereas the health hazards related to the production of food are limited to a relatively small number of agricultural and food processing workers, the health hazards related to the consumption of food affect the whole population. Diet is directly related to the changing pattern of disease in modern industrial societies. We can illustrate this proposition by looking at the pattern of sugar consumption. Sugar is probably the only known serious dietary cause of tooth decay (Sheiham, 1983). In Norway, Finland, Austria, Holland, Denmark and Britain the rate of tooth decay fell by half during World War II when sugar was rationed (Sognnaes, 1948). In Britain, in 1952 (at the end of rationing) on average a 15-year old had four teeth decayed, but by 1959 the average had increased to ten. During the same period the consumption of sugar had increased markedly (James, 1965).

Processed sugar is not the only dietary change which has influenced our health. Changes in the consumption of roughage (the fibre content of the diet) have been related to changes in the pattern of diseases affecting the digestive system. In particular, highly processed foods like modern white bread usually contain very little roughage. As the consumption of roughage has decreased there has been an increase in incidence of diseases of the digestive tract (Burkitt & Trowell, 1975).

Lack of fibre also encourages obesity because, without the fibre, the food is less bulky (Van Itallie, 1978); to compensate, one tends to eat more food, and as a result ends up eating an excess of calories (Fig. 4.2). Obesity is also related to an increase in the consumption of sugar and fat (Royal College of Physicians of London, 1983). This increase in obesity has been associated with an increased risk of heart disease, high

Fig. 4.2 'Junk food' for lunch can easily become the norm (courtesy of Rik Walton)

blood pressure, diabetes, and arthritis (Chiang et al, 1969; Tansey et al, 1977; Royal College of Physicians of London, 1983).

The level of consumption

Like tobacco consumption, food consumption is considered to be a relatively free choice. Yet like tobacco consumption it is affected by a variety of social influences. Perhaps the greatest influence on individual consumption is the pressure of advertising, which is determined by the manufacturers' need to sell their products. Manufacturers are also concerned with making a profit. The production of meat products, wheat products, and sugar products is encouraged because they are more profitable—they cost less to cultivate and transport than, for example, fresh vegetables. The Politics of Health Group (1980) have described the incentive to manufacturers to manufacture these products in the following way:

'White flour is more profitable than brown, because the bran and the germ can be sold separately, so people tend to eat more of them. Sugar can make products more satisfying to taste, particularly if we were encouraged as children to enjoy highly sugared products. As we have seen, sugar and white flour are among foods causing ill-health. Animal fats have been associated with cancer of the bowel and the breast, and with heart disease. Yet some of the most profitable products of the meat industry, such as sausages and pies, are particularly high in fats.

The food industry has a particular problem. It cannot expect us to consume more of their products when our incomes rise. There is, after all, a limit to the amount we can eat, so that with a rise in real wages we do not buy more and more of the same sort of food. So in order to keep up their profits, the industry encourages us to shift our purchasing of food with less profit to food with more profit.' (p. 7).

The impact of the food industry has also had a great impact on the health of people in the Third World. Perhaps the most serious has been the export of formula milk for babies. With a static home market, dried milk producers can only expand their markets by selling to the Third World. Although health professionals tend to support the view that breast milk is best for a newborn child, there is less evidence, nowadays, that babies born in Britain and *fed correctly* on formula milk are seriously disadvantaged (Thomson & Black, 1975). This is not the case in Third World countries, where bottle feeding has been lethal. In the West Indies to feed a three-month-old baby on formula milk can take up to a third of a family's income. Often mothers resort to watering down feeds, which causes malnutrition. In contrast to modern industrial societies the preparation of feeds is usually undertaken in conditions which are far from ideal and which encourage gastroenteritis. In the Caribbean and Africa a combination of gastroenteritis and malnutrition is known as the *lactogen syndrome* (Jelliffe & Jelliffe, 1978).

Diet and social stratification

In Chapter 3 we reviewed inequalities in health and found that people from lower social strata in Britain had a shorter expectation of life, higher rates of infant mortality and higher rates of acute and chronic sickness.

A number of researchers have emphasised the importance of diet on the health of individuals. Thomas McKeown (1979), in his review of the role of medicine, describes the historical determinants of improved nutrition and relates this to the decline of mortality from infectious diseases. Lord Taylor (1975), from a review of the factors influencing the rate of infant mortality, concluded that maternal and infant nutrition were the most important. Wilkinson (1978) has shown that diet is probably the main factor responsible for class differences in life expectancy. He made a number of dietary comparisons for the decade 1964–74 and found that there were marked differences in the consumption of fruit, fresh vegetables, cheese, milk and meat. People from the lower social classes consumed far less of these than those from the higher social classes. The lower social classes also consumed more sugar and refined wheat.

Our discussion of the effects of food and nutrition on the health of individuals has been somewhat speculative, since much of the data are based on observational studies alone. However, nutritionists are convinced by these data (NACNE, 1983). The possibility of comprehensive prospective data being collected on the relationship between food policy and health is slight. Unlike health care, where evaluation of new treatments, particularly medicines, before their widespread use by health professionals is accepted practice, the introduction of new food lines or new food additives are not usually the subject of a full-scale evaluation. These data do, however, indicate some of the ways in which the structure of society can be said to be a cause of illness because of its association with diet.

ILLNESS AND THE INDIVIDUAL

We now focus our attention on the question: Why is it that individuals from similar social backgrounds and life-styles have differential morbidity and mortality experiences? One fruitful line of research has been life events research. The basic premise of life-events research is that the incidence of stressful life change, such as bereavement or unemployment, is related to the onset of illness. A causal relationship between life-events and illness is postulated. This relationship has been confirmed by a number of studies in recent years. For a review of these we suggest you consult Dohrenwend and Dohrenwend (1974). In this section we consider three kinds of stressful life events: bereavement, social change and unemployment.

Bereavement

It is now reasonably well established that there exists a causal relationship between bereavement and subsequent ill health. Colin Murray Parkes, in his book on bereavement, catalogues the numerous cross-sectional studies which report the strong association between mortality and bereavement and between morbidity and bereavement (1975, pp. 29–45, 227–249). One explanation of these data is that couples who have shared a similar life-style for a number of years would be expected to experience similar patterns of morbidity and mortality. While this could explain the increase in the mortality rate among the widowed population as a whole, it does not explain the peak of mortality in widows and widowers during the first year of bereavement, as first reported by Michael Young and his colleagues (Young, Benjamin & Wallis, 1963) and confirmed by a number of subsequent smaller studies. Of course these studies do not indicate that bereavement is the *cause* of death of the remaining spouse. They do not even tell us whether bereavements cause the illness which causes death or simply aggravates an existing condition.

Other studies have identified recently bereaved people and collected data at a later time about the period since bereavement. Peter Marris interviewed widows two years after the event and asked them to report their general health during that period (Marris, 1974). These women reported a high proportion of headaches, digestive upsets, rheumatism and asthma. Similar data have been collected by other researchers and are reported by Parkes (1975). From these studies Parkes concludes that bereavement does influence the pattern of physical illness but as yet the causal mechanisms are not fully understood.

Many of these studies suffer from what is called *retrospective bias*. Since data about an event is collected after the event has occurred, the choice of data to be collected and the way the data is recorded and interpreted can be unconsciously influenced by the scientist's ideas about the relationship between the event, i.e. bereavement, and outcome, i.e. death of the remaining spouse. *Retrospective studies*, in which data about the event is collected after the event has occurred, provide scientists with a simple and effective method of identifying possible relationships. *Prospective studies*, in which data is collected longitudinally from the point where an event is first identified, provide a sounder basis on which to test relationships between the event and its outcomes, but are often more complicated and expensive to undertake.

Social change

Peter Marris has described a number of similarities between bereavement and other types of social change. In his book *Loss and Change* Marris (1974) applies the concept of grieving to situations of change where people suffer loss: a woman losing her husband; a household being evicted by a slum clearance scheme; a son of a peasant farmer launching a modern wholesale business in his village; and a new plan of action setting out to challenge the jurisdiction of established bureaucracies. In each of these situations, a familiar pattern of relationships has been disrupted; and in each of them the disruption seems to provide similar reactions. Whenever people suffer loss their reactions express an internal conflict, whose nature is fundamentally similar to the working out of grief.

We can understand broadly how this is so. When a sudden change occurs there is a need to deny and also a need to accept that the change has occurred. This ambivalence generally inhibits straightforward adjustment. Adjustment to a major change involving loss is likely to be both painful and erratic. Our ambivalence at times of change reflects what Marris terms as our *conservative impulse*. We depend on the fact that the meanings we give to daily events are essentially predictable. The loss of someone close to us can strike at this very sense of purpose or meaning. Of course, this loss is not necessarily only the loss of the object, but will also involve a loss of *role*. As we shall see, this loss of role can also be applied in the context of unemployment, and it applies to bereavement when the remaining spouse must alter his role.

Peter Marris does not claim to have discovered the causal link between social change and health. His argument is based on selected evidence from his own research. It would be an almost impossible task to review all the relevant evidence. However, the diversity of the examples presented illustrates the possible wide application of his theory, which deserves more formal testing.

Unemployment

It is generally accepted that unemployment is not only undesirable but has detrimental effects on health (Colledge, 1982). A number of writers have postulated that unemployment is a stressful life event which is causally related to ill health. At times of relatively low levels of unemployment following the 1939–1945 war, research about unemployment and health was unable to establish whether unemployment caused ill health or ill health caused unemployment. During that time most of the research about unemployment was concerned with the characteristics of the unemployed rather than on the effects of unemployment.

Technological innovation and the recession in the world economy during the eighties provides a unique opportunity to study the effects of unemployment on health, since unemployment levels are so high that living without work is the experience of the young and the old, men and women, non-manual and manual workers.

The findings and methods of most studies of unemployment have been reviewed by Ken Mullen and Raymond Illsley. Their review describes the effects of unemployment on health under three main headings: studies of the unemployed, correlation studies, and studies of factory closures or redundancies (Mullen & Illsley, 1981).

Most of the studies of the unemployed reported by Mullen and Illsley make little attempt to compare the health status of the unemployed with the employed. The studies generally show that the unemployed are unhealthy mentally and, not so conclusively, physically. However, they are unable to indicate whether ill health is caused by unemployment. People may be unemployed because they were less healthy. They may also be less healthy because of the conditions in which they live so that it is difficult to identify which of many social influences such as unemployment, poverty, bad housing or geographic location are the cause of ill health. A major problem with these studies is that they are usually too small to account for all the possible explanations.

Some researchers have used econometric models similar to models used by economists in predicting the state of the economy. The models used have attempted to relate unemployment to macro health indicators like psychiatric admission rates, health trend data and mortality statistics. This approach is similar to that used by Emile Durkheim in his classic study of suicide which we have already mentioned in Chapter 2 and will consider again in Chapter 12. Of course nowadays, with the help of computers, complex multi-variate statistical models, models which can take account of more than one variable at a time, are used. This approach to the relationship between unemployment and health is surrounded by controversy. An advanced knowledge of statistics is required to understand many of the nuances in the arguments. Two kinds of conflicting explanations have emerged. Some writers claim that unemployment causes increased mortality while other writers using apparently similar models and data suggest that economic booms are the cause of increased mortality and psychiatric illness, not unemployment. Such disagreements are not unknown between economists using similar econometric models. We must await the outcome of further studies of this kind before concluding who is right.

The third group of studies reviewed by Mullen and Illsley suggest a more fruitful line of approach. Unfortunately studies of redundancy or factory closure are few in number. Redundancy or factory closure afford the opportunity of studying the health status of workers over time: before and after termination of employment. Such prospective or longitudinal enquiries are the only reliable way of establishing causality. However, longitudinal studies are not without their problems. In the case of unemployment, the unemployed worker can be re-employed or move to another area. Both starting a new job and moving home to a new area have been identified as potential stressful life events. In such studies we would need to identify the effects of unemployment *and* other life events.

In this section we have tried to examine the evidence that stressful life events such as bereavement, social change and unemployment are causally related to ill health. Another way of exploring this relationship is to take a single medical condition or group of conditions and seek explanations for these conditions in terms of stressful life events. To illustrate this approach let us consider depression among women.

The social origins of depression

Our heading for this section is taken from the important work of George Brown and Tirril Harris. In Chapter 3 we discussed differences between the social classes in their experience of illness. The prevalence of clinical depression is one condition which was found to be significantly higher among 'working-class' women than among 'middle-class' women. Brown and Harris (1978) discuss why this might be. They studied women from an inner-city area in London, using detailed accounts of women's daily lives and recent experiences and systematic descriptions of any psychiatric symptoms. Their data suggest that certain kinds of severe life events, especially losses, and major long-term difficulties are significant in the aetiology of depression. Other psycho-social factors also emerged as important determinants of women's vulnerability to such events and difficulties, and of the severity of the depression. The nature of these other factors help account for the higher prevalence of clinical depression among 'working-class' women and help us understand some of the other inequalities discussed in Chapter 3.

The essential features of the model used by Brown and Harris are shown in Figure 4.3. It identifies two important components of the model: provoking agents and vulnerability factors. The data collected by Brown and Harris suggested that severe life events occurring at a particular time, such as losing a job, and severe long-term difficulties, such as a husband's alcoholism, were both causally related to depression. Yet a number of women who experienced severe life-events or long-term difficulties did not develop depression. The data was used to identify a second component of the model: vulnerability factors, such as low intimacy with husband or loss of a mother before the age of eleven. Vulnerability factors were found only to be capable of increasing the risk of depression in the presence of a provoking agent.

Although the model identifies the negative role of vulnerability factors, Brown and Harris emphasise the importance of the positive role of what they call protective factors. High in-

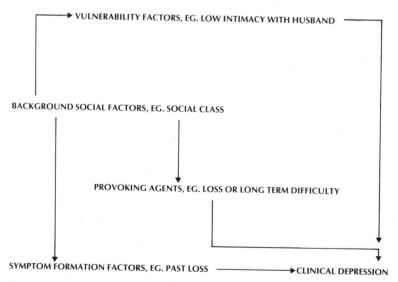

Fig. 4.3 A simple causal model of depression (adapted from Brown & Harris, 1978).

timacy with husband and no loss of mother before the age of eleven are examples of such factors.

A third set of factors identified by the model are symptom formation factors. Such factors appear only to influence the severity of depression once established. Previous history of psychiatric illness, age of the woman, and a past loss were all identified as important symptom formation factors.

In summary: there are three major components to the model. The provoking agents influence when the depression occurs, the vulnerability factors influence whether these agents will have an effect, and the symptom formation factors influence the severity and the form of the depressive disorder itself. The model tells us only that in some way the factors are causally linked to the disorder. It does not tell us how and why.

HEALTH, STRESS AND COPING

Much of the life-events research has focused on the causal relationship between a stressful life event and illness. This research has contributed little to the explanation of why stressful life events should be a cause of illness. Another way of looking at the relationship between stressful life events and illness is to seek explanations about why some people experiencing stressful life events remain healthy while others become ill. This has been the central concern of Aaron Antonovsky over a number of years, which is embodied in his search for the origins (*genesis*) of health (*saluto*). An explanation of why people remain healthy is provided by the *Salutogenic Model* (Antonovsky, 1979). A simple outline of the model is shown in Figure 4.4. Let us run through each of the components in turn by first defining the sense of coherence, which Antonovsky presents as the core of his answer to the question of the origins of health (*salutogenesis*).

Sence of coherence

'The *sense of coherence* is a global orientation that expresses the extent to which one has a pervasive, enduring though dynamic feeling of confidence that one's internal and external environments are predictable and that there is a high probability that things will work as well as can reasonably be expected'.

(Antonovsky, 1979, p. 123).

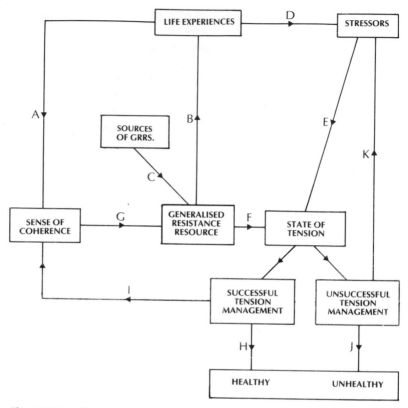

Fig. 4.4 Simplified diagram of the Salutogenic Model (adapted from Antonovsky, 1979).

We can see similarities here with Marris's concept of *conservative impulse*. Both are concerned with the predictability of life experiences, but a sense of coherence implies something more: that we are in control of our own situations.

Life experience. Our *life experiences* are crucial in shaping our sense of coherence (Arrow A). Throughout life, from birth to death, we experience a variety of social situations. When such experiences are characterised by consistency, then the meanings and purpose we give to events are predictable, and we see the world as coherent and predictable. When people's lives are characterised by total predictability, however, they are likely to have a weaker sense of coherence than people experiencing some unpredictable events, which force the individual to adapt and maintain a more flexible approach to life. There is therefore benefit in a degree of unpredictability, too much of it and, on the other hand total consistency are harmful.

Our sense of coherence develops at different stages of our life. In childhood the individual is to some extent protected from unpredictable events. He will experience a limited number of relationships with others and therefore gets feedback from relatively few people. In adolescence a sense of coherence is reinforced by similar experiences but at this stage there is a far greater choice of experiences available. As the individual moves into adulthood more changes are in store for him: marriage, employment, new relationships. Usually these provide a fairly stable life experience which further strengthens the sense of coherence.

Sudden life events such as divorce or unemployment will force an individual to modify his sense of coherence. How we adapt to these life experiences will depend on our ability to cope or our *generalised resistance resources.*

Generalised resistance resources. At the most general level the generalised resistance resources (GRR) are the resources at our disposal which enable us to resolve tension. More specifically Antonovsky defines the GRR using the following mapping sentence:

'A GRR is a
$$\left\{\begin{array}{l}\text{physical}\\\text{biochemical}\\\text{artifactual-material}\\\text{cognitive}\\\text{emotional}\\\text{valuative-attitudinal}\\\text{interpersonal-relational}\\\text{macrosocio-cultural}\end{array}\right\}$$
characteristic of an

$$\left\{\begin{array}{l}\text{individual}\\\text{primary}\\\text{group}\\\text{subculture}\\\text{society}\end{array}\right\}$$
that is effective in $\left\{\begin{array}{l}\text{avoiding}\\\text{combating}\end{array}\right\}$ a wide variety

of stressors and thus preventing tension from being transformed into stress.' (1979, p. 103).

Source of GRRs. Antonovsky identifies two primary sources of GRRs: child-rearing practice, and the roles assigned to us in particular cultures (Arrow C). The kinds of social roles, whether they be gender, occupational or family roles, will be a major influence. The importance of chance and serendipity also should not be ignored. Thus the sociocultural and historical context in which an individual lives will influence the development of his GRRs.

Stressors. Stressors are a part of life. They will depend not only on biological forces but on our own life experiences. As a response to stressors we develop a state of tension (Arrow E). What are stressors? One definition suggests that stressors are *'demands that tax or exceed the resources of the system* or, to put it in a slightly different way, demands to which there are no readily available or automatic adaptive responses' (Lazarus & Cohen, 1977, p. 109, emphasis in original). We must not forget that different individuals will perceive stress in different ways. To many people normal activities of daily life like going outside in the open or using an escalator are stressful. However in terms of the Salutogenic Model this may not be particularly important, although it makes prediction of stressful events about some of us more difficult. Stressors, therefore, affect each of us in different ways.

Tension management. As we can see from the model, how we manage the tensions created by stressors (Arrow E) will depend to a large extent on our generalised resistance resources (Arrow F) which in turn are mobilised by our sense of coherence (Arrow G). Successful tension management may lead not only to a healthy outcome (Arrow H) but will also reinforce our sense of coherence (Arrow I). In contrast, unsuccessful tension management will lead to an unhealthy outcome (Arrow J) and will increase the stressors affecting each of us (Arrow K).

This is a much simplified summary of the salutogenic model, which itself may even be too simplistic. However, the full model is too complex to explain adequately here. We can only direct you to Antonovsky's book *Health, Stress and Coping* which is devoted entirely to an explanation of the model. This model still requires empirical testing, a not insubstantial task! It does, however, provide a theoretical framework in which the individual might find a solution to the *private trouble* of how to promote personal health. For society it highlights the *public issue* of how to prevent stressors.

PREVENTION

It is now appropriate to recall the short story which we quoted at the beginning of the chapter. The moral of this story is, of course, that *prevention* is better than cure. If we can stop people being pushed in upstream then we will not need to expend so much effort in pulling people out downstream. However, the relevance of this story to many health professionals is that they have little time for prevention because they spend most of their time caring and curing; that, rather than a health service, we have an illness service. What do we mean by prevention?

Prevention of ill health can be classified as primary, secondary or tertiary (Report of the Royal Commission on the National Health Service, 1979). Primary prevention involves taking measures which prevent disease or injury occurring. The discouragement of smoking, legislation to make the wearing of seat belts in motor vehicles compulsory and the provision of adequate sanitation and nutrition provide good examples of primary prevention. Secondary prevention refers to health care measures which are concerned with identifying and treating ill health. The early detection of disease through screening programmes such as antenatal care, breast screening or hypertension clinics are common examples of secondary prevention. Tertiary prevention is concerned with mitigating the effects of illness and disease which have already occurred. Surgery to remove cancerous tissues, rehabilitation following a stroke and the aftercare of diabetics are examples of tertiary prevention. Health services have concentrated on tertiary prevention, and to a lesser extent on secondary prevention. In contrast, primary prevention, for the reasons illustrated by the story, has been virtually ignored.

The focus of this chapter has been on those features of social life which contribute to health or ill health. From the examples cited primary prevention would appear to be much more a social and political activity than the other two kinds described. We might then be justified in thinking that primary prevention is outside the sphere of health professionals' work. Certainly the historical evidence suggests that changes in standard of living conditions, such as the provision of a clean water supply and an efficient sewage system, and improved nutrition and standards of food hygiene, were responsible for the improvements in the nation's health (McKeown, 1979). Medical advances may have had little effect on mortality rates and there is little clear evidence that the health services are improving our experience of disease and illness. We make this point not to belittle the achievement of the National Health Service or those professionals working in it, but to put their role in primary prevention into perspective.

We have already referred to a number of targets for primary prevention such as, for example, additional help to the most disadvantaged groups and the control of food, alcohol and tobacco consumption. In these, health professionals, in both their professional and their private lives, can play an important role. Our way of life, we have argued, is the central contributory factor in the majority of conditions. Theoretically, then, most illness or disease is preventable. The Report of the Royal Commission on the National Health Service (1979) advocates that *society* should act to discourage smoking, prevent accidents and encourage the 'right' kinds of food. But how might society act to achieve such ends? The literature on smoking indicates that psycho-social factors influence whether or not an individual starts smoking, but it is psychological and pharmacological ones that play a part in its continuance (Raw, 1978). Smoking has come to be interpreted as a form of rational action by individuals under certain circumstances, even though it may have some negative consequences (Calnan, 1982).

It is in the explanation of why people *start* smoking that sociological factors are paramount. Bynner (1969) describes a recruitment model which identifies barriers to taking up smoking and factors which increase the chances. Major barriers are negative parental and school attitudes toward smoking and perceived health risks. On the other hand, factors influencing young people to smoke include the availability of cigarettes, curiosity, rebelliousness, a desire to appear tough, anticipation of adulthood, social confidence, and parents, older siblings and friends smoking. It is the young person's social environment that plays a crucial part in influencing whether he starts smoking.

McKennell and Thomas (1968) demonstrated that a large proportion of young regular smokers persist in the habit when they grow up. An analysis of types of adult smoker suggests that the career of the smoker starts off with socially oriented motives and then moves to the stage where smoking is nicotine motivated (Russel, 1976). Nicotine dependence is then crucial but it is supported by the social environment in which the smoker lives, including images created by advertising.

Calnan (1982) points out that present models of cigarette smokers fail to explain why people have different levels of cigarette consumption and why it is that many smokers state that they smoke when under stress (Schachter, 1978). We have already indicated that stressors include a number of life events but also continuing social circumstances. If smokers smoke heavily because they believe it eases tension, anxiety or stress, then smoking can be interpreted as not only meeting a person's perfectly rational need for coping with stress but also indicating that stress is generated by events outside his control. If, as the Royal Commission advocates, 'society' should act by discouraging smoking then, by Calnan's argument, policies would require either to provide a substitute or alternative coping mechanism, or to attempt to eradicate the sources of stress. We would live in a different type of society if the primary goal was health. We should not travel in cars, eat refined foods or use aerosols. Some health professionals, as well as laymen, may consider health to be *the* primary goal, but we suspect that they are a very small minority.

As it is, health education remains the major vehicle for attempts to achieve a healthier society. Health education is typically based on the belief that responsibility for health lies with the individual, and therefore health education involves changing the individual's attitudes and knowledge. However, the resources devoted to health education represent a very small proportion of the total resources devoted to either health or education. While laying stress on the importance of designing and regulating appropriate occupational, environmental and social structures, the *Black Report* recommended 'that a greatly enlarged programme of health education, with a particular focus on schools, should be sponsored by the government. The DHSS and the DES, as well as other departments, would be involved, and at the local level health education in schools should be the joint responsibility of AHAs and LEAs.' (Townsend & Davidson, 1982, p. 161).

Health education is central to the health professional's role. But in undertaking health education our sociological understanding will identify that different social groups respond to health education in different ways. Take the issue of smoking again. Once doctors had taken the lead in reducing their personal consumption of tobacco products, there was a slow reduction among similar professional groups. Although considerable numbers of people from the professions and other high socio-economic groups have stopped smoking, this has been matched by an increased consumption among people from the lower socio-economic groups, particularly women (OPCS, 1982). For health education to be effective it would appear, from these data, that new ways of influencing smoking behaviour among the lower socio-economic groups are required, especially among young people. We have noted that the major influences on smoking behaviour among the young are parents, peers and friends. Thus for health education to become more effective it must use social networks for social change, or at least recognise that health education measures need to take account of the social context in which people live.

When certain groups of people behave in ways which are detrimental to their own or other peoples' health there is a tendency to blame them. Bronchitics who smoke, mothers of unvaccinated children with whooping cough, and women who have difficulty when delivering their babies may be blamed by health professionals for their behaviour. Clearly they all theoretically could influence their own or their children's health, by not smoking, by getting their children vaccinated or by attending antenatal classes. However, in this chapter we have identified both structural and personal constraints which make it difficult for some people to adopt standards of behaviour considered acceptable by some health professionals.

SUMMARY

This chapter has raised what we consider as important issues on the relationship between social factors and health. Our discussion on diet, health and illness is an example of the ways in which social, political and economic forces, as well as patterns of production and consumption interact to influence the health of the population. Since this chapter was written, the report produced by a Working Party of the National Advisory Committee on Nutrition and Education—NACNE Report—lends weight to the arguments about dietary composition and health.

The link between events which individuals find stressful and ill health was explored with reference to studies of a range of such events. There is now a large body of evidence pointing to a causal relationship between stressful life events and illness and evidence is now developing from the study of depression among women that it is causally linked to social factors. Why some people should become ill while others do not when exposed to objectively similar circumstances is explained by Antonovsky in terms of the coherence an individual is able to attribute to his life and what happens to him. This model is one attempt to explain the processes at work but it remains to be empirically tested. Given the current interest in health, stress and coping, it is likely that other models will be developed which will influence ideas about prevention of stress and facilitating coping strategies.

It is evident that while individuals are in large part responsible for their health, their health related actions which permeate most of their daily lives, are inexplicably linked with social processes. It is by understanding these processes that health professionals will appreciate and relate to the difficulties that many of us have in conforming to a lifestyle which maximises our health.

REFERENCES

Antonovsky A 1979 Health, stress and coping. Jossey Bass, San Francisco
Brown G W, Harris T 1978 Social origins of depression. A study of
    psychiatric disorder in women. Tavistock Publications, London
Burkitt D P, Trowell H C 1975 Refined carbohydrate foods and disease:
    some implications of dietary fibre. Academic Press, London

Bynner J M 1969 The young smoker: a study of smoking among schoolboys carried out for the Ministry of Health. Government Social Survey No. SS 383 HMSO, London

Calnan M 1982 Non-governmental approaches to the control of cancer. In: Alderson M (ed) The prevention of cancer. Edward Arnold, London, ch 7, p 210–226

Carson R 1963 Silent spring. H. Hamilton, London

Chiang B N, Perlman L V, Epstein F H 1969 Overweight and hypertension. A review. Circulation 39: 403–421

Colledge M 1982 Economic cycles and health. Towards a sociological understanding of the impact of the recession on health and illness. Social Science and Medicine 16: 1919–1927

Dohrenwend B S, Dohrenwend B P 1974 Stressful life events: their nature and effects. Wiley, New York

Doyal L, Pennell I 1979 The political economy of health. Pluto Press, London

James P M C 1965 The problem of dental caries. British Dental Journal 119: 295–299

Jellife D B, Jellife E F P 1978 Human milk in the modern world: psychological, nutritional, and economic significance. Oxford University Press, Oxford

Kinnersley P 1973 The hazards of work: how to fight them. Pluto Press, London

Lazarus R S, Cohen J B 1977 Environmental stress. In: Altman I, Wohlhill J F (eds) Human behaviour and environment. Advances in theory and research, vol 2. Plenum, New York, ch 3, p 89–127

McKennell A C, Thomas R K 1968 Adults' and adolescents' smoking habits and attitudes. Government Social Survey No SS 353/B HMSO, London

McKeown T 1979 The role of medicine. Dream, mirage or nemesis? Basil Blackwell, Oxford

McKinlay J B 1979 A case for re-focusing upstream: the political economy of illness. In: Jaco E G (ed) Patients, physicians and illness. A source book in behavioural science and health, 3rd edn. Free Press, New York, ch 2, p 9–25

Marris P 1974 Loss and change. Routledge & Kegan Paul, London

Mullen K, Illsley R 1981 Unemployment and health: a review of findings and methodology. MRC Medical Sociology Unit, Institute for Medical Sociology, Aberdeen

National Advisory Committee of Nutrition Education 1983 A discussion paper on proposals for nutritional guidelines for health education in Britain. The Health Education Council, London

Office of Population, Censuses and Survey 1982 General Household Survey 1980. HMSO, London

Parkes C M 1975 Bereavement: studies of grief in adult life. Penguin Books, Harmondsworth

Raw M 1978 The treatment of cigarette dependence. In: Israel Y, Glaser B, Kalant H, Popham R E, Schmidt W, Smart R G (eds) Research advances in alcohol and drug problems, vol 4. Plenum, New York, ch 11, p 441–485

Royal College of Physicians of London 1983 Obesity. Journal of Royal College of Physicians of London 17: 5–65

Royal Commission on the National Health Service 1979 (The Merrison Report), Cmnd 7615. HMSO, London

Russell M A H 1976 Tobacco smoking and nicotine dependence. In: Gibbins R J, Israel Y, Kalant H, Popham R E, Schmidt W, Smart R G (eds)

Research advances in drug and alcohol problems, vol 3. Wiley, London, ch 1, p 1–47

Schachter S 1978 Pharmacological and psychological determinants of smoking. In: Thornton R E (ed) Smoking behaviours. Churchill Livingstone, Edinburgh, ch 17, p 208–228

Sheiham A 1983 Sugars and dental decay. Lancet I: 282–284

Smith D M 1977 Health care of people at work: agricultural workers. Journal of the Society of Occupational Medicine 27: 87–92

Sognnaes R F 1948 Analysis of war time reduction of dental caries in European children. American Journal of Diseases of Children 75: 792–821

Tansey M J B, Opie L H, Kennelly B M 1977 High mortality in obese women diabetics with acute myocardial infarction. British Medical Journal 1: 1624–1626

Taylor Lord 1975 Poverty, wealth and health or getting the dosage right. British Medical Journal 4: 207–211

The Lancet 1977 Nitrate and human cancer. Lancet II: 281–282

The Politics of Health Group 1980 Food and profit—it makes you sick, Pamphlet No. 1. The Politics of Health Group, London

Thomson A M, Black A E 1975 Nutritional aspects of human lactation. Bulletin of World Health Organisation, 52: 163–177

Townsend P, Davidson N (eds) 1982 Inequalities in health. The Black Report. Penguin Books, Harmondsworth

Van Itallie T B 1978 Dietary fibre and obesity. American Journal of Clinical Nutrition 31: S43–S52

Whorton D, Krauss R M, Marshall S, Milby T H 1977 Infertility in male pesticide workers. Lancet II: 1259–1261

Wilkinson R G 1978 A classy way to die. Ecologist Quarterly Summer: 102–113

Young M, Benjamin B, Wallis C 1963 The mortality of widowers. Lancet II: 454–456

FURTHER READING

Antonovsky A 1979 Health, stress and coping. Jossey Bass, San Francisco

McKinlay J B 1979 A case of re-focusing upstream: the political economy of illness. In: Jaco E G (ed) Patients, physicians and illness, 3rd edn. Free Press, New York, ch 1, p 9–25

National Advisory Committee of Nutrition Education 1983 A discussion paper on proposals for nutritional guidelines for health education in Britain. The Health Education Council, London

5

The family and the life career

In Chapter 3 we introduced the concept of social stratification and indicated the importance of social class and other similar concepts in the development of a sociological understanding. We saw how a sociological understanding extended and modified conventional interpretations of health inequalities. In Chapter 4 we described how illness was caused and prevented by social factors and how these could be interpreted in relation to social structure. Before turning to a fuller discussion of these health-related concepts in Chapter 8 we wish to focus on another important aspect of social structure, namely, the family.

We shall introduce different definitions of what constitutes a family and consider how 'family' has been handled by different sociological perspectives. In order to place the family in a broader social context, we introduce the concept of the life career and discuss processes of socialisation as well as transition points in the life career. Finally we turn to more generalised aspects of social change.

Almost all of us have an intimate knowledge of at least one family. It is a universal institution which takes many forms both within one culture and between different cultures. All of us will have experienced, at some time in our lives, differences between the way our own families and those of acquaintances are organised: families which are mother-centred, or what in sociology we call the *matriarchal family*; families which are father-centred—the *patriarchal family*; families which are neither mother-nor-father centred; and single parent families. Think of your close acquaintances and see whether you can identify an example of each of these. Of course many of the families we each know will exhibit characteristics which are due not to the social structure of the group but to differences in the personalities of family members.

Much of what we know about the family we take for granted. Our intimate knowledge of our own families makes it difficult to transcend all that we already understand about them. In making a study of *the* family as an institution we must confront a major problem of sociological research—we must learn to understand our own values while gaining an understanding of the way others define their situations. But there is a third obstacle to a sociological understanding of the family. In our culture we define family relationships as intimate and private. People are not always willing to respond to detailed study of their family life and those who do respond to questions are likely, as are the sociologists studying them, to couch their answers to conform to society's normative expectations of the family.

Family, therefore, is a concept which has significant personal meaning; it also has a variety of distinct sociological interpretations, which we shall turn to shortly.

A second concept we want to develop in this chapter is *career*. This equally has both everyday and sociological interpretations.

We generally use the word career to refer to a person's advancement through life, especially in relation to his or her profession or occupation. In sociology the concept of career has been applied to a number of very different situations, although retaining the general meaning of progression through life. In this book we shall use the concept in relation to the *life career*, the *patient career* (Ch. 8) and the *professional career* (Ch. 11).

Common to each of these careers are a number of related sociological concepts. In this chapter we focus on two—*socialisation* and *social change*—and, in the process, introduce a number of others.

Fig. 5.1a

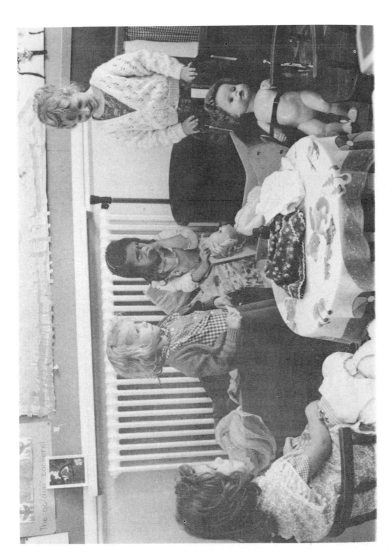

Fig. 5.1a, b Five-year olds already showing stereotyped roles in their play (courtesy of Rik Walton).

Everyone, everywhere, is subject to the process of socialisation by virtue of being born into and continuing to learn the ways of a given society or social group. (Fig. 5.1a, b) Children learn the meanings of different ways of dressing for social events like going out to play, going to church or going to school; patients learn when and in what terms it is appropriate to talk about their illness to different kinds of hospital staff, to other patients and to their families; and students learn the expected ways of acting in front of hospital consultants, senior members of their own profession and their peers.

Like socialisation, social change is not only a common but also a taken-for-granted feature of social life and exerts influence on different kinds of career. Social change affects us all, both in the short and in the long term. In the short term technological innovations such as the telephone have revolutionised many aspects of everyday life: at home, at work and at leisure. In the long term, changing patterns of social behaviour influence the development of our life careers. Employment patterns, leisure activities and family life have been influenced markedly in the last twenty years by social changes such as the changing pattern of female employment and the shorter working week.

In this chapter we shall illustrate the variety of forms the family can take in the context of the life career, and we shall describe the related concepts of marriage and kinship. We shall look at changes in the role of the family in modern Britain, describing two contrasting sociological explanations of the functions of the family. We reserve our discussion of the role of the family in health care until Chapter 6, when we also describe some implications of illness for families.

THE FAMILY

The term family, like the term career, is widely used in everyday speech. People may refer to their relatives as 'the family' and may use it to include or exclude their relatives through marriage. Sometimes it is used in a more restrictive sense to refer to parents and their offspring, while on other occasions the term will refer to the household. What do sociologists understand by the term family? Worsley (1977) identifies three central elements of family: marriage, parenthood and residence. The important thing about these three elements is that they are neither necessary nor sufficient parts of the definition but do, in various combinations, delineate a definition of the family. Let us examine each of these three elements in turn.

Marriage

Traditionally *marriage* has been seen as a relatively unitary concept consisting of a relationship between two adults, one male and one female, which was legally recognised through participation in a religious or civil marriage ceremony. The Report of the Royal Commission on Marriage and Divorce (1956) defined marriage as a 'voluntary union for life of one man and one woman to the exclusion of all others' (p. 7). That is a union which is voluntary, permanent and strictly monogamous. Thirty years on, since the publication of this Report, marriage remains very popular. In 1980, 92% of men and 95% of women aged 45–59 were or had been married (OPCS, 1982, p. 38). Traditional monogamy, that is having one spouse for life, is relatively less common than it used to be. Increasingly modern Britain is characterised by serial monogamy—the practice of having a sequence of spouses, one at a time. In 1965, 11% of marriages involved a divorced bride or groom; this increased to 22% in 1972 (Leete, 1976, p. 6–7) and 35% in 1979 (OPCS, 1981a). More difficult to enumerate (Brown & Kiernan, 1981) is the increasing trend toward common-law marriages—cohabitation. Cohabitation is often short term, and such liaisons are regularly legalised at the appearance of the first child. In 1980 three per cent of women were cohabiting (OPCS, 1982, p. 27). Even more difficult to enumerate is the not insignificant increase in the number of stable homosexual relationships.

Traditionalists may well argue that some of these modern trends do not constitute marriage. But from a sociological perspective what *would be* the characteristics of a particular form of social organisation which can be embraced by the term marriage? To help answer this question let us consider an early sociological definition. Westermark (1926) defined marriage as a relation 'of one or more men with one or more women which is recognised by custom or law, and which involves certain rights and duties, both in the case of the parties entering the union and in the case of the children born of it' (p. 1).

This definition is useful because it highlights the fact that marriage has wider social implications than merely biological mating. An important feature is the emphasis on rights and obligations of marriage, which are common to many societies. Thus marriage may exclude casual sexual relationships and other social relationships not approved by the particular society. Westermark excludes homosexual 'marriages'. But in the fifty years since this definition was penned homosexuality has become more acceptable. Arguably, then, given the breadth of his definition, he would have included homosexual relationships if he had been writing in the 1980s.

We can see that traditional monogamy is just one of many patterns of marriage embraced by Westermark's definition. Group marriage, either polygyny—where a man has more than one wife—or polyandry—where a woman has more than one husband, are included. Marriages can be either permanent or transitional, by divorce or death the latter also permitting serial monogamy. Marriage can be involuntary, as well as voluntary. In many societies, including our own, marriages are arranged by parents.

Britain had absorbed a great many different cultural traditions, and many of these different patterns of marriage exist. British law however decrees polygyny and polyandry illegal, while group common-law marriages are not sanctioned in law. Serial monogamy, as we have already noted is increasingly common, and among some ethnic minorities marriages are still arranged in accordance with the normal customs of the sub-culture, causing some young women to ask to be made 'wards of court' in order to avoid having to enter such a marriage. Marriages of convenience provide a means of overcoming immigration laws.

Parenthood

Parenthood is also socially constructed. Biological parenthood is the basis of many types of families in different cultures.

However, the identification of the biological father can often be a matter of conjecture. As a result, fathers will assume paternity without necessarily being the biological father. Recognition that a parent is not the biological parent takes a number of forms in modern society. Being a step-parent, an increasing likelihood nowadays, has rights and obligations almost identical to those of parenthood. Similarly step-children have rights and obligations similar to those of biological children but, until recently, illegitimate children were deprived of many of these. Adoptive parents, foster parents and grandparents acting as adoptive or foster parents are further examples of social parenthood.

Similar problems of definition surround a number of taken-for-granted relationships. Brother and sister are both kinship terms used to describe offspring of the same parents. They are also used by the Black Power movement in the United States and Trade Union movement, for example, to signify comradeship. The term uncle has been used in at least three ways: a brother of a person's mother or father; an adult friend of a person's parents; and a mother's lover. In studying family relationships we must be careful to be aware of these taken-for-granted uses of the terms, and to remember that other cultures will describe the family in different ways.

Residence

We have already introduced the idea of *residence* in our discussion of marriage. Childless common-law marriages or 'living together' illustrate the importance of residence in defining the family. Like marriage and parenthood, residence is not a sufficient definition of the family. Parents may be married but not living together, for instance in families where one or other parent is at sea, in prison or working abroad, or where parents have temporarily separated. Laslett (1965) describes how, in pre-industrial societies, families would include not only close kin but also servants and other workers—in other words, all of those living in the household. A similar emphasis on residence rather than marriage or parenthood as a definition of family is used by the Census Office, who categorise 'family groupings' into households defined as follows:

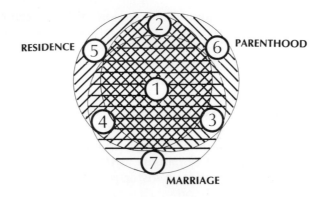

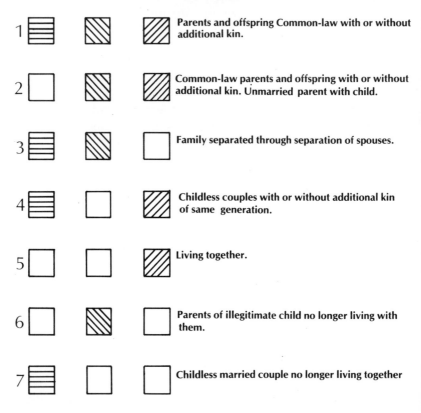

Fig. 5.2 Overlap of the three elements of the family showing seven possible combinations of marriage, parenthood and residence (adapted from Worsley, 1977).

A household is either one person living alone or a group of people (who may or may not be related) living or staying temporarily at the same address with common housekeeping (OPCS, 1981b, p. 6).

Figure 5.2 attempts to illustrate the overlap between the three elements of the family identified by Worsley (1977). Sociologists studying the family have often followed traditional ideas of what constitutes the family. They have focused in particular on the family as man, woman and their offspring. To some extent this conception of the family is an ideal type. It masks the considerable variations which are highlighted by Figure 5.2 and which are indicated in the Rapoports' collection of essays on the family in modern Britain (Rapoport et al, 1982).

Kinship terms

Conjugal family. Sometimes the terms *conjugal family* and *nuclear family* are used to define a social group consisting of a man and woman and their dependent offspring. The term nuclear family is limited to this grouping which subscribes to the view that this is the 'nuclear' unit of social organisation. The term conjugal family while including the above social group is sufficiently inclusive to describe four of the seven categories defined in Figure 5.2 (categories 1, 2, 3 and 6). The central element of the conjugal family is parenthood. Marriage and residence are not necessary for the species to survive.

Family sociologists have generated a confusing list of terms. Their ambiguity has led Harris and Stacey (1969) to identify five key terms: *the family of origin, the family of marriage, ego's kinship core, the T-core* and *the near kin.* We illustrate these in Figures 5.3–5.5, using normal anthropological notation. Three symbols are used. A triangle represents the male of the group, a circle the female and the equals sign between a circle and a triangle represents marriage or common-law marriage. The person who is defining the situation is called the ego.

The family of origin. This is the first of two ways of looking at the conjugal family. The family of origin, sometimes referred to as the family of orientation, refers to the kin grouping of ego, her parent(s) and siblings(s) (see **Fig. 5.3**).

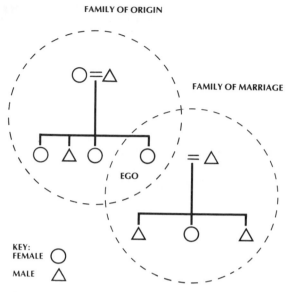

Fig. 5.3 Family of marriage and family of origin.

The family of marriage. This is the second way of looking at the conjugal family. The family of marriage, sometimes referred to as the family of procreation, refers to the kin grouping of ego, her spouse and their children (see Fig. 5.3).

Ego's kinship core. The kin grouping consisting of both the family of origin and the family of marriage is called ego's kinship (see Fig. 5.3).

The T-core. This kin grouping consists of the couple's kinship core: ego's family of origin, her spouse's family of origin and their common family of marriage (see Fig. 5.4).

Near kin. This term refers to ego's *first and second degree kin.* In other words the kinship cores of ego, ego's spouse (the T-core), ego's children, ego's father, ego's mother, and ego's siblings (brothers and sisters). Figure 5.5 shows the kinship universe within which ego's near kin exist.

While there are different structural family arrangements and families have different degrees of permanence, the family is an enduring institution. Any one of us in our lifetime is likely to be a member of more than one family. We progress

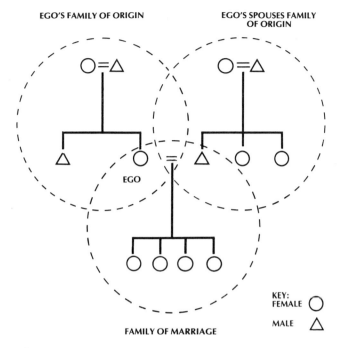

EGO'S FAMILY OF ORIGIN

EGO'S SPOUSES FAMILY
OF ORIGIN

EGO

FAMILY OF MARRIAGE

KEY:
FEMALE ◯

MALE △

Fig. 5.4 The T-core

through life, engaging in different kinds of family relationships, in what can be termed our life careers.

THE LIFE CAREER

All of us are born and in the end we all die. Some people survive in this world for only a few minutes while others last a
century. The concept of *life career* embraces this time span
representing one way in which we can look at our collective
biographies. Figure 5.6 shows the various stages of the life
career starting with birth and ending with death. Along the
way typically the individual will be socialised as a child (and
subsequently at all stages of the life career), be educated,
raise a family, work, become a patient, and live through old

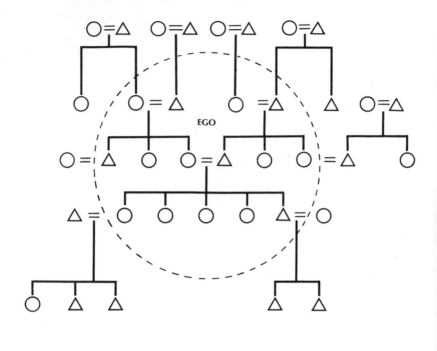

Fig. 5.5 Ego's near kin

age. At different points in the career the typical individual will pass some important milestones: reaching the age of majority, obtaining a job, getting married and retiring.

Ideal type

This illustration of the life career exemplifies the notion of *ideal type*, which was used by the influential sociologist, Max Weber, for comparing social phenomena (Gerth & Mills, 1948). An ideal type is not a moral judgement in the sense of ideal as best morally; neither is it ideal as the best or average example of a social phenomenon; its is an abstract tool, which

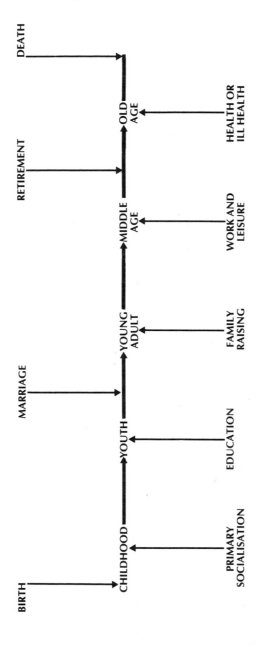

Fig. 5.6 The life career

focuses our attention on a certain range of factors which are regarded as of particular sociological importance. In constructing ideal types the sociologist is asserting that some features of social reality are more sociologically interesting and more worthy of attention than others. Our concept of life career illustrated in Figure 5.6 is not the average life career of a person or indeed the best, but an ideal type constructed as an explanatory device. It has not included features like moving home or getting the sack, which are important to the individual but of less sociological importance for understanding the life career.

Family cycles

In the context of the family, the life career is concerned with the family cycle, which is sometimes referred to as the family life cycle or the cycle of family development. Individual families change in structure: an ideal type would be courtship to marriage, to procreation, to child rearing, to children leaving home and then to dissolution. These phases are determined by biological factors such as the fertility and life span of individuals and the rate of physical maturation of children, and social factors such as the legal definition of adulthood, mating patterns and retirement. A variety of biological and social factors help to determine the length and duration of each phase of the family cycle. Such factors will, of course, vary between different cultures, different historical periods, and different economic conditions.

For the typical individual the first experience of the family will be the family of origin. At this phase of life primary socialisation (in the family) and secondary socialisation (education) will be prime characteristics of the career. When the individual reaches adulthood he may leave the family of origin and, with marriage, enter the family of marriage. This transition will be followed by the period of family-raising. This phase ends when all offspring have reached adult status and have left their family of origin, ego's family of marriage, to begin a new family cycle. The original family of marriage will then enter a phase of independence, probably during middle age, when work and leisure are predominant aspects of the life career. Old age and retirement from major life roles signal the final drama of the life career and the family cycle.

SOCIALISATION

A person's biography begins with his birth. At this point, and continuously through his life, he is subject to the process of *socialisation*. Elkin has defined it 'as the process by which someone learns the ways of a given society or social group so that he can function within it' (Elkin, 1960, p. 4).

Fig. 5.7 Two ends of the life career (courtesy of Rik Walton).

In the first few months of life infants experience numerous stimuli. They experience hunger, thirst, pain, discomfort and pleasure. Although these are physical experiences they are often mediated by society. Infants learn when and where to eat, sleep and defaecate according to a set of predefined rules adhered to by their parents. Of course, such rules will vary between different societies and between different social groups within a particular society. Even within a society child-rearing practices and associated rules vary between different social groupings (Newsom & Newsom, 1965). Young babies will experience and learn, for example, the different rules of demand feeding and regular scheduled feeding according to the social group of their mothers and the feeding policies of different maternity hospitals.

Primary and secondary socialisation

We call the socialisation of an individual in early childhood *primary socialisation*. The learning of more complex social rules in later childhood and adulthood is known as *secondary socialisation*.

Secondary socialisation is experienced throughout the life career. In order to function in a socially appropriate manner we have to learn new rules when we enter any new and strange situation. How many of us would know how to behave when presented to the Queen? When we begin training for a profession, when we start working in a new hospital department, or ward, when we travel abroad on holiday, we are learning the rules appropriate to the social setting in which we are currently interacting. From the cradle to the grave we are being socialised.

Anticipatory socialisation

How does socialisation proceed? Socialisation is often referred to as *anticipatory socialisation* because during the learning of new social rules we anticipate our future behaviour when we have learned these rules. In the socialisation of young children a crucial step is what Mead (1934) called 'learning to take the attitude of the other'. A child will not only learn to recognise a certain attitude in someone else and understand its meaning, but will learn to adopt the attitude himself.

This is readily observed in young children who engage in games of mothers and fathers with their dolls. When the doll 'wets' his clothes the child will imitate both verbally and non-verbally the expressions and gestures of the parent in the real-life situation.

Similarly during training the student nurse will anticipate his future role as a qualified professional by acting out that role during training. He will at first 'play nurse' rather than be a 'real nurse' and hope that those watching him will approve the performance. Through time and with practice the student will gain the conviction that the practices are authentic because others will respond to him as competent and legitimate in the role. Try to think how you yourself have behaved when you were faced with a new situation and had somehow to manage through it. How did you react, for instance, the first time you had to break bad news to a family, or the first time a patient had an extreme emotional outburst?

DEFINITION OF THE SITUATION

As part of the socialisation process an individual learns particular ways of defining the situations in which they find themselves. In other words, 'it all depends on how you see it'. The basis of any definition of a situation described by an individual is rooted in his past social experience. It is affected by the norms and values of his social group which have been learnt through socialisation. Thus the *definition of the situation* is the typical meaning which members of a social group attach to any given social event. For example, people define social roles according to their social experience. Thus the role of husband in relation to child-rearing practices varies between social groups (Newsom & Newsom, 1965). This has the potential for generating conflict in some working-class women when they receive advice from middle-class professionals about the role their husbands *should* play as fathers-to-be, because they hold different normative expectations of what is appropriate. Therefore in order to understand how men and women will act their social roles it is necessary to know and understand how they define a given situation, and to do this we need to know something about what they take for granted.

If a nurse's and patient's definition of the situation, say the
patient's normal bathing patterns, are different, then unless
the nurse is willing to appreciate the patient's point of view,
social understanding and consequently social interaction will
be impaired. A patient who is used to bathing once a week
may find it difficult and distressing to comply with hospital
routines which expect a daily bath. Similarly the male patient
suffering from a myocardial infarction who is washed and
shaved by the nurse may resist this attention because he feels
it reflects adversely on his manliness, and feels distaste at
being attended by a young girl carrying out such personal
tasks. He does not understand or appreciate the nurse's attempts to do everything to help him rest. Their definitions of
the situation are entirely at odds. They need to be given the
opportunity to clarify their varying perspectives to each other
for care to proceed more effectively.

NORMS, VALUES AND ATTITUDES

The specific things that people learn and the way that they are
socialised into a particular mode of behaviour will depend on
a variety of factors: where they live, who they live with, who
they talk to, and where they work. The socialisation process
will be influenced by the *norms, values* and *attitudes* of the
people who are their agents of socialisation.

Norms. Norms refer to those patterns of behaviour in society which are more or less taken for granted. When we meet
people we greet them in different kinds of ways; if we want
something we say please and when we receive it we say thank
you. Similarly men will normally wear trousers and we would
not expect them to wear skirts although in Scotland we would
not be surprised if they were wearing kilts, and female physiotherapists and teachers now often wear trousers at work.
Norms are dependent on given social situations. In hospital
professional staff are expected to look at and touch parts of
the body of the same and opposite sex as they carry out their
professional functions. The same behaviour outside hospital,
or out of context in hospital, would be a gross violation of
society's norms. Male nurses have recently been disciplined

for having sexual relationships with female patients in the patients' own homes but no action would have been taken had the women not been patients.

Values. Values may also be taken for granted but they differ from norms in that they are ideas which we hold to be right or wrong. So for example, in some social groups it would be regarded as wrong to break into someone's house and remove their possessions, but those same people might consider it all-right to use an employer's telephone to make private calls or 'borrow' the odd envelope, paper tissues or bandage. In an absolute sense, all are forms of theft.

Within British society there are variations in both norms and values. In some areas it is taken for granted that women do not frequent certain pubs or areas within them, whereas in other parts of the country it is taken for granted that women may visit any bar or pub. Similarly, different social groups hold different values. In some families where the man is the main wage-earner and undertakes manual work, it is not thought right that men should tell their wives how much they earn, whereas among non-manual workers the opposite generally holds.

Attitudes. Attitudes are more specific than values and often less enduring; like values they are always present, but not necessarily taken for granted. Thus it is taken for granted that children of doctors, teachers, lawyers and people like that will have what we call 'middle-class values'. They will have certain tastes in food and drink, for example they may have a preference for brown bread rather than white or a preference for Brie rather than Cheddar cheese; they may see an importance in school work which other children might not. Although we shall not always be able to predict the values of individual middle-class children we know 'something of the group's values. Their attitudes, however, are something quite different. These are more likely to change over their lifetime and are more likely to be specific and unpredictable—for example, their attitudes towards nuclear weapons, music, euthanasia or abortion. We must also remember that attitudes are more likely than values to be highly emotional issues, both in the sense of being irrational and illogical and in the sense of arousing powerful defences.

AGENCIES OF SOCIALISATION

We have suggested that a person's norms, values and attitudes are influenced by the norms, values and attitudes of their agents of socialisation—those people or groups who participate in the socialisation process. If we look again at Figure 5.6 of our ideal type of life career we can identify a number of phases in the career where major socialisation processes will take place. The prominent agents of socialisation in our society are the family, school, peer group, mass media and work-place. We are all influenced to different degrees by institutions such as the church, the pub or the discotheque. At different points in the life career other institutions such as hospitals, prisons and old people's homes may teach us new rules to follow.

All of us, as well as being socialised, are also agents of socialisation at some time in our lives. In the family the parent teaches the infant a set of roles appropriate to her age, gender and social class. Further on in the life career the teacher will guide pupils towards ways of acting while peers will lead in other and sometimes conflicting ways. In hospital the staff and other patients teach new patients the role of patient while students learn the role of the professional group toward which they aspire. Perhaps, with the exception of professional teachers, the role of socialisation agent is not obvious to those acting it, but informal teaching or role modelling is often a far more important mechanism of socialisation than what is formally taught in class rooms.

CULTURE AND SUB-CULTURE

Perhaps one of the most striking influences on the individual through the socialisation process is the effect of an individual's culture or sub-culture. In sociology the term culture is often used in such a way as to include almost every aspect of human action. In this broader sense culture consists of the entire pattern of beliefs, attitudes, values, ideas and knowledge that members of different social groups hold about themselves.

Within any society there are a number of distinctive smaller cultures called sub-cultures. These develop their own particular cultural patterns. A true sub-culture develops when its members as a group work or live in relative isolation, such as a village of coal-miners or fishermen; when a group perceives external threats to its welfare, for example battered wives or homosexuals; or when a group has a common interest to defend against others, such as black immigrants in a white society. As sub-cultures develop their members may acquire preferences for different kinds of material objects such as clothes or music, and they may develop norms, values and attitudes of their own. Sometimes these involve a rejection of the norms, values and attitudes of the larger culture. We have only to look at many teenagers to see how their sub-cultures reject traditional modes of dress and behaviour. In some sub-cultures values are reversed. Petty crime and drugs use may be admired among sub-cultures which would be termed delinquent by the larger society.

AGEING

Throughout the life career individuals also undergo a process of ageing. Ageing is both a biological and a social process; it involves interaction between the social and physical environment and the individual's biological state. From a biological perspective ageing in individuals can be defined as a deteriorative process through which the resistance of the organism to the pressure of the environment progressively diminishes, until it can no longer withstand them and dies. Thus throughout an individual's life there will be a decline in biological functioning; in basal metabolic rate, in cardiac output, in the vital capacity of the lungs, in breathing capacity, in nerve conduction velocity, in body water content, in kidney plasma flow and in the filtration rates of the kidney. A similar dynamic set of processes, which operate at all stages of the life career, can be seen from a sociological perspective. However, from a sociological perspective ageing does not necessarily imply social decline; rather it is an example of social change.

Social change

We experience change at various stages throughout out life careers. We get married, we move house, we divorce and we retire. A number of important changes occur to many of us in our lives and the socialisation process prepares each of us for some of them, although inevitably we are left unprepared to deal with others.

Status passage. To describe such changes in our life careers we use the concept of *status passage*. A status passage is a significant event in the life career which marks the change from one social position to another. Thus birth, graduation, marriage, divorce, redundancy, and death are all examples of status passage.

Rites de passage. The status passage is often marked by ritual ceremonies called *rites de passage*. In native African and South American culture these may take the form of ritual dances and feasts. In contemporary Britain the presentation of the hospital badge to newly qualified nurses, the graduation ceremony, and the lavish presentation of gifts at the birth of a new baby and marriage are common examples. Perhaps the best illustration of the status passage and its associated *rites de passage* is retirement. People's experience of retirement and their reactions to the process will be numerous. However, changes for the individual throughout the life career are often predictable, like retirement, and represent persistent patterns of action.

Retirement

We tend to use the concept of retirement in two complementary ways: to describe the transition from the role of worker to the role of retired person and to describe the social status of the retired person. In the first sense retirement is a *rite de passage*. In many primitive societies the various *rites de passage* provide a smooth transition from one social status to another. Three kinds of rites can be distinguished for any given status passage: rites of separation, rites of transition and rites of incorporation (Van Gennep, 1960). Marion Crawford has described the experiences of a small number of men before and after retirement. She suggests that in British society retirement includes rites of both separation and transition but not of incorporation (Crawford, 1973).

Rites of separation. The experiences of the worker during his last week at work may be described as *rites of separation.* For part of this time he would be expected to leave his normal task and spend some of the time saying his farewells to his fellow workers. The time spent participating in this ritual will be determined not only by the size of the establishment in which he works but the significance of it to workers.

Retirement not only means relinguishing the status of worker; it also implies giving up the status identity associated with a particular kind of job—electrician, driver, lawyer, speech therapist or whatever. This identity will have more chance of continuing where a job is taken over by someone else. Thus an important aspect of the rites of separation includes the handing over of the job to someone else.

Rites of transition. The retiring worker will signify the 'sacred' status of the transition by not being subject to the ordinary disciplines of the work place. For example, the blue-collar worker may wear more formal clothes which would normally be inapprorpriate for the tasks usually undertaken. The *rites of transition* may include a number of symbolic acts such as visits, exchange of gifts, final drinks or special meals and outings away from the work place. In contemporary retirement ceremonies the presentation of gifts from colleagues and employers appears to be the most common *rite.* Gifts, as well as showing real appreciation to a retiring colleague, also provide a focus for the leaving ceremony.

Rites of incorporation. The social group to which the retired worker is incorporated is the family. This is the group with which in retirement he will spend most of his time and will be most closely identified by the rest of the community. Such rites of incorporation would include celebration meals or retirement parties for family and friends. Rites of incorporation do not appear to be such a common practice among retiring workers in Britain (Crawford, 1973). Since the rites of incorporation are an important part of a *rites de passage* in helping the individual to adjust to his new role, the absence of such rites during retirement might be greeted with some concern.

In the second sense in which we commonly use the term 'retirement' it represents a social status often identified as synonymous with old age. In the life career described earlier in this chapter we have constructed an ideal type which implies this synonymity. However it is more appropriate to talk about 'old age' and reserve the term 'retirement' to describe the process of transition between the status of worker and status of retired person. It is particularly inappropriate to use the term retirement to describe the status of elderly women if they have never been formally employed.

Characteristics of contemporary social change

Not only does the individual face change throughout the individual life career; he must also learn to recognise and adapt to structural changes in society. Before concluding this chapter with a discussion about social changes and the contemporary family we shall identify a number of common characteristics of change.

Social change influences all aspects of our lives. In contrast to earlier periods of history the 20th century has experienced dramatic social changes, and according to writers like Toffler (1970) changes are coming about even more rapidly. The rate at which changes occur influences our sense of time. Yet the strength of ancient Islamic traditions in the Middle East, the revival of African culture among American blacks and the continuing importance of the family in contemporary Britain might suggest that major social change in the world at large has not been very rapid. However, relative to other historical periods, there is little doubt that for most societies more rapid social change is now occurring, sometimes bringing strife as new and old values clash.

Social change in contemporary British society is piecemeal rather than revolutionary or utopian. Institutions such as the family, the church or Government, are constantly subject to change but it is neither sudden nor violent. The changes which have taken place in the reorganisation of the National Health Service since it was established in 1948 show that while change is not revolutionary, the rate at which changes have been introduced has increased over time and when changes are regarded as occurring too frequently this can cause social unrest. Usually, in our society, changes are piecemeal, evolutionary, less dramatic and are therefore less obvious.

In the past social change was unplanned. Nowadays much social change is planned, as for example the creation of employment opportunities in Special Development Areas, or results from the deliberate introduction of technological innovation such as using computerised records to call babies for immunisation. The introduction of silicon chip technology has led to increased automation and information processing is changing dramatically. Such technological innovation has profound social consequences—higher residual unemployment, early retirement, shorter working weeks and longer holidays. The obsolescence of some procedures and forms of organisation in our worlds of work have been matched by new ways of working. In addition, new forms of employment and leisure activities have been established.

The consequences of current social change to the individual can be severe. Families are uprooted; people change occupations and homes more frequently; new relationships have to be established. We all need to learn ways adaptiving to our changing social environment or milieu. Social change affects every feature of modern life and every stage of the life career.

SOCIAL CHANGE AND THE FAMILY

In Chapter 2 we identified a number of sociological theories. Two of these, both in the structuralist tradition, are relevant to our discussion of social change and the family: structural functionalism, which provides a consensus perspective, and Marxism, which provides a conflict perspective. Both perspectives have focused on the family as central to their theories about society and, not surprisingly, offer different interpretations of the relationship between social change and the family.

The study of the family presents a number of theoretical difficulties. As we have described in this chapter, the individual family is a constantly changing structure; moving from courtship to marriage, to procreation, to child-rearing, to children leaving home, and then to dissolution. A study of the same family cannot easily be made over its natural life-cycle since the sociologist undertaking such a study might not survive that long! Sociologists attempt to overcome this difficulty by comparing different families at various stages of the life-cycle, in other words using a cross-sectional rather than a longitudinal approach. This method is not without its own problems, however. It is difficult to distinguish between differences in study families which are due to the various stages of their life-cycles from those which are due to more general changes in the structure of modern families over time; this is typical of problems which particularly haunt students of social change.

Most institutions such as hospitals or schools have clearly identifiable boundaries, formal structures and a set of clearly specified functions. Whereas hospitals are usually defined by a physical area, have explicit structures and exist for the care and cure of patients, the family is more difficult to define, has little formal structure and functions variously as a vehicle for procreation, and as an agency of socialisation and social control. Indeed, different theoretical perspectives identify different structures and functions as being differentially important.

Structural functionalism

Talcott Parsons (1951, 1954, 1964) provides the fullest account of the functionalist perspective of the family. His analysis identifies two major functions of the conjugal family. First, families exist to facilitate the procreation of children and to socialise them into adult roles of the kind which are accepted and expected by the social group in which they live. For example, the Western family plays a major role in teaching adult gender roles to children; the way children are dressed, the games they are allowed to play and the different attitudes of parents toward their children's behaviour are all part of a process in which children identify with a gender role.

Second, the family acts to reinforce primary and secondary socialisation and is used to stabilise adult behaviour to adopt the stereotyped roles of husband and wife. Thus in traditional conjugal families men and women not only influence the way their children identify adult gender roles as described above, but they also act as role models for their children. Men have as their primary duty the earning of money to support the family, and as a result their activities and interests are more often focused outside the home than are those of women, whose main occupations are domestic and who are therefore homecentred.

Thus the functionalist perspective views the relatively autonomous conjugal family, with its emphasis on free mate-selection and relatively weak kinship ties, as the family structure most appropriate for modern industrial society. This kind of structure facilitates free mobility of labour, on the one hand, which is essential for economic growth in a modern industrial society and, on the other hand, a supportive relationship for men and women which acts as an emotional balance to the stresses and tensions of modern life (Parsons, 1964).

Marxism

Marxist theory also stresses the importance of the relationship between the family and the functioning of the economy. However, the emphasis is different. In Marxist theory the family is the institution within capitalist societies by which capitalism reproduces itself. In addition, as a unit of consumption, the family reinforces capitalism. The family provides workers to operate the system and also provides the mechanism for the socialisation and social control of both men and women. A similar view of gender roles is described for both functionalist and Marxist theories. The feminine role consists of one which supports the male worker by fulfilling various physical, sexual, social and emotional needs. The masculine role is one which disciplines individuals to sell their labour to the capitalist system. The influence of the Marxist perspective is evident in the feminist critique of the family.

Feminism

The feminist critique of the family identifies the inherent contradictions of the family. On the one hand, the family unit has been established to serve the function of procreation and to provide practical and emotional support to male workers. On the other hand, the family is a major source of emotional tension between men and women. Whereas Marx's perspective blames the oppression and exploitation of women on the class system, the feminist perspective blames both the class system and the family (Segal, 1983).

Weaknesses of functionalist and Marxist theory

There are three important differences between the two theoretical approaches we have described above. First, whereas
functionalism emphasises the needs of industrial society,
Marxism emphasises the needs of capitalism. Second, from a
functionalist perspective the relationship between the family
and the economy is one of reciprocity whereas from a Marxist
perspective it is a relationship in which the economy is the
dominant partner. Third, as we described in Chapter 2, the
functionalist perspective postulates a relatively stable equilibrium within the social system, while the Marxist perspective
postulates conflict between two antagonistic social classes
which will lead to social change.

Neither theoretical tradition has been substantiated through
the collection of empirical data. As we have shown above,
although there exists no generally recognisable family unit,
other than the conjugal family, in both functionalist and Marxist theory, the variations of the basic structure are numerous
and significant in number. Neither perspective really explains,
for example, the emergence of the dual-career family or the
single-parent family. Nor do they explain the changes in the
relationship between the family unit and other sectors of society, particularly the economy. For example, there has been
little attempt by either the functionalists or the Marxists to
accommodate in their theories the increasing rate of economic activity among women outside the home.

Although we do not feel that these two theoretical perspectives provide an adequate explanation of the functions of
the family, they are important for our understanding of modern society. In particular they are important to our understanding of the family in a changing society and of the modern
debate over gender roles.

The family in a changing society

In our discussion of what constitutes a family we indicated
substantial changes in the prevalence of different family structures. The traditional conjugal family still dominates, but the
increase in divorce and remarriage, in single parent families
and in other family forms fuels the ideological debate about
changing values of the family.

At the centre of this debate are three areas of family life which have been the subject of rapid social change since the Second World War, namely gender roles, family planning, and child-care practices and rights.

It is maintained by many commentators that within the family there has been a marked change in gender roles. Elizabeth Bott (1971) in her seminal study of gender roles noticed that in small conjugal families partners substituted for each other when either was ill or away from home. It is much easier to maintain gender differentiation in a larger family unit when someone of the same gender is usually available to perform the duties of a member who is not present. Young and Willmott (1973) in their study of *The Symmetrical Family* report an increase in the substitution of partners' roles. More married women are working in paid employment and their husbands are sharing more domestic tasks. However, Young and Willmott note that it as still the wives who made household decisions and lived with the pressures of 'two jobs'. How many truly egalitarian families do you know? We suspect that even among the examples of the fairly rare *dual-career family* (Rapoport & Rapoport, 1971) there will be few in which traditional gender roles are fully shared. Observed changes in gender roles are another example of evolutionary social change, in this case toward a more egalitarian family structure.

The increasing availability of abortion and contraception means that women are less likely to spend such a large proportion of their lives bearing and rearing children, and are more likely, therefore, to seek employment outside the home.

As well as changes in the relationship between men and women, it is argued that there have been similar changes in relationships between adults and children; child-care has become more 'permissive', so that children can play some part, albeit a small one, in the decision-making processes of the family. Ideological debates about the permissiveness of current child-rearing practices have been encouraged by changes in the behaviour of adolescents. Yet there are no strong data to show actual levels of change in permissiveness.

Data from the Newsoms' study of infant care (now 20 years old) suggest that changes have been subtle: from physical to emotional means of controlling children (Newsom & Newsom, 1965). While there certainly has been a development of a prominent youth culture, this may be largely independent of child-rearing practices and due to, for example, changes in the economy, peer-group influences or even television.

The interpretation of these three examples of social change and their relationship to the family varies enormously between the two sides of the feminist ideological debate. Feminist rhetoric focuses on egalitarian gender roles. They demand 'equal rights' for all in the public sphere. This ideal is based on the assertion that all differences in occupational positions are the result of discrimination, i.e. they are socially constructed. Much feminist rhetoric denies any innate differences between men and women, while a minority of feminists believe that, far from being equal with men, women are superior. We suspect, however, that a majority of women who consider themselves to be feminists would adopt a 'differential-egalitarian position' (Berger & Berger, 1983). That is, they would demand equality of opportunity but accept some innate differences between men and women, such as physical strength.

Traditionalist rhetoric has opposed these views, arguing strongly that a woman's role is first and foremost in the home 'servicing' husband and family. Ideologically this approach is probably widely approved, but in practice the economic needs of families are an incentive for families to become more egalitarian.

Abortion and contraception are probably taken more for granted than is gender-role egalitarianism. Yet the issue of abortion has recently galvanised far more passion that any other issue concerning the family—even than divorce. This is perhaps not surprising, given the gulf in ideals between the two groups. Feminists argue that it is the fundamental right of a woman to have control over her own body and her own life. Others defend the right of society to protect even its weakest members—in this instance, unborn children. The debate centres on the issue of whether the fetus is a person or not. One side argues that the fetus is just a part of a woman's body and that she should therefore decide on its future, while the other side argues that the fetus is a separate body. The only definite statement we should wish to make is that the answer to this particular debate will be socially constructed, and that different cultures and sub-cultures will give different answers.

The third area of family life which has also attracted bitter argument is that of child-rearing practices. We look at this issue in some detail in the next chapter when we consider the role of the family in the maintenance of health. For the present it is probably sufficient to say that the black-and-white dichotomy which summarises the position of the feminists and traditionalists is, as with our other two examples, too over-simplied. In between, there are various shades of grey representing a large number of viewpoints.

SUMMARY

This chapter has introduced a number of new concepts, each of which helps us to understand our ideal type of life career and the family. We have indicated the methodological difficulties in studying the family, and highlighted the extent to which different groups in society take up ideological positions based on different definitions of the situation.

It is our assumption that, universally, human beings in all societies arrange themselves into families. However, different societies have constructed the family in different ways and, indeed, in modern Britain individuals modify and interpret their own families in the light of their own experiences, expectations and perceptions. Therefore for us the meaningful question is not *whether* the family will survive, but, rather, *what kinds* of family will occur in the future. We do not think that the rhetoric of either the feminists or the traditionalists will provide an answer to this question. Consideration of their debates should, however, encourage you to think carefully and question your own fundamental and taken-for-granted ideas about *the* family and *your* family.

In this chapter we describe the inter-relationship between the family and the life career. We saw that for all of us our experience of family life will change as we move through life from childhood, through adolescence, young adulthood, child-rearing, middle-age, and old age. Of course, as we proceed along our life career we will also have different experiences of health and ill health. The chapter was also concerned with showing the effects of social change on the structure of the family and identifying the various competing explanations of the function of the family.

REFERENCES

Berger B, Berger P L 1983 The war over the family. Capturing the middle ground. Hutchinson, London
Bott E 1971 Family and social network, 2nd edn. Tavistock, London
Brown A, Kiernan K 1981 Cohabitation in Great Britain: evidence from the General Household Survey. Population Trends 25: 4–10
Crawford M P 1973 Retirement: a rite de passage. Sociological Review 21: 447–461
Elkin F 1960 The child and society. The process of socialisation. Random House, New York
Gerth H H, Mills C W 1948 From Max Weber: essays in sociology. Routledge & Kegan Paul, London
Harris C C, Stacey M 1969 A note on the term 'extended family'. In: Stacey M (ed) Comparability in social research. Heinemann, London, ch 2, p 56–64
Laslett P 1965 The world we have lost. Methuen, London
Leete R 1976 Marriage and divorce: trends and patterns. Population Trends 3: 3–8
Mead G H 1934 Mind, self and society. University of Chicago Press, Chicago
Newsom J, Newsom E 1965 Patterns of infant care in an urban community. Penguin Books, Harmondsworth
Office of Population, Censuses and Surveys 1981a Marriage and divorce statistics, 1979. England and Wales. HMSO, London
Office of Population, Censuses and Surveys 1981b Census 1981. Definitions. Great Britain. HMSO, London
Office of Population, Censuses and Surveys 1982 General Household Survey, 1980. HMSO, London
Parsons T 1951 The social system. Routledge & Kegan Paul, London
Parsons T 1954 Essays in sociological theory, Revised edn. The Free Press, New York
Parsons T 1964 Social structure and personality. Free Press, New York
Rapoport R, Rapoport R N 1971 Dual-career families. Penguin Books, Harmondsworth
Rapoport R N, Fogarty M P, Rapoport R 1982 Families in Britain. Routledge & Kegan Paul, London
Royal Commission on Marriage and Divorce 1956 Report 1951–1955, Cmnd 9678. HMSO, London
Segal L (ed) 1983 What is to be done about the family? Penguin Books, Harmondsworth
Toffler A 1970 Future shock. Bodley Head, London
Van Gennep A 1960 The rites of passage. Routledge & Kegan Paul, London
Westermark E 1926 A short history of marriage. MacMillan, London
Worsley P (ed) 1977 Introducing sociology, 2nd edn. Penguin Books, Harmondsworth
Young M, Willmott P 1973 The symmetrical family. Routledge & Kegan Paul, London

FURTHER READING

Rapoport R N, Fogarty M P, Rapoport R 1982 Families in Britain. Routledge
  & Kegan Paul, London
Worsley P (ed) 1977 Introducing sociology, 2nd edn. Penguin Books,
  Harmondsworth, ch 4, p 165–209

The family and the
  maintenance of health
The family in the context
  of health
The family's response to
  illness

6

Health and the family

Arguably, the family provides the most important social context within which health is maintained and illness occurs and is resolved. The manner in which the individual reacts to his illness, and the nature of the family's response to it, may influence not only the course of the patient's illness but the health and happiness of the family as well. The effects that an individual's illness has on his family will depend on the characteristics of his particular family, on such factors as the allocation of roles within the family and the extent of emotional support available, as well as the family's financial stability or vulnerability. A long-term illness of the mother in a single-parent family is likely to have different effects on the family than would the same illness on a non-employed mother in a traditional conjugal family. These considerations led Theodore Litman (1974) to argue that the family serves as the primary unit in health and medical care.

The inter-relation between the family and health is a highly dynamic one which has a number of facets. In this chapter we shall explore this relationship in three ways:

1. We shall consider the role of the family in the maintenance of health
2. We shall discuss the the role of the family at times of illness
3. We shall explore the role of the family in community care, and discuss competing explanations for this role.

THE FAMILY AND THE MAINTENANCE OF HEALTH

Empirical studies of the role of the family in the maintenance of health have been relatively few. A World Health Organisation report observed:

'In spite of its central position in society, the family has been infrequently studied from the public health point of view. The complex interrelationships between health and the family virtually constitute *terra incognita*. In the form presented or available statistics too often tell very little about the family setting although this is undoubtedly a major factor, in, for example, the rearing of children and the development and stabilisation of adult personality. Many of the strains and maladjustments which place an increasing burden on paediatric, general medical and psychiatric services can be understood and efficiently tackled only after due attention has been given to the family setting. The fact that the family is a unit of illness because it is the unit of 'living' has been grossly neglected in the development of statistical tools suitable for coping with this set of problems, and in the provision of statistical data essential for an investigation of the individual as part of the family in illness as well as health.' (WHO, 1971, p. 2).

The few studies which have looked at the role of the family in the maintenance of health have focused more on the family as a social cause of illness. In Chapter 4 we identified a number of social causes of illness. Here we deal only with the relationship between family structure and health and illness, and in particular we focus on the role of the family in the aetiology of psychiatric illness, on parental and maternal deprivation and on inter-generational influence on health and illness behaviours.

Schizophrenia and the family

In Chapter 8 we develop the concept of *labelling* which refers to a social process by which individuals or groups classify the social behaviour of other individuals. Labels are social constructions which change through time. For example, the American Psychiatric Association recently decided that homosexuality is no longer a psychiatric illness. Patients are no longer admitted to hospitals for the mentally handicapped as 'morally defective'.

The psychiatrist R.D. Laing has argued, from the labelling perspective, that schizophrenia is not so much an illness as a label given to people who react to a family life in a specific way within its own rationality (Laing, 1965). Such a view, of course, challenges the everyday assumptions of the psychi-

atric profession and is a view which appears highly speculative. It is also a view which challenges normative views of the
ideal type of family, which we have suggested is not necessarily the only family structure in contemporary society. Laing
(1967) argues that case studies of families of people regarded
as schizophrenic show that the apparent irrationality of the
individual appears quite rational in the context of the schizophrenic's family. By living in a particular family we all absorb
our family's system of role-relationship. In other words, 'to be
in the same family means having the same family inside oneself' (Laing, 1967, p. 119). The absorption of our family's role
system threatens us all with the possibility that our individual
identities may become seriously confused through conflicting
self-images received from different family members. In order
to establish individual autonomy in this situation, Laing argues, the individual will reject his family role system and exhibit what conventional psychiatrists interpret as 'schizophrenic
behaviour'.

Through Laing's case study of Jane we can get some idea of
how this happens. Jane experienced a change in her personality from an active, friendly, involved seventeen-year-old, to
an inactive, self-absorbed and silent figure. During psychotherapy she described herself as a tennis ball being passed to
and fro in a game of mixed doubles. This fantasy, Laing argues, is derived from her role relationship in her family in
which she acted as the message-carrier between different family members: father, mother, mother's father and father's
mother. For weeks at a time all communication would pass
through Jane. 'Mother would turn to Jane and say, 'Tell your
father to pass the salt', Jane would say to her father 'Mum
wants you to pass the salt' and so on' (Laing, 1967, p. 122). The
purpose of psychotherapy would be to establish for Jane the
connection between her world of 'mixed doubles' inside her
head and the world of her family outside. The aim would be
to get Jane to understand that her response was an essentially
rational reaction to her family situation.

While these theories apparently conflict with mainstream
psychiatry, we must be careful not to reject radical reinter-
pretations out of hand. To reject such ideas could be like continuing to accept the notion that the earth is flat. Before
Columbus there was little or no evidence to suggest that the

world was not flat. We have only a series of case studies to support Laing's theories, and these may be open to alternative interpretations. For example, it could be that Jane's behaviour was in some sense causing the 'tennis-ball' effect on other family members. Also, thinking of all the families we know with adolescent members, we are surprised there is not a greater prevalence of schizophrenia! In other words our sociological concern is not so much one of why Jane was labelled schizophrenic but why so many other Janes are not.

Brown et al (1972) were also concerned with the part the family plays in schizophrenia, not in its aetiology, but in the course of the illness. They studied a group of patients already diagnosed with different forms of schizophrenia, and their families, over a two-year period. The hypothesis being tested was that families in which there was a high degree of expressed emotion were likely to cause a florid relapse of symptoms independently of other variables such as length of history of the illness, severity of previous behaviour disturbance or type of symptoms. The concept *expressed emotion* among relatives was constructed from a number of measures including critical comments about others at home, expressed hostility towards family members, expressions of dissatisfaction about several areas of family life and emotional over-involvement of parents with the patient. It is a measure with mainly negative connotations.

Brown and his colleagues examined the course of the illness over two years, and particularly whether patients relapsed. Relapse was related to major variables, shown diagrammatically at Figure 6.1. A high degree of emotion expressed by relatives at the time of a key hospital admission was found to be strongly associated with subsequent symptomatic relapse in the nine months following discharge from hospital. Previous work impairment and behavioural disturbance were also associated with relapse. This was becuase of their high association with level of expressed emotion. No other factor was able to predict symptomatic relapse. Two factors, however, could mitigate the effects of high expressed emotion by family members. One was regular phenothiazine medication for the patient, and the other was reducing the amount of contact between the patient and a highly emotional relative. Social

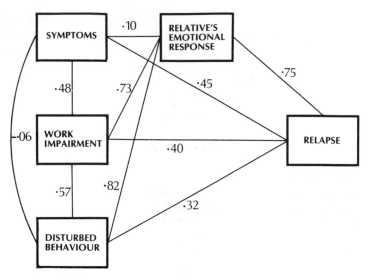

Fig. 6.1 Relationship of main variables to each other and to relapse (Brown et al, 1972).

withdrawal from the family could, therefore, be a protective mechanism for some patients.

Expressed emotion within families is one factor which influences relapse. So too does previous history and type of schizophrenic condition. However, expressed emotion is strongly associated with patients' behaviour and work record and the direction of cause and effect is interpreted by Brown and his colleagues as mutually dependent, i.e.

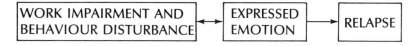

They relate the deleterious effects of living in a family with high expressed emotion to patients experiencing high levels of arousal over long periods. When a critical life event occurs (see our discussion of life events in Chapter 4) and patients are already in a state of high arousal, then they are particularly likely to suffer relapse. While elements of the environment other than family life are likely to influence arousal, they have not yet been systematically studied. However, the interaction between biological and social factors in the course of illness in this context adds to our developing stock of knowledge about the complex nature of illness and its management. A major recommendation of Brown and his colleagues' study is that 'The optimum social environment would be structured with clearcut roles, only as much complexity as any individual can cope with and with neutral but active supervision to keep up standards of appearance, work, and behaviour' (1972, p.256).

Parental and maternal deprivation

The family has also been 'blamed' for other social abnormalities. Many of these hypotheses focus on *parental deprivation*, and in particular *maternal deprivation*. A wide range of social abnormalities have been attributed to parental deprivation including developmental retardation, affectionless psychopathy, delinquency, growth failure, and depression in adults (Rutter, 1972). Many of these hypotheses assume certain expectations about parenting.

First, the family provides stable bonds or relationships which may serve as the basis for the child's growing circle of relationships outside the family (Bowlby, 1971). Second, as we described in Chapter 5, the family is a primary agent of socialisation, so that parents will provide a child with a set of values and attitudes which he may accept or reject. Third, the family will provide the necessary life experiences which the child requires for 'normal' development. Finally, the family provides a secure background to act as a base from which the child can explore his world (Rutter & Madge, 1976).

Such expectations of the family have what Rapoport et al have called a *biological emphasis*. The biological emphasis suggests that parental behaviour is biologically rooted. This view implies that mothers are primary nurturing parents; fathers are peripheral and, while they are expected to protect and provide for the mother and child, substitutes are more acceptable for them than for mothers; and the domestic division of labour that reflects the above is the most natural and appropriate one (Rapoport, Rapoport and Strelitz, 1977). The reader will note a number of similarities between this view of parenting and the functionalist theories of the family described in the previous chapter.

Functionalist theories also form the basis for the *systems emphasis* to parenting. Parenting behaviour mirrors social structure and adapts responsively to social values. Thus the functionalist view of the family emphasises the gender-linked division of labour which fits the environment and is functional both for the individual family members and for wider society. From a functionalist perspective it is logical to blame the changes in family structure and parenting behaviour for the wide range of social abnormalities attributed to the family, since the conjugal family with stereotyped gender roles would satisfy the requirements of modern industrial society: labour mobility, stability of income and reliability of personal relationships. This view of parenting and the family has come under increasing attack both ideologically and theoretically. In addition, Rapoport, Rapoport and Strelitz (1977) have shown that many of the theoretical assumptions do not stand up to empirical investigation.

Another way of looking at parenting is with a *cultural emphasis*. The family is considered to be the universal social institution for reproduction and socialisation of infants, but its structure and norms for parenting vary according to the cultural context. Thus the experience of the Israeli *kibbutzim* suggests that maternal deprivation as such does not exist in all societies (Oakley, 1976). Indeed it is probable that maternal deprivation as strictly defined does not truly exist in contemporary British society. If it did, with the increasing proportion of mothers working we would expect a corresponding increase in maternal deprivation and its consequences. It is now apparent from a number of studies 'that working mothers have children with no more problems than the children of women who remain at home' (Rutter & Madge, 1976, p. 213). In addition, as Anne Oakley has pointed out, the empirical evidence of the concept was based on the juxtaposition of maternal child care, which was regarded as inevitably good, with institutional child care, which was interpreted as bad (Oakley, 1976). Of course, this is not the case.

The evidence that parental deprivation makes an individual extremely vulnerable has been examined by Chen and Cobb (1960). They found that tuberculosis patients, accident victims and parasuicidals reported being parentally deprived. A common factor linking the backgrounds of this vulnerable group was found to be social isolation. However, Chen and Cobb advise caution in the interpretation of these data since they only suggest that certain individuals are at risk; we cannot conclude that parental deprivation is a *cause* of these illness events.

Intergenerational influences and health

In Chapter 3 we looked at inequalities in health which persist between different social groups in society. One explanation for the persistence of such inequalities, which has gained acceptance among health professionals becuase of its common-sense usefulness, is what Oscar Lewis termed the *culture of poverty*. Lewis (1964) argues that in anthropological usage the term culture implies a design for living which is passed down from generation to generation. (This is a slightly different meaning of the concept which we described in Chapter 5.) 'In short, it is a way of life, remarkably stable and persistent, passed down from generation to generation along family lines' (Lewis, 1964, p. xxiv). Both Rutter and Madge (1976) and Townsend (1979) have criticised the 'culture of poverty' thesis, but does it have any credibility in regard to the transmission of health attitudes between generations?

Blaxter and Paterson (1982) set out to examine the hypothesis that individuals' health experience might, in poor socio-economic circumstances, create attitudes of apathy toward health care and conflict with health professionals, and that these attitudes might be transmitted through generations among female members of the family. The study set out to obtain from an older generation of women (the grandmothers) information about their past and present perceptions of the structure and functions of health services. These are compared with the attitudes of their daughters (the mothers) to see to what extent values and beliefs are transmitted or recur throughout generations.

Of major importance are the behavioural consequences of attitudes, since it is behavioural variables which will influence the health of the next generation of children. The health care behaviour of the mothers was therefore documented over a six-month period by obtaining regular reports from them of illness among their children and their response to such episodes. The focus was on women, because there is some agreement about the central role of the mother in coping with illness in the family (Locker, 1981), about her role in the transmission of attitudes (Pratt, 1973), and about the continuing importance of the mother-daughter relationship (Young & Willmott, 1957; Litman, 1974).

In this study the effect of social change was minimised by excluding upwardly mobile families. The study was therfore confined to 58 three-generation families from the Registrar General's Social Classes IV and V living in one Scottish city. The interview data obtained from grandmothers and mothers was supplemented by data on health behaviour of the grandmother group from an extension study carried out when they were having their first babies in 1950–1953 and followed up five and ten years later.

Analysis was carried out to determine the mothers' and grandmothers' concepts of health, illness and disease, and a detailed analysis of all reported illness episodes among children and of the use of health services was completed. As well as mothers' perceptions of, and behaviour toward, symptoms of acute illness among their children, also documented were chronic and handicapping conditions, accidents, dental care, immunisation, fertility control, infant feeding and child nutrition and the pattern of lay remedies and lay referral.

Grandmothers' and mothers' attitudes toward available health services were examined. Of course the relationship between attitudes and behaviour is complex, and other influences on the use of health services like economic constraints, transport, location of services and other practical contingencies were included in the study. While the emphasis was on the clients' attitudes, it is important to remember that how professionals respond to clients is influential in shaping these attitudes.

To what extent is the conventional wisdom—'like mother, like daughter'—upheld? There was some evidence that lay remedies and methods of child-care in illness were passed on. However, it appears that only in the area of the early introduction of solid foods to young babies were the grandmothers particularly influential. When comparisons were made between grandmothers' and mothers' accounts of advice given, they were very consistent. Only two of 47 comparisons showed contradictory accounts. Most respondents agreed that, although there was often discussion between grand-mothers and mothers, the mothers usually went their own way. The advice most usually given was to go to the doctor. Grandmothers helped in emotional and practical ways, but demonstrated little overt influence on health-care or child-rearing practices.

Both grandmothers and mothers were characterised by early childrearing and high rates of youthful, illegitimate and prenuptial pregnancies. The grandmothers, however, were likely to have large and unplanned families while mothers had no intention of following this example. The norms of behav-iour in relation to family size and to other aspects of child health have so changed that inter-generational comparisons mean little. This is certainly so in such areas as contraception and infant feeding.

Thus, in a community characterised by close family net-works, no consistent relationships were found between the attitudes of grandmothers and mothers. More important than direct family transmission were inter-generational changes bound up with changes in lifestyle and circumstances, service provision and more widespread changes in public attitude—that is, wider social change.

The examples of 'health-deprived' children were often in part associated with the mother's behaviour. Of more major importance, however, were aspects of a disadvantaged en-vironment and organisation of services. It was in circumstances where the environment had changed least and the young mothers were in the most disadvantaged positions that their attitudes resembled those of their mothers. Both generations exhibited a disorganised and apathetic approach to preventive care.

Thus inter-generational continuity is present only in some ways and under some circumstances. The study serves to demonstrate the complexity of family studies and the need for sophisticated methods of data collection and analysis. These complexities indicate some reasons why only a few such stud-ies exist.

With these three examples we have tried to indicate some

of the ways in which the contemporary family interacts with health. Each of the examples chosen challenges conventional and often professional wisdom.

THE FAMILY IN THE CONTEXT OF HEALTH

When a person is ill it is generally the family that copes. The family will offer remedies and advice; it will take over roles that the ill person is unable to undertake and it will provide the care necessary for recovery or for long-term dependency. However, because of traditional gender roles within families, the burden of illness will usually fall on the women of the family: the mother or the daughter. When we talk about care by the family in our everyday lives we are usually talking about care by women. This pattern is reflected in public policy, and care by women is what is implied by community care (Walker, 1982).

Community or family care

Community is one of the unit ideas identified by Robert Nisbet in his analysis of the sociological tradition (Nisbet, 1967). Unfortunately the concept is vague and presents numerous problems in sociological analysis. These difficulties stem partly from the lack of clear definition as well as from the value-laden nature of the concept. Bell and Newby (1971) prefer a territorial approach to community, which implies a distinct area within which a more or less distinct group of people interact. Others, notably Stacey (1969), use the term to identify a specific pattern of social organisation.

Wilson argues that it is the value-laden nature of the concept which is more important than problems of definition. Community is an emotive word, which produces images of what is a good life, what kind of life is desirable and what kinds of social arrangements promote intimacy and stability. This vision of life idealises the rural community with intimate personal relationships, constructive methods of social control, the transfer of knowledge between generations and respect for authority and for the status quo. This contrasts dramatically with life in modern conurbations (Wilson, 1982).

Similar confusions in the meaning of the concept of *com-*

munity care are documented by Walker (1982). This confusion is perhaps best summarised by Michael Bayley's distinction between *care in the community* and *care by the community* (Bayley, 1973). Care in the community refers to the trend of replacing large and often geographically remote institutional facilities with smaller units of residential provision which would, if possible, be familiar to individual residents. This was replaced by the notion that 'community care' referred to the fact that carers resided in the community, incorporating the notion of *the community* actually doing the caring. Nowadays, the concept of care by the community dominates:

> The primary sources of support and care for elderly people are informal and voluntary. These spring from ties of kinship, friendship and neighbourhood, and they are irreplaceable. It is the task of the public authorities to sustain and where necessary to develop this vast grass-roots network, but the responsibility is one for the community as a whole. Care *in* the community must increasingly mean care *by* the community.
>
> (DHSS, 1982, p. I)

An examination of the reality of community care revealed that the provision of support and care for elderly people falls not upon the 'community' but upon the family in general and women in particular. Janet Finch and Dulcie Groves express this conclusion in terms of the double equation: 'in practice community care equals care by the family, and in practice care by the family equals care by women' (1980, p. 494) (Fig. 6.2). Of course, although there has been a shift in emphasis from care in the community to care by the community, numerous studies testify that care by female members of the family has remained the main source of support for the disabled and the old. (See for example Moroney, 1976; Wicks and Rossiter, 1982, for reviews of this literature.) Studies which have documented reasons for admission to institutional care have also shown that the absence of family support is a major predicator of admission to an institution (Townsend, 1965; Isaacs et al, 1972; Bond & Carstairs, 1982).

THE FAMILY'S RESPONSE TO ILLNESS

Few studies of the family's response to illness have highlighted the different ways in which men and women react.

Fig. 6.2 Care in the community means family care, means women's care (courtesy of Rik Walton).

Indeed, most have focused on the family as a unit. One such study is Davis' study of 14 child victims of spinal paralytic poliomyelitis (Davis, 1963). Even though polio has now ceased to be a prevalent illness this study provides major insights into the way that families identify and react to a life-threatening illness and subsequent chronic disability.

Following the initial appearance of symptoms the 14 families exhibited a common pattern in the process of identification, interepretation and reaction. Davis identifies four stages in this process: *prelude, warning, impact* and *inventory*. In the prelude stage the family will perceive the symptoms as an ordinary childhood illness. Unusual symptoms will be ignored when they do not fit into a commonsense explanation such as the diagnosis of colds or 'flu'. The warning stage usually commences with some dramatic change in symptoms or the behaviour of the child. For example, the cue to something more serious was read by one father at the sight of his three-year-old winning a fight with his six-year-old. The differential perception of such cues affects the timing of consultations with the medical profession. During the impact stage many families had difficulty in accepting a diagnosis of polio. This may have been affected by the doctor's reluctance to provide a definite diagnosis, encouraged by a desire not to be seen to make a mistake, combined with a protective attitude toward the family. The impact stage is characterised by extreme reactions of fear, grief, and loss. The inventory stage emerges once the acute condition has abated. It is a period of taking stock and re-appraising the situation in readiness for the long-term effects of the disease.

A diagnosis of leukaemia or cystic fibrosis, like that of polio will have both immediate and long-term consequences for the families of affected children. One approach to understanding the implications of having such a severe illness has been to consider their diagnosis as a particular form of stressful event or crisis (Kaplan, et al 1973). Vincent (1967) states that the family is uniquely organised to carry out its stressmediating responsibility and is in a strategic position to do so. Given our early discussion of the variety of forms that family units now take, it is noteworthy that Venters (1981) found that single-parent families of cystic fibrosis children functioned less well through the course of the illness than did 'intact families'.

The effects of chronic illness

The effect of chronic illness on other family members can be considerable. Venters (1981) reviews a range of consequences in families where a child has cystic fibrosis, including financial strain, increased communication difficulties between husband and wife as well as other family members, accentuation of pre-existing marital problems, increased social isolation of the family unit and disorganisation of family routines resulting in role disorganisation. Such negatives only occur in certain families, as it appears that some are more vulnerable than others. Harrisson, in her study of the long-term medical treatment of children and parental stress, provides a number of useful case-studies with highlight these kinds of outcomes (Harrisson, 1977).

Another outcome, which was reported by Litman (1974), is

that mediation of the stress of illness or coping can have very different effects, by bringing one type of family unit closer together in a corporate attempt to deal with problems, while for others family relationships are made far more difficult than before the onset of the illness.

The impact of chronic illness on the family in terms of psychiatric morbidity among family members has also been documented by a number of writers about a variety of chronic conditions. For example, Allan et al (1974) explored the psychological impact on the individual family members of cystic fibrosis, while Sainsbury and Grad (1970) have described some of the psychological effects on family members of psychiatric illness.

Venters (1981) links better quality of family functioning, assessed by a composite measure, with two coping strategies. One is endowing the illness with meaning. Rather than living with uncertainty, some families find it positively helpful to interpret the illness and its causation according to a pre-existing religious, medical or scientific philosophy and to go on to define the hardships caused by the disease with optimistic explanations. The second coping device was sharing the burden of the illness within and beyond the immediate family, so that an equilibrium between family loyalty and social participation provided social support.

She considered family adjustment to cystic fibrosis as a process which provided for more positive functioning after the first year once families had progressed beyond initial confusion and depression. The earlier findings, which typified familial response as social isolation and a reduction in positive communication between family members, could have been distorted by considering only the early phase of adjustment, before longer-term reorganisation and recovery of family functioning had been established.

Comaroff and Maguire (1981) regard the process of establishing meaning in the case of leukaemia as rather more problematic in the sense of emphasising the uncertainties of leukaemia. Like cystic fibrosis, leukaemia was once inevitably fatal. Advances in treatment now mean that its most striking feature is the unpredictability of its course and outcome. Thus families are preoccupied by the hope of long-term and perhaps complete remission, despite unfavourable odds.

Early in the course of the illness parents react by feeling singled out by an affliction of the type that usually seems 'only to happen to others'. The families of polio patients reacted in the same way in Davis's study (1963). At this time, too, the uncertain duration and consequences are handled by attempting to construct some norms against which to measure their present state and future prospects. This is achieved by parents collating all available information in an attempt to postulate timetables and probabilities but, while so doing, maintaining an optimistic definition of their own case for as long as possible. Selective information-seeking and avoidance persists for as long as the illness, its nature changing as the course of the illness progresses. Oscillation between contradictory responses—repugnance, guilt, optimism, pessimism—are a regular feature. Comaroff's and Maguire's (1981) analysis is grounded in the need for parents to complete their inadequate clinical knowledge by transcending the boundaries between what is formally 'known' and 'unknown' about leukaemia.

As well as the more clinical definition of the illness, the moral implications, the explanations of why it happened, were also a recurrent feature of 'meaning'. This was clearly tied to attempts to allocate responsibility for its occurrence. Seeking explanations for cause typically progressed from biological or medical to more ultimate questions of 'Why us?', 'Why now?'. Such questions appear typical of all chronic childhood illnesses. Parents of Davis's (1963) polio victims were asking the same kinds of questions. In so doing, parents reviewed their own biographies of potential events or factors which might have caused the illness, even to invoking metaphysical explanations: 'It's a punishment for something we've done'. Comaroff and Maguire (1981) suggest that this seeking for meaning is not resolved, unlike Venters who found resolution in the majority of the families. In part this might be attributable to the different clinical courses of leukaemia and cystic fibrosis, as well as to the stubbornly unknown features of the former. For example, the aetiology of leukaemia remains a total mystery, while treatment efforts are progressing; prognosis is crucially uncertain and there is an ever-present threat of fatal relapse. The uncertainty of prognosis has social implications. It affects social encounters between the family and others who are likely to respond with embarrassment or emotion. Their behaviour can be interpreted by the family as being patronising or sympathetic while they may respond as if the illness was contagious. More crucial are the relationships within the family. While parents may try to conduct as 'normal' a mode of existence as possible, the meaning of the whole domestic context is radically altered. This entails not only the child's perceptions of illness and treatment, but also parents' relationship with him, which stem from an uncertain future. Situations and cultural constraints often entail efforts to stifle overt acknowledgement of the illness, while at the same time it is responsible for radically altering the meaning of their lives and the future. While most families resist collapse, the disruption of family relations raises searching questions about the meaning of survival.

The implications of severe childhood illness, especially where uncertainty is high, highlight for professional policy the differences between clinical and family values and meanings. The families in these studies of children with different chronic diseases doubted the value of clinical investigations, as well as interpreted their childrens state of health and wellbeing differently from the assessments offered by professionals. Sociological investigations try to encompass the processes by which families respond to having an ill child, or the outcomes for families in terms of the quality of family functioning or psychiatric morbidity. What these studies emphasise are the social implications of developments in modern treatment, which have the effect of exaggerating rather than reducing remaining uncertainties for the families involved.

Families' responses to chronic illness among older people have not been documented in quite the same way. However, the effects on the family can be equally devastating, particularly to the female members. Financial strain, stress on family relationships, increased social isolation of some family members and the disorganisation of existing family roles and routines are likely for all families caring for a family member with a chronic illness as well as when life-threatening conditions such as myocardial infarction are diagnosed (McEwen & Finlayson, 1977).

In later life a stroke is one chronic illness which dramatically affects family life. One writer, describing his own dysphasia, termed stroke 'a family illness' (Buck, 1963). In a recent study John Brocklehurst and his colleagues described some of the social effects of stroke (Brocklehurst et al, 1981). Their longitudinal study found that three-quarters of the chief carers were women, and of these three-fifths were under the age of 60. Thus the largest group of chief carers were women aged less than 60; and a significant proportion were also responsible for other people. During the first year of the stroke 14% of the carers in employment gave up their jobs because of the stroke and there was a noticeable deterioration in the health of carers during that period. The major problems arising for the chief carers were related to the patients' behaviour, the need for constant supervision and the carer's loss of sleep. These families were providing considerable support to patients. In over a quarter of cases the patient was dependent for feeding, dressing and toileting, and a further third for everything except for personal care. This caring role is not unique to the families of stroke patients. In a study of the terminal year of life (Cartwright et al, 1973), many patients with other chronic illnesses were found to be as dependent as stroke patients. Similar difficulties were experienced by the main carers, and again they were mainly women. These data reinforce our view that the family is the basic unit in health and medical care, and that female members of the family are the key individuals.

SUMMARY

This chapter has shown that the family has a pervasive influence in matters of health. While it remains speculative that family relationships may cause psychiatric illness, there is now evidence that they influence the course of schizophrenia.

Child health is in part determined by the behaviour of parents. It is important therefore to discover the social influences on such behaviour. Inter-generational studies are one way of looking at the transmission of health culture. Blaxter and Paterson's study of mothers and daughters found that the inter-generational transmission of health culture was much more complex and relied on broader social changes to a greater extent than might have been supposed.

Illness among family members can have devastatingly negative effects as well as, at times, positive consequences. While families are subjected to social, financial and emotional stress, some also gain in mutual strength and understanding, finding resources previously untapped. While the effects of chronic illness, or the long-term caring for handicapped or elderly family members, has pronounced family effects, the major consequences are for the female members of society. The movement to increase care by the community, maintaining the chronically ill, the old and the handicapped within their families, has profound consequences for women—married and unmarried, daughters, mothers and wives. Government and health service policy to expand community care needs to examine and take into account the consequences of such policies for the health and wellbeing of the family and, in particular, of its female members.

REFERENCES

Allan J L, Townley R R W, Phelan P D 1974 Family response to cystic fibrosis. Australian Paediatric Journal 10: 136–146

Bayley M 1973 Mental handicap and community care: a study of mentally handicapped people in Sheffield. Routledge & Kegan Paul, London

Bell C, Newby H 1971 Community studies: an introduction to the sociology of the local community. George Allen & Unwin, London

Blaxter M, Paterson E 1982 Mothers and daughters: a three generational study of health attitudes and behaviour. Heinemann Educational Books, London

Bond J, Carstairs V 1982 Services for the elderly: a survey of the characteristics and needs of a population of 5000 old people. Scottish Health Service Studies No. 42. Scottish Home and Health Department, Edinburgh

Bowlby J 1971 Attachment and loss, vol 1. Attachment. Penguin Books, Harmondsworth

Brocklehurst J C, Morris P, Andrews K, Richards B, Laycock P 1981 Social effects of stroke. Social Science and Medicine 15A: 35–39

Brown G W, Birley J L T, Wing J K 1972 Influence of family life on the course of schizophrenic disorders: a replication. British Journal of Psychiatry 121: 241–258

Buck M 1963 The language disorders. Journal of Rehabilitation 29: 37–38

Chen E, Cobb S 1960 Family structure in relation to health and disease. A review of the literature. Journal of Chronic Diseases 12: 544–567

Comaroff J, Maguire P 1981 Ambiguity and the search for meaning: childhood leukaemia in the modern clinical context. Social Science and Medicine 15B: 115–123

Cartwright A, Hockey L, Anderson J 1973 Life before death. Routledge & Kegan Paul, London

Davis F 1963 Passage through crisis: polio victims and their families. Bobs-Merrill, New York

Department of Health and Social Security 1982 Ageing in the United Kingdom. DHSS, London
Finch J, Groves D 1980 Community care and the family: a case for equal opportunities? Journal of Social Policy 9: 487–511
Harrisson S P 1977 Families in stress. A study of the long term medical treatment of children and parental stress. Royal College of Nursing, London
Isaacs B, Livingstone M, Neville Y 1972 Survival of the unfittest: a study of geriatric patients in Glasgow. Routledge & Kegan Paul, London
Kaplan D M, Smith A, Grobstein R, Fischman S E 1973 Family mediation of stress. Social Work 18: 60–69
Laing R D 1965 The divided self. An existential study in sanity and madness. Penguin Books, Harmondsworth
Laing R D 1967 Family and individual structure. In: Lomas P (ed) The predicament of the family. Hogarth Press, London, ch 6, p 107–125
Lewis O 1964 The children of Sanchez. Penguin Books, Harmondsworth
Litman T J 1974 The family as a basic unit in health and medical care: a social-behavioural overview. Social Science and Medicine 8: 495–519
Locker D 1981 Symptoms and illness. The cognitive organisation of disorder. Tavistock, London
McEwen J, Finlayson A 1977 Coronary heart disease and patterns of living. Croom Helm, London
Moroney R M 1976 The family and the state. Considerations for social policy. Longman, London
Nisbet R A 1967 The sociological tradition. Heinemann, London
Oakley A 1976 The family, marriage, and its relationship to illness. In: Tuckett D (ed) An introduction to medical sociology. Tavistock, London, ch 3, p 74–109
Pratt L 1973 The significance of the family in medication. Journal of Comparative Family Studies 4: 13–35
Rapoport R, Rapoport R N, Strelitz Z 1977 Fathers, mothers and others. Routledge & Kegan Paul, London
Rutter M 1972 Maternal deprivation reassessed. Penguin Books, Harmondsworth
Rutter M, Madge N 1976 Cycles of disadvantage. A review of research. Heinemann, London
Sainsbury P, Grad de Alarcon J 1970 The psychiatrist and the geriatric patient. The effects of community care on the family of the geriatric patient. Journal of Geriatric Psychiatry IV: 23–41
Stacey M 1969 The myth of community studies. British Journal of Sociology 20: 134–147
Townsend P 1965 The effects of family structure on the likelihood of admission to an institution in old age: the application of a general theory. In: Shanas E, Streib G F (eds) Social structure and the family: generational relations. Prentice Hall, Englewood Cliffs, N J, ch 8, p 163–187
Townsend P 1979 Poverty in the United Kingdom. A survey of household resources and standards of living. Penguin Books, Harmondsworth
Venters M 1981 Familial coping with chronic and severe childhood illness: the case of cystic fibrosis. Social Science and Medicine 15A: 289–297
Vincent C E 1967 Mental health and the family. Journal of Marriage and the Family, February: 18–39
Walker A (ed) 1982 Community care: the family, the state and social policy. Basil Blackwell & Martin Robertson, Oxford

Wicks M, Rossiter C 1982 Crisis or challenge? Family care, elderly people
and social policy. Study Commission on the Family, London
Wilson E 1982 Women, the 'Community' and the 'Family'. In: Walker A (ed)
Community care: the family, the state and social policy. Basil Blackwell &
Martin Robertson, Oxford, ch 2, p 40–55
World Health Organisation 1971 Report on the statistical aspects of the
family as a unit in health studies. December 14–20, 1971, DSI/72–6. WHO,
Geneva
Young M, Willmott P 1957 Family and kinship in East London. Routledge &
Kegan Paul, London

FURTHER READING

Blaxter M, Paterson E 1982 Mothers and daughters: a three-generational
study of health attitudes and behaviour. Heinemann Educational Books,
London
Walker A (ed) 1982 Community care: the family, the state and social policy.
Martin Robertson & Basil Blackwell, Oxford

7

Health care organisations

INTRODUCTION

So far in this book we have introduced two universal features of modern societies and discussed their importance in the context of health. First, we identified the concept of social stratification as a cornerstone to understanding the structure of societies, and showed how social stratification could be related to health. We then focused on the family, and in the last chapter, contended that the family is the most important social group within which health is maintained and illness occurs and is resolved. In this chapter we turn to a third universal feature of modern societies, namely organisations, and discuss the relevance of organisation theory for understanding health care organisations.

As with other sociological concerns, the study of organisations can be approached from a variety of perspectives. David Silverman (1970), in his influential study of organisations, identifies two broad approaches, each of which comprises a number of perspectives. One approach, generally referred to as *systems theory*, emphasises explanations of behaviour in terms of the interaction of systems attempting to satisfy their organisational goals. Systems theory is dominated by structural functionalism and often uses the organic analogy discussed in Chapter 2 to explain the nature of the relationships between different parts of the system. Other perspectives within systems theory do not adopt a sociological frame of reference. Human Relations theory and Organisational Psychology owe most to psychology; Socio-Technical Systems theory straddles psychology and economics; and Decision-Making theory is grounded in economics and cybernetics as it applies to automatic communication and control.

The other main approach, *action theory*, argues that attention should be focused on the participants in organisations. Each participant might experience and perceive the organisation and its relationship to the wider social world in which they live in different ways. Action theory emphasises the ability of individual participants to create, sustain and change the social environment and nature of organisations.

In this chapter we review these two theories of organisation and major concepts like bureaucracy and power. In particular we show how the functionalists rely on the concept role and the idea of organisational goals is expanded in a systems theory approach to studying the care of inmates of long-stay institutions. In contrast, action theory relies heavily on the perspectives of those within organisations determining how they operate and we use a study of play leaders in childrens' wards as an example of this interpretation. We then turn to the negotiated nature of social processes in organisations. We begin this chapter with a discussion of the concept institution, a term which is often used synomously with organisation.

Institutions. Sociologists use the concept of institution to describe the way we order social life so that we can make sense of each other's actions—*a regulatory pattern* which is programmed by society and imposed on the conduct of individuals. Institutions are experienced as having external reality, objectivity, coerciveness, moral authority and historicity (Berger & Berger, 1976).

Externality and objectivity. Institutions have *external reality*. They are not just things we humans imagine as existing. Like rocks, trees or houses, a hospital has a physical presence or like love or thought, medicine has an abstract presence. In either case we cannot ignore them when they occur in our daily lives. They will also have objectivity since in general we all agree that they exist.

Coerciveness. The possession of external reality and objectivity gives an institution *coerciveness* or *coercive power*. We have all experienced the power of the school or the hospital in our everyday lives, perhaps in the way that these institutions get us to wear their distinctive uniforms and arrive and depart at specific times. We would not normally question the power of institutions like the law or medicine for example, to detain a patient under the Mental Health Act, whether or not we agree with the way this power is used. In some instances, however, such as in the case of patients who discharge themselves, people might try to ignore the power of the institution. When this happens the coerciveness of the institution will become explicit. Specific sanctions will be used to bring the defaulting patient into line. Similarly, mechanisms are available to persuade radical members of hospital staff to adhere to hospital customs and practices.

Moral authority. Institutions also have what Max Weber called *moral authority*—a concept we described in Chapter 3. In other words the institution has *legitimacy*. The institution will have legitimacy when it is generally accepted that the authority of the institution is just and rightfully given. Thus, the psychiatric hospital which prevents a patient from discharging himself has the moral authority as well as the physical ability to do so. Of course, the moral authority will only exist while society agrees that it is the right of the psychiatric hospital to determine which patients should be discharged.

Historicity. Finally, a basic characteristic of most institutions is their enduring nature. Most institutions have a history which extends beyond the life careers of the authors and readers of this book. The family has been in existence and is likely to endure for a considerable time, as we saw in Chapter 5.

The sociological use of the term institution has a wider meaning than just physical structures. Similarly when we talk about health care organisations we shall be concerned not only with the physical structures of hospitals or professional occupations but with the social organisation of health care. This approach differs from that adopted by many sociologists, particularly the structural-functionalists who have emphasised that organisations are physical entities persisting over time, which are specifically set up to achieve certain aims.

ORGANISATIONS AS SYSTEMS

The structural functionalist perspective on organisations, in common with other systems' theories, is based on a number of functions. These are that organisations comprise a set of interdependent parts; organisations have needs which are necessary for their survival; they also have goals; and organisations take actions.

Such assumptions, in the context of health care, appear trivial and common sense. Most health systems, whether they be primary care teams, hospital clinics or whole health districts, can be divided into 'sub-systems' by occupational group, speciality or some other ascriptive category. Thus the antenatal clinic in one hospital observed and described by MacIntyre (1978) would provide an example of an organisation with interdependent parts: consultants, junior medical staff, midwifery staff, clerical staff, patients and patients' relatives. The stated goals of the antenatal clinic are to screen the total population of pregnant women; to select high- and low-risk groups; and carefully to monitor high-risk groups. This example illustrates a major problem for systems theory. MacIntyre's study shows that not all those attending or working in the clinic share the same goals as the medical and nursing staff running the clinic. Indeed, there may also be disagreements between different doctors or midwives as to the appropriate goals of this particular example of an organisation. Thus in gaining a sociological understanding of the antenatal clinic we need to recognise that different individuals may hold different goals. Systems theory ignores this fact.

This kind of criticism of systems theory has led to the distinction being made between the *formal organisation*, based on rationality and efficiency, and the *informal organisation* based on sentiment. Yet if we recognise that formal and informal organisations can coexist, we shall see that these concepts are problematic. The formal organisation is something defined by one set of personnel, in our example the obstetricians, who consciously attempt to impose their definition of the situation throughout the antenatal clinic. However, within the informal organisation the goals of midwives and mothers may differ. The aims and interests of midwives and mothers will influence their commitment to the rules and routines of the clinic. If their commitment declines, their performance of roles in the organisation may be affected.

The study of roles

A persistent feature of structuralist theories of organisations is the static rather than dynamic nature of the roles occupied by its participants. Our discussion of socialisation in Chapter 5 implies that one of the functions of socialisation is to prepare the individual for different roles in the social system. The concept of *role* implies not only an expected pattern of behaviour but also that the occupier of the role—what we shall call the *role incumbent*—shows appropriate feelings and values. A patient is expected to comply with a doctor's orders, but he is also expected to feel that it is right and proper that the doctor issues such instructions. For the patient to tell the doctor how to treat him or to refuse to accept a doctor's prescription would be regarded as inappropriate behaviour.

Multiple roles. The concept of role has a theatrical analogy (Goffman, 1971) in that we are all engaged in acting our various roles. The role is like the part in the play (Brutus) while the way that the individual acts the role is analogous to the performance of the part by a particular actor ('John Gielgud's Brutus'). In real life, as on the stage, we can act more than one role. We act some roles, such as gender roles, throughout our lives, while others such as those of parent, occupational therapist or goalkeeper, will be acquired. We all act *multiple roles* (Fig. 7.1). At the same time as being a doctor a female person can be a feminist, daughter, mother, rate-payer, preacher, cardriver and patient.

Role-set. Robert Merton (1957) coined the term *role-set* to describe the array of roles and expectations that any individual will confront while taking a particular role. The doctor, while acting as doctor and not in any of her multiple roles, will be interacting with several other roles: pharmacist, hospital administrator, nurse, dietitian, physio-therapist, patient and patient's relatives. (Fig. 7.2) When she acts the role of mother the role-set will include other mothers, son, daughter, daughter's friend, son's teacher. A more complex example of a role-set is illustrated by Phyllis Runciman (1983) in her study of the

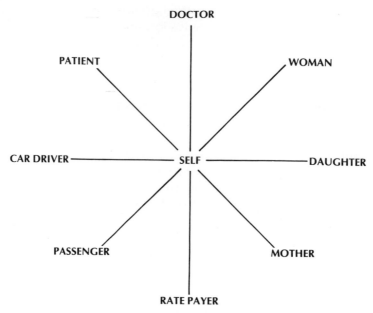

Fig. 7.1 Multiple roles.

work of the ward sister. As a ward sister her own role-set consisted of over 100 role relationships.

These formal descriptions of multiple roles and role-sets give an impression that roles are uniform and static. Ralph Turner (1962) emphasises the important distinction between *role-taking* and *role-making*. The idea of role-taking suggests that all roles are prescribed and defined by a specific set of rules which all actors comprehend and to which they conform. Military and bureaucratic roles are probably the minority which easily fit this model, since the formal regulation systems of most bureaucracies prevent individual actors from making any modification to the behaviour and decisions prescribed for their roles. In contrast, the idea of role-making suggests that actors will usually create and modify roles according to their own interpretation of the role and in response to the ways others interpret their own roles in the role-set. This is especially the case when new roles are emerging in organisations—roles such as joint clinical-teaching appointments or clinical specialists in nursing organisations.

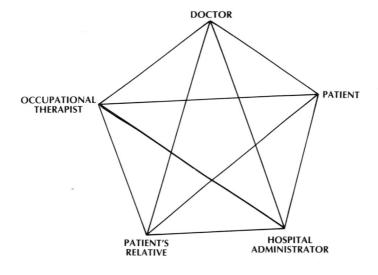

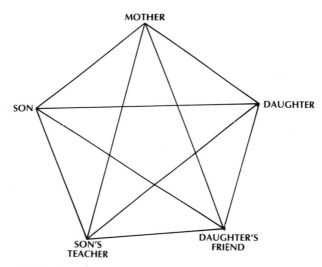

Fig. 7.2 Simplified role-sets.

In her analysis of the role of the occupational therapist Eileen Fairhurst (1981) shows how, even in a bureaucratic organisation like a District General Hospital, actors are able to make their roles. Fairhurst found that the definition of what constituted occupational therapy advanced by 'official' ideology was not the one shared by the occupational therapists in the hospital studied. They felt unable to *take* the role of occupational therapist as defined by 'official' ideology. By devising their own strategies, manipulating other people's roles and suspending others' versions of their own roles they were able to *make* their own version of the role of occupational therapist. Thus it is useful to see roles as dynamic and something which the individual develops rather than as static features of the individual's life to which he moulds his performance. Nevertheless, roles are to some degree constrained by the social environment, and there are limits to the behaviour tolerated by others in their expectations of appropriate role behaviour. Bond (1978) observed that some nurses strongly criticised one who regarded it as within her interpretation of the nurse's role to tell patients with cancer their diagnosis if the patient asked her. Others regarded this as a medical prerogative and exerted sanctions to persuade their colleague to limit this kind of behaviour.

Role conflict

Most of us will act multiple roles throughout our lives, such as doctor and mother, and as a result will experience *inter-role conflict*. Holding a perception of the role of doctor which differs from official ideology or of mother which differs from traditional beliefs can lead to *intra-role conflict*.

Inter-role conflict means conflict between two simultaneously held roles. The working mother who is at work on the afternoon of her daughter's birthday party experiences *inter-role conflict*. Doctors are expected to work specific hours according to the rota worked out some time in advance. Mothers are also expected to be present at their childrens' birthday parties. Since none of us is capable of being in two places at once we should all experience inter-role conflict in this kind of situation, and the degree of conflict will reflect strength of attachment to the two roles.

Intra-role conflict. In contrast, the mother who disagrees with the expectation that a mother should be present at a daughter's birthday party will experience *intra-role conflict.* Her interpretation of the role of mother conflicts with the dominant view of other similar role incumbents—other mothers. In other words, she does not agree with the general consensus of her social group about the patterns of expected behaviour in mothers. In contemporary Britain there are appreciable differences in opinion about a mother's role between on the one hand the 'feminists' and on the other hand the 'traditionalists'. These differences are often expressed in terms of whether or not mothers should go out to work and in terms of the demands made in particular kinds of work. It is still the case that women with young children are not acceptable to some hospitals to undertake nurse training, the prevailing view being that they cannot give sufficient time, energy and commitment to both the job and the family. Are male recruits ever discriminated against in this way? They are probably not. In such hospitals mothers of young children wishing to undertake nurse training would experience inter-role conflict, while the fathers of young children would probably not. However, they may have problems reconciling the role of man with the role of nurse, since the latter is often regarded as a feminine role.

This approach to role conflict proceeds as if the actor is forced to choose between two competing sets of expectations, between the 'traditional' and 'modern' views of the feminine role. However, in its most general sense, intra-role conflict exists when there is no immediately apparent way of simultaneously coping effectively with two or more expectations of the role. The problem for the individual actor is more fundamental. How should a woman interact with men, some of whom have modern and some traditional and some mixed conceptions of the masculine role, and with women who may have the same or different conceptions of the feminine role? To some extent women learn to modify their role in line with the expectations of other men and women who have different conceptions of it.

OPEN SYSTEMS

In Chapter 2 we described how functionalism often uses the analogy of the biological organism. This is the model proposed by the open systems approach which developed in response to certain criticisms against the systems approach. The model emphasises a social organism, existing in relationship to the social environment, and proposes four basic requirements for the functioning of the system:
1. The organisation takes some input from the environment.
2. The organisation processes this input.
3. The organisation produces an output for the environment.
4. The organisation retains sufficient resources from the process of production to allow its survival.

Clearly this cyclical pattern is well illustrated in industrial society by the successful commercial enterprise which adapts its activities to the environment in which it operates. Thus an open-systems model will predict diversification of interests in the major cigarette manufacturers if health education and other pressures encourage a reduction in the demand for cigarettes. A number of cigarette manufacturers in recent years have diversified into other markets, such as food, in preparation for a contraction in their traditional markets. However, the open-systems model does not highlight *how* organisations adapt to their changing environments.

The open-systems model has been used by Miller and Gwynne (1972) in a study of institutions for the physically handicapped and the chronic sick. The four basic requirements identified above are illustrated by Miller and Gwynne (see Fig. 7.3). The inmates of the institution represent the throughput of the organisation. Caring and other staff are the human resources and equipment the physical resources. Death or discharge of an inmate represents the output of the system.

This study illustrates some of the difficulties associated with the identification of the organisation's goals and the pursuit of these goals within the framework of a shared set of values. The logical output of this kind of organisation is dead inmates, even though inmates, staff and the outside world find such explicit goals unpalatable. Miller and Gwynne report that the implicit output of dead inmates leads to the development of

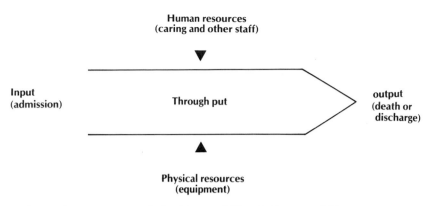

Fig. 7.3 An open system in health care (Miller & Gwynne, 1974).

two contrasting types of value systems, which they refer to as psychological defences.

First, staff, who were committed to preserving life at all costs, were described as providing a humanitarian defence. Thus, although the handicapped inmate may be socially dead, the pressure of humanitarian values attempts to maximise the interval between social and physiological death. In Chapter 10 we explore the notions of social and physiological death in some detail. Here Miller and Gwynne are using the term 'social death' to describe the implicit rejection by society of the handicapped inmate.

Second, staff who attempted to deny that the handicapped are abnormal, were described as providing a liberal defence. Liberal values aid the handicapped inmate whose capacities should be fostered to their full potential. Physical and social rehabilitation are therefore encouraged.

The type of care provided in the organisation was found to relate to the type of value system present. In institutions where staff were committed to preserving life at all costs the *warehousing* model of care was dominant, while in institutions where staff defined the inmates as normal the *horticultural* model of care persisted.

The warehousing model. In the warehousing model care is provided for the primary task of prolonging physical life. Effective warehousing requires that the patient or resident remains dependent and depersonalised, and accepting of his own dependency. Any attempts by the patient or resident to assert himself, or to display individual needs other than those previously defined by staff, will be a constraint on the achievement of the primary task. Independence is therefore discouraged. The ideal patient or resident is the one who accepts the staff's assessment of his needs and the treatment they prescribe and administer.

The warehousing model has been refined by Helen Evers in her study of work organisation in geriatric hospitals (Evers, 1981). She describes two kinds of warehousing: *minimal warehousing*, where patients' care is organised entirely on a routinised basis in order to achieve the primary tasks of prolonging life, and *personalised warehousing*, (Fig. 7.4) where some attempt is made to provide a personalised service to patients, albeit within a life preservation ideology.

The horticultural model. The horticultural model is a relatively recent development, which is more an aspiration than a reality. Needs for physical care are the constraints in the horticultural model. The primary task of the model is to develop an individual's capacities to their optimum by encour-

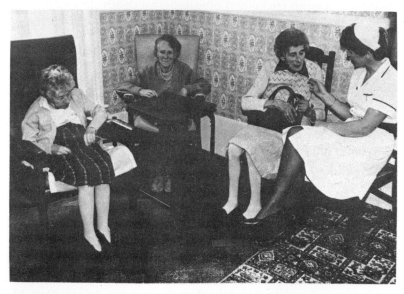

Fig. 7.4 Warehousing may be characterised by the extent to which it is personalised (courtesy of Nursing Standard).

aging independence. This might be achieved through the process of *normalisation*: by organising caring activities around social activities and by providing an environment which approximates to life outside the institution. Privacy, choice and independence should all be respected. The development of small domestic units for the mentally handicapped and experimental NHS nursing homes for long-stay elderly people are recent examples of an attempt to encourage the horticultural model in institutional care (Graham, 1983).

The limitation of using the open systems model in this kind of study is that it provides no explanation as to *why* different value systems develop within different institutions or *how* these different value systems lead to the contrasting kinds of care regimes described. This led a number of people to adopt a social action approach which, while recognising the structural constraints on action, asks how individuals concerned carry on their interactions within that framework.

ACTION THEORY

Action theory has been an influential perspective in the study of health care organisations. The approach is probably exemplified by Erving Goffman's analysis of the *total institution*.

A number of institutions for the elderly, disabled and young chronic sick exhibit the characteristics of the total institution. The essential feature of the total institution is that, unlike life outside, there is no separation between the three central spheres of modern life: work, leisure and family. All aspects of life are conducted within the boundaries of the institution and under the control of a single authority. Each phase of daily activities is shared with a large number of other people, all of whom are treated alike and are required to do the same thing together. These activities normally follow a strict routine imposed from above by a system of explicit formal rulings and a body of officials. The routine of daily activities comprises a single rational plan which has been designed to fulfil the official aims of the institution (Goffman, 1961).

British studies of long-stay institutions exemplify Goffman's model. The survey by Peter Townsend (1962) of residential institutions and homes for the aged in England and Wales remains, after 25 years, the best description of the ubiquity of the total institution. His case studies of residents in old workhouses, which provided the mainstay of local authority residential services for the old and handicapped, vividly describe the isolation of residents from the outside world, the lack of individual privacy and independence, the routinisation of activities, and the separation between residents and staff. Miller's and Gwynne's study of residential institutions for the physically handicapped and young chronic sick describes a similar situation in some of the organisations they studied. Dorothy Baker (1983) and Helen Evers (1981) in their studies of staff and patients in geriatric hospitals found that the concept of the total institution is also relevant to contemporary British long-stay hospitals.

The characteristics of the total institution identified by Goffman describe a form of organisation in which the prevailing definitions of the situation derive from within the organisation itself. General goals for psychiatric hospitals or prisons may be proposed by society, but the rules as to how these are achieved will generally emerge from within the institution. We draw on Goffman's analysis again in Chapter 8 when we describe how patients are socialised into their new roles as inmates. Members are cleansed of their outside identities by having to undergo a mortifying process during which their personal possessions are almost entirely removed; they may be made to wear a uniform or to answer to a number only. They may often react to such treatment by intransigence or withdrawal, both of which are interpreted in some institutions as signs of the disease for which the patient has been institutionalised. After long periods of stay Goffman observed that inmates may generate the adaptations of *colonisation* by establishing an identity within the organisation, which they perceive as being more important than previous identities they experienced in 'normal' society, or *conversion* by appearing to accept the staff's views of them. Both these adaptations are vividly described in his study of *Ways of Making Out in a Mental Hospital* (Goffman, 1961), and show how some inmates are able to increase their power and status relative to other inmates, and even sometimes to staff members.

David Hall, in his study of the introduction of play leaders into two children's wards, also illustrates the usefulness of action theory (Hall, 1977). His approach stresses the different perspectives of those involved: the children, the nursing and medical staff, the play leaders and teachers, and the domestic staff. Each participant was shown to construct his or her own definition of the situation which guided his or her actions. Such a model would seem to fit Hall's view of disturbances in hospital being caused by threats to the continuity and persistence of individual interpretations of the situation. The recognition of various interest groups at ward level helps us to understand resistance to any kind of innovation. This can be seen as a rational response to threatened disruption of existing social relationships, which carries implications for the rights and obligations attached to socially defined roles. In Hall's study different participants regarded play in different ways, having different conceptions of its value for the care of children in hospital. For the play leaders, play was the *raison d'être* of their role. Nursing staff saw play as a subsidiary part of their role; they appeared to value the play leaders because, by keeping the children occupied, this allowed them to concentrate on the more technical aspects of their job. For domestic staff play in the ward, and the greater mobility of children as a result of play, could easily create more work despite any attempts by play leaders to keep their areas tidy. Indeed, the emphasis on play goes against the traditional values of order and cleanliness at all times, to which many cleaners and nurses subscribe. Hall's analysis also shows that teamwork, the official ideology of the organisation, was neither believed to be achieved nor actually achieved.

TEAMWORK AND HEALTH CARE ORGANISATIONS

It is perhaps assumed that health care organisations are essentially teams of professionals working together to achieve a common goal. We have reported a number of studies in this book which suggest that this official view of health care organisation is not often supported by empirical data. Indeed, a number of writers such as Dingwall (1980) and Reedy (1980) have questioned the usefulness of 'teamwork' as a term which is open to so many interpretations. Reedy (1980) prefers to use the concept of collaboration to describe those characteristics central to many of the notions of teamwork. Armitage (1983), in a recent paper about primary health care organisation, identifies inter-professional collaboration as 'the exchange of information between individuals involved in the delivery of primary health care, which has the potential for action in the interests of a common purpose' (Armitage, 1983, p. 75). Although this definition focuses on just one aspect of collaboration, namely information sharing, it is arguably more realistic and useful than those used to define teamwork.

Armitage goes further than this, in that he identifies a taxonomy of collaboration consisting of five stages (Table 7.1). Although these stages refer only to the level of interaction, it may be possible to use them as signposts to other aspects of inter-professional collaboration. This construction still requires empirical testing and this is currently the subject of research by Reedy and colleagues, who are attempting to measure collaboration between district nurses, general practitioners and health visitors, focusing on this same taxonomy (Reedy et al, 1983). Interpretation of these data will not be easy since collaboration in health care organisations is most often an association of unequal partners in which participants are rarely equal in status, prestige or power and, as we have

Table 7.1 A taxonomy of collaboration (From Armitage, 1983)

Stages of collaboration	Definitions
1. Isolation	Members who never meet, talk or write to one another
2. Encounter	Members who encounter or correspond with others but do not interact meaningfully
3. Communication	Members whose encounters or correspondence include the transference of information
4. Collaboration between two agents	Members who act on that information sympathetically; participate in patterns of joint working; subscribe to the same general objectives as others on a one-to-one basis in the same organisation
5. Collaboration throughout an organisation	Organisations in which the work of all members is fully integrated

seen, do not necessarily share the same values or goals. As McIntosh and Dingwall (1978) note:

> '. . . the status of many nurses and health visitors in practice attachments is equivocal. On the one hand they are superficially members of the team, they have direct contact with doctors, and their advice is sought. However, they do suffer a certain subtle, but no less potent, undermining of any aspirations to partnership they may have. If partnership with doctors exist at all it can best be described as a "junior partnership"' (1978, pp. 130–131).

The British Medical Association's evidence to the Royal Commission on the National Health Service states:

> 'No doctor fails to recognise the necessity of co-operation with the nursing profession and *with other medical workers.* But this does not mean that the doctor should in any way hand over his control of the clinical decisions concerning the treatment of his patient to anyone else or to a group or team' (*British Medical Association*, 1977, p. 303.).

Although *teams* may exist and *team* conferences are held in hospitals, a clear division of accountability takes place at the consultant level across all medical specialities (Illsley, 1980) and, in practice, decisions by doctors are those likely to carry most weight.

Thus although teamwork, or more specifically collaboration, is a dominant ideology of most health care organisations, most doctors will support the view that the doctor should provide leadership. We suspect that a number of other health professionals might also support this ideology; and if there is general support then we must consider how co-operation and consensus work out in practice.

POWER IN HEALTH CARE ORGANISATIONS

We have argued that any consideration of interactions between members of health care organisations must take account of structural constraints. In the above discussion of teamwork we have ignored the role of patients and other lay members of the organisation. This has been intentional. We defer our discussion of interaction to Chapter 9. However, structural constraints affect patient and professional alike, albeit in different ways. One such constraint is the bureaucratic setting in which care is usually delivered.

Bureaucracy

Central to any bureaucratic setting is the feeling of *being processed*. (Fig. 7.5). This underlying experience is common to all of us when we deal with bureaucracies, whether as students, patients, tax-payers or consumers. What is a *bureaucracy*? Few sociologists have attempted a simple definition, and most refer to the basic characteristics of a bureaucracy first delineated by Max Weber.

Bureaucracies are characterised by a separate organisation with full-time staff—a feature common to all health care organisations. As in the total institution described above, the work of such organisations is segregated from the private lives and activities of staff members, and not infrequently is characterised as impersonal and creating loss of dignity for clients. The work of bureaucracies is usually arranged around fixed areas in which they hold authority legitimated and ordered by specific regulations. The various National Health Services Acts delineate the areas of concern for different health care organisations.

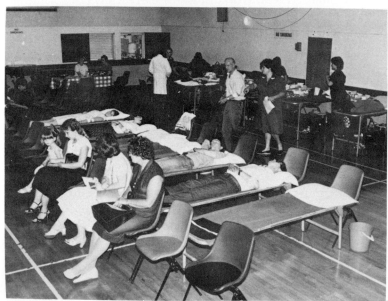

Fig. 7.5 'Being processed' at a blood donation session (courtesy of Nursing Standard).

A bureaucracy will assume that each staff member is trained in a rational manner, an assumption taken for granted by health professionals working in the health service. Part of this training includes the development of an ethos of 'objectivity'. Each client or patient is supposed to be handled according to the rules of the organisation, regardless of the personal feelings of staff and clients. Attempts to be objective encourage the impersonal atmosphere associated with many health service institutions.

Bureaucracies, in order to accomplish objective activity within a defined area of jurisdiction, are organised in orderly and stable hierarchies. It is this characteristic of health care systems which is particularly important for the understanding of interactions between health professionals and patients.

At the top of the power hierarchy are senior doctors who achieved their dominance by virtue of being regarded as having expert knowledge as well as holding socio-legal responsibility for patients (Freidson, 1975). The work of other professional staff is organised by doctors' orders. Thus other staff may be regarded as doctors' agents in dealing with patients. While remedial therapists, social workers and chaplains, like doctors, can lay claim to professional expertise they tend to be 'staff' rather than 'line' personnel and so lack the authority awarded to doctors (Katz, 1969). Their subordination to medical authority extends into areas of *non-medical* expertise, so that doctors can instruct others what to say and what not to say to patients about their illness (Bond, 1978).

Nurses are even more lacking in autonomy. While often acting as the representative of the doctor, they are reluctant to give care based on their own initiative or to assume personal accountability. Rather, deriving from Florence Nightingale's view of nursing, 'what the nurse did for the patient was function of what the doctor felt was required for the patient. Even such unskilled tasks as feeding a patient were thus defined as part of the medical regimen. All nursing work flowed from the doctors and thus nursing became a formal part of the doctors' work . . . . Nursing was thus defined as a subordinate part of the technical division of labour surrounding medicine' (Freidson, 1975, p. 61). As well as being subject to the orders of doctors, nurses are also subject to the authority of the nursing administrative hierarchy which (Fig. 7.6) has become for-

Fig. 7.6 The nursing hierarchy reflected at a ward report (courtesy of Nursing Standard).

malised in Britain through the implementation of the Salmon and Mayston Reports (Ministry of Health, 1966; DHSS, 1969) as well as the re-organisation of the National Health Service in 1974 and again in 1982. More will be said about this aspect of work in Chapter 11.

Nurses and paramedical workers are, therefore, constrained in their relationships with patients by the medical profession as well as by the organisation; but they are still in a position to exert relative power and authority over patients. This aspect of health care organisations is developed in Chapter 9.

Negotiation

Action theory has questioned the use of the rational-bureaucratic model in the study of health care organisations, arguing that the power structure in any complex organisation is amenable to modification by individual actors. Within any health care organisation there is a variety of personnel: patients, doctors, nurses, administrators, porters, cleaners, physiotherapists, social workers, clerical workers, volunteers and many others, all in the same place and ostensibly working toward the primary goal of the organisation, which is to restore and maintain patients' health. These groups bring together different personal backgrounds, different types of training and professional socialisation (a subject we discuss in Chapter 11) and varying amounts of experience, and, significantly, as we have seen, they occupy different hierarchical positions in the organisation. Between them they will hold a multitude of views and perspectives about the restoration and maintenance of health and about dying. Due to these divergent orientations and interests, differences of opinion will regularly emerge in matters of patient care and organisational policy. For example, Bucher and Stelling (1969) found that the different perspectives of the basic science and clinical faculties in the medical schools they studied led to competition for resources and recognition in the curriculum. Even organisations with unusually high levels of consensus between individuals on these issues have the problem of practical implementation of ideas and the assignment of specific tasks.

According to the rational-bureaucratic model the organisation turns to its rules and regulations whenever internal problems occur. However, most personnel do not know all of these rules nor how to apply them, and indeed the rules are often neither very extensive nor explicit. Consequently conflict of interest will not be resolved by the straightforward application of rules, nor even by relying upon the exertion of hierarchical authority within the organisation.

The inadequacy of formal rules and structures to govern activities in organisations sustains an informal structure in which the parties involved maintain social order by *negotiation*. This is done by a continuous process of give and take, diplomacy, bargaining, withholding information and displaying different degrees of co-operativeness (Strauss et al, 1963). This happens between staff groups as well as between individual staff and individual patients. In Chapter 5 we discussed how individuals are socialised into particular roles, with orderly relationships a function of appropriate role expectations, co-operation and reciprocity. Negotiation is another important process through which social action takes place.

Initially negotiation was studied in long-term settings. Strauss and colleagues articulated the theory on the basis of their study in two psychiatric hospitals. They found that psychiatrists often disagree among themselves on such matters as diagnosis, ward placement, therapeutic regimes, and prognoses in individual cases. This is, of course, a feature of professional practice which is not unique to psychiatric hospitals. We have all experienced similar differences of opinion between professionals in all health care organisations and other organisations such as schools, government agencies and commercial enterprises. Such disagreements do, however, create problems for other staff. For example, when a psychiatrist decides to transfer an extremely rumbustious patient from one ward to another, it creates numerous problems for that ward's staff and their manner of dealing with the 'problem' may be to transfer the patient to still another ward behind the physician's back (Strauss et al, 1963).

Within the hierarchical structure of most health care organisations, negotiations between professionals may be extremely subtle. Leonard Stein provides a vivid illustration of the subleties of negotiation between doctors and nurses in his account of *The doctor-nurse game* (Stein, 1978). The object of the game is for the nurse to be responsible for making significant recommendations which must nevertheless appear to be initiated by the doctor. To do this the nurse makes her recommendations without appearing to be making a recommendation statement. At the same time a physician making a request for a recommendation from a nurse should do so without specifically asking for one.

Stein provides the following dialogue to illustrate how the game is played. In this example the medical resident on hospital call is awakened by telephone at 1.00 a.m. because a patient on a ward, not his own, has not been able to fall asleep. The medical resident answers the telephone:

This is Dr Jones. (*An open and direct communication.*) Dr Jones, this is Miss Smith on 2W. Mrs. Brown, who learned today of her father's death, is unable to fall asleep.
(*This message has two levels. Openly, it describes a set of circumstances, a woman who is unable to fall asleep and who that morning received word of her father's death. Less openly, but just as*

directly, it is a diagnostic and recommendation statement; Mrs Brown is unable to sleep because of her grief, and she should be given a sedative. Dr. Jones, accepting the diagnostic statement and replying to the recommendation statement, answers.)
What sleeping medication has been helpful to Mrs Brown in the past?
(Dr Jones, not knowing the patient, is asking for a recommendation from the nurse, who does know the patient, about what sleeping medication should be prescribed. Note, however, his question does not appear to be asking her for a recommendation. Miss Smith replies.)
Pentobarbital mg 100 was quite effective night before last.
(A disguised recommendation statement. Dr Jones replies with a note of authority in his voice.)
Pentobarbital mg 100 before bedtime as needed for sleep, got it?
(Miss Smith ends the conversation with the tone of the grateful supplicant.)
Yes I have, and thank you very much doctor.

(Stein, 1978, p. 110)

This example illustrates one way the doctor-nurse game is played. It also illustrates that doctors and nurses hold different types of power.

Types of power

In practice there are a limited number of issues which are amenable to negotiation. One criticism of negotiated order theory is that it focuses on the minutiae of everyday life in organisations and ignores the wider aspects of power. The presence of power structures within an organisation puts people in unequal positions before the processes of negotiation even begin. However, as the negotiated order model indicates, most members of an organisation will have some power, albeit rather limited, for some personnel.

One way of looking at social power is to attempt to observe the influence that one person has over another. French and Raven (1968) have identified several types of power by describing the ways in which 'person A could cause person B to do something which was contrary to B's desire'.

Reward power

The power holder may influence behaviour by controlling rewards or resources which are valued by the subject. Hospital cleaners might reward the play leaders for keeping their area tidy by agreeing to the establishment of a sand box in the children's wards. Doctors might reward patients for not complaining by discharging them home earlier than expected. Ward sisters might reward student nurses for extra help by giving them a good report. General practitioners can reward district nurses and health visitors by the amount of space provided for them in the GPs premises.

Coercive power

The power holder may influence behaviour by controlling the punishments. A nurse may punish an elderly patient for being incontinent by being too busy to attend to him. Any professional can be punished by another professional in cases of professional misconduct by reporting them to the relevant disciplinary body.

Coercive and reward power are similar in that the power holder is in a position to manipulate the environment by withholding or threatening to withhold resources considered necessary for the maintenance of a satisfactory environment.

Legitimate power

We have already discussed the concept of legitimacy in relation to social stratification in Chapter 3. Legitimate power is the result of an individual's position within an organisation. It stems from the moral authority of a particular position in the organisation, which allows the role incumbent the right to prescribe particular behaviour. Legitimate power gives the power holder control over invisible assets, particularly information, right to access and right to organise.

Information. The power to withhold information is often a very evident form of legitimate power. In Chapter 9 we describe the ways information is controlled in staff-patient interactions. Doctors control information on diagnosis and prognosis, so that other professionals as well as patients are dependent on the doctor for this knowledge. In primary care organisations the GP may control information by, for example, insisting that all patients on a practice list are seen by a GP before they are referred to other primary care professionals. The administrator may control access to the notes of meetings of the Health Authority. The well-known saying that 'information means power' is well founded.

Right to access. Legitimate power gives the power holder the right of access to a number of individuals and networks. This right to access not only leads to more information, but the familiarity which often occurs can be used to the advantage of the power holder. The establishment of a general manager in Health Service Management Teams would reduce the legitimate power of other members by restricting their right of access to the Chairman.

Right to organise. Legitimate power gives the power holder the right to organise one's own work and the right to make decisions. All professionals, to different degrees, are given this kind of power.

Expert power

Expert power is based on the subject's belief that the power holder possesses superior knowledge and ability. As Michael Young's monograph *The Rise of the Meritocracy* (1961) suggests, this form of power is the most acceptable since we all have the opportunity to become experts, even if only in small ways. People also tend not to resent being influenced by experts, except when their power has not been legitimated.

Referent power

This kind of power relates to the prestige of individuals and to some extent relates to the status of a person in society. Thus people who invoke high prestige or charisma are endowed with referent power. The higher status usually attributed to doctors means that they have higher referent power than social workers or nurses. Thus patients or clients may be more influenced by doctors, because of their status, than by other health professionals.

This approach to the study of power helps to illustrate the variety of influences, interests and conflicts inherent in any organisation before negotiation begins. It also helps to explain why, in social interaction, different actors are able to 'negotiate' different outcomes. Power is a multi-dimensional concept, so that individuals who have a great deal of legitimate power may have little power on other dimensions and, as a result, are relatively weak in influencing decisions. It may be that these other types of power have a greater influence on people's daily lives than legitimate power.

UNDERSTANDING HEALTH CARE ORGANISATIONS

Health care organisations occur in a variety of forms, from a single-handed general practice in rural Sutherland to a large teaching hospital in Central London. However, in this chapter we have suggested that whatever the diversity of size and specific function, health care organisations, like other organis-ations, exhibit essentially similar characteristics. We have also shown that the physical and social boundaries of organisations do not necessarily coincide. We may have a clear idea about the physical boundary of a hospital, perhaps by the presence of a perimeter fence, but we will have more difficulty in de-termining its social boundary. Both patients and professionals are part of that particular organisation even though they may not reside within its physical boundaries.

In this chapter we have seen how different sociological per-spectives have been used to analyse health care organisations. Systems theory emphasises the formal rules of organisations which guide members' performance of their roles to achieve defined organisational goals. These rules include definitions of organisational goals, definitions of the relative power of members, and rational procedures for identifying methods of achieving organisational goals.

Action theory describes the limitations of this rational-bureaucratic model, emphasising the variability of members' definitions of goals, the way members manipulate the different kinds of power and the variability of methods used to achieve organisational goals.

However, in understanding health care organisations, both perspectives provide useful insights, albeit at different levels of analysis. In attempting to understand the day-to-day rou-tines of an organisation and the processes of conflict and change as they occur at the individual level, action theory and, in particular, negotiated order theory are directly relevant. Together they suggest why different professional ideologies develop and are maintained, why within organisations there is a resistance to innovation and change, but mostly why there is so much variability within and between organisations. Most of these issues are highlighted by our discussion of Hall's study of the introduction of play leaders into two children's wards. Used in this way, action theory illustrates a *micro-sociological* approach to the study of organisations.

A number of writers, notably Day and Day (1977), have been appreciative, but critical of this micro-sociological approach. From a *macro-sociological* perspective action theory in general, and the negotiated order theory in particular, fails to explain the ways in which forces external to the organisation do in fact affect the negotiations, relationships, and structures within it. How, for example, are the power relationships which we have identified as being common to most health care organisations contingent on the power relationships of society in general, summarised in our earlier discussion of social stratification (see Ch. 3). Systems theory too, though to a lesser extent, focuses on the organisation in isolation from the wider social structure. A wider discussion of health care organisations in the context of British society is not presented here, although we have indicated in both Chapters three and four how the social, political and economic structures of society interact to influence health, the maintenance of health and the prevention of illness.

REFERENCES

Armitage P 1983 Joint working in primary health care. Nursing Times, Occasional Papers 79: 75–78
Baker D 1983 'Care' in the geriatric ward: an account of two styles of nursing. In: Wilson-Barnett J (ed) Nursing research: ten studies in patient care. John Wiley & Sons, Chichester, ch 5, p 101–117
Berger P L, Berger B 1976 Sociology: a biographical approach. Penguin Books, Harmondsworth
Bond S 1978 Processes of communication about cancer in a radiotherapy department. Unpublished Phd. thesis, University of Edinburgh
British Medical Association 1977 Royal Commission on the National Health Service. Report of Council to the Special Representative Meeting, London, 9th March 1977. Submission of evidence. British Medical Journal 1: 299–334
Bucher R, Stelling J 1969 Characteristics of professional organisations. Journal of Health and Social Behaviour 10: 3–15
Day R, Day J A V 1977 A review of the current state of negotiated order theory: an appreciation and a critique. In: Benson J K (ed) Organisational analysis. Critique and Innovation. Sage Publications, London, p 128–144

Department of Health and Social Security 1969 Report of working party on management structure in the local authority nursing services (The Mayston Report). DHSS, London

Dingwall R 1980 Problems of teamwork in primary care. In: Londsdale S, Webb A, Briggs T L (eds) Teamwork in the personal social services and health care. Croom Helm, London, ch 7, p 111–137

Evers H K 1981 Tender loving care? Patients and nurses in geriatric wards. In: Copp L A (ed) Care of the aging. Churchill Livingstone, Edinburgh, ch 3, p 46–74

Fairhurst E 1981 What do you do? Multiple realities in occupational therapy and rehabilitation. In: Atkinson P, Heath C (eds) Medical work: realities and routines. Gower, Farnborough, ch 11, p 171–187

French J R P, Raven B 1968 The bases of social power. In: Cartwright D, Zander A (eds) Group dynamics. Research and theory, 3rd edn. Harper & Row, New York, ch 20, p 259–269

Freidson E 1975 Profession of medicine. A study of the sociology of applied knowledge. Dodd, Mead & Co, New York

Goffman E 1961 Asylums. Essays on the social situation of mental patients and other inmates. Anchor Books, New York

Goffman E 1971 The presentation of self in everyday life. Penguin Books, Harmondsworth

Graham J M 1983 Experimental nursing homes for elderly people in the National Health Service. Age and Ageing 12: 273–274

Hall D J 1977 Social relations and innovations. Changing the state of play in hospitals. Routledge & Kegan Paul, London

Illsley R 1980 Professional or public health? Sociology in health and medicine. The Nuffield Provincial Hospitals Trust, London

Katz F E 1969 Nurses. In: Etzioni A (ed) The semi-professions and their organisation. The Free Press, New York, ch 2, p 54–81

McIntosh J, Dingwall R 1978 Teamwork in theory and practice. In: Dingwall R, McIntosh J (eds) Readings in the sociology of nursing. Churchill Livingstone, Edinburgh, ch 8, p 118–134

McIntyre S 1978 Obstetric routines in antenatal care. In: Davis A (ed) Relationships between doctors and patients. Saxon House, London, ch 4, p 76–105

Merton R K 1957 The role-set: problems in sociological theory. British Journal of Sociology 8: 106–120

Miller E J, Gwynne G V 1972 A life apart. A pilot study of residential institutions for the physically handicapped and the young chronic sick. Tavistock, London

Ministry of Health 1966 The report of the committee on senior nursing staff structure (The Salmon Report). HMSO, London

Reedy B L E C 1980 Teamwork in primary health care: a conspectus. In: Fry J (ed) Primary care. Heinemann, London, ch 6, p 108–138

Reedy B L E C, Barton A G, Gregson B A 1983 A review of British experience in teamwork for primary care. Proceedings of the 5th Annual Conference on Inter-disciplinary Health Care Teams. University of Rochester, Rochester, New York

Runciman P J 1983 Ward sister at work. Churchill Livingstone, Edinburgh

Silverman D 1970 The theory of organisations. A sociological framework. Heinemann, London

Stein L 1978 The doctor-nurse game. In: Dingwall R, McIntosh J (eds) Readings in the sociology of nursing. Churchill Livingstone, Edinburgh, ch 7, p 107–117

Strauss A, Schatzman L, Ehrlich D, Bucher R, Sabshin M 1963 The hospital and its negotiated order. In: Freidson E (ed) The hospital in modern society. Collier-MacMillan, London, ch 5, p 147–169
Townsend P 1962 The last refuge. A survey of residential institutions and homes for the aged in England and Wales. Routledge & Kegan Paul, London
Turner R H 1962 Role-taking: process versus conformity. In: Rose A M (ed) Human behaviour and social processes. An interactionist approach. Routledge & Kegan Paul, London, ch 2, p 20–40
Young M 1961 The rise of the meritocracy 1870–2033. Penguin Books, Harmondsworth

FURTHER READING

Goffman E 1961 Asylums. Essays on the social situation of mental patients and other inmates. Anchor Books, New York
Hall D J 1977 Social relations and innovations. Changing the state of play in hospitals. Routledge & Kegan Paul, London
Silverman D 1970 The theory of organisations. A sociological framework. Heinemann, London
Strauss A, Schatzman L, Ehrlich D, Bucher R, Sabshin M 1963 The hospital and its negotiated order. In: Freidson E (ed) The hospital in modern society. Collier-MacMillan, London, ch 5, p 147–169

8

The patient career

INTRODUCTION

Within the life career, most people at one or more times become a patient. Health professionals have little difficulty in defining the meaning of 'patient', but we shall show in this chapter that 'patient' can take a number of different meanings. We shall also explore how people become patients, how they adopt the patient role and how they follow a career which is explained by the same kinds of sociological concepts as the life career.

In order to consider the patient and his career, we need first of all to draw on the idea of illness. A great deal is taught to health workers about signs and symptoms which are the diagnostic features of various diseases. Sociologists, however, distinguish between *disease* as a concept, with its origins in medicine, and *illness*, which has a social basis. Appreciating the social basis of illness is important if we are to understand the behaviour of individuals, patients as well as those with whom they relate, when they are ill, and why different people may behave in very different ways. Why is it that some people with a bad cold retire to bed until it has cleared up while others, with ostensibly the same symptoms, carry on with their work? Why is it that some people who discover a lump in their

breast very quickly go to their doctor, while others procrasti-
nate for weeks or months before seeking help? Sociologists
call this *illness behaviour*. We shall examine two contrasting
models which have been developed to help explain such differences in behaviour.

WHAT IS A PATIENT?

As members of society, and particularly as health care workers, you may think it a little strange and perhaps trivial that
we should ask 'What is a patient?'. How would you answer it?
Someone in hospital? Someone receiving medical treatment?
Someone attending for a routine chest X-ray? Someone suffering pain? These would all be suitable answers, and point
to characteristics of some people we would call patients.

When we begin to answer the question in sociological terms
the notion of patient becomes less self-evident and, as a result, more useful in analysing the 'patient career' (Fig. 8.1). An
important aspect of sociological enquiry is to question many
of the taken-for-granted definitions of things, events and actions which occur in our society. We have already noted (in
Ch. 5), when discussing definition of the situation, that people
hold different perspectives about social life. It is, important, therefore, before proceeding further that we establish a
common notion of 'patient'. Let us examine some of our taken-
for-granted understandings of the term 'patient'.

A patient is someone who receives services from a doctor
or other health professional—nurse, physiotherapist, chiro-
podist among others. In Britain almost everyone is a patient
because, in our system of health care, our names are registered with a general practitioner. His patients are all those
currently on his list. This is purely our administrative definition of the patient, since all are patients irrespective of
whether medical treatment is currently being received or, indeed, has ever been received. In contrast dentists do not have
patient lists. Dentists' patients always receive attention of
some description, even if it consists of only an examination
to show that there is no need for any other intervention.
These administrative definitions and distinctions of what constitutes a general medical practitioner's or a general dental

Fig. 8.1 Achieving patient status in a hospital casualty department (courtesy of Nursing Standard).

practitioner's patient stems from the different ways that they receive payment for the work that they do. General medical practitioners receive much of their income on the basis of the number of people for whom they can be called upon to give treatment, that is all those on their list, *whether or not* they receive any treatment. They can supplement this income by carrying out other work, for example carrying out cervical cytology tests on women in the 'at risk' age groups, by providing immunisations, and, by attending the birth of a baby in hospital. Dentists, on the other hand are paid only on the basis of the work that they do, that is the number of people whom they actually examine or treat.

Someone under medical treatment constitutes a second definition of 'patient'. In the same way, of course, what constitutes treatment is an administrative definition. Social workers, health visitors, nurses, remedial therapists as well as doctors all provide some kind of treatment, although not necessarily medical treatment. Yet social workers call people to whom they provide 'treatment' clients, as do health visitors.

Nurses and therapists, like doctors, usually provide 'treatment' to patients.

Medical treatment can only be given by doctors or by people who are under the supervision of a doctor. If we try to define medical treatment we can engage in circular definitions such as 'medical treatment is treatment normally given to patients by doctors'. Such definitions are not necessarily unhelpful, in that they imply that there is a social basis for the administrative definition of what constitutes medical treatment. It is the medical profession with its monopoly of practice which defines the content of medical treatment and regulates who can give it. We return to this subject again briefly in chapter 11.

Our third taken-for-granted understanding of a patient is someone who bears and suffers pain. Now although many illnesses cause people a certain amount of discomfort, there is no doubt that only a proportion of patients bear or suffer pain. This understanding of the term patient is, therefore, too narrow to be helpful.

How, then, do sociologists explain the labels 'patient' and 'client', applied to different persons by different professionals? In order to understand their explanations we must turn to two important sociological concepts: *labelling* and *deviance*.

LABELLING AND DEVIANCE

The term labelling refers to a social process by which individuals or groups classify the social behaviour of other individuals. In sociology we are generally interested in understanding the processes by which labelling of particular individuals or groups evolves and the characteristics of the groups which fall within a given label. We include social groups regularly in our conversations—criminals, agnostics, feminists—and we label individuals—old, mad, sexy—in order to classify them. The important thing to note about these examples is that the nouns refer to deviant groups, and the adjectives describe deviant attributes. They imply a shift in some respect or attribute which is away from the norm and valued attributes of the society. In the same way a state of health is the norm and is valued by society while illness is deviance.

Everyone experiences deviance at some time in their lives: attending a funeral without a black tie or turning up to a wedding in a pair of jeans are examples of deviant acts. In pluralistic societies—societies in which different social groups preserve their own customs and rules—the distinction between deviant and non-deviant behaviour is blurred. In British society it is now quite common and regarded as normal for couples to have sexual relationships outside marriage, yet for many religious groups this remains an immoral arrangement. Thus for a large proportion of the population this behaviour is not deviant, but for others it would be considered a deviant act.

There is general agreement that 'deviance always refers to conduct that is a violation of the rules constructed by a given society or group' (Berger & Berger, 1976). Deviance is therefore a matter of social definition. Sociologists have identified two types of deviance: primary and secondary (Lemert, 1964).

Primary deviance. Whether or not a given label will have meaning within a social group will depend on whether that label is permanent and this, in turn will depend a great deal on whether the person applying the label has the authority to do so. For example, if a man is labelled mentally ill by his spouse or his lawyer, this may not be accepted by others in society until a psychiatrist has legitimated this label by diagnosing the behaviour of this individual as clinical depression or whatever. Legitimation may not occur until he has been given hospital treatment which reinforces that he is indeed mentally ill.

Another example of primary deviance concerns the person seeking a sick note from the general practitioner. In order that they shall receive sickness benefit, or continue receiving their wages or salaries, the DHSS requires that sick people off work for more than one week have their deviant status of being a sick person legitimated by their general practitioner signing the appropriate forms.

Secondary deviance. One of the important features of labelling is the *effect* it has on both the person being labelled and other people around them. We call this secondary deviance, to distinguish it from the attributes which initially triggered the label. Being given a label is likely to affect the way the individual behaves with others. In time he is likely to come to act the role which the new label implies, because of the way others have behaved towards him, the possessor of the label. For example, if we start to call elderly relatives senile and, perhaps more important, to treat them as if they were senile, it is amazing how quickly they begin to behave in somewhat bizarre ways. This process is sometimes called a 'self-fulfilling prophecy'.

As the above example shows, secondary deviance can have negative effects. This is well illustrated by Goffman (1968) in his book, *Stigma—notes on the management of spoiled identity*, who shows that certain categories of patient, once labelled, become stigmatised and that the effect of this stigma is to reinforce the deviant behaviour of such patients. This helps to explain why in psychiatric settings patients labelled as 'violent' and responded to in particular ways may exhibit more rather than fewer violent episodes, and why patients in general hospitals labelled as 'demanding' are responded to in such a manner that their 'demanding' behaviour is perpetuated. We return to the concept of stigma again in the next chapter, when we consider how labelling patients influences interaction with them.

We are now in a better position to answer our initial question: What is a patient? We have seen that we use the labelling process to categorise people. Being ill is a form of deviance. People who are ill, and who are diagnosed as ill by doctors, are given the label 'patient'.

Similarly being poor, living in a single-parent household, or experiencing social problems are all forms of deviance. In these cases it is the social worker, among others, who legitimates this status by giving the status of 'client'. As we have tried to show, such labelling processes are essentially arbitrary, and are also essentially social.

BECOMING A PATIENT

In describing the life career we introduced the reader to Weber's notion of *ideal type* (Ch. 5). The patient career is a similar ideal type; and it most closely approximates the experience of people entering hospital.

The notion of patient career owes a great deal to the work of Goffman (1961). The value of the concept, as Goffman describes it, is that it has two sides. One concerns the private side of the individual concerning the patient's feelings, image of self and felt identity. The other relates to the patient's public image reflected in his status, life-style and relationships with others. Goffman writes of the '*moral* career' of the mental patient; that is, the regular sequences of changes that occur in an individual's private image of himself and those changes which affect his public image in the course of becoming a psychiatric patient. He describes the moral career of a patient as a series of *status passages* through initial identification of symptoms, diagnosis, treatment and outcome. Although the model described by Goffman is of psychiatric patients, there are close parallels with long-stay patients in non-psychiatric hospitals and, to a lesser extent, shorter-stay patients. Following Goffman, our ideal type of a patient career is shown in Figure 8.2.

The concept of the patient career illustrated in Figure 8.2 is not the average patient career, not indeed the best, but an ideal type. We consider that this very simple model of progression through symptom identification, diagnosis, treatment and outcome illustrates the variety of patient careers. As with

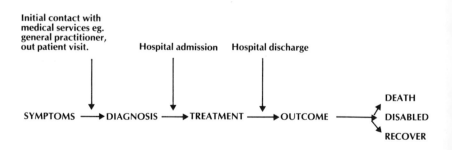

Fig. 8.2 The patient career.

some other aspects of the life career, some patients will pass the career milestones of symptoms, treatment, diagnosis and outcome on a number of occasions. In some instances some of these milestones may be omitted: for some patients symptoms like abdominal pain will be treated without a diagnosis ever being made, while for others symptoms will be identified and the patient will die or recover without a diagnosis being made or treatment being given. Patients with chronic illness will have extremely complex careers.

As a patient follows his individual career he will perceive a change in his public image—in his status and role—and will privately re-assess his self-image to match this changing status. For example, the middle-aged man who seeks medical attention because of mild chest pains, may alter his self-image of a youthful squashplayer to that of invalid if a doctor signs him off work as sick because of heart trouble. As Goffman describes for the psychiatric patient, this process of re-assessment will not necessarily take place simultaneously with the person's changing role or status. It may take time and, as in the life career, it happens through a process of socialisation.

Patient socialisation

How does a person with signs and symptoms become a patient? In the context of the hospital, becoming a patient entails behaving differently from how one would behave in other settings. Sometimes it entails removing outdoor clothes and wearing night attire. The new patient learns the role and expected status of patients within the particular ward. It may be different from some other wards in which he has spent some time. If he is to obtain information about his condition he must learn who to ask, when to ask and how to ask. Some patients leave behind their adult independence and ask, for example, if they may make a telephone call or take a bath. If they exert their usual degree of independence and take their own medication, on the other hand, they may receive a reprimand from the staff. The role of patient, like other roles in life, has to be learned. This is achieved by talking with other patients and observing how they behave, as well as being explicitly taught and controlled in certain ways by hospital staff.

Patients learn very quickly where you can smoke, when it is most appropriate to ask for a bedpan and when are the best times to have a word with sister. In other words, new patients are socialised into their role as patient.

The process of learning the role of patient is well illustrated by Goffman (1961). In his essay, *The moral career of a mental patient* Goffman is concerned with the processes by which patients reassess their self-image, and in particular he draws attention to the ways in which patients distinguish between right and wrong ways to behave. Goffman follows the career of psychiatric patients through the process of *institutionalisation*. That is a process by which patients lose autonomy and function completely within and are dependent upon the institution in which they live. When patients become *institutionalised*, when they learn to conform to the rules and routines of the institution, they will lose their 'old' self and obtain a new institutionalised identity. Not only will their public image conform to the institution's routines for eating, sleeping, relaxing, working and bathing, for example, but also the private self-image will conform eventually to this public image.

On entry to hospital some patients refuse to accept that their roles have changed. They may avoid talking with other patients, regarding themselves as different, and they may respond to hospital staff in a manner different from that of other patients. After a while the new patient gradually increases social interaction with other patients, and begins to act more like other patients in patient groups as well as with doctors and nurses. The psychiatric patient may gradually accompany other patients to the cafeteria to spend some time talking, smoking and drinking tea rather than spending the time alone in the ward or garden. Instead of sitting back and waiting for his name to be called to receive his medication, or waiting for it to be brought to him by a nurse, he joins the queue in the ward with other patients at the usual times.

While engaging in this behaviour, however, he may still attempt to withdraw from the patient role in other ways. For example, the businessman waiting for a routine operation or recovering from a heart attack may attempt to continue working while in hospital. In the psychiatric hospital Goffman observed that patients would continue to use nicknames they had earned in 'outside' life and to use the 'cover' address tact-fully provided by some psychiatric hospitals, since admitting to being a mental patient would be socially stigmatising and contradictory to their own self-image.

In time the new patient begins to realise that he is really no different from other patients. Irrespective of other roles in life—plumbers, mothers, fathers, teachers—all act similarly as patients. There is a common core to the patient role—and as with all roles, there are acceptable and less acceptable ways of acting it. The process of adapting or being socialised into the role of patient involves beginning to accept restrictions of freedom and movement, to accept community living arrange-ments and to conform to ward routines. These become nor-mal as opposed to alien experiences of the patient's new social status. A good literary example of socialisation into the patient role is described in *Cancer Ward* (Solzhenitsyn, 1971).

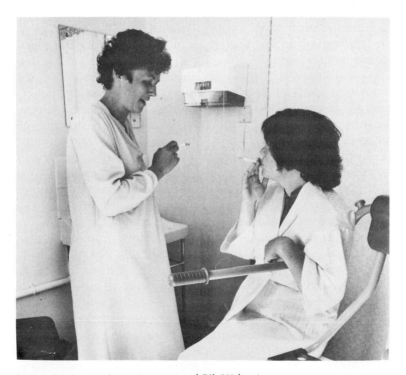

Fig. 8.3 Deviant patients (courtesy of Rik Walton).

Of course, some patients never learn to act the correct patient role as defined by other patients and also by professionals— they become part of a deviant sub-culture inside the wider patient culture of the hospital. Anyone who has read or seen *One flew over the cuckoo's nest* (Kesey, 1973) will very readily recognise this (Fig. 8.3).

We have described how patients become socialised into the patient role and, in extreme circumstances, some patients become 'institutionalised'. This presents a problem when attempts are made to rehabilitate the long-stay patient from hospitals for the mentally handicapped or mentally ill. These patients need to adopt new private and public images through similar processes; they must unlearn their patient role and become resocialised into a more adaptive social role in the community.

HEALTH AND ILLNESS

In the context of an ideal type of patient career people become patients because they are ill. Illness and health or wellness are aspects of everyday life, which occur at opposite ends of a continuum. Where a person is located on that continuum depends very much on what he himself perceives as health and illness and what others, particularly doctors, also perceive. Illness is differently defined by different people.

A simple distinction we need to make here is between *illness* and *disease*. Disease refers to a medical concept of pathology, which is indicated by a group of signs and symptoms. The presence or absence of a disease, as indicated by signs and symptoms, is clinically defined by the medical profession. The doctor or his substitute, using a common body of knowledge, makes the decision as to whether or not a person has a disease. In contrast, illness is defined by the person who had the signs and symptoms. It refers primarily to a person's subjective experience of 'health' and 'ill-health' and is indicated by the person's reactions to the symptoms; such reactions include stopping eating, staying off work, going to bed and taking pills. If two or more people are defining the situation in the case of a particular set of signs and symptoms—'the patient' and 'the doctor'—it follows that some people can feel ill without having a disease, while others will have a disease without feeling ill. We can illustrate this diagrammatically as shown in Figure 8.4.

Sometimes the two definitions of the situation will coincide—when the individual and the medical practitioner agree that the person is well, and when they agree that he is unwell and has a disease. On other occasions disparities arise. The individual may go to the doctor feeling unwell but the doctor may find no reason for this and, while remedies may be prescribed, the patient is not classified as diseased. The individual may also feel perfectly well but at a routine examination a very high blood pressure may be discovered together with changes in the optic discs, indicating hypertensive disease. Medication is prescribed and the patient is faced with adjusting to the fact that he has a serious chronic condition but knew nothing of it.

In this distinction between what Western medicine calls disease and what lay people call illness we have emphasised that different definitions of phenomena—signs and symptoms—can exist within the same culture. Between cultures definitions of what constitutes illness and disease can differ markedly. A commonly cited example is that of a South American tribe where a certain facially disfiguring skin disease is so common that it is those members of the tribe without the disease who are considered 'abnormal' or diseased, and who seek treatment from the local medicine man. We therefore emphasise that definitions of disease and illness are socially

| | | Medically identified signs and symptoms | |
		NO	YES
Signs and symptoms identified by subject and interpreted as 'abnormal'	NO	WELL	WELL BUT DISEASED
	YES	UNWELL	UNWELL AND DISEASED

Fig. 8.4 Relationship between disease and illness.

determined. In this country there was a time when people sought help from their priest for particular problems rather than from a doctor; this indicates a historical shift in definitions of what constitutes illness.

ILLNESS BEHAVIOUR

Epidemiological and social research have shown that many people with signs and symptoms do not obtain professional advice and treatment. For example Dunnell and Cartwright (1972), in their study of medicine-taking, found that fewer than one in five people who reported symptoms to their interviewers had consulted their general practititioner about them. Hannay (1979), in a study of symptom prevalence, found that two in every three physical symptoms were not reported to the general practitioner. A number of studies of chronic physical and psychiatric illnesses have shown consistently that for every person with a particular disorder and receiving some kind of treatment from medical services, one or more people exist with the same disorder who are not receiving treatment. Williamson and colleagues (1964), in a seminal work about the unmet medical needs of old people, reported that 58% of their sample had disabilities unknown to the doctor. Brown and Harris (1978) have shown that of 69 women who were suffering from a definitive affective psychiatric disorder in the three months prior to being interviewed in their survey, only four had received psychiatric care during the previous year, and almost half were not being treated by a general practitioner. Why is it that some people with particular symptoms consult doctors or other health professionals, while others do not? The concept which helps us explain this phenomenon is *illness behaviour.*

Illness behaviour is concerned with those social factors which affect definitions of health and illness and which influence, among other things, the demands people make for medical care. The term was first coined by Mechanic (1962) who defined illness behaviour as 'the way in which symptoms may be differentially perceived, evaluated and acted upon by different kinds of persons'. In other words, illness behaviour is about the social factors which influence the way individuals view signs and symptoms, and the kinds of action engaged in to deal with them. Individuals may recognise signs and symptoms as a medical problem, but they may or may not choose to ignore them, or they may or may not deal with the problem without seeking formal medical care. What are the social factors which influence the use of medical services?

A number of British studies have identified some broad characteristics of people in the four categories shown in Figure 8.4. They have looked at the social characteristics of users of different health services such as general practitioners, outpatient, hospital and antenatal services (Carwright, 1967; McKinlay & McKinlay 1972, 1979; Cartwright et al, 1973; Robinson, 1973; Cartwright & Anderson, 1979). Common social factors were found to be associated with the use of services; for example, age, gender, marital status, social class, religion, employment status and education are all associated with health service utilisation. We know that middle-aged women visit their general practitioner more often than younger women, and more often than younger and middle-aged men (OPCS, 1982). Working-class people make less use of dental services than their middle-class counterparts (Gray et al, 1970).

These studies have shown that the use of medical services is associated with certain social characteristics; in other words, they tell us which kind of person is most likely to use the different services. However, they throw little light on *why* it is that people do or do not use the various medical services. This has implications for policy makers. It is only by establishing these reasons and explaining the differences that policy decisions can be influenced in an attempt to alter the utilisation of services by groups 'at risk' to health problems.

EXPLANATIONS OF ILLNESS BEHAVIOUR

A number of writers have devised conceptual models to help in our understanding of illness behaviour. Many are fairly similar, but we have selected two contrasting models to illustrate not only the complexity of illness behaviour, but also the variation in sociological perspectives which have been used to study it. Broadly speaking these two models are representative of the structuralist and the interactionist approaches in sociology.

A structuralist approach

The first model is taken from a review article by Kasl and Cobb (1966). The model was developed using the findings from a large number of studies, which were undertaken mainly in the United States, in order to explain why individuals will or will not go to the doctor with their symptoms. Their model is presented schematically in Figure 8.5.

Kasl and Cobb have listed in the top left-hand corner a number of characteristics of individuals, which have been shown in earlier research to be associated with illness behaviour and with psychological distress, perceptions about the value of

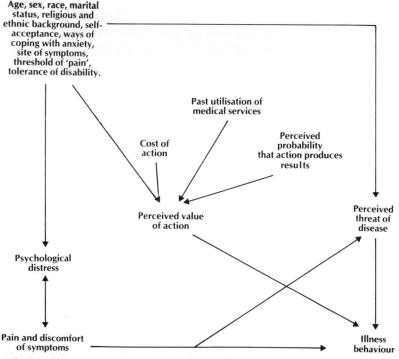

Fig. 8.5 The postulated relationship between symptoms and illness behaviour (Adapted from Kasl & Cobb, 1966).

seeing a doctor and perceptions about the threat of disease indicated by symptoms. In this scheme it is assumed that if an individual regards the symptom as a threat and he believes that a visit to the doctor will be of some benefit, then he is more likely to seek medical aid than another individual who, for example, perceives a visit to the doctor to be of little value. The model identifies a number of factors which might affect a person's perception about the threat of disease and about the value of different actions.

The first factor identified is psychological distress. People react in different ways to symptoms. Many can cause distress, which will mediate a person's way of looking at the threat of disease. For example, two women both find lumps in their breasts. Both might consider that they could be malignant. One may immediately seek medical aid while the other delays, not wishing to confirm whether the lump is indeed malignant. Research has shown that psychological distress in response to symptoms varies according to the characteristics of individuals as listed in the top left of the diagram.

The other mediating factors identified in the model relate to the perceived value of action. The cost to the individual of seeking medical care in terms of loss of earnings, loss of leisure time, cost of travelling, for example, or the previous experience of seeking help and the perceived probability that seeking medical aid will have any effect on the symptoms, are all factors which an individual may take into account when deciding whether or not to take his symptoms to the doctor.

The approach to illness behaviour which Kasl's and Cobb's model represents has been used most often to explain the use of services by different social groups in society. However, illness behaviour takes many forms apart from this. To ignore symptoms is a form of illness behaviour just as going to bed without seeking any professional help is equally illness behaviour. The particular form of behaviour engaged in depends on the individual's perception and definition of the situation. A number of writers have identified what Goffman (1961) terms *career contingencies* triggering mechanisms to describe the influences that social factors have on illness behaviour. The person due to start a new job ignores today the symptoms which last week or next week would have kept him off work. Some career contingencies are inevitable. For example, the old lady with rheumatism ignores the pains in her legs until she is unable to get into the bath. Others are more fortuitous. Take the case of the alcoholic who commits some crime in his need for alcohol. He is caught and goes to court for his misdemeanour, but whether he is given psychiatric treatment in hospital or is sent to prison depends on the availability of a place in an appropriate psychiatric institution. Contingencies determine whether he will embark on a patient career or prisoner career.

We can now see that the Kasl and Cobb model, elegantly described as it is, identifies a number of personal and broad social factors which help us understand why people attend or do not attend for medical care. It also provides a basis for making predictive statements in this context about the behaviour of individuals with defined characteristics. It does not, however, explain why people with similar social characteristics respond differently to similar signs and symptoms.

An interactionist approach

In contrast Dingwall (1976) provides an interactionist perspective on the study of illness behaviour. Unlike the previous model, which draws on a large number of studies, Dingwall supports his *Illness Action Model* with empirical data from only four substantive studies—on psychoactive drugs (Becker, 1967), poliomyelitis (Davis, 1963), myocardial infarction (Cowie, 1976) and childbirth (Dick-Read, 1958). This does not, in our view, limit the usefulness of his model, which is illustrated in Figure 8.6. If this is a useful model, it will give rise to studies which will test it and perhaps lead to modifications to fit the data obtained.

The first thing to note about Dingwall's model is that some of the terminology is different. The title refers to *illness action* rather than *illness behaviour*. What at first reading might appear to be a trivial difference is in fact a crucial distinction between the structuralist and interactionist perspectives. We refer the reader back to chapter 2, in which we discussed the distinction between *behaviour* and *action*. Behaviour, as we said, implies an automatic reaction to a given stimulus whereas action involves notions of intention or purpose stemming from within the individual. The person, therefore, makes

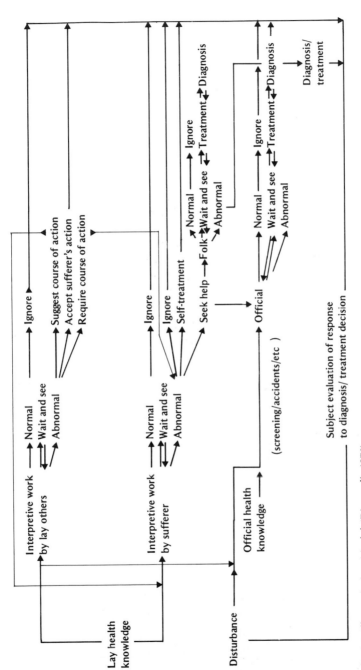

Fig. 8.6 Illness Action Model (Dingwall, 1976).

choices about if and how he will respond, and the complex array of possible outcomes is included in the model.

Let us now work through this rather complex model which, you will note, has no beginning or end—it forms a loop. We will begin at the left-hand side and explore some of its components.

We immediately come across a second terminological difference from the first model. Instead of talking about signs and symptoms Dingwall refers to disturbance—meaning *disturbance of equilibrium*—as the initiating phenomenon. Three main types of disturbance of equilibrium can be identified. These are symptoms, changes in the individual's lay health knowledge and the identification of signs of disease through routine screening.

Recognising disturbance by symptoms indicates awareness of some abnormal state for this individual. It could refer to symptoms like backache, heartburn or blood loss but the important feature is that the individual interprets this as abnormal for him. Therefore the office worker who has spent the previous day enthusiastically digging his garden only to find that he has a stiff back would feel discomfort but would probably not define his condition as abnormal, and would continue his usual lifestyle. However, if his discomfort continues for longer than he thinks it should, then there is a disturbance in his equilibrium which will prompt some kind of action.

The onset of symptoms need not be a sudden event. In fact, symptoms may be present for some time, but it is not until the pain becomes so severe that we cannot walk or the headache so intense that we can no longer concentrate that the disturbance of equilibrium is sufficient to influence the course of action.

Whereas symptoms may be a triggering mechanism in many acute illness, this will not necessarily be the case for chronic illness, where symptoms in the usual sense of the word are a constant feature of the person's life. What tends to happen is that the ill patient who has a chronic condition, for instance obstructive airway disease, comes to perceive his morning cough, sputum and breathlessness as normal for him. When this 'normality' is disturbed and there is an exacerbation of bronchitis the individual can follow the pathways through the

Illness Action Model. He has perceived a disturbance from his own equilibrium.

The second form of disturbance, changes in the individual's lay health knowledge, can come about through watching a television documentary about the dangers of asbestos, for instance, or through reading an article on the harmful outcomes of gross obesity. Disturbance is therefore created by the individual re-evaluating the significance of his lack of breath and cough, which in turn leads to some form of action.

The third type of disturbance comes about after some asymptomatic disease has been discovered through participation in a routine health check. The person who is discovered to have an abnormal cervical smear or high blood pressure is informed and this leads to some form of action.

After an individual has become aware of a disturbance in his equilibrium, the model shows three possible parallel pathways which he could follow. Some individuals following screening or accidents, for example, will already be in contact with medical services, without the sufferer being able to make decisions. Dingwall calls this official health knowledge.

In most situations, however, the disturbance will lead to an interpretation of its meaning by the sufferer within the framework of his own lay health knowledge. This interpretation will be influenced by his previous personal experiences of a similar condition, his knowledge of others with that condition or what he may read or hear about it. At the same time, the interpretation of the disturbance by significant others such as a spouse or friend may be sought and this may also influence the actions of the individual.

The result of the interpretation produces in each case three possible outcomes.

One of the recurrent possibilities we see throughout this model is to wait and see what happens. No judgement need be made immediately. It is not unusual in everyday life to delay and wait and see what develops before we act. For example, we tend to wait to see whether a headache develops and persists before resorting to analgesics. Of course, what is important to note is that we all make such judgements differently, using different health knowledge and experiences. In the above example what constitutes a headache for the individual concerned would become a central question. During this waiting time the nature of the disturbance will be re-appraised; hence there are arrows in two directions in the model to indicate this.

The other ways of interpreting the disturbance are to define it as normal or as abnormal. The sufferer, as well as significant others, will engage in forming these conclusions, and folk medicine and official medicine do likewise. What is important to note here is that definitions of what constitutes normality and abnormality can differ between those involved. If the disturbance is defined as normal then it is ignored by everyone. Should early morning sickness occur after a woman has learned she is newly pregnant, then this would be likely to be interpreted by everyone as normal and to be ignored after the episode is over. Each of the interpretations as normal lead straight to the righthand side of the model. If, on the other hand, a disturbance is interpreted as abnormal, then the model indicates a number of different outcomes for each of the groups which may be involved.

If we focus on the sufferer we see that he can do one of three things: ignore the disturbance, undertake some sort of self-treatment such as taking an aspirin, or seek help. There are two sources from which help may be sought—from traditional medical services or from *folk* or *alternative medicine*. A good example of folk medicine was the granny midwife, who used to help local women in childbirth. Homeopathic clinics, osteopaths and those who practice acupuncture are examples of alternative medicine. Individuals providing traditional, folk or alternative medicine will make their own interpretations of the disturbance and act accordingly. If they regard it as abnormal, then diagnosis and treatment will follow. This takes us to the bottom right of the model.

Once an episode of disturbance is complete, and remembering that this may take from minutes to months to accomplish, the sufferer will engage in a re-valuation of the disturbance, informed by his evaluation of the diagnosis and treatment decisions. If all is well, the outcome will be a re-establishment of the original equilibrium from which the disturbance was first noted, and the individual will return to his own normality. Depending on the nature of the disturbance, however, the original equilibrium may never be regained, and the sufferer may come to re-define a new equilibrium as normal. The person who had originally thought himself perfectly well, but who suffers a coronary thrombosis necessitating a change in life-style and life-long medication, will re-define his equilibrium and this will influence any future episodes of disturbance and their interpretation. Less dramatically, the hill-walker who one day cannot reach his favourite summit will re-define his health status and act accordingly. The model, therefore, is circular and demonstrates how past experiences, as they are subjectively interpreted and acted upon, will influence future actions.

Appreciating the subjectivity of interpretations of health, illness and action, and regarding the origin as a definition of disturbance rather than imposing the notion of symptoms which are defined through medical knowledge, provides for a less rigid approach to the study of illness behaviour.

We have discussed these two models at some length and attempted to show that while they provide different interpretations and explanations of illness behaviour, they both demonstrate that illness behaviour can only be understood by looking at it within its social context. To ignore the social realities of an individual's situation is to misunderstand the meaning of an illness to that individual.

Illness is, therefore, both a biological and a social event. It involves changes in both biological function as a result of disease and changes in social function: changes in behaviour and changes in a person's relationship with others. We can now see that people seek medical care and become patients, not because they have a disease, but because of the social response to that disease, as it is defined and dealt with by them. Being ill or being a patient refers not only to a clinical or biological state but also to a social position or role.

THE SICK ROLE

Being a patient implies that you are ill. Parsons (1951) developed the concept of the *sick role* to describe the expectations of people in a society which defines the rights and duties of its members who are sick. Like any of the other social roles we have mentioned—father, plumber, teacher, nurse—adopting the sick role requires co-operation and recognition of that role from all of those around us. The behaviour of the sick person and the behaviour of others around him must conform to the particular pattern of expectations that surround the sick role.

In his analysis of the sick role, Parsons identified four principal elements. Two of these elements represent the rights and the other two elements the obligations associated with the sick role. The first right that the sick person, that is the one occupying the sick role, can claim is the exemption from normal activities and responsibilities. Being off work, staying at home in the evenings instead of going out and being relieved of domestic chores are exemptions which some sick people achieve. Sick women often have more difficulty in obtaining these rights, since domestic work might have to be continued whereas employment outside the home would not.

It is clear from our earlier discussions that adoption of the sick role, being ill, will not be directly related to any objective or subjective assessment of symptom severity. The variability of these play some part, but what we have already described as career contingencies interfere with such an apparently straightforward relationship. Claiming the rights of the sick role is also contingency dependent. If there is no one else there to feed the baby, the woman with 'flu will struggle to do it despite feeling extremely ill.

The second right which Parsons identifies that the sick person can expect, is assistance from or dependency on others. Sick leave and other welfare practices are society's recognition of the special status of illness. Similarly, the assistance given by relatives and friends at a time of illness is recognition of the sick role, as is admission to hospital or attendance by nurses at home. While the individual can lay claim to these rights, he must also meet obligations.

The first of the obligations associated with the sick role is that the incumbent should want to get better and to get out of the sick role as soon as possible. At times we may have come across someone whom we regard as clinging to the sick role for longer than we think is appropriate; the patient appears not to want to get better, wants to stay in bed or in hospital for longer than is thought necessary or wants to deter resuming normal activities for a period longer than the time normally regarded as acceptable for a particular condition. They are not meeting their obligations.

At this stage it is necessary to identify one of the difficulties of Parsons' analysis, one which we have already discussed in terms of Dingwall's use of the term normality, that is the difference between acute and chronic illness. When we are ill we all, generally, want to get better. To this extent we should be conforming to the expectations of the sick role. However for most chronic conditions, by definition, there is no getting better in absolute terms.

The second obligation of the sick role which Parsons identifies is that the sick person should not only try to get better but should do so by acting in an appropriate manner: staying in bed as necessary or seeking medical care when required. Leaving aside the problem of the person with a chronic illness, the major difficulty with this obligation is that there are at least two perspectives as to how to define what is appropriate behaviour. As Dingwall's *Illness Action Model* implies, the sick person, other lay people and the doctor may well hold different views about the relevance or appropriateness of specific treatments. The patient with an arthritic hip may decide to attend a homeopathic clinic and use their remedies, while her family may know of an osteopath with a very good reputation in dealing with 'hips' and the orthopaedic surgeon representing official medical knowledge may consider that the only effective treatment would be hip replacement. Who is to say what is appropriate?

As an ideal type the *sick role* is particularly useful in providing an insight into the way an individual is expected to behave in the face of acute illness. It is less useful when considering chronic illness or disability. Many writers consider that the concept has been over-used (Mechanic, 1978) and to some extent it has become a term used by health professionals to label certain categories of patients. From the perspective of labelling theory, playing or being in the sick role becomes the label we use for groups of patients who are 'normally' ill, i.e. acutely ill. We reserve labels like cripple, geriatric, or alcoholic for people with chronic illnesses or disabilities. However, as an ideal type, the sick role is useful in helping us understand some characteristics of the patient career.

SUMMARY

In this chapter we have focused on some of the issues which influence how we regard patients, health and illness. The meanings that these terms hold have been explored in some detail to show that they are socially defined and can differ in meaning according to various cultures and sub-cultures, education, age, gender and social origins. This helps us to understand more clearly the World Health Organisation's definition of health which is 'the state of complete physical, mental and social well-being and not merely the absence of disease and infirmity' (1983, p. 1). Health is not an absolute state of affairs. Rather it is a variable status between different countries, cultures and social groups. This definition is also noteworthy since, as well as physical and mental well-being, health includes a social component. This very broad definition of health clearly implies that it is not the prerogative of medicine to define health, just as we have shown that illness is not medically defined. Being ill and subsequent behaviour depends on how the individual regards and is influenced by his own particular circumstances.

Equally, how health care professionals regard patients and illness is determined by their own experiences, and to the extent that these differ from those of their patients, so interpretations will differ. Health care professionals deal with illness for much of their working time and come to make assumptions about patients and patient behaviour. They may come to forget that while they regard tests or procedures as routine, they are new and can be frightening to patients, and their beliefs about the reason for a patient's behaviour may be totally alien to the patient's own explanation. Therefore, if health care professionals are to understand their patients—why they discontinue breast feeding within a few weeks, fail to bring children for immunisation, wish to discharge themselves from hospital or do not practice their exercises—it is necessary to find out the patient's version of events rather than impose their own views.

In understanding the concept of patient career we note that people coming into hospital have to learn how to become patients, indeed how to become good patients if they want a smooth passage. Simply becoming a patient involves an interactive process between the person and his social and physical environment. Understanding how this comes about and some of its implications will be examined in further detail when we consider staff-patient interaction in chapter 9 and death and dying in chapter 10.

Another useful way of incorporating patient career into ideas about professional practice is to consider the organisation of care from the patient's perspective rather than from the perspective of a single form of care-giving organisation. Patients may follow extremely complex career pathways, being treated by different doctors, nurses and various kinds of therapists not only in different hospitals as well as at home but even in different wards and departments within a single hospital. With conditions like rheumatic disease or cancer, the career can extend over many years and involve many different care-givers. By focusing on the patient and the continuous nature of the career rather than on discrete elements within it this may provide for a more rational and cohesive way of planning and delivering care.

REFERENCES

Becker H S 1967 History, culture and subjective experience: an exploration of the social basis of drug induced experiences. Journal of Health and Social Behaviour 8: 163–176

Berger P L, Berger B 1976 Sociology: a biographical approach. Penguin Books, Harmondsworth

Brown G W, Harris T 1978 Social origins of depression. A study of psychiatric disorder in women. Tavistock, London

Cartwright A 1967 Patients and their doctors. A study of general practice. Routledge & Kegan Paul, London

Cartwright A, Anderson R 1979 Patients and their doctors 1977. Journal of the Royal College of General Practitioners, Occasional Paper 8

Cartwright A, Hockey L, Anderson J 1973 Life before death. Routledge & Kegan Paul, London

Cowie B 1976 The cardiac patient's perception of his heart attack. Social Science and Medicine 10: 87–96

Davis F 1963 Passage through crisis: polio victims and their families. Bobs-Merrill, New York

Dick-Read G 1958 Childbirth without fear. The principles and practices of natural childbirth. Heinemann, London

Dingwall R 1976 Aspects of illness. Martin Robertson, London

Dunnell K, Cartwright A 1972 Medicine takers, prescribers and hoarders. Routledge & Kegan Paul, London

Goffman E 1961 Asylums. Essays on the social situation of mental patients and other inmates. Anchor Books, New York

Goffman E 1968 Stigma. Notes on the management of spoiled identity. Penguin Books, Harmondsworth

Gray P G, Todd J E, Slack G L, Bulman J S 1970 Adult dental health in England and Wales in 1968, SS 411. HMSO, London

Hannay D R 1979 Factors associated with formal symptom referral. Social Science and Medicine 13A: 101–104

Kasl S V, Cobb S 1966 Health behaviour, illness behaviour, and sick-role behaviour. Archives of Environmental Health 12: 246–266 and 531–542

Kesey K 1973 One flew over the cuckoo's nest. Picador, London

Lemert E 1964 Social structure, social control, and deviation. In: Clinard M B (ed) Anomie and deviant behaviour. A discussion and critique. Free Press, New York, p 57–97

McKinlay J B, McKinlay S M 1972 Some social characteristics of lower working class utilisers and underutilisers of maternity care services. Journal of Health and Social Behaviour 13: 369–382

McKinlay J B, McKinlay S M 1979 The influence of premarital conception and various obstetric complications on subsequent prenatal health behaviour. Epidemiology and Community Health 33: 84–90

Mechanic D 1962 The concept of illness behaviour. Journal of Chronic Diseases 15: 189–194

Mechanic D 1978 Medical sociology, 2nd edn. Free Press, New York

Office of Population, Censuses and Surveys 1982 General Household Survey, 1980. HMSO, London

Parsons T 1951 The social system. Routledge & Kegan Paul, London

Robinson D 1973 Patients, practitioners and medical care. Aspects of medical sociology. Heinemann, London

Solzhenitsyn A 1971 Cancer ward. Penguin Books, Harmondsworth

Williamson J, Stokoe I H, Gray S,.Fisher M, Smith A, McGhee A, Stephenson E 1964 Old people at home. Their unreported needs. Lancet II: 1117–1220

World Health Organisation 1983 Basic documents, 33rd edn. WHO, Geneva

FURTHER READING

Dingwall R 1976 Aspects of illness. Martin Robertson, London

9

Interaction with patients

INTRODUCTION

In this chapter we focus on interaction between patients or clients and health professionals. Investigation of types and processes of interaction has proven to be a fruitful area for sociological research and the amount of attention reflects the importance attached to this aspect of the professional's work. It reminds us also of Christine Chapman's definition of nursing as a process of social interaction, a view of professional work which is equally relevant to all professional groups.

We begin by discussing some aspects of the relationship which may be said to exist between professional and client and how these may be very similar but also vary in relation to time, place and context. The roles played by participants are important here. We introduce another of Goffman's ideas, namely that *frames* provide structure and meaning for social interaction. Professional-client interaction can also be viewed as the same kind of negotiated order as was discussed in Chapter 7 to explain interaction between different professionals within an organisation.

We then explore the ways in which patients are inevitably classed or typed, in relation to understanding the distinction between 'good' and 'bad' patients, and the effects of such typification on the way staff frame their interactions with patients, the way work is carried out and patient outcomes. Particular attention is given to the way nurses deal with patients classified as neurotic. Finally different aspects of work involving pain is used as an example to describe the way professionals, especially nurses, manage interaction with patients.

RELATIONSHIPS BETWEEN CLIENTS AND PROFESSIONALS

The term relationship does nothing more than indicate the relative position of two objects in time and space or in a classification system. When we consider social relationships, we refer to situations in which two or more persons are involved and in which 'in its meaningful context, the action of each takes into account that of the other and is oriented in these terms' (Parsons, 1937). This implies that the participants have some understanding of each other's behaviour and act in ways that take this into account. In order to do this, participants have expectations about each other which influence the particular forms actions will take. Sociologists are concerned with the social positions that participants occupy and the roles they act, and this includes those of professional and client.

One of Goffman's most recent contributions has been to provide an analysis of how social actions proceed by conceiving them as on-going within particular kinds of *frame*. In his book *Frame Analysis* (1974) Goffman tries to analyse the basis of our social experience. He suggests that we rely on a number of primary frameworks each of which 'allows its user to locate, perceive, identify and label a seemingly infinite number of complete occurrences defined in its terms' (1974, p. 21). When we attend a doctor's surgery, then, we are likely to behave in a fashion which is framed or structured by both the doctor's and our own shared view of the form of this kind of interaction. Frames, therefore, can be regarded as providing a structure for interactions but, simultaneously, the actors negotiate and structure the meaning of their experience—that is, you and your doctor interpret what is going on, interact taking this into account, and achieve a level of inter-subjective communication because of the frame in which you are operating. Important here is that a good deal of our activity is reflexive; our understanding of what our activities mean depends on understandings gained from other bits of behaviour, or the same behaviour under different conditions for which we have established a sense of reality. In this way frames provide a means of attending to and interpreting social experiences, as well as providing a structure and definition for them.

Goffman describes different kinds of framing, and ways of moving out of the primary social frameworks which provide background understanding for events. For example, we generally know when a fight is serious and when not. We are generally adept at constituting what we see in accordance with the framework that officially applies. Goffman uses the example of the right of medical personnel to approach the human naked body and the special efforts taken to infuse procedures with terms and actions which keep sexual readings of the interaction in check. Others have also reported the difficulty of keeping the sexual implications of mouth to mouth contact out of resuscitation practice sessions. The human body, and touching it, is thus one relevant feature of different kinds of primary frame and we must rely on our interpretative competency to distinguish what is meant and act appropriately. Needless to say, each framework will comprise a host of different features.

Another important notion is that of distinctiveness. We regularly hear such phrases as 'doctor-patient relationship' or 'client-therapist relationship'. This implies that the special relationship a person has with his doctor is different from the special relationship he has with his therapist, which is again different from that he has with his wife or his milkman or the person on the cashout register at the supermarket. But is the relationship between nurse X and patient A the same as that between nurse X and patient B, C, D, E, F, etc. or between nurses W, Y, Z etc. and patients A, B, C, D, E, F, etc.? Goffman draws a distinction between the *person* or individual participating and the *particular role* that the person realises during the interaction. There is therefore a blend of person and role, insofar as the individual is never either completely free from the role they are in, nor completely constrained by it. To every encounter nurse X will bring herself, X, and her role, nurse, the components of X and nurse varying depending upon the frame, one component of which is the patient A, B or C, etc. and their distinctive person-role blend.

The particular roles that individuals are permitted to perform, however—say in a nurse-patient encounter—are socially limited. There are questions about role rights and obligations—that is, the right to participate in the application of a particular frame—but also character rights—the right to participate in that role in a particular way. We discussed this issue in Chapter 8 in relation to the patient career.

This kind of analysis helps us to understand why relationships between professionals and patients will have certain aspects in common, because of the roles of the participants, but relationships will also vary because of how the participants characterise those roles as well as the personal elements which are added to them. There will also be situational variations and there will be different kinds of frames depending on such features as the degree of autonomy of the professional, the awareness contexts pertaining (discussed in Chapter 10) and the prevailing ideology.

The construction of nurse-patient relationships

David Armstrong (1983) in a recent paper contends that while the word 'relationship' has continued to be applied the actual form and nature of the relationship between patient and nurse has undergone a fundamental reformulation within the past decade or so in general nursing and rather earlier in psychiatric nursing. The analysis is based on an examination on what has been written about nurse-patient relationships in popular nursing textbooks, which 'attempt to distil the essence of nursing for the benefit of the student' (p. 457).

Contrasting the position in the late 1960s with that currently portrayed, the nature of what is implied in nurse-patient relationship changes dramatically. His analysis begins earlier, however, and draws on the currently fashionable writing of Foucault (1973). Foucault's thesis is that traditional perceptions of the patient as a discrete, analysable, passive body did not emerge in medicine until the end of the 18th century when various techniques were developed by which to explore the human body. Despite the apparent biological entity which constitutes the body, its social meaning, is constructed through social practices and as well as the kinds of procedures and techniques carried out. Foucault further identifies the body as having an objective and individual status developed contemporaneously in a variety of institutional settings— schools, prisons, workshops, barracks as well as hospitals— which were emerging at the same time as theories of localised pathology. In Nightingale's *Notes on Nursing* (1859) a century later, emphasis was given to the physical environment in which the patient's body was nursed, together with careful and accurate observation of the body. The patient thus become objectified in these physical and physiological realities.

It was not until the 1950s and early 1960s that medical writers began to find the patient's personality, as opposed to his body, a factor of importance. This was related to response to treatment, focused on problems of compliance and identified doctor-patient communication as problematic (Armstrong, 1982). This subsequently gave rise to a considerable literature on the nature of doctor-patient relationships with importance given to work such as that of Balint (1956). This work served to establish doctors and patients as 'real' people. This is, rather than being objects, they were regarded as having personalities and as subjective beings.

There has been a similar change in how nurse-patient relationships are defined and how that definition comes about. Armstrong uses the analogy of that between supermarket customer and cashier. Both parties have well defined roles, their interaction is usually minimal and neither party expects to have to negotiate differences of meaning or mutual anxieties. Imagine now a large research grant being awarded to investigate the relationship. Both parties would have to start examining their relationship so that they could relate their feelings to the research team: the confession of silent thoughts would be encouraged and new problems or misunderstandings would be identified. Gradually a mechanistic relationship—virtually between a bag of shopping and a cash till—becomes problematic in that as the customer comes to look for and respond to the personal meanings of the cashier, so that cashier becomes more than an extension of the till but a 'whole person' in her own right. Armstrong writes, 'Until recently the relationship between the patient and nurse was similar in its mechanistic passivity to that between customer and cashier' (1983, p. 458); that is, extremely limited in the identity it provided for its participants.

The more recent nursing literature examined by Armstrong suggests that the nurse-patient relationship has been reformulated from being a passive one, with the identities of participants described in such a manner that patients only obeyed and showed respect while nurses were limited to being biddable and showing appropriate demeanour and manner. In other words, the patient was a biological object and the nurse was part of the machinery of surveillance. The re-definition of the relationship in general nursing in the past decade portrays the patient as a subjective rather than an objective being, with nurses responsible for monitoring and evaluating the patient's personal identity, constructing and sustaining that identity. This is particularly evident in the emphasis on 'individuality' and the 'nursing process' (Kratz, 1979; Roper et al, 1981).

Accounts of nursing before 1960 therefore will deal with the patient as objective while subsequent histories, for example Davies (1981), reveal patients as subjective. In this sense Armstrong considers that recent writings on nurse-patient relationships and analysis of nurse-patient interactions are a reflection of current interpretations of the subjectivity of both nurses and patients.

Studying relationships by studying interactions

As Altschul (1972) noted, 'The concept of relationship remains elusive, even when qualified by such attributes as 'personal' or 'impersonal' and even more so when terms like 'possessive, emotionally involved relationship' are used'. (p. 9). Because of this elusiveness, research has tended to focus on the less emotive and observable *interaction* between clients and professionals.

Generalising about interactions between professionals and patients is complicated however by the extreme diversity of situations in which patients are cared for, the kinds of problem they present, the kinds of knowledge and skills drawn upon, and the nature and intent of the relationships formed. In the United Kingdom particular attention has been given to psychiatric settings (Altschul, 1972; Macilwaine, 1983), intensive care units (Ashworth, 1980), general hospital wards (Clark,

1983; Faulkner, 1980), geriatric wards (Wells, 1980; Evers, 1981; Fairhurst, 1981) and to patients in their own homes (McIntosh, 1981). Interaction with different client groups has been the focus of research: cancer patients (McIntosh, 1977; Bond, 1978), antenatal patients (McIntyre, 1982), patients in labour (Kirkham, 1983), parents of chronically ill children (Comaroff & Maguire 1981), parents of children with Perthes disease (Harrisson, 1977) and stroke patients at home (Kratz, 1978). There is also a growing body of work on the analysis of consultations in general practice and in out-patient clinics (e.g. Bloor, 1976; Strong, 1979).

These studies have variously investigated methods of soliciting information from patients as a basic of making decisions; ideological influences on communication practices; value assumptions as they influence communication and the subsequent treatment of social groups. From these and other studies we can draw on some general ideas about interactions with patients and some influences on them. What professionals bring to an interaction will depend in part on the organisational context in which it takes place—whether a general or psychiatric hospital ward, an outpatient clinic or casualty department, a well baby or venereal disease clinic. Overriding these are constraints of law, professional ethics, time, space, inter-professional relations and the organisation of the profession.

PROFESSIONAL-CLIENT INTERACTIONS AS NEGOTIATED ORDER

In Chapter 7 we developed the idea that institutions are socially created and an important feature of their construction is their negotiated order. This concept is equally relevant to interaction between professionals and clients as they intersubjectively produce a social order.

Power and control

Central to an analysis of the relationship between client and professional is an appreciation that they bring to the relationship different definitions of the situation, different needs and different aspirations. While these may coincide, the professional and the client may have different ways of achieving them. Both mother and midwife wish to see a successful birth but the midwife may wish to minimise her patient's discomfort by encouraging the use of drugs for pain relief while the mother may prefer to stay alert throughout her labour without drugs. Somehow they must arrive at a decision about how to proceed.

Interactions between clients and professionals often take place in institutions and an earlier discussion of the nature of institutions provides a broad framework for their interpretation. Riley (1977) in commenting on the structural organisation of Maternity Hospitals suggested that institutions which depend on rigidly maintained hierarchy and strict division of labour among their personnel cannot fail to transfer the results in some form to the treatment of patients. 'The difficulties of acquiring a theoretical appreciation are as nothing compared with the difficulties of *enacting* flexibility within an inflexibly organised system' (p. 69–70). This extreme view of hierarchy and division of labour reflects the structuralist position that professionals have more power than clients, and that all professional groups are likely to be dominated to some degree by doctors. However as Davies (1983) points out, relationships in hospitals are likely to be as much related to the wider social divisions and ideological positions as the constraints of bureaucracy and profession. Therefore the way that professionals interact with patients will be influenced by their social structural-class positions as well as ideological views of the relative positions of professional and client.

Nevertheless, one way of analysing professional-client relationships is in terms of the relative power each brings to them. Freidson (1975) has invested this power in *functional autonomy*, in the independence of the professional from lay evaluation and control. Functional autonomy is imputed as a structural property of a particular class of occupations, namely professions. Those occupying professional positions will inevitably carry out their work with clients from this dominant position. The view of the professional as dominant places the client in a reciprocal subservient position. The professional view in this analysis will therefore prevail because clients and professionals occupy different structural positions.

This is reflected in the different ways that professionals exert control, even to the extent of regulating access to the sick role, as discussed in Chapter 8. Professionals exert control in areas as different as deciding which patients should be resuscitated (discussed in Chapter 10), when they should be discharged home (Armitage, 1981), or when they should be offered an aspirin (Fagerhaugh & Strauss, 1977). The amount of autonomy available, however, will depend upon the occupational group to which the professional belongs (doctors being more autonomous than other health professionals) and on their authority position within that group. Moreover, while relationships may be asymmetrical this is not to suggest that patients are either unable to make their voices heard or bound to do as they are bidden.

Controlling information

One aspect of inequality between the client and professional is that the professionals can be interpreted as having more knowledge and information, which they are at liberty to withhold from clients. This view is upheld by the many studies which have shown that a major source of dissatisfaction among patients is a feeling of not being kept informed (Cartwright, 1964; Reynolds, 1978; Report of the Royal Commission on the National Health Service, 1979; Kirkham, 1983). While information may be actively sought by patients, it is the conscious or unconscious control by professionals which creates uncertainty and anxiety as well as a feeling among patients that they are ignored (Waitzkin & Stoeckle, 1972; Ley, 1977; Report of the Royal Commission on the National Health Service, 1979). There are many alleged reasons for not keeping patients informed—not least that they would rather not know—which are used to justify staff behaviour.

Professionals regularly act on the basis of *assumptions* held about patients' desire for information, assumptions which can often be quite erroneous (Bond, 1978; Madge & Fassam, 1982). The effect of information restriction is to deny the patient responsible status, and this denial implies that the patient is incapable of intelligent choice and self-control (Slack, 1976).

A major concept in information control is the management

of patients' *uncertainty*. As Waitzkin and Stoeckle (1972) wrote:

> 'a physician's ability to preserve his own power over the patient in the doctor-patient relationship depends largely on his ability to control the patient's uncertainty' (p. 187).

Power therefore rests on the control of uncertainty which in turn rests on the management of information. Davis (1963) distinguished two types of uncertainty. *Clinical uncertainty* exists when there is real uncertainty about clinical matters and when information of this kind is withheld. However, uncertainty can be projected into a situation where there is no clinical uncertainty in order to manage interactions. This is called *functional uncertainty* and may be used to avoid patients demanding reasons for treatment or explanation of events as well as, when the news is bad, emotional or disruptive outbursts. In order to maintain information control, staff may resort to a number of linguistic devices and interactional tactics including structuring interactions so that the patient has no opportunity to ask questions. In turn patients resort to counter-tactics including bargaining techniques, such as appealing against established norms, applying the pressure of a barrage of questions or enlisting the aid of intermediaries (Roth, 1963).

As in any bargaining situation, the relative power of participants is an important feature. Patients can increase their power by behaving irresponsibly or threatening to withhold co-operation. However, since health professionals are privy to the information first it is they who decide how, when and what to tell patients. As well as not telling, they can invoke postponement, selective information-giving and deception. On the whole paramedical staff concur with medical decisions regarding information. While they may express opinions about the negative effect such practices may have on patients, on the whole they prefer to avoid conflict with medical colleagues by maintaining their silence on the subject (Bond, 1978).

Negotiating information and other aspects of care

Initially negotiation was studied in long-term care settings

(Roth, 1963) and was conceived as a series of 'offers and responses' (Scheff, 1966). Negotiation also occurs in short-term
contacts, however. We observed our daughter, aged 6, who
had fallen badly on her shoulder, successfully negotiate that
she would not have it examined at the local casualty department unless by a female doctor. The staff on duty reorganised
the flow of work so that when it was her turn to be seen, a
female casualty officer was allocated and treatment was successfully instituted. We eagerly await her next visit to the den-
tist when a milk tooth extraction is anticipated! Because she
has not yet been socialised into the patient role occupied by
adults, she is responded to by professionals as a child patient
and so treated differently (Dingwall & Murray, 1983). Her demands, which in adults would have caused them to be categorised as deviants, were met, whereas in adults they would
have resulted in particular sanctions. For example Jeffrey's
(1979) analysis of 'bad' adult patients in casualty departments
showed them to be subjected to delay, inattention, verbal
hostility and vigorous restraint. Thus child-patients are treated
in a different frame in casualty, as they are by physiotherapists
attempting to carry out particular therapeutic regimes (Davis
& Strong, 1976).

Negotiation can also take place through a third party. During fieldwork one of us observed a female patient in a radiotherapy ward who was thought to require psychiatric
treatment. When this was suggested to her husband he in-
terceded on her behalf, expressing his belief that this would
be premature and likely to prompt his wife to discharge herself. In this sense the patient, through her husband, had negotiated her treatment. Through asserting themselves in
different ways patients can obtain and retain some measure
of control which may be regarded as counteracting that of
professionals. Where relationships are harmonious then all
parties must be reasonably satisfied with the negotiated order
they have created and must feel reasonably in control (Rosenthal et al, 1980) or accept their power deficit as legitimate or
inevitable. Where either party is dissatisfied then problems of
interpersonal relationships will persist.

Of course there are limits to the extent that negotiation can
take place, with both staff and patients drawing their own de-
marcations. Formal policy can limit the extent to which pa-

tients may negotiate, for example, a home confinement. While midwives are bound by rules to attend a woman wishing a home confinement, there is no silimar rule which governs the attendance of a general practitioner, who can refuse to do so. Therefore, in choosing a home confinement, some patients choose to do so without medical cover. In other circumstances they may negotiate that their general practitioner will attend. More informal rules govern length of stay in hospital after confinement, and though patients may wish to go home earlier than the routine number of days, whether they can successfully negotiate this will depend on how they are regarded by the medical staff who agree their discharge. In extreme circumstances, of course, where hospital staff refuse to negotiate, patients can discharge themselves. This right of patients has been publicised recently. The Association for Improvements in the Maternity Services notes:

'A mother may discharge herself and her baby from hospital at any time. An early discharge is sometimes looked upon with disfavour by hospital staff who may require the mother to sign a form stating that she has discharged herself against medical advice. If the mother does not wish to sign this form she is under no obligation to do so'.

(Beech & Claxton, 1980, p. 21)

Yet patients are under strong pressure to sign such documents.

The asymmetrical nature of relationships between professionals and patients is more pronounced in hospital than it is in the patient's own home. McIntosh (1981) observed that district nurses saw themselves very much as guests in patients' homes, and this determined to a considerable extent the way in which they managed their interactions and the position from which they could negotiate. For example, a guest does not lay down rules and regulations for her hosts, whereas the nurse as professional has to do so in the course of her duties. Thus nurses had to learn to exert sufficient control to establish their authority in respect of the nursing care of patients, but at the same time to be enough of the 'guest' to let patients and families feel that they were in control.

Kirkham (1983) observed that patients having home confinements behaved much more assertively than their hospital counterparts. Midwives' relationships with home patients were described as more colleague-like. In the absence of pro-

---

fessional colleagues, the midwives shared what they were doing with their patients, giving them running commentaries about what was happening and announcing their intended actions in advance. This information gave patients the opportunity to refuse procedures which some did, unlike hospital patients. Therefore the standards by which patients conformed were different at home. Those delivering in hospital had very quickly to learn the standards of the institution, since their negotiating position was that much weaker.

Control of work

Control of work involves controlling patients who constitute work. Like all other workers, health professionals try to arrange their work to be conveniently and easily performed. One way of achieving this is to establish a number of *routines* and develop procedures which will encourage patients to accept routine forms of treatment.

One vivid example of routinisation of care is the clerking procedure employed at women's first visit at an antenatal clinic (McIntyre, 1978). A midwife asks a number of medically predetermined standard questions and carries out physical checks, the results of which are entered in the case notes. In this context there is no negotiation about the nature of patients' problems. Any problems identified for the doctor will conform to those predetermined by the questions. Should the patients themselves raise any questions then the observed standard response is to tell them to speak to the doctor about it. In this routinised fashion large numbers of patients with similar conditions are processed in such a way as to conserve the time of doctors and, to a lesser extent, that of midwives.

In other settings a variety of routines are identifiable, corresponding to particular patient types. Bond (1978) observes that what nurses tell cancer patients about their treatment and condition is reduced to a number of routine explanations appropriate to the categories defined by the nature of the patient's diagnosis, and type and stage of treatment. We will confront routinisation of care again when we discuss the management of dying patients in Chapter 10.

In using routines health professionals are drawing on their habitual knowledge developed over repeated experiences of the same kind of clinical situations. In so doing, the application of routines serves to embody the professionals' functional autonomy because they reflect the purposes of the professional without necessarily taking account of those of the patient. At the same time routines, because of their structure, serve to deny patients any potential influence (Bloor, 1976). However the extent to which standard routines apply will vary according to the various resources and constraints that clients and professionals feel that the particular setting affords them or imposes upon them.

While routinisation of care may go against an expressed ideology of individualised care (Bond, 1978), it is regarded as an inevitable aspect of work when a high client-worker ratio is involved (Davies, 1976). Routinisation of work goes hand in hand with how patients are classified or, as sociologists would say, *typified*. Routines are developed and applied differentially to the appropriate patient type. These types will be specific to the work problems and situations involved.

Typification

Typification is a process of categorising individuals or events into types. It is a concept particularly associated with phenomenological perspectives. The act of slotting things, events and people into types helps to reduce the complexity of the social world by narrowing the focus of interaction to a small number of recognised types. Available typifications are a major determinant of how subsequent relationships are managed. This is because participants take more account of the characteristics of the type than of the characteristics of those who constitute the type.

An important feature of typifications is that they are 'plan-determined' (Schutz & Luckmann, 1974). That is, the practical purposes underlying typification and the circumstances in which it occurs will influence the particular types constructed. A general case of this arises in the typification of good patients and bad or problem patients. From nurses' descriptions of patients Duff and Hollingshead (1968) concluded that '*problem* patients obstructed work and *no problem* patients facilitated work' (p. 221–222). What constitutes obstruction and facilitation of work is, of course, context-specific. Murcott

(1981) identified cancer specialists' typification of 'bad' patients as those who delayed seeking attention for their condition. This was derived from the particular medical concerns of oncology, where the likelihood of successful treatment diminishes the longer a patient delays. In any context it is theoretically possible to determine what kind of patient falls into the problem category.

However there are different views of the process of constructing typifications (Hargreaves, 1977). One way is to compare individual patients against an ideal (Becker, 1952). British and North American studies undertaken in general hospitals arrive at very similar descriptions of ideal patients (Ujhely, 1963; Stockwell, 1972; Rosenthal et al, 1980).

> 'Ideally, from a nurse's perspective, all patients should be sick when they enter hospital, should follow eagerly and exactly the therapeutic programme set up by the staff, should be pleasant, uncomplaining, fit into the hospital routine, and should leave the hospital 'cured'. Good patients handle their illness well, are co-operative, as cheerful as possible, comply with treatment, provide the staff with all the relevant information, follow the rules, and do not disrupt the ward or demand special privileges and excessive attention.' (Rosenthal et al, 1980, p. 27).

Nurses identified two main types of problem patient—'forgivable' and 'wilful' (Lorber, 1975). The former needed a lot of time and resources from staff, were anxious and complained a great deal. They were, however, severely ill and their behaviour and the problems they created were not viewed as their fault. They were given the attention they demanded, especially if they showed gratitude. Patients categorised as 'wilful' were not seriously ill from the staff's point of view, but acted as if they were. They complained, were emotional and uncooperative and were regarded as deliberately deviant, wilfully causing extraordinary trouble. Rosenthal et al (1980) identified similar characteristics which gave rise to the designation 'problem patient'. Some are described as manipulative, demanding or complaining excessively. Some are physically abusive in ways which are bizarre or threatening to staff. Others have unpleasant personalities. Another problem category related to excessive complaints about pain or excessive dependence on medication. Finally some patients described as 'career patients', who sought hospitalisation for its own sake, were not considered to be legitimate patients. Included were patients judged not sufficiently ill to warrant hospitalisation or who were inappropriate for a particular ward.

After their thorough review of the literature, Kelly and May (1982) attribute nurses' definition of patients as good and bad to the way in which they either provide or withhold legitimisation of the nurses' role. The role of the caring professional is only viable with reference to an appreciative patient; therefore the good patient confirms the role of the nurse while a bad patient denies that legitimation. This analysis is borne out in the nursing of neurotic patients.

Caudill (1958) reported American nurses' problems in dealing with neurotic patients '. . . I don't think the nurse has any security. No definite body of knowledge to hang her hat on with neurotics. With psychotics you can read and study what their behaviour means. There are innumerable books on how to handle psychotics but nothing for nurses on neurotics' (p. 184). Caudill concluded that 'the nurse was fairly clear about how she was to act toward psychotic patients, but she felt uncomfortable and unsure of herself in her contact with neurotic patients' (p. 336).

John (1961) noted a similar phenomenon among British psychiatric nurses '. . . one frequently heard comments that neurotics were just in to 'dodge responsibility' or 'you don't know how much of the illness is genuine and how much is imaginary' or 'they were too pampered'. This was particularly astonishing in view of the obvious handicaps under which certain patients were placed by their illness, for example, fear of being left alone or even stepping outside their own front door. The attitudes, however, were interesting in the light of the amount of sympathy which was extended to patients with evidence of tangible illness, for example, vomiting' (p. 124).

More recently Towell (1976) found nurses describing patients with non-psychotic disorders as not being ill and, of course, patients who were not regarded as 'ill thereby lost their claims to receive help' (p. 80). Similarly Altschul (1972) observed '. . . the label of neurotic does act as a disincentive to interaction' (p. 80). This has been verified subsequently by MacIlwaine (1983) who also observed that many psychiatric nurses felt insecure in dealing with patients who were not easily cast in the sick role. She judged that nurses were happy *only* with patients who were obviously sick or disturbed and neurotic patients do not fit what nurses regard as an appropriate sick role.

May and Kelly (1982) carried out detailed investigation of the interactional and developmental process of a patient being labelled 'problem' and the consequences of her behaviour in terms of the feelings aroused in the psychiatric nurses who had to deal with her. This particular patient had a whole string of diagnoses attached to her over her 20-year patient career. Nurses were confronted with major difficulties in attempting to cope with the extremes of the patient's behaviour, which they attributed in part to her own wilful attention-seeking. The patient's 'behaviour and attitudes involved a rejection of the help nurses felt uniquely able to provide and the giving of which is central to the activities and a necessary part of their self esteem and professional image. In short (she) denied nurses professional competence and undermined their authority' (p. 288). This applies particularly to the relevance or legitimacy of nurses' therapeutic aspirations. To fail to acknowledge that psychiatric nurses have such a role is to restrict them to a peripheral role in the treatment process and underline their subordinate status positions in the health care hierarchy. The issue of problem patients is therefore intimately bound up with the nurses' sense of professional identity and with it, their authority and therapeutic competence. While May and Kelly's paper is grounded in empirical observations, it applies to a particular psychiatric setting. It would be useful to test their interpretation more broadly.

It certainly shows similarities to Jeffery's (1979) work in Casualty Departments. Patients labelled 'bad' or 'rubbish' were mostly of four kinds: trivial complaints, drunks, overdoses and tramps. Jeffery argues that they are defined as 'bad' patients because they break one or more rules:

1. Patients must not be responsible, either for their own illness or for getting better; casualty staff can only be held responsible if, in addition, they are able to treat the illness.
2. Patients should be restricted in their reasonable activities by the illness they report with.
3. Patients should see illness as an undesirable state.
4. Patients should co-operate in trying to get well.

Patients who are 'bad' or deviant, in the sense that they

break the rules about the kind of patient who is appropriate for casualty treatment, evoke particular kinds of interactions. Because they may be time-consuming they may be detained until there is sufficient slack time; they are managed in unpleasant and otherwise abusive ways or with superficial politeness, subject to post-hoc attacks in departmental gossip. Millman (1976) provides a similar example from 'The backrooms of medicine':

> 'Standing around, waiting for the police to arrive, the resident and the intern make bets on whether the case would be a real emergency or just a teenager who had swallowed too much aspirin. But at least, they assured one another, this time it wouldn't be some old alcoholic who would 'waste' all of their time in the Coronary Care Unit' (p. 49).

'Good' or legitimate patients evoked different types of interactions. This analysis has been extended by Dingwall and Murray (1983) using children as casualty patients to force a reconstruction of types, shown in Figure 9.1. In this reconstruction the category of 'deviant patient' is extended and, rather than all 'not bad' patients being placed in the good half of the dichotomy, they are further categorised as either conforming to what is normal, or preclassified before their arrival in casualty as 'interesting'. Deviant patients and conforming patients can also be reclassified after examination as 'interesting' on the basis of their clinical condition. The category into which patients are mentally slotted will influence how subsequent interactions proceed.

Therefore bestowing even informal labels on patients can have major and minor consequences. Meyer and Mendelson (1961) studied psychiatric referrals in general hospitals. They found that those labelled as disruptive, because they refused to submit to hospital routines, were referred to a psychiatrist and so became labelled as someone with a psychiatric problem. Roth and Eddy (1967) noted that rehabilitation patients typified as abusive and uncooperative were discharged from the ward and subsequently denied retraining. Laryea (1984) observed post-natal care in hospitals and found that how midwives categorised mothers in terms of their mothering ability influenced the extent to which they were perceived as requiring assistance in feeding their infants. This had repercussions for their eventual success in feeding, as well as for the mothers' own perception of their mothering ability.

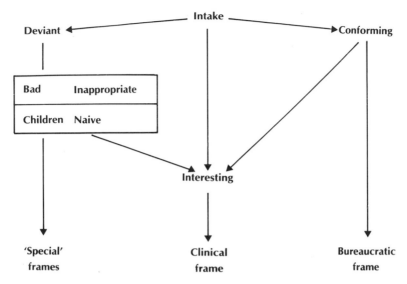

Fig. 9.1 How casualty patients are typified according to frames (Dingwall & Murray, 1983).

These examples, drawn from different areas, demonstrate the fundamental nature of typification and the way that typifications provide for systematic variations in the manner in which staff frame their encounters with patients. As such they influence the control of work and have consequences for patient outcomes.

Let us now consider some of the determinants of interaction between professionals and patients as they relate to a particular phenomenon—the management of pain.

PATIENT-STAFF INTERACTION IN THE MANAGEMENT OF PAIN

An examination of the literature about pain shows that much attention has been devoted to physiological, pharmacological, surgical, clinical and psychological aspects. This reflects the immense importance attached to the management of pain in the work of health professionals. However, there is a marked absence of sociological studies which deal with the organisational aspect of the settings in which pain is managed, or the interactions which take place, in dealing with pain, between patients and their families with hospital staff and among hospital staff themselves. Yet as Stacey & Homans wrote:

> 'The sociology of health and illness is unlikely to be able to go forward if it fails to recognise the impact of suffering upon social relationships. . . . It is, after all, the existence of human suffering, of the body and the mind, and the desire to avoid it, which have led to the development of elaborate health care systems.
>   Social relations in health and illness may perhaps have a unique quality for this reason'.

(1978, p. 297–298).

A notable exception to the dearth of work is a study by Fagerhaugh and Strauss (1977) which deals with sociological aspects of pain management in a number of hospitals in the United States. While this is entirely an American study, using an interactionist perspective, much of the theory it develops is immediately applicable to situations met in British hospitals, although the details are different in some respects. We have found no comparable British work.

Earlier in our discussions of patient-professional relations we touched on some of the features that characterise them. Important among them were power and political differentials. We related these to how patients may negotiate to obtain particular information or, to manage their treatments. Other tactics include persuasion, appeals to authority, threatening and coercion. These determine what gets done, how, when, where and by whom, and are as relevant to the management of pain as to any other aspect of health care. However, as we pointed out, any examination of what goes on in hospitals must not only take account of what happens between individuals and groups but also set these actions within the broader context of the organisation and, beyond that, the prevailing ideologies of the groups involved and more generally the social structure.

Ideology and organisation

Ideologies are ideas and beliefs, which are regarded by those who hold them as true and adequate explanations of phenomena and as furnishing sufficient grounds for them to plan and carry out courses of social action. In Chapter 8 we discussed how the major medical ideology was disease-oriented with its emphasis on an acute-care model characterised by patients with a short-term episode of illness, having treatment and being cured. It has been argued that this is inappropriate as a guiding principle for long-term and chronic care; it also poses problems for the management of chronic pain, which comprises a substantial amount of pain related work in hospitals (Kotarba, 1983).

Of course other ideologies cross-cut the dominant one. The caring which takes place in some hospitals and hospices represents a contrasting ideology emphasising patient comfort, and the management of pain in such organisations has developed along lines very different to those in traditional acute hospitals. As an example of how an organisational setting influences interaction, studies in intensive care units show that interaction between patients and staff is much more a function of monitoring machines and biological systems (Kilgour, 1972; Ashworth, 1980) than are interactions in postnatal or geriatric wards. All hospital wards will have identifiable organisational variables. Here we shall attend primarily to the interactional aspects of pain management—but urge that the organisational and ideological contexts are borne in mind.

Pain work

Interactions involving pain can have a number of different dimensions and functions. The *relief* of pain by staff and by patients readily springs to mind as most salient. (Fig. 9.2) A few moments reflection gives rise to a number of different dimensions—the handling of *expressions* of pain by patients and response to such expressions, *diagnosing* the meaning of pain, *inflicting* pain in order to carry out procedures, *preventing* and *minimising* pain if possible, and *enduring* pain, which involves short- or long-term coming to grips with pain. It would be possible to draw up profiles for different wards showing how these dimensions are differentially salient.

Of course for staff to accomplish pain work the patient's co-operation must be sought. This may be at a simple level as when the patient is asked to relax a muscle to minimise the pain of an injection, or to lie still and not interfere with a painful procedure. When the patient's view or definition of the

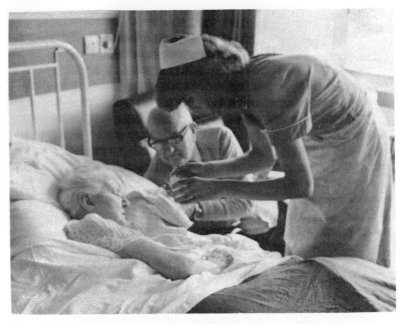

Fig. 9.2 Pain relief at the end of life involving the family, a fundamental aspect of hospice care (courtesy of Derek Bayes).

situation coincides with that of the staff, then there are likely to be no problems. If co-operation is not forth-coming then it may have to be elicited by any of a number of tactics: persuasion, appeal to sense or to authority and, above all, negotiation. In any negotiation, power and authority lie primarily with the staff. Their overriding aim is not necessarily the alleviation of pain; it may be establishing a diagnosis or providing treatment of the disease. Negotiations may relate to actions or procedures particularly painful, such as coughing after abdominal surgery or debridement of sloughing wounds. Negotiations can also cover who carries out the procedures, when they will be carried out, and even the kind of substances used. We have all met this with children afraid of the sting of lotions applied to a cut knee, or the removal of a splinter with a needle, and the kind of negotiation which goes on to allow the action to proceed. It also happens with patients.

In delivery areas of obstetric units there are likely to be a range of cultural, ideological and personal perspectives on birth and its accompanying pain. The longer labour continues, the more likely it is that discrepant positions between the mother and her attendants will be thrown into relief with regard to pain and its expression. At these times negotiations take place which can resolve in compromises between the mother experiencing her pain and delivery in the way she chooses and the staff imposing and instituting their views about pain control. Conflicting views can lead to interactional difficulties, with each party attempting to assert control over the birth process, and negotiated decisions taking place about whether and when the staff can institute pain relief measures.

In any setting there will be various degrees of professional tolerance for lay management of pain and this has recently achieved prominence in the case of birth pain. In other settings it applies to the extent that patients may use their own tried and tested remedies for relief—the trusted hot water bottle, lying in what, to observers, seem to be weird positions or pacing up and down; again, interaction with negotiation will determine the extent to which patients are permitted to institute their own remedies.

Pain trajectory

One facet of pain work which is important is the expected *pain trajectory*, that is, the course that the pain will take. In specific wards and departments staff will have had repeated experience of pain and are able to anticipate the normal trajectory for particular conditions. In surgical wards, for instance, the trajectories for common operations like herniorrhaphy or cholecystectomy are well defined. It is when some unexpected pain trajectory appears, such as genuine intractable pain in an acute surgical ward or a patient insisting that relief measures are not controlling pain when the normal measures have been tried, that problems become apparent.

The television play *Minor Complications* showed how difficult it was for staff to believe that a patient who had a routine sterilisation operation could possibly experience the kind of pain she reported, and the kind of extreme tactics the patient had to resort to in order to stimulate them into doing something about it. This dramatisation of a real person's pain showed vividly how staff had expectations of the appropriate pain trajectory for the operation, and failed to recognise the pain of peritonitis.

The ward is not organised, or the staff psychologically prepared, to deal with such events. When patients do not fit either accepted types or the routines established for pain management in a particular ward then they are amongst those likely to become labelled 'uncooperative or difficult'. This happens in part because of the time and energy demanded by these patients amidst a whole lot of other work requiring sometimes prompt attention. It is also occasioned by the interactional difficulties created for both patients and staff, by the patient having to legitimise pain and manage his expression of it while the staff may become frustrated and feel helpless in the face of unpredictable pain. It is not a matter of either patients or staff being at fault, but when mutual blame and recrimination occur they will create a downward and often irretrievable spiral in the quality of relationships.

Other patient trajectories

Of course the pain trajectory is only one of a number of trajectories relevant to patients. Illness, medical care and social trajectories are features of the patient career and biography. We know, for instance, that different cultural groups have different ways of expressing pain (Zborowski, 1969) and that different people control their pain in very different ways (Copp, 1974). Patients with long-standing pain will have worked out a drug regime which is tolerable and controls the pain; yet on coming into hospital the staff take over the relief work and an effect of drugs or allergens can be ignored to their cost. Previous experience of hospitalisation, which could have involved misdiagnosis, iatrogenic trauma, or rejection of their complaints, will create specific interactional problems on their next admission. Patients who have repeated admissions will be able to compare different hospitals and individual personnel in terms of what they regard as competence in pain control and its antithesis, incompetence resulting in unnecessary pain. An examination of patients' notes will tell us how little of what could be available to us about patient biographies is actually written for others to see. To what extent do the social and medical histories of patients really deal with such matters?

Professionals' interpretation of pain

Professionals are charged with deciding whether the patient is in pain and whether he or she is suffering. Edwards (1984) has recently considered the distinction between pain which is located in a specific bodily area and spiritual pain which is non-localised and has no specific bodily place. Bodily pain can of course give rise to mental or spiritual pain, but spiritual pain often exists alone due to loneliness, knowledge of terminal illness or what are usually referred to as psychiatric conditions. Edwards' view is that by far the greater emphasis has been given to the alleviation of bodily pain.

> 'The imperative to assist the patient gain relief from the unnecessary mental pains arising from his illness should be at least as strong as, if not stronger than, the imperative to assist in the relief of unnecessary bodily pain. Yet, it is precisely in this area that there seems to be the greatest patient neglect . . . for it happens that a patient's suffering is dismissed as 'psychological', 'imaginary' or 'unreal' when it is thought not to be bodily localised in nature . . . Those who believe that pains of soul are somehow unreal also find it easy to convince themselves that the ethics of pain management does not apply to that kind of suffering.'
> (Edwards, 1984, p. 516)

How professionals interpret pain therefore will be affected by their orientation towards bodily and spiritual pain and by how they interpret different indicators or cues provided by the patient.

If any professionals accept an obligation to help relieve the unnecessary pains of patients then it falls to them to be able to determine with reasonable accuracy not only *that* the other is suffering but also the kind of pain and its intensity and duration. However, only the person who is feeling pain can directly perceive it. This information has to be relayed to others. It can be done verbally, but onlookers expect to see signs of pain: pallor, clenched fists, perspiring, wincing or groaning. For pain to be attributed, these signs are particularly important when a pain trajectory is not normal for the ward or condition. Patients are sometimes accused of reporting more pain than they have or of complaining of pain when they have none, and this is more so when they have acquired a repu-

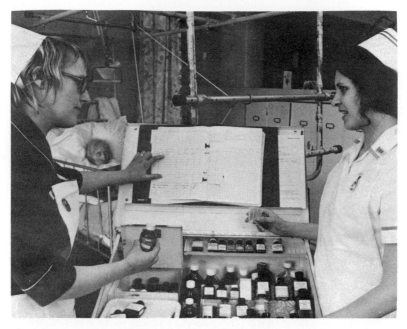

Fig. 9.3 P.R.N. pain relief is rarely the most effective (courtesy of Nursing Standard).

tation. In pain work assessing pain and legitimising pain are associated processes. Pain assessment has a number of dimensions. Listen for them when you are in any ward. You are likely to hear questions like: Does she really have pain? Is it as bad as she is making out? Is it getting worse? Is the pain real or psychological? What is causing this pain?

Staff base their assessment on their ability to read the signs, the patient's expression and other evidence of pain. This will be influenced by the staff's experience and it is not unknown for an inexperienced midwifery student to dismiss a patient's backache, in the absence of other signs, only to discover she is well advanced in labour. Patients, in order to have their pain accepted, need to be aware of the social rules that apply in a particular setting and what they need to do. It is no use waiting and tolerating, expecting to be asked about pain, in a setting where the staff wait for patients to report it before they act.

Davitz and Davitz (1981) found cultural differences among nurses' perceptions of pain and suffering. Of 12 countries studied, English nurses were ranked ninth in their inferences of psychological distress and inferred the least amount of physical pain. They report that when English nurses work in the United States, they find difficulty in adjusting to the apparently low tolerance of their patients, which is in striking comparison to the British 'stiff upper lip'. Nurses' own inferences of pain and suffering are their learned behavioural responses of their culture or sub-culture. However, these are influenced by perceptions of patients' characteristics. In general, lower-class patients were regarded as experiencing a greater degree of physical pain than middle-class patients. While patients' age made no difference to nurses' perceived physical pain, children were viewed as experiencing less psychological suffering than patients in other age groups. Nurses, therefore, interpret from an adult perspective.

Patients' ethnic origin also influenced nurses' perceptions. Jews were consistently rated as having greater physical pain regardless of age, diagnosis and social class, with the ratings moving down through Spanish, Negro, Mediterranean to Anglo-Saxon and Oriental as lowest. While such cultural differences exist both in influencing nurses' responses and in how patients are perceived, other patient characteristics are also influential. Patients who are believed to be responsible for their own conditions, such as a drunk driver or those in Jeffery's (1979) 'rubbish' category, are treated differently. Conditions difficult to diagnose precisely also raise doubts for some staff about the reality of the pain being reported. This necessitates that at times patients have to work to legitimise that they have pain and its severity.

Legitimising pain

In different contexts pain is perceived as having different degrees of legitimacy. In particular, Fagerhaugh and Strauss (1977) found that both physiotherapists and nurses tended to discount the severity of patients' low back pain and this created a breakdown in co-operation over pain work. This rejection of patients' expressions of pain occurs because of professionals' interpretation of behaviour.

Physiotherapist: 'You can tell by the way she moved around the room; if you are in a lot of pain you just can't do that. She acts as though it were a hotel rather than a hospital room'

(Fagerhaugh and Strauss, 1977, p. 120).

Tactics can then be adopted to deal with this appraisal. One tactic is to disregard complaints of pain, telling the patient she is doing well, on the assumption that if there is no real pain, then providing one waits long enough, the patient will stop or reduce claims to pain. Patients who send out the wrong behavioural cues or employ unfavourable tactics come to be negatively stereotyped, which makes the job of convincing staff about the meaning of the pain all the harder. In time, patients may just give up trying to persuade staff of the legitimacy of their pain. Patients with back pain have especially difficult problems stemming from the enduring and measureless nature of their pain compared with more easily managed post-operative pain of which well recognised trajectories exist.

Most often patients do not need to legitimise their pain but on occasions when staff, unknown to them, may be sceptical, then they need to find ways of telling them and convincing them. They may show more obvious outward signs like crying, banging, complaining regularly, growing more demanding in their requests for relief or becoming angry. If they convince the staff then attempts at relief will be instituted. However, if staff are not convinced, then they are likely to become labelled as over-demanding and dishonest about their assertions. In order to assess the 'real' nature of pain staff may resort to more extreme tactics like giving placebos instead of analgesics or observing patients' behaviour without them knowing. The interactional difficulties this creates can then become extreme.

Petrie (1967) demonstrated that there are natural variations between individuals in susceptibility to pain. Therefore as well as social differences, there are also physiological differences, giving rise to three groups of people—'The reducer, the augmenter, and the moderate' (p. 1). By definition 'The reducer tends subjectively to *decrease* what is perceived; the augmenter to increase what is perceived; the moderator neither to reduce nor to augment what is perceived' (pp. 1–2). These three types, and particularly the reducers who tend to be regarded as stoics, and the augmenters, create interactional difficulties. Stoical patients may be experiencing severe pain yet do not show signs of it. Staff must find methods of establishing and managing their pain without making patients feel loss of face or that they are giving in. On the other hand augmenters may be subject to various forms of staff abuse which not only challenge their claims concerning their own suffering or need for help but more widely their moral standing in the ward and broader community.

Balancing

The control of pain involves the balancing of priorities. We have all met this ourselves. We have to decide whether to endure a headache, which may be short-lived, or resort to aspirins which will relieve it which involves taking medication, which we dislike. There are equally simple choices to be made by patients—whether to endure a minor pain of a procedure which will increase the chance of a better diagnosis. There are also more complex and difficult decisions such as whether to undergo neurosurgery which will almost certainly yield pain relief but can also produce blindness or other sensory deficits.

Staff as well as patients are involved in a balancing process. For staff this may involve balancing the likelihood of producing addiction in non-terminal patients versus providing reliable pain relief. Patients and staff will become involved in interactions which take balancing from their different perspectives as the focus and which create contests over control. Hospital patients temporarily cede to staff members considerable control over some, although not all, aspects of their lives, behaviour and bodies. There is not always agreement about how much control has been handed over—how much right the staff have to continue with therapy despite the pain it may cause, whether as well as managing and taking decisions about some aspects of medical therapy, the staff may control pain medication in its entirety. It is because they do not wish to hand over control that some patients choose to have their babies at home and to die at home, they want to be sure of maintaining their essential rights and conducting their lives and deaths in their own style.

In every situation there are a number of choices or options

and these will be different for different people. Surgery to relieve pain which will also severely restrict mobility has very different consequences for the patient and for other family members. Extending the time between drug administrations to fit in with a routine drug round has different implications for nurses and for patients. Differential judgements in balancing pain work can have personal, cultural and social roots; they also depend on the position of the individual in the organisation—patient, relative, nurse, nursing auxiliary, doctor or physiotherapist. When decisions have to be made they will each weigh somewhat different considerations or the same ones differently. In addition, balancing will be profoundly affected by the information available. A patient cannot weigh potential addiction in the balance if he does not know of its possibility; nursing staff will be aware of the possibility of addiction but may not realise the patient's terminal condition.

SUMMARY

Patients and staff may disagree over choices, and disagreements can be implicit or explicit. They may lead to controversy and disagreement between patient and staff, as well as between staff members themselves. Unforeseen yet profound consequences can emerge, with mutual antagonism; staff withdraw from patients and patients reject staff—to the point of self-discharge and even attempted suicide.

The interactional consequences of the care of patients with pain are relevant for both patients and staff. For patients, this not only involves the amount of suffering and relief they experience but also overlaps their feelings about hospitals and their staff, their own self-concept, family relationships and the way they manage their lives. For staff, depending on how they have managed pain, there may be a growth in professional stature brought about by a job well done or a blow to personal identity when incompetence has caused or failed to reduce pain. The experience of intense involvement with a patient with pain can hold major personal significance.

In this chapter we have dealt with some of the important determining features of relationships between patients and nurses. These apply to some extent to relationships between any group of clients and professionals but, as we have pointed out, a major influence for paramedical workers is their standing in relation to medicine. We introduced this in Chapter 7 and will do so again in Chapter 10.

Our major example of interaction concerns the management of pain. While pain is a unique experience for every patient it is such an ubiquitous aspect of health professionals' work that it tends to be taken for granted as a routine aspect of work. On occasions, it becomes a major problem for staff to manage. It is when non-routine measures come into operation that profound interpersonal consequences can emerge. However, even in *routine* pain management, as in other everyday contexts, we have shown that issues of power and control are all-important, together with such features as patient typification, negotiation, persuasion and legitimation which arise in interaction. Careful sociological analysis of relationship between clients and professionals assist us understand how interaction proceeds and why at times this may become difficult for everyone. By learning to place particular interactions in work and organisational contexts we see there is nothing *abnormal* in regarding patients as popular or ideal, or as difficult or unpopular—it is a perfectly rational response to attempting to get through the work. By drawing awareness to these factors which influence interaction it may be possible to increase professionals' understanding of them and to enable them to come to terms with some of them. To do so will certainly mean attending to the organisational structure in which care is given as well as to the behaviour of the individual practitioners. This is clearly the case in the management of patients with *non-routine* pain.

We take up some of the issues of interpersonal aspects of care again in the next chapter.

REFERENCES

Altschul A 1972 Patient nurse interaction: a study of interaction patterns in acute psychiatric wards. Churchill Livingstone, Edinburgh

Armitage S K 1981 Negotiating the discharge of medical patients. Journal of Advanced Nursing 6: 385–389

Armstrong D 1982 The doctor-patient relationship 1930–80. In: Wright P, Treacher A (eds) The problem of medical knowledge. Examining the social construction of medicine. Edinburgh University Press, Edinburgh, ch 5, p 109–122

Armstrong D 1983 The fabrication of nurse-patient relationships. Social Science and Medicine 17: 457–460

Ashworth P 1980 Care to communicate: an investigation into problems of communication between patients and nurses in intensive therapy units. Royal College of Nursing, London

Balint M 1956 The doctor his patient and the illness. Pitman, London

Becker H 1952 Social class variations in the teacher-pupil relationship. Journal of Educational Sociology 25: 451–465

Beech B A, Claxton R 1980 Health rights handbook for maternity care. Association for Improvements in the Maternity Services and The Birth Centre, London

Bloor M 1976 Professional autonomy and client exclusion: a study in ENT clinics. In: Wadsworth M, Robinson D (eds) Studies in everyday medical life. Martin Robertson, London, ch 4, p 52–68

Bond S 1978 Processes of communication about cancer in a radiotherapy department. Unpublished Phd thesis, University of Edinburgh

Cartwright A 1964 Human relations and hospital care. Routledge & Kegan Paul, London

Caudhill W A 1958 The psychiatric hospital as a small society. Harvard University Press, Cambridge, Mass

Clark J McL 1983 Nurse-patient communication—an analysis of conversations from surgical wards. In: Wilson-Barnett J (ed) Nursing research: ten studies in patient care. Wiley, Chichester, ch 2, p 25–56

Copp L A 1974 The spectrum of suffering. American Journal of Nursing 74: 491–495

Comaroff J, Maguire P 1981 Ambiguity and the search for meaning: childhood leukaemia in the modern clinical context. Social Science and Medicine 15B: 115–123

Davies C 1976 Experience of dependency and control of work: the case of nurses. Journal of Advanced Nursing 1: 273–282

Davies C (ed) 1981 Rewriting nursing history. Croom Helm, London

Davies C 1983 Professionals in bureaucracies: the conflict thesis revisited. In: Dingwall R, Lewis P (eds) The sociology of the professions. Lawyers, doctors and others. MacMillan, London, ch 8, p 177–194

Davis A, Strong P 1976 The management of a therapeutic encounter. In: Wadsworth M, Robinson D (eds) Studies in everyday medical life. Martin Robertson, London, ch 8, p 123–137

Davis F 1963 Passage through crisis: polio victims and their families. Bobs-Merrill, New York

Davitz L J, Davitz J R 1981 Nurses' response to patient's suffering. Springer, New York

Dingwall R, Murray T 1983 Categorisation in accident departments: 'good' patients, 'bad' patients and children. Sociology of Health and Illness 5: 127–148

Duff R S, Hollingshead A B 1968 Sickness and society. Harper & Row, New York

Edwards R B 1984 Pain and the ethics of pain management. Social Science and Medicine 18: 515–523

Evers H 1981 Tender loving care? Patients and nurses in geriatric wards. In: Copp L A (ed) Care of the ageing. Churchill Livingstone, Edinburgh, ch 3, p 46–74

Fagerhaugh S Y, Strauss A 1977 Politics of pain management: staff-patient interaction. Addison-Wesley, California

Fairhurst E 1981 What do you do? Multiple realities in occupational therapy and rehabilitation. In: Atkinson P, Heath C (eds) Medical work: realities and routines. Gower, Farnborough, ch 11, p 171–187

Faulkner A 1980 Communication and the nurse. Nursing Times, Occasional Papers 21 76: 93–95

Freidson E 1975 Profession of medicine. A study of the sociology of applied knowledge. Dodd, Mead & Co, New York

Foucault M 1973 Birth of the clinic: an archeology of medical perception. Tavistock, London

Goffman E 1974 Frame analysis: an essay on the organisation of experience. Penguin Books, London

Hargreaves D H 1977 The process of typification in classroom interaction. British Journal of Educational Psychology 47: 274–284

Harrisson S 1977 Families in stress. A study of the long-term medical treatment of children and parental stress. Royal College of Nursing, London

Jeffrey R 1979 Normal rubbish: deviant patients in casualty departments. Sociology of Health and Illness 1: 90–107

John A L 1961 A study of the psychiatric nurse. Churchill Livingstone, Edinburgh

Kelly M P, May D 1982 Good and bad patients: a review of the literature and a theoretical critique. Journal of Advanced Nursing 7: 147–156

Kilgour D Y 1972 In intensive therapy units are nurses more concerned with machines than with patients? Nursing Times 68: 529–530

Kirkham M J 1983 Labouring in the dark: limitations on the giving of information to enable patients to orientate themselves to the likely events and timescale of labour. In: Wilson-Barnet J (ed) Nursing research: ten studies in patient care. Wiley, Chichester, ch 4, p 81–99.

Kotarba J A 1983 Chronic pain, its social dimensions. Sage, Beverley Hills

Kratz C R 1978 Care of the long-term sick in the community: particularly patients with stroke. Churchill Livingstone, Edinburgh

Kratz C R 1979 The nursing process. Balliere Tindall, London

Laryea M G 1984 Postnatal care—the midwives' role. Churchill Livingstone, Edinburgh

Ley P 1977 Psychological studies of doctor-patient communication. In: Rachman S (ed) Contributions to medical psychology, volume 1. Pergamon Press, Oxford, ch 2, p 9–42

Lorber J 1975 Good patients and problem patients: conformity and deviance in a general hospital. Journal of Health and Social Behaviour 16: 213–225

Macilwaine H 1983 The communication patterns of female neurotic patients with nursing staff in psychiatric units of general hospitals. In: Wilson-Barnet J (ed) Nursing research: ten studies in patient care. Wiley, Chichester, ch 1, p 1–24

McIntosh J 1977 Communication and awareness in a cancer ward. Croom Helm, London

McIntosh J 1981 Communicating with patients in their own homes. In: Bridge W, Clark J Mc (eds) Communication in nursing care. HM + M, London, ch 7, p 99–114

McIntyre S 1978 Obstetric routines in antenatal care. In: Davis A (ed) Relationships between doctors and patients. Saxon House, London, ch 4, p 76–105

McIntyre S 1982 Communications between pregnant women and their medical and midwifery attendants. Midwives Chronicle and Nursing Notes 95: 387–394

250 / *Sociology and health care*

Madge N, Fassam M 1982 Ask the children: experiences of physical disability in the school years. Batsford Academic Book, London

May D, Kelly M P 1982 Chancers, pests and poor wee souls: problems of legitimation in psychiatric nursing. Sociology of Health and Illness 4: 279–301

Meyer E, Mendelson M 1961 Psychiatric consultations with patients on medical and surgical wards: patterns and processes. Psychiatry 24: 197–220

Millman M 1976 The unkindest cut: life in the back rooms of medicine. Morrow, New York

Murcott A 1981 On the typification of 'bad' patients. In: Atkinson P, Heath C (eds) Medical work: realities and routines. Gower, Farnborough, ch 8, p 128–140

Nightingale F 1859 Notes on nursing. Blackie, London

Parsons T 1937 The structure of social action: a study in social theory with special reference to a group of recent European writers. McGraw-Hill, New York

Petrie A A 1967 Individuality in pain and suffering. University of Chicago Press, Chicago

Reynolds M 1978 No news is bad news: patients' views about communication in hospital. British Medical Journal 1: 1673–1676

Riley E M D 1977 What do women want? The question of choice in the conduct of labour. In: Chard T, Richards M (eds) Benefits and hazards of the new obstetrics. Spastics International Medical Publications, Heinemann, London, ch 4, p 62–71

Roper N, Logan W W, Tierney A J 1981 Learning to use the process of nursing. Churchill Livingstone, Edinburgh

Rosenthal C J, Marshall V W, Macpherson A S, French S E 1980 Nurses, patients and families. Croom Helm, London

Roth J A 1963 Timetables: structuring the passage of time in hospital treatment and other careers. Bobs-Merrill, New York

Roth J A, Eddy E M 1967 Rehabilitation for the unwanted. Atherton, New York

Royal Commission on the National Health Service 1979 (The Merrison Report), Cmnd 7615. HMSO, London

Scheff T J 1966 Typification in the diagnostic practices of rehabilitation. In: Sussman M B (ed) Sociology and rehabilitation. American Sociological Association, Washington, p 139–144

Schutz A, Luckmann T 1974 The structures of the life world. Heinemann, London

Slack P 1976 Planning training for coping with non-accidental injury. Nursing Times 72: 1561–1563

Stacey M, Homans H 1978 The sociology of health and illness: its present state, future prospects and potential for health research. Sociology 12: 281–307

Stockwell F 1972 The unpopular patient. Royal College of Nursing, London

Strong P M 1979 The ceremonial order of the clinic. Parents, doctors and medical bureaucracies. Routledge & Kegan Paul, London

Towell D 1976 Understanding psychiatric nursing—a sociological study of modern psychiatric nursing practice. Royal college of Nursing, London

Ujhely G B 1963 The nurse and her problem patients. Springer, New York

Waitzkin H, Stoeckle J D 1972 The communication of information about illness: clinical, sociological and methodological considerations. Advances in Psychomatic Medicine 8: 180–215

Wells T J 1980 Problems in geriatric nursing care: a study of nurses' problems in the care of old people in hospitals. Churchill Livingstone, Edinburgh
Zborowski M 1969 People in pain. Jossey Bass, San Francisco

FURTHER READING

Fagerhaugh S Y, Strauss A 1977 Politics of pain management: staff patient interaction. Addison-Wesley, California
Kelly M P, May D 1982 Good and bad patients: a review of the literature and a theoretical critique. Journal of Advanced Nursing 7: 147–156
Wilson-Barnet J (ed) 1983 Nursing research: ten studies in patient care. Wiley, Chichester

10

Dying, death and bereavement

INTRODUCTION

In this chapter we deal with the end of the life career: *dying* and *death*, and for those who remain, *bereavement*. We will show that, like other social phenomena, dying is socially defined and that, while definitions of clinical death are relatively straightforward, social death is far more complex.

We then turn to the social behaviour of health professionals around patients who are dying and how this is influenced by factors like age, mode of dying and the status of the dying person. Important also is the patient's level of awareness and we discuss how patients become aware that they are dying and how staff manage patients' awareness. The different interactional problems created by different awareness contexts are described.

Finally, we turn to the consequences of bereavement and influences on how individuals adjust to bereavement and the process of grieving. Bereavement is discussed specifically in the example of loss of a new baby. This highlights the often erroneous common sense beliefs held about the severity of different kinds of loss. The importance of an identity for the baby and its influence in the grieving process, and how maternity unit staff influence this identity are considered. The implications for the care of the bereaved parents are discussed.

Sociological as well as clinical aspects of dying have received a tremendous increase in attention in recent years, paralleled by the growth of alternative care institutions, particularly hospices, for the dying. Despite this growth of interest and knowledge, death is still a 'taboo' topic to be avoided in both personal and prefessional lives. Our parents steadfastly refuse to discuss with us the kind of funeral arrangements they would prefer. Dying patients are not welcomed by many wards in our hospitals.

Because childhood and infant deaths are now relatively rare (see Tables 4.3–4.5) and life expectancy has increased dramatically this century (Central Statistical Office, 1981, p. 119), many of us are well advanced in years before we actually experience the death of close family or friends. In professional life, on the other hand, death cannot be avoided although it can be minimised by choosing to work in particular settings. Death, as some people see it, is the one certainty in life. As the poet Stevie Smith wrote 'I first thought of suicide when I was eight—the thought cheered me up enormously. One might not be able to rely on life but one could always rely on death.' Some would say that we are dying from the moment of birth.

Death is something all of us will experience, although the timing and nature of our own deaths and the quality of our dying is infinitely variable. Death and dying therefore have significance for us as individuals but, in C. Wright Mills' terms, it is also a *public issue*. A situational analysis of dying— the role one is forced to play, the expectations that others have, the social space available within the context of staff-patient dichotomies, the degree of self-integrity versus isolation and depersonalisation all play their part in influencing the kind of dying which will be experienced by patients, their families and the health staff involved. In some settings, such as intensive care units and hospices, caring for the dying is much more an aspect of the day-to-day organisation of work than, for example, in a maternity or gynaecological ward. The organisational and interpersonal dynamics of particular settings strongly influence definitions of dying and death and their management. The nature of dying as a process and its categorisation is another example of *status passage* which assists our understanding of this final drama of life as a social phenomenon.

DYING AS A SOCIAL STATE OF AFFAIRS

A major impetus to providing a sociological understanding of dying was a study of 'death work' in two United States hospitals by David Sudnow (1967). Sudnow raised to the level of consciousness and social investigation, issues about the definitions hospital workers used of dying and how they arrived at the belief that someone was dying. He did not begin with any taken-for-granted meaning of dying that any one of us working in hospital will certainly have. Using *ethnographic* methods, he attempted to make explicit how health workers came to categorise patients as dying and as dead.

The social construction of particular states of being has been demonstrated recently by debates about the nature of brain death. While much of the debate has been grounded in medical-physiological definitions, it serves to highlight that there is nothing straightforward about the definition of death. Neither is the pinpointing of the point at which the patient's 'dying' begins a straightforward matter.

The dying trajectory

Recognising dying is not the same kind of activity as noticing bleeding or tachycardia. Neither is it a diagnosis and, should a patient ask 'what is the matter with me?', he is not likely to be told that he is dying. He would probably be given a disease label or an appropriate euphemism for it. Dying is a *predictive* term, indicating the likelihood that someone will die within a socially agreed time perspective. This time perspective has been called the *dying trajectory* by Glaser and Strauss (1968). They describe it in this way:

> 'When the dying patient's hospital career begins—when he is admitted to the hospital and a specific service—the staff in solo and in concert make initial definitions of the patient's trajectory. They expect him to linger, to die quickly or to approach death at some pace between the extremes. They establish some degree of certainty about his impending death—for example, they may judge that there is 'nothing more to do'

for the patient. They forecast that he will never leave the hospital again, or that he will leave and perhaps be admitted several times before his death. They may anticipate that he will have periods of relative health as well as severe physical hardship during the course of his illness. They predict the potential modes of his dying and how he will fare during the last days and hours of his life . . .' (p. 30).

Dying trajectories therefore have two characteristics. They have duration but they also have 'shape' in the sense that the dying process can be represented graphically as plunging straight down, moving up and down before the final descent, or moving onto a plateau for a considerable time.

Dying as a social construction

To be regarded as dying, the patient must fall within some set of circumstances as defined by the staff. Sometimes this prediction is well agreed. This is often the case with cancer patients, since a great deal of effort has gone into developing prognostic indicators, but even here there is a tendency to over-estimate remaining life (Parkes, 1972a) and errors regularly occur (Wright, 1981).

Even if a very specific prognosis is given this does not mean that the person will be defined as dying by those who care for him. Sudnow observed that a person would be labelled as 'dying' only if the prediction of death would involve those who made such predictions in organisational, interactional or prefessional problems. Patients in hospital in objectively the same state and with the same prognosis are defined as dying if they remain to be cared for over the duration of their last illness or if they involve the staff in making arrangements for their transfer to a hospital for the terminally ill. In both cases hospital staff will be involved in a variety of activities. Patients discharged home are far less likely to fall within the 'dying' category since their discharge absolves staff from death-related work. Definitions of dying by hospital staff therefore depend on the patient's death impinging on their work. Arguably the same happens in home care—the patient comes to be defined as dying by professionals when this process directly involves the primary health care team or indirectly involves them in making alternative arrangements for his care.

A second important feature of who is defined as dying is age relative to prognosis. Should a prognosis of two or three years be given to a 30-year-old, this has different social relevance from the same prognosis given to an 80-year-old. The patients are in very different positions in their life careers. The younger patient is still very early in his work career; he may have a young family, an active leisure and sports life and, in the normal run of things, could look forward to a long, happy and fruitful life ahead. This is not so for the aged who are already oriented towards forthcoming death. The family is increasingly independent, references to the future are curtailed and the life career is regarded more in retrospect than in prospect (Cummings & Henry, 1961). The death of an old person requires less drastic revision of others' life plans than when a young adult is dying. As we shall see, the social consequences of death are important for interactions with and around the dying person.

The process of becoming a dying person influences and is influenced by orientations towards the future rather than the past or present. Activities of families and hospital staff become organised around expectations of death. To be dying places a framework of interpretations around the individual which influences social activites. Attributes of social significance, other than age, influence both the definition of dying and activities associated with maintaining life.

Sudnow observed tremendous efforts to keep alive those who were 'special cases'—particular individuals whose lives were considered especially worthy of saving. On the other hand, those deemed socially unworthy—drunks, suicide attempts and other types of morally improper persons—had far less attention given to them to sustain life. Particularly in the case of those brought into the Emergency Unit as possibly 'Dead on Arrival', the social status of the patients as much as their physiological status influenced subsequent events. Depending on the category into which patients were slotted, they were treated in organisationally routine ways. When patients did not fit neatly into prevalent classifications—atypical deaths like that of a child or a young adult or on the other hand a morally imperfect citizen—then disruption of routinised meanings, activities and consequences was observed. The types of disruption depended on the social status and worth of the individual involved.

Types of death

In chapter 8 we discussed different definitions of illness and disease. Similarly there are different definitions of death. Sudnow has distinguished between *clinical death*—the appearance of death signs upon examination—*biological death*—the cessation of cellular activity—and *social death* when the individual is treated essentially as a corpse although still clinically and biologically alive.

Sometimes patients are clinically and biologically dead while treated as alive. A student nurse was observed by one of us changing the pyjamas of a patient who had 'died' biologically minutes before while the nurse had been cleaning him after he had been incontinent. As she rolled him onto his back she had not heard that he had stopped breathing nor did she look at his face. She then proceeded to attempt to put on clean pyjama trousers, asking the patient to assist by raising his leg. The nurse was unaware that the patient was dead clinically. For her he was not dead socially.

This may be a relatively rare instance of clinical death genuinely preceding social death. More often this happens consciously when patients are adjusted to look *as if* they are still alive when in fact they are clinically dead, or when staff prolong a meal break or busy themselves with other tasks to avoid contact with the patient. The function of such behaviour is to avoid having to carry out 'last offices', a task not welcomed by most staff members irrespective of their competence.

More regularly, the patient is treated as socially dead while still alive in biological terms. Examples of social death include seeking permission to carry out post-mortem examinations before the person has actually died. The patient can also be said to be socially dead when the doctor passes by and no longer pays attention to the patient on the ward round. He is no longer of interest in respect of further diagnosis or treatment. Nurses treat patients as socially dead when they pack up their belongings for removal prior to the patient's clinical death. Physiotherapists do so when they cease attempts at treatment while relatives, by stopping visiting, terminate social life.

Observation of the management of dying patients demonstrates the definition of the patients' state. At one time, in

Nightingale-type wards, when patients were moved to the bed adjacent to the door this was an indication that they were dying. One of our grandmothers was admitted to hospital as an obstetric emergency. She was placed in a small room immediately beside the front door of the hospital. This was a cue to the family that she was not expected to survive. She did survive, however, and was subsequently admitted to a ward. In effect she had been treated as a corpse until, despite the expectation of dying, she lived and was subsequently afforded patient status. This is an example of transitions between life and death, with social life reinstated. The movement of patients who are dying still occurs in hospitals. In a radiotherapy department patients were regularly moved to a single room from a four-bedded ward when their deaths were predicted within a few days or within a few hours (Bond, 1978).

Closer still to death, behavioural changes of staff toward the patient can be observed. As observation of biological life signs show a decline and death approaches, attention shifts from caring for the patient's possible discomforts and carrying out regular physical treatments to defining biological events. Traditional practices of suctioning, mouth care and repositioning the patient diminish while observation of pulse volume and respiration depth and rhythm become important. Routine drug therapy may be omitted.

Staff themselves also categorise deaths as 'good' or 'bad'. Wright (1981) comments on a formal reviewing system of all recent deaths by hospice staff. Deaths are evaluated on a ten point scale. In this case staff have formally defined what they regard as the characteristics of a 'good' death. High on the list is dying free from pain and with 'dignity'. Less formal accounts of what constitutes 'good' or 'proper' deaths are likely to be along similar dimensions, although they will be context specific. A 'good' death in a special care baby unit will not be the same as that in an adult intensive care unit or in a geriatric ward.

Wright found difficult deaths characterised by ineffective pain control and feelings of inadequate interpersonal relations with the patient concerned. A major contribution to a 'bad' death in the context of the hospice was the occurrence of an atypical trajectory. These may be deaths judged as abnormally quick or lingering and which, as a consequence, influence the feelings the staff have about the adequacy and appropriateness of the care given. Also patient behaviour during dying, defined by the staff as inappropriate as judged against standards of proper conduct, can render a death 'bad'. Wright (1981) cites the case of a male patient, known to be adulterous and known to grab the nurses in an affectionate way, who was labelled uncooperative.

Glaser and Strauss (1965) note two kinds of obligations which staff expect to be met by dying patients who are aware of their terminal Status. First they should not act to bring about or hasten their own deaths, for example by attempting suicide. Second are certain positive obligations about standards of courageous and decent behaviour. Their partial list includes:

> 'The patient should maintain relative composure and cheerfulness. At the very least he should face death with dignity. He should not cut himself off from the world, turning his back upon the living; instead he should continue to be a good family member, and be 'nice' to other patients. He should co-operate with staff members who care for him, and if possible should avoid distressing or embarrassing them.' (p. 86).

It is much easier for staff to appreciate those who exit with courage and grace, not merely because they create fewer scenes and cause less emotional stress but because they evoke feelings of professional usefulness. It is far less easy to endow a death with positive evaluation when the patient behaves improperly, from the staff's perspective, even though it is possible to sympathise with his terrible situation.

Awareness of dying

Many of the patients observed by Sudnow died very shortly after their admission to hospital. This was a function of acute care facilities, the most expensive type of care in the United States, and so patients stay there for the minimum number of days. His focus was on sudden rather than lingering deaths so that for many patients awareness of dying was not an issue. Comatose patients and babies also do not present problems in terms of their awareness.

Awareness is more of a problem for staff and families as well as for patients themselves when there is lingering death and patients remain alert. Cancer patients as well as those with progressive motor neurone disease fit this kind of trajectory. The close association in peoples' minds between dying and cancer may not be a function solely of the persistent high mortality rates but also the unpleasant and protracted dying which many patients still experience (Cartwright et al, 1973).

How patients become aware that they are dying and how hospital staff manage patients' awareness was the focus of work carried out by Glaser and Strauss (1965). In this study the definition of dying was not regarded as problematic. What was important was how staff managed their social interactions (Fig. 10.1) with dying patients in such a way as to attempt to exert control over how much patients were aware of their condition and how much patients could express of their awareness. Sudnow described how patients were treated—the handling of bodies, administering the flow of incoming and outgoing patients, doing diagnoses, prognoses, teaching and so on—in such a way as to fit the institutionalised daily ward routines, 'routines built up to afford mass treatment on an efficiency basis'. Glaser and Strauss observed what happened within interpersonal interactions with dying patients and how they differed according to the awareness context in which they took place.

Fig. 10.1 Medical staff learn how to manage open communications with dying patients at St Christopher's Hospice (courtesy of Derek Bayes).

Awareness of death

Glaser and Strauss found that the kinds of interactions which occurred between dying patients and hospital personnel could be explained in terms of what each party knew of the patients' prognosis at any particular time. What was important was knowledge of certainty of death—that the patient would die—and time of death—when death would be likely to occur or when this question would be resolved. Patients can be placed in any of the four categories, as demonstrated in Table 10.1. These categories represent a movement from living to dead and each is essentially a different point in a status passage. Patients move through these statuses; they are transitional points along two continua.

Let us consider an example. A man falls into category 4 before he is ill. He loses a considerable amount of weight, has problems in eating and retaining his food and develops abdominal pain. He consults his general practitioner, who refers him straight away to a surgeon. It is decided to carry out some tests and exploratory surgery. The man now shifts into category 3; there is not yet certainty about the nature of his illness or whether he will die, but we know when the question will be resolved. In theatre a stomach cancer is found. At this point he moves into category 2; that is, he will die because of his pathology but we are left with uncertainty about when he will die. He can continue to exist in category 2 until the point comes when time of death is clear. In this sense dying is a status passage, although variations in the timing of the schedule, its onset and transitions between stages can vary enormously. This variability, which is beyond our control, caused Glaser and Strauss to call dying *a non-scheduled status passage*.

An important part of this status passage is the legitimate determination of when the patient is in passage and changing his status. It is regarded as doctor's work to make definitions of the time scale involved, to announce such definitions at appropriate times to professional colleagues, relatives, perhaps even to patients and to co-ordinate the passage. The doctor decides what and when to communicate to others. He may attempt to withhold information completely from patients and staff or to withhold partial information. The patient's be-

Table 10.1 Certainty and time of death

		Time of death	
Certainty of death	Yes	1. Certain death at known time	2. Certain death at unknown time
	No	3. Uncertain death but known time when the question will be resolved	4. Uncertain death and unknown time when the question will be resolved

lief about his position will depend on what and how the doctor and others communicate, formally, and informally, verbally and non-verbally as well on as other cues in the environment. He may interpret correctly or wrongly depending on his sophistication as well as the view of his circumstances which he wishes to maintain. A recent example of a wrong definition was when a hospital patient thought he was in category 2. He thought he had a malignancy and would die of it although the time of his death would remain uncertain. In this belief he attempted suicide by jumping from the window. In fact he was mistaken in his belief, he had no malignancy and was in category 4. He had interpreted the behaviour of others as signifying a cancer diagnosis, and his beliefs about cancer were such that he thought his own death would be both inevitable and unbearable.

Awareness contexts

Interaction between individuals takes place in what Glaser and Strauss term *awareness contexts*—what each knows about the identity of the other and his own identity in the eyes of the other. Four awareness contexts are identified:

1. *closed awareness* in which the patient does not recognise impending death although everyone else does,
2. *suspicion awareness* in which the patient suspects what the others know and he attempts to confirm his suspicions,
3. *mutual pretence awareness* in which both patient and others define the patient as dying but each pretends the other does not know,
4. *open awareness* in which both staff and patients define the patient as dying, are openly aware that each holds this

definition and act relatively openly in response to this knowledge.

The tactics used by hospital staff in their interactions with patients are determined, in part, by their expectations of certainty and timing of the patient's death. How they talk with patients, the time spent with them, how the ward atmosphere is controlled are related to expectations of the patient's death and also the patient's state of awareness.

If the patient is not defined as dying then there is no particular reason to avoid discussion of death, apart from the fact that it is still a relatively undesirable topic and could potentially lead into discussing other patients. If the patient is dying, however, this can create many more problems. The nature of these problems is in part determined by the awareness context in which the interaction is taking place.

The different awareness contexts pose different kinds of problems. With closed awareness, the problem is essentially one of maintaining the patient in that state. Staff are in the position of having to construct an account of the patient's future biography that he will accept. As an example, a young boy in category 1 was moved to a single room. He was thought not to be aware of his impending death. The reason given for his move was that he had developed an infection, which explained why he felt so ill, and which necessitated barrier nursing. Fiction was enhanced by the use of gowns and masks and much handwashing. The staff attempted to maintain a closed awareness context for as long as possible to avoid the patient knowing the real state of affairs and the more difficult problems they assumed would follow from a change to another context. For the same reasons delaying tactics are engaged in when patients are to be transferred from a general hospital to a hospital or home for the terminally ill. To divulge this would certainly create suspicions which some patients would then attempt to confirm. The resulting interactional problems are largely avoided when patients are genuinely unaware.

In suspicious awareness one difficulty staff face is whether the patient is really suspicious or may even know. You may hear staff discussing whether or not a patient knows that he is terminal, and what kinds of cues he gives which lead to the staff's feeling that he is suspicious. If it is recognised that the

patient has suspicions that he is dying, then tactics are frequently adopted to avoid disclosure of information which
would reduce the patient's level of uncertainty. It is unlikely
that certainty about dying would be increased intentionally by
professionals other than, on rare occasions, by doctors and
then in response to a patient's obvious efforts to find out.

It is possible to maintain uncertainty in many ways—verbally
by referring to the future, being brisk and cheerful within normal limits, by chatting about anything and everything and so
preventing opportunities for 'difficult' conversations to arise.
It is also possible to avoid patients except to carry out 'essential' care, to linger for as little time as possible and then to
avoid creating intimacy by involving others. In short, if the
staff behave as if the patient is not dying, and act in such a
way that there is no time to talk, patients respect this right that
'other work' is more important. Should the patient ask directly, and they rarely do, then some stock response may be
produced such as 'I don't know, I'm not the doctor' or 'only
God can answer that' or, more simply, the carer may carry on
as if the question had never been asked.

Students very quickly learn how to control patients. They
observe the common tactics available in the different settings
in which they work, and how to have their own rights
honoured. Learning is achieved more by observation and imi-
tation of their seniors than by formal teaching. Professionals can
claim the right not to respond to a difficult question by just
staying silent—in effect, saying 'I will not answer that, I do not
need to.'

Mutual pretence awareness is perhaps the most common
context in hospitals. The staff know the position and know
that the patient *must* know although neither openly acknowl-
edges this to the other. There are two rationales for this pretence from the perspective of hospital staff. First, it is argued
that this is the best thing for the patient and no good would
come of open discussion; both the patient and staff would
become upset by it. Second, not to have to confront the patient
with the subject allows for better forms of care to be carried
out.

Glaser and Strauss comment that for mutual pretence to be
sustained there is extensive use of props. This includes continuing to carry out particular forms of care—not only those

associated with keeping the patient comfortable (e.g. by maintaining adequate hydration and clean and intact skin) but also,
for example elaborate drug therapy for no therapeutic benefit
in a physical sense. Routines such as recording temperature
and writing up fluid balance charts are continued. As Sudnow
observed, when nurses see death approach they may omit
some of their routines; in other words some of the props are
dispensed with. However, by this time the patient would not
be in a state to notice. So long as the patient is sufficiently
alert to know what is going on, then the props must be sustained if mutual pretence is to continue.

Avoidance of dangerous topics is important. If the patient
chooses to refer to the future *as if* it will be then staff will go
along with this just as they will allow him to totter to the toilet
unaided in a brave show of pretence. While the aim is to focus
on safe topics which suggest that life is going on as usual, if
there is a slip then *both* parties will minimise and conceal it,
each actively sustaining the status quo. Otherwise mutual
pretence would change to an open awareness context.

Open awareness reduces some of the interactional problems just described, but other complexities take their place.
Two important types of difficulty are associated with time of
dying and the nature of dying. While patients may know that
they are dying, they may not know when. They may or may
not wish to confirm this. Patients may also have definite ideas
about how they wish to die and these ideas may or may not
be in accordance with those of their families or the
professionals charged with their care. Their main concern may
be freedom from pain, irrespective of drug dosage, while the
staff may remain concerned about frequency and levels of
narcotics being administered. They may wish to die at home,
while their family fears having them home because they
cannot cope. Being able to discuss these things can create all
manner of problems.

This can be exacerbated by expectations held by
professionals of how patients *should* behave. If nurses
consider the maintenance of appropriate fluid intake
important, whereas the patient has decided that he does not
want to drink or eat any more, he will resist attempts to
persuade him. The patient who is afraid of dying may want
someone by him almost constantly, whereas nurses have

other demands on their time and some cannot tolerate long periods with dying patients. We have already touched on some of the behaviours defined as 'appropriate' and which give rise to categorising deaths as good and bad. Some patients themselves attempt to act as if dead before they die—by refusing to talk and hiding themselves below their sheets. Open awareness is acceptable only so long as the patient shows courage and grace, does not create scenes and does not make emotional demands. Patients who die gracefully are often long remembered by staff.

PROFESSIONAL COMPOSURE

In their interactions with dying patients and their families it is important for professionals to maintain their composure. Glaser and Strauss stress the importance of nurses in supporting other staff members during this time. Composure is largely determined by awareness of certainty and time of death. We have described the transitions through which patients pass; the stages in this process exert a strong effect on the appropriateness of the strategies to maintain composure. Always there are competing conditions which, on the one hand, assist the maintenance of composure and, on the other hand, tend to break it down.

A major strategy is the degree of involvement between patients and professionals. At one level the *sentimental order* of the ward influences involvement. *Sentimental order* is a construct derived from the collective expression of attitudes and mood and the forms of behaviour used to manage different kinds of work pressures. One aspect of the sentimental order of wards is the death ratio—the proportion of patients who will die. The socially determined appropriate level of involvement with patients depends on the death ratio, with higher levels of involvement permitted where there is a low death ratio.

While it may be possible to gauge the level of involvement deemed appropriate for a particular ward, over-involvement by individual members of staff can happen by virtue of their particular relationship with a patient; they may have cared for him in an earlier admission, the patient may resemble a close relative or friend, the illness may be like that of a family member, it may be easy to identify with the patient's age or other social attributes. Close involvement is far less problematic when death is uncertain than when death and time of death become progressively defined. On the other hand an inappropriately low level of involvement can also create problems. Distance with the patient may have been established because death was expected and, for some reason, dying has become protracted and time of death less certain.

Composure is also influenced by the extent to which staff feel negligent, either about particular features of care or about standards of professional conduct. Saving a patient is a high achievement and failure to save can seriously threaten composure when death becomes inevitable. When a patient moves into the 'nothing more to be done' phase, even while time of death is unknown, a major goal of care is comfort. Providing good quality comfort care can counter balance previous feelings of negligence. However, it is not always possible to achieve this goal. Then, as at other times, a major composure strategy is to forget the patient—out of sight out of mind—but this is incompatible with giving good comfort care, involving regular and sometimes prolonged contact. Thus composure is threatened.

We have already discussed social death. A less extreme form of this is to carry out tasks for patients using expressive avoidance. This way of managing patients is increased in potency if the patient is sedated. In this way the patient's physical needs are met but his being as a person is avoided by the wearing of blank expressions, exuding dignity and efficiency, avoiding conversation, and spending as little time as possible carrying out the tasks. Only routine care is carried out, so that feelings of helplessness and negligence, as well as the risk of emotional involvement, are minimised.

Depersonalisation is less easy when long-term and lingering patients have become friends. Attachment may be to the patient as well as his family and the dying becomes harder for everyone. This constitutes a real threat to composure and it is here that group strategies may take over to share care and lessen the burden on any one person. The intensity of feeling is increased when a closed awareness context prevails, yet staff feel that the patient would be served best by talking openly about the implications of dying. In this context, being able to behave in what would be a more natural way by displaying involvement would aid composure and reduce the possibility of losing the patient's trust. As it is, there are strong pressures not to change to open awareness.

Collective moods among staff serve to reduce involvement and maintain composure when death is certain. By viewing it together as inevitable and even desirable, there is a move towards preparation for the ordeal. This is assisted by developing collective rationales to explain and condone their acceptance of a death—be it as best for the family or release for the patient. There is also a feeling of relief among the staff, that certainty about what to expect has been achieved and, once the patient dies, relief that the ordeal is over for the staff, the patient and the family.

While the dying and death of a patient may be long remembered by those who looked after him and the feelings of loss involve both personal and professional dimensions, it is the bereaved family that has most to bear.

BEREAVEMENT

The preceding discussion has indicated that how people are bereaved can vary enormously but, irrespective of its nature, bereavement can be identified as a specific event. One way of conceptualising bereavement is to regard it as a loss—in this case the irretrievable loss of a person. As we discussed in chapter 4, theoretically, the idea of loss and consequent reaction to it has encapsulated such diverse areas as loss of a limb, spouse or home (Parkes, 1972b) and even more diffuse types of social discontinuity (Marris, 1974).

Bereavement is characterised by two components—grief, involving psychological and physiological response patterns; and mourning, behaviour influenced by custom and mores (Averill, 1968). Marris (1974) describes the recent English traditions of mourning and how they symbolise grief.

'Traditionally, full mourning in England would begin with the shuttering of the house, and the hanging of black crepe, while the dead person was laid out in his or her old home. The funeral procession itself was decked with as much pomp as the family could afford, or its sense of good taste suggested. Thereafter, the nearest relatives wore black for several months, and then half mourning for a while, gradually adding quiet colours to their dress. They lived in retirement, avoiding public pleasures or any show of gaiety until their mourning was over. Cheerful events in the family, such as a marriage, were postponed a while: and a widow or widower could not decently consider proposals for remarriage until the mourning had run its term. But the term was limited by convention, and the social pressure which would condemn too hasty a return to normal life also reproved an overprolonged indulgence of grief. At first, the family might visit the grave often, laying fresh flowers there; in time they would go less and less, but a visit on the anniversary of the death might become a perennial ritual of remembrance. Such customs symbolise the stages of grief: at first the household withdraws, shutting out life; then, by the ceremony of the funeral, it emphasises its concern for the dead; then, through the months of mourning, it gradually comes to terms with its loss. And when the period of mourning is over, it can take up the thread of life without guilt, because the customs of society make this its duty. At the same time, the observance of these rituals sustained a relationship with the dead: it was done for their sake, as much as for the world. Conventional Christianity allowed the bereaved to imagine that the dead looked down from Heaven, saw the flowers on the grave, and appreciated them. Thus the relationship was not broken abruptly, but attenuated through all the acts that turned the harshness of death into the gentler sorrow of laying to rest. Yet these acts also acknowledge death – they related to one who had died, not a pretence of a living person.'

(Marris, 1974, pp. 29–30)

In all societies the rites of mourning interpret a conflict between the acknowledgement of death and the continuity of life. Changes in social behaviour in Britain—the absence of public expression of mourning by dispensing with black, the interest in secular rather than Christian funerals, increase in cremation rather than burial, high re-marriage rates among the young—stress the living rather than the dead.

Bereavement may proceed through distinct stages. The first is identified as shock, sometimes accompanied by denial of the death. The next stage involves intense grief, involving a search for the lost person and, as the loss in realised, resulting in depression and apathy. To achieve resolution a stage of reorganisation is reached and life taken up again (Parkes, 1975a; Lindemann, 1944).

Shock

This process of adjustment to bereavement has been conceptualised as a *psycho-social transition*, defined by Parkes (1971) as major changes in life space which are lasting in their ef-

Fig. 10.2 The symbolism of a State funeral (courtesy of BBC Hulton Picture Library).

fects, which take place over a relatively short period of time and which affect large areas of the assumptive world. The assumptive world implies the world which a person assumes to exist on the basis of his previous experience. In the context of bereavement, the dead person has been one such influence on this world and, where the relationship has been that of husband and wife, then major modifications of the assumptive world are likely.

Grief and grieving

The process of grief involves comparing the assumptive world that was with the new external situation. Parkes (1982) attributes the sense of loss of purpose or meaning in life that typically follows a major loss to the perceived discrepancy between what was and what is the new situation. For Marris (1974) grief 'is the expression of a profound conflict between contradictory impulses—to consolidate all that is still valuable and important in the past, and preserve it from loss; and at the same time, to reestablish a meaningful pattern of relationships in which the loss is accepted' (p. 31). In order to review and revise assumptive models the person involved will turn to others to whom he is attached, in the hope that they will help him cope during this period. However when the death of a loved one has occurred, the person to whom the bereaved would normally have turned is no longer there. Indeed, the death of a spouse probably has greater impact on people in terms of their ability to adjust than any other event in their lives (Holmes & Rahe, 1967). Hence the generalised finding that those under adversity who have few 'available attachments' are at special risk of developing neurotic symptoms (Henderson, 1982).

Studies which have monitored the responses of bereaved widows and widowers [by Maddison and Walker (1967) and Raphael (1977)] have demonstrated the importance of the remaining family as an influence on grieving. The poorest health outcomes were observed in those who perceive the family as 'unhelpful'. Poorer outcomes are also demonstrated when multiple losses are involved.

It is not necessarily the intensity of love in the relationship which governs the perceived degree of loss. Parkes (1975b) found that ambivalent relationships and those characterised by clinging were more likely to give rise to pathological grief reactions. The survivors of unhappy marriages may harbour bitterness, resentment and guilt and, as a consequence, are less able to handle their grief (Bowling & Cartwright, 1982).

The loss of a spouse forces the bereaved individual to make profound and lasting changes in both his or her personal and social environments. This will involve adjustments to living alone, isolation and loneliness, taking on new roles and tasks and dealing with financial changes. These constitute the *normal* tasks which the bereaved spouse must work through in order to come to terms with his loss. This can take from months to years to accomplish and, in some cases, will never be achieved. The death of Prince Albert and the ensuing chronic mourning of Queen Victoria demonstrated this.

Grief, as well as becoming chronic, may be arrested or magnified in intensity. On the basis of clinical and research studies Parkes (1982) has postulated a number of causes of pathological grief.

Overt grieving may be avoided by social pressures, which demand 'a stiff upper lip', and when family pressures are such that its expression is avoided. In some cases the bereaved consider the demands of dependents; for instance mothers of young children often 'avoid' grieving in order to protect them. The bereaved may fear being labelled as having a 'breakdown', attributed by others to loss of emotional control, and so may inhibit expressions of grief and situations which evoke it. Fear of the physiological accompaniments of distress, which may be interpreted as evidence of incipient breakdown, at times leads to their blocking by the use of tranquillizers, sedatives or antidepressants. These serve only to delay or distort expressions of grief, rather than to promote working through it. Yet Bowling and Cartwright (1982), from a sample of elderly bereaved, found a tendency for general practitioners to prescribe such drugs for widows with whom they had had little home contact before their bereavement. These general practitioners were described by widows as less caring than those who avoided prescribing drugs to control grief.

Rather than avoiding grief, other circumstances may predispose to chronic grief. Again, social influences are prevalent rather than biological ones. In some circumstances others idealise the mourner, for example, children may identify the bereaved parent as a living memorial to the dead. Their behaviour in response to their remaining parent's attempts to achieve autonomy, especially in the resumption of sexual relationships, perpetuates grieving. In instances where the loving relationship was ambivalent, chronic self-punitive grief may persist to produce psychopathology (Parkes, 1965). When the lost person has fostered a sense of inferiority or insecurity, the remaining spouse is left with little confidence to survive the loss. Undue pressure on the survivor to undertake tasks and responsibilities for which he does not believe himself qualified or capable or the absence of satisfactory alternatives to the mourning role—those who believe themselves to be on the 'scrap heap'—can find themselves unable to develop constructive solutions to their loss.

Several determinants influence the magnitude of grief. A number of studies have established that the magnitude of grief is greater following deaths that were both unexpected and untimely. The exception is in the elderly where death, while sudden, is not entirely unanticipated (Clayton et al, 1973; Bowling & Cartwright, 1982). It is proposed that anticipation facilitates modification of internal models of the world; new expectations and plans evolve which make it easier to approach the problems of bereavement. When anticipatory grief has not been established such a model is lacking, and lasting difficulties can be created by defences which avoid realisation of what has happened, or by overwhelming disorganisation of the psychic world. The magnitude of the transition, the amount of change in the assumptive world will relate to the amount of grief. There would be, in most instances, a sizeable difference in response to loss of a wife and loss of an old umbrella. The extension of this is to multiple losses—not only of persons, but of jobs, self-respect and homes. When a survivor is himself physically or physiologically incapacitated then reduced psychophysiological resistance will magnify the grief response.

Let us now consider in some detail a special form of loss—that of a new baby.

MISCARRIAGE, STILLBIRTH AND PERINATAL LOSS

Just as the past 20 years have shown an increased concern in understanding the social consequences of bereavement, so this concern has extended to miscarriage, stillbirth and perinatal loss (Bourne, 1968; Giles, 1970; Lewis, 1976). Miscarriage is often not considered as bereavement, since there is no person for whom to grieve. Childbirth and childcare literature, in concert with society generally, studiously avoids reference to such events. Recently Alice Lovell (1983) examined some of the ambiguities which arise in pregnancies which do not result in the delivery of a live baby, or where the baby dies shortly after birth.

A common-sense view is that the earlier the pregnancy fails, the 'less' the loss and the 'less' the grief. In this case miscarriage would be less sad than stillbirth which would be less sad than losing a baby who lived, however briefly. This is linked to ideas of babies becoming persons. All live births require a birth certificate; stillbirths require a document of still birth, and both must be given some form of burial or cremation. Miscarriages, on the other hand, may be treated as gynaecological scrapings and either incinerated or macerated and flushed away. Lovell quotes from some correspondence in *The Lancet* in 1981 which shows that since weeks of gestation are inexact, some probable stillbirths and neonatal deaths are incorrectly recorded as miscarriages in order both to save the expense of a funeral and to reduce distress to parents. This rests on the assumption that not having to arrange a funeral and categorising the loss as a lesser one will make it easier to bear. Lovell's findings challenge this view. It was mothers whose babies had lived, even fleetingly, who made better sense of their tragedy. Those who saw their dead babies regarded this as a positive action and none regretted it. Having seen their babies was associated with feelings of having accepted the loss of their dead child, as was knowing what had happened to the baby subsequently. These factors appear to assist in building up memories and constructing an identity for the lost baby.

This idea of identity is associated with being able to grieve. However, under certain conditions, being able to construct an identity for the baby was interfered with. Having a damaged or imperfect baby inhibited hospital staff from showing the baby to parents. It is as if babies who do not look right are morally as well as physically imperfect. Since well formed babies are described in terms of their 'perfectness', mothers of deformed babies felt guilt and doubts about their own self-worth, since their babies were defined to them by hospital staff primarily in terms of their abnormality and physical appearance.

By contrast, perfectly formed babies, beautiful babies who die are, by implication, a tragic loss. Rather than being unfit to be seen, unfit to be loved, unfit to live and so not worthy of mourning, babies defined as beautiful fall into the stereo type 'beautiful is good'. Mothers whose babies were normal in appearance were not discouraged from seeing them in the same way as mothers of deformed babies. While professionals may believe that the sight of a deformed baby would be distressing, arguably fantasies about the baby are more frightening than reality. And, while there would be initial distress, this presupposes that there is a single adverse response rather than a process of adjustment to the loss. None of the people in the study had photographs of their dead babies.

Loss of the baby also produces loss of the anticipated role of mother into which women are progressively socialised during the antenatal period. The women described feeling that they were regarded as an embarrassment to staff in postnatal wards. The problem of what constitutes a baby, in respect of gestational age, applies similarly to the social construction of mother. At what point do midwives' patients become mothers? Sudnow (1967) observed this happened when the head was crowning but before a live birth was assured. It did not happen when a non-viable baby was expected, and when a stillbirth occurred all references to 'mother' were suspended. Lovell noted that women were referred to as 'mother' from the beginning of antenatal care. In her assumptive world, in a very short space of time a woman can become a *mother* and not a mother, and also lose her anticipated new baby.

She can also be stripped of her status as patient. Since maternity units are geared to the production of live babies, non-mothers present problems by having no babies to feed, bathe and weigh. Lovell observed that they had no legitimate role; this problem was solved at times by isolating the women from other mothers, not performing routine postnatal care, avoiding them for long periods and at times, sending them home with what was felt as indecent haste. When women felt a 'strong sense of dismissal', which might not be related to actual days spent in hospital after the birth, they were less able to come to terms with their loss. This was exacerbated when they felt that their loss might have been avoided.

The feelings expressed by some mothers about the absence of postnatal assistance to deal with the loss can be associated with the feelings of the staff about such losses. The goal of midwifery is healthy mothers and live babies. Feelings of failure associated with deaths and the difficulties associated with such feelings can be reflected in the way mothers are handled. Often midwives, when discharging such patients, will say 'see you next year', implying another and more successful attempt at producing a baby—in which case the mother will be more acceptable. Ejection into the community does not necessarily entail any more comforting an environment, since lay and professional attitudes reflect and reinforce each other—the life and death of the baby were treated as if the latter cancelled out the former, and renderered the baby 'invisible'.

SUMMARY

In this chapter we reached the end of the life career and explored the social construction of death and dying. The impact of the final stages of life on those remaining after death is also described. As we have seen in a number of other chapters, a sociological perspective on everyday events provides us with new insights. The major advantage of gaining a sociological understanding of dying, death and bereavement is to assist both professional and lay carers to make these events more bearable to all involved. Dying contravenes the ideological basis of health care provision in our society, which focuses on 'saving' patients and restoring them to health. Just as this high technology ideology is inappropriate in the care of those with chronic illness, so it creates problems for those who are charged with the care of the dying and bereaved. In this chapter we refer to a variety of studies which highlight the difficulties that health professionals face when coping with the final drama of life. This was most vividly described in midwifery where miscarriages, still-births and perinatal loss are at odds with the production of live healthy babies. We noted that when they happen staff do not always cope in ways which are in the best interest of patients and their families. A sociological understanding might help staff to overcome their feelings of failure. These feelings were shown to correlate strongly with the way staff coped and managed the 'bereaved mothers'.

Most deaths are unavoidable; they are the natural conclusion to the life career. Death is normal and inevitable. So is grief. Yet society as a whole, and health professionals, at times inhibit its expression and fail to recognise the normality of its psychological and physiological concomitants which are inextricably associated with death in its social context.

In chapter 4 we discussed how different individuals cope in different ways with bereavement, some better than others. Bereavement, and especially inhibited processes of grieving, are an obvious social cause of illness. Again we can recognise an important role in primary prevention, not of death, but of the untoward consequences of bereavement. Parkes (1979, 1980) has shown that it is possible to identify those survivors most 'at risk' and to intervene in such a way as to provide supportive care for those who are otherwise bereft of supportive relationships. Group interventions for losses other than bereavement reflect positive efforts (Rahe et al, 1979; Dammers & Harpin, 1982), but such developments remain the exception. This is partly a result of the dominance of the medical model with its emphasis on the diagnosis and treatment of disease; but in the case of dying and bereavement, social taboos complicate and inhibit progress. An understanding of the social context of bereavement may lead to health professionals becoming more supportive of the bereaved.

One sub-culture in the health care system, the hospice movement, has changed the approach of some health professionals but it is doubtful to what extent it has influenced those working in general hospitals and the community services. Continued sociological interest in this topic may not only add to our understanding of social behaviour in the context of death but make a positive contribution to the changing

of practice to the benefit of patients, their relatives and professionals alike.

REFERENCES

Averill J R 1968 Grief: its nature and significance. Psychological Bulletin
    70: 721–748
Bond S 1978 Processes of communication about cancer in a radiotherapy
    department. Unpublished Phd thesis, University of Edinburgh
Bourne S 1968 The psychological effects of stillbirths on women and their
    doctors. Journal of the Royal College of General Practitioners 16: 103–112
Bowling A, Cartwright A 1982 Life after a death. A study of the elderly
    widowed. Tavistock, London
Cartwright A, Hockey L, Anderson J 1973 Life before death. Routledge &
    Kegan Paul, London
Central Statistical Office 1981 Social Trends No 12. HMSO, London
Clayton P J, Halikas J A, Maurice W L, Robins E 1973 Anticipatory grief and
    widowhood. British Journal of Psychiatry 122: 47–51
Cummings E, Henry W E 1961 Growing old: the process of disengagement.
    Basic Books, New York
Dammers J, Harpin V 1982 Parents' meetings in two noenatal units: a way
    of increasing support for parents. British Medical Journal 285: 863–865
Giles P F H 1970 Reactions of women to perinatal death. Australia and New
    Zealand Journal of Obstetrics and Gynaecology 10: 207–210
Glaser B G, Strauss A L 1965 Awareness of dying. Aldine, Chicago
Glaser B G, Strauss A L 1968 Time for dying. Aldine, Chicago
Henderson S 1982 The significance of social relationships in the etiology of
    neurosis. In: Parkes C M, Stevenson-Hinde J (eds) The place of attachment
    in human behaviour. Tavistock, London, ch 11, p 205–231
Holmes T H, Rahe R H 1967 The social readjustment rating scale. Journal of
    Psychosomatic Research 11: 213–218
Lewis E 1976 The management of stillbirth: coping with unreality. Lancet
    II: 619–620
Lindemann E 1944 Symptomatology and management of acute grief.
    American Journal of Psychiatry 101: 141–148
Lovell A 1983 Some questions of identity: late miscarriage, stillbirth and
    perinatal loss. Social Science and Medicine 17: 755–761
Maddison D, Walker W L 1967 Factors affecting the outcome of conjugal
    bereavement. British Journal of Psychiatry 113: 1057–1067
Marris P 1974 Loss and change. Routledge & Kegan Paul, London
Parkes C M 1965 Bereavement and mental illness. Part 1. A clinical study of
    the grief of bereaved psychiatric patients. British Journal of Medical
    Psychology 38: 1–12
Parkes C M 1971 The first year of bereavement. A longitudinal study of the
    reaction of London widows to the death of their husbands. Psychiatry
    33: 444–467
Parkes C M 1972a Accuracy of predictions of survival in later stages of
    cancer. British Medical Journal 2: 29–31
Parkes C M 1972b Components of reaction to loss of a limb, spouse or
    home. Journal of Psychomatic Research 16: 343–349
Parkes C M 1975a Bereavement: studies of grief in adult life. Penguin
    Books, Harmondsworth

Parkes C M 1975b Determinants of outcome following bereavement. Omega 6: 303–323

Parkes C M 1979 Evaluation of a bereavement service. In: De Vries A, Cormi A (eds) The dying human. Turtledove, Ramat Gan, Israel, p 389–402

Parkes C M 1980 Bereavement counselling: does it work? British Medical Journal 281:3–6

Parkes C M 1982 Attachment and the prevention of mental disorders. In: Parkes C M, Stevenson-Hinde J (eds) The place of attachment in human behaviour. Tavistock, London, ch 14, p 295–309

Rahe R H, Ward H W, Hayes V 1979 Brief group therapy in myocardial infarction rehabilitation: three to four year follow up of a controlled trial. Psychosomatic Medicine 41: 229–242

Raphael B 1977 Preventive intervention with the recently bereaved. Archives of General Psychiatry 34: 1450–1454

Sudnow D 1967 Passing on. The social organisation of dying. Prentice-Hall, Englewood Cliffs, NJ

Wright M 1981 Coming to terms with death: patient care in a hospice for the terminally ill. In: Atkinson P, Heath C (eds) Medical work: realities and routines. Gower, Farnborough, ch 9, p 141–151

FURTHER READING

Glaser B G, Strauss A L 1965 Awareness of dying. Aldine, Chicago

Oakley A, McPherson A, Roberts H 1984 Miscarriage. Fontana, London

Parkes C M, Weiss R S 1984 Recovery from bereavement. Harper and Row, London

Sudnow D 1967 Passing on. The social organisation of dying. Prentice-Hall, Englewood Cliffs, NJ

Professions and
  occupations
Becoming a professional
Profession and gender
Profession and the future

11

The professional career

INTRODUCTION

In this chapter the word career is used in its more traditional sense to describe occupational or professional progress. We focus on three main themes: the characteristics of occupations which give them professional status, professional socialisation and the significance of gender in the understanding of professionalism.

An understanding of the professional career requires that we distinguish between the sociological uses of the terms *occupation* and *profession*. In so doing we shall introduce the concepts of *semi-profession* and *para-profession*. To do this we shall draw on some of the themes, concerned with the organisation of health care, already identified in earlier chapters, particularly themes concerned with inter-professional relations in Chapters 7, 9 and 10.

We introduced some general ideas about socialisation when discussing the life career in Chapter 5. Now that we are focusing on the professional career our attention turns to professional socialisation in particular the process of becoming a professional, of moving out of the world of laymen and into that of professionals.

During this status passage, the individual acquires the knowledge, skills and sense of occupational identity characteristic of the professional (Moore, 1970). This is achieved by moving through educational programmes in well identified and often cohesive cohorts. Roles as students are structurally tied to future roles in the occupational system and there are clearly identifiable procedures for entrance to and exit from professional education.

While the formal educational programme is of particular importance in professional socialisation, other important influences exert their effects on students. As Becker (1972) wrote in a chapter entitled 'School is a Lousy Place to Learn Anything':

> 'Students do not learn what the school proposes to teach them. Colleges do not make students more liberal and humane . . . nor do they have any great effect on students' intellectual development and learning . . . Medical school training has little effect on the quality of medicine a doctor practices . . . Actors considered expert by their peers have seldom gone to drama school . . . The spectacle of elementary and secondary education gives credence to Herndon's . . . wry hypothesis that nobody learns anything in school, but middle class children learn enough elsewhere to make it appear that schooling is effective . . .'
>
> (Becker, 1972, p. 90)

Of course the process of socialisation begins long before entry to a professional career. Its roots lie much earlier when the individual is faced with an array of possible occupations. The answer to 'what will you do when you grow up?' will change for some children many times over the years until a stable career choice is reached. Early experiences will contribute to the wish to join a particular occupational group. Particularly important is gender. However, before considering gender and professions as particular occupations let us turn, first, to the concept of profession itself.

PROFESSIONS AND OCCUPATIONS

When a number of people perform the same work using common methods, which are passed on to new recruits, we may say that workers have become organised into an occupational group. *Profession* is subsumed under the general category *occupation*, but it is usually regarded as a special kind of occupation. The concept of profession is more complex than this, however, having many usages and definitions (Freidson, 1975). One use of the concept is a means of flattery (Becker,

Fig. 11.1 Fed-up with their 'shop-assistant' type uniform, nurses designed their own style with different colours for each grade, 'It will do wonders for the nurses' morale and professional image', said the District Nursing Officer (courtesy of Nursing Times).

1971). It may distinguish the bona fide worker from one who is not, the professional from the amateur, as applied to musician, home decorator or engineer. Sociologists further add to the confusion by using it in different ways; some use it to characterise a broad social stratum including many different occupations for example the Registrar General uses the term to classify occupations in Social Class I (see Ch. 3) and includes university teachers, lawyers, doctors and civil engineers. Others use it to characterise very particular occupations.

One way in which sociologists have tried to reach agreement about professions, albeit unsuccessfully, is to define the characteristics which differentiate them from other occupations. This *attribute approach* to professions rests on the basic assumption that it is possible to draw up such a fixed list of attributes which will transcend time and place. A number of such lists have been drawn up over the years; these have overlapped but have also differed in a number of ways (Roth et al 1973). In defining such a set of criteria, an ideal type of professional occupation can be identified.

Such an approach was developed by Flexner, who identified six criteria of profession:

> '. . . professional activity was basically *intellectual*, carrying with it great personal responsibility; it was *learned*, being based on great knowledge and not merely routine; it was *practical* rather than academic or theoretic; its techniques could be taught, this being the basic of professional education; it was strongly organised *internally*; and it was motivated by altruism, the professionals viewing themselves as working for some aspect of the good of society'.
>
> (Becker, 1971, p. 88)

Another occupation could therefore be matched against such a list and some judgment made about its eligibility. Freidson (1983) rejects such a method of definition and argues that profession is defined and used in two very different ways. First is the concept of profession that refers to a broad group of relatively prestigious but quite varied occupations whose members have all had some kind of higher education and who are identified more by their educational status than by their occupational skills. This applied initially to medicine, to law and the clergy. Second is the concept of profession that is limited to a number of occupations which have particular institutional and ideological traits, more or less in common. In this sense *professionalism* is a way of organising an occupation (Johnson, 1972). It provides not only for status but also produces distinctive occupational identities and market rights for clients, which sets occupations apart from, and often in opposition to, each other. Status is achieved not primarily from the educational institutions themselves but rather from the actual professional training and the sense of identity achieved by particular corporately organised occupations to which specialised knowledge, ethicality and importance to society are imputed, and for which privilege is claimed (Freidson, 1983). It is Freidson's argument that profession is a historically based and socially valued concept and that it is inevitable that disagreements exist about the social, economic, political and

symbolic rewards which should accrue to those labelled professional, and about those individuals and occupations which
are entitled to be so labelled. While definitions of profession
require to be made explicit by those studying them in order
that readers know what they mean, such definitions may arise
from folk concepts, i.e. that professions are what the man in
the street says they are. However, it would be naive to consider that there is a single folk concept of profession, just as
there is no single definition of such concepts as social class.
Different answers would be obtained depending on who was
asked—for example, among those in 'aspirant' occupational
groups seeking the rewards of a professional label. Recently
Dingwall (1976) has argued that rather than sociologists attempting to provide a single definition of profession they
would do better to devote themselves to studying and explaining the ways that ordinary members of particular occupations employ and invoke the term during the course of their
everyday activities. That is, to study how members 'accomplish' profession independently of any imposed sociological definition. Of course to accomplish profession relies on
taking into account the projected conceptions of other occupations with which interaction takes place and negotiating
with them some workable agreement on usage and the activities and relationships it implies. In order to be able to gain
an official title of 'profession' Freidson (1983) argues that it is
insufficient that occupations accomplish profession in their
interpersonal relations or negotiate it through their daily tasks
with those with whom they work. The ability to do so is predefined by the nature of the job and only certain jobs have the
resources for negotiation. These reside in the institutional
characteristics of the occupation and in such characteristics of
its members as their formal education, both of which must
conform to *official* criteria of profession. Thus administrative
categorisations of profession and indeed sociological ones, influence whether occupations can negotiate and achieve
profession.

Professional autonomy

Freidson (1975), who has concentrated on medicine as the
prototype profession, argues that the most strategic distinc-

tion between professions and other occupations lies in their legitimate organised autonomy. '. . . the only true important and uniform criterion for distinguishing professions from other occupations is the fact of autonomy—a position of legitimate control over work' (Freidson, 1975, p. 82). This is a deliberately granted right, by society, for a group to control its own work. This includes the exclusive rights to determine who can legitimately do its work, how the work should be done, and to declare any outside evaluation of its work illegitimate and intolerable. Freidson's work is concerned with the medical profession in the United States where, because of the different organisation of health care, they have far greater autonomy than do British doctors working in the National Health Service. Nevertheless, medical autonomy in Britain is enormous. That it remains autonomous to judge performance is reflected in the fact that the Health Service Commissioner (the Ombudsman) has no powers to comment on the clinical decisions of doctors in the cases brought before him. The statements can also be made that 'the operation was a success although the patient died', and 'it was an excellent book, but it did not sell', demonstrating a particular focus of professional concern about performance which is different from lay concern.

Autonomy has two components. First, autonomy in the immediate execution of work and second, autonomy in the institutionalised regulation of the relations between experts and clients. Rueschemeyer (1983) comments that the irreducible core of autonomy, in the actual delivery of expert services, remains a resource of power and influence that can become the spring-board for even more extended institutional independence and other privileges. In Britain doctors have retained the right to determine which conditions shall be deemed medical and, as individual practitioners, what given treatment any individual patient shall receive. However, they have had to cede ground to administrators over resource allocation and policy decisions which influence patients as well as the conditions in which doctors themselves work.

Horobin's (1983) analysis of profession emphasises its non-amateur status; services performed for gain rather than satisfaction or obligation, skills acquired rather than endowed and dependent on the availability of clients for its practice. He points up two specific features—profession as morality and as mystery. The former rests in making moral judgments about work and the people doing the work—the idea of service as a moral imperative. Aspects of how that work is performed remain mysterious to the layman, the professional holds the position of expert in relation to the non-expert layman. However, the degree of expertness varies. In Horobin's analysis, patient, general practitioner and hospital specialist conform to what Schutz (1964) terms man in the street, well informed citizen and expert respectively.

So where does this leave nursing and para-medical groups?

Professions and semi-professions

In a somewhat dated analysis relying on the attribute approach, Etzioni (1969) has called nursing and related occupations the *semi-professions*. While there are courses of professional study, a licence to practise is not always required. Appropriate qualification is certainly required in health visiting and midwifery; but the right to use the word 'nurse' is not limited to those with a statutory qualification, since nursing auxiliaries are referred to as 'nurse', as are student nurses. Employment as a 'qualified nurse' of course demands production of a current registration or enrolment number.

The mandatory requirement of appropriate training and a qualification to practise as a District Nursing Sister is very recent. It was also opposed by some because of the costs involved, since mandatory certification would involve the training of some nurses currently employed as District Nursing Sisters, as well as a longer training period. In community nursing a number of different levels of preparation exist, and only the 'district nurse' has to have specific training. Other grades without such educational preparation are employed under different names, thus diluting the profession.

The same licensing situation does not prevail among such groups as chiropodists and physiotherapists. While employment in the NHS would require a licence to practise, there is nothing in law which prevents individuals practising and advertising their services as chiropodists or physiotherapists. Unqualified persons are of course employed in the NHS—as helpers to occupational therapists for instance, and as nursing auxiliaries. The nearest thing to the American doctor's aide is probably a practice nurse (Reedy, 1978), although there is emerging in the United Kingdom a role as nurse practitioner (Reedy et al, 1980) which is already established in North America (Yakauer & Sullivan, 1982). This role carries greater autonomy than do traditional nursing roles (see, for example, Stilwell, 1982).

Semi-professions typically have less autonomy or control over training and practice than is the case with full-fledged professionals. Work is organised by bureaucracies and by higher-ranking professions and also, to a greater extent than in medicine, by elaborate legal restrictions. Attempts to develop their own bodies of knowledge on which to base claims to collegial authority have met with limited success (Strauss, 1966).

The work of the semi-professions is organised both *vertically* and *horizontally*. In the sense of horizontal organisation, work is performed in different settings, there are different functions and different work hours. In this way they are similar to professions. Cross-cutting horizontal organisation is vertical organisation created by bureaucracy and controlled by external sources. Work roles are arranged vertically so that they differ in terms of authority and prestige. This arrangement undermines collegialism by creating invidious distinctions and power differences among workers who claim to be in the same professional group (Simpson, 1979). This is demonstrated by the fact that every level in nursing, from Staff Nurse through to District Nursing Officer, is entitled to call itself nurse but each has very different amounts of power and control. This is most obvious in times of industrial strife; nurses as 'managers' are in direct confrontation with nurses as 'workers'. At other times too, tension over issues of resource allocation are bound to exist between them, as well as between the different tiers within management. Great emphasis has been laid on the enhanced status of senior nurse managers in equal partnership with administrator, treasurer and medical officer at Regional and District Health Authority levels. Because of this form of organisation and identification of senior nurses with other management colleagues at this senior level, loyalties to their professional group of origin are challenged.

Rather than semi-professions, Freidson (1975) calls groups organised around a dominant profession *para-professions*. In the case of nursing and remedial therapy Freidson's categorisation is reflected in titles of organisations like 'the Council for Professions Supplementary to Medicine' as well as such official classifications as 'paramedical groups' (DHSS, 1972). While it is legitimate for paramedical professions to take orders from and be evaluated by doctors, it is not legitimate for the reverse to occur. Freidson argues that close proximity to the truly professional group encourages paramedics to take on professional attributes and to claim to be a profession. Indeed the nursing students studied by Melia (1983) called 'real nursing' those aspects of their work which was technical or medically delegated and was contrasted with the kind of work carried out by nursing auxiliaries.

The professions have followed a route of basing their professional education in universities. The semi-professions or para-professions have done likewise as a means of attempting to increase occupational control and to generate a codified body of knowledge. The movement towards degree courses in nursing was begun with the establishment of a Nursing Studies Unit at Edinburgh University in 1956 with the first undergraduate degree beginning in 1960 (Scott-Wright, 1973). More recently the Council for the Professions Supplementary to Medicine has pressed for the introduction of degree level courses. It states 'the main argument for degree studies is the requirement for a mode of learning geared to the stimulation of genuine scientific enquiry, in order to foster a climate in which provenly ineffective methods, whether new or old, can be abandoned in the search for effectiveness and efficiency' (Council for Professions Supplementary to Medicine, 1979, p. 4). While such developments may alter the cognitive abilities and the knowledge base from which to progress, the move also provides for greater control of student selection and ultimately the award of qualifications from the institution itself rather than a statutory body. It also confers a professional image embodying greater 'status', 'prestige', and 'professional autonomy'. Autonomy, however, remains very partial although Alaszewski (1977) sees a strengthening of the power position of therapists vis-a-vis doctors.

Hughes (1961) has noted that schools of semi-professions,

in an attempt to upgrade their status, also extend their periods of training. The rationale is that more time is necessary to teach the generalised knowledge which is drawn upon in making professional decisions. In practice, what Hughes observed was the addition of liberal arts courses in the early years of professional training and a borrowing of general concepts and methodology of other disciplines as 'sensitising ideas for students'. The inclusion of ideas and methods of sociology in courses for health professionals could be interpreted in this light. By adding 'academic' subjects to the course, it can be argued that this increased the status of the occupation more than increasing the knowledge base of the actual work the occupation does.

BECOMING A PROFESSIONAL

As we would expect, different sociological perspectives give rise to very different views of what it means to become a professional. However, it is not only a matter of looking at the same things and explaining them differently. Different perspectives of professional socialisation have examined different phenomena. The functionalist position emphasised the socialisation of 'professional' trainees. From this point of view it is the process of socialisation which reconciles the opposition between the functioning of the social system and the actions of individual members of society. The core values are internalised through this process so that there is a correspondence between the norms and values of the system and the subjective meanings of the actors in it.

A functionalist view of medical education (Merton et al, 1957) focused on the medical school and its faculty as a subsystem of the wider professional system. They regarded student doctors more as student-professionals than as students *per se.* They became professionals by a process within the professional system of the school, with didactic teaching as well as involvement with professionals as important features of the learning that develops them into 'full professionals'. According to this model, socialisation consists of transmitting professional culture to students who are eager to learn it through role relationships with the professional teachers, from whom they learn expectations of the professional role.

For this to happen teachers and other significant professionals who interact with students must uphold definitions of professional roles in their contact with students and the training experience provided for students must enable them to see the connection between the skills they learn and the carrying out of the professional role. The emphasis therefore is on socialisation by professional education into a professional role. Simpson (1979) comments that this approach fails to consider whether what students learn formally persists into their work as professionals. Nor has it examined the students' motivation to pursue the professional role. A more fundamental criticism is that, rather than focus on medicine as an example of a profession, greater sociological insights would be gained from considering a range of occupations, identifying similarities among diverse examples.

Interactionists believe that the search for criteria of 'profession' is quite misconceived. Profession is regarded by them as a 'lay' term, which some occupations claim at some time under certain conditions. Despite the connotations of the term itself, there is nothing inherent in the work, training, values or whatever to distinguish occupations designated as professions. By the same token there is no assumption of consensus. Bucher and Strauss (1961) remark that 'the assumption of relative homogeneity within the profession is not entirely useful; there are many identities, many values and many interests'. Different segments press their own particular interests, for example District Nurses and Health Visitors, clinical nurses and nurse managers.

In line with their interests in day-to-day survival two interactionist studies of professional socialisation, Becker et al's, (1961) *Boys in white* and Oleson and Whittaker's (1968) study of nursing students, focus on what happens to *students* and not on the professional role. By regarding students as students, they examine how they deal with the problems of getting through school and not as student-professionals. Oleson and Whittaker note that the important issues for analysis are the 'learners' self-awareness', situational management and integration of multiple roles and selves (1968, p. 15). They do not consider it useful to take the view that a professional is produced during professional education. It is not until the individual actually occupies that status that he can learn appropriate behaviour. Thus while students learn attitudes as well as skills and knowledge during professional education, these are not regarded as the major influences on the behaviour of practitioners. Rather they argue that the organisation of the environment *after* leaving professional education influences performance. The interactionists are more concerned with the here and now, how students cope with and negotiate demands of the curriculum and other experiences in professional school rather than what they might do once they are professionally qualified.

An essential feature of socialisation, however, is continuity and in this case, the continuity of behaviour between the status of student and that of professional. The functionalists do not see this as problematic since the student acquires professional culture through the educational process and so membership is assured by provision of appropriate norms and attitudes as well as knowledge. The interactionists make no such assumption since behaviour in unknown future situations depends on transactions between the individual and the particulars of the situation he will meet. The student nurse, who moves into the new status of professionally qualified nurse, will behave and respond to others' behaviour according to the way he and others perceive his role at that time.

Simpson identifies three requirements for continuity of behaviour between the worlds of training and work.

(1) Enough cognitive preparation for the person to perform their role.
(2) Orientation that forms a person's perception of demands of the role and behaviour to meet the demands.
(3) Motivation sufficient to make the transition from one situation to another (Simpson, 1979, p. 13).

These three requirements are regarded as dimensions of socialisation—education, orientation, and relatedness to the occupation. Conceiving socialisation as multidimensional involved Simpson in studying the processes of development of each distinct dimension and the conditions in which they develop. The timing of their experiences was important for the nursing students studied by Simpson, as was the way in which the students' orientations to the occupational role differed from ideology as well as their original expectations of nursing. However, Simpson (1979) suggests that the purpose of her study was not so much to understand the socialisation of students as such, but was to test the efficiency of this multi-dimensional and dynamic model. So what do we understand of this socialisation process?

Davis (1975) advocates a model which relies on Hughes' earlier conceptualisations of how the status passage from layman to professional is achieved. It is like 'passing through the mirror . . . (to create) . . . the sense of seeing the world in reverse' (Hughes, 1958, pp. 119–20). He deals with the subjective perceptions of those experiencing this process. This he calls *doctrinal conversion*, which describes the transition from the lay imagery of the novice entering nursing to the institutionally approved imagery of the qualifying student. Although this is an American study where the organisation of nurse education is somewhat different from that in the U.K., the six stages of transition identified by Davis are interesting.

Stage 1—Initial innocence

Student nurses arrive with a lay imagery of nursing comprising 'a strong instrumental emphasis on *doing* alongside a secularised Christian-humanitarian ethic of care, kindness and love for those who suffer' (Davis, 1975, p. 242). This lay conception is at once at odds with what they are taught and what is expected of them. While they look forward to developing skills in practical procedures, they are asked to go to the wards to 'observe' patients and learn how to 'communicate' with them. Because they are taught few practical skills in the early weeks, time spent on the wards creates feelings of embarrassment, uselessness and personal inadequacy. They are unable to act as they imagine a 'real nurse' does. Comparisons with their lay ideals are of no help in understanding what is being asked of them by their teachers.

Stage 2—Labelled recognition of incongruity

At this stage students collectively share the problems with each other—in handling their feelings about not being taught what they expected and their inability to act as nurses rather than on a social level with patients. Large numbers openly question their choice of nursing and consider other occupations. This recognised misalignment of their own expectations with those of teaching staff causes some to leave while those who remain progress to other ways of dealing with the incongruity.

Stage 3—Psyching out

Next students try to find out what their teachers want from them and how to provide it. This requires the setting aside of their initial imagery of nursing. The students then work to develop ways of identifying what is regarded as desirable behaviour by their teachers—either asking outright or noting what it is that makes a teacher 'light up'—and providing it. While this may be effective to satisfy teachers, it can leave students with a feeling of moral discomfort because they are discrediting their own initial and dearly held ideals. To relieve this feeling for themselves as well as to acknowledge to their peers that they are not *truly* as they appear before staff, students describe themselves as 'putting on a front'.

Stage 4—Role simulation

Role simulation is the performance of 'psyching out'. This entails highly self-conscious manipulative behaviour of students which aims at constructing teacher-approved performances of the nurse's role. It is not truly 'doing nursing' because it embodies self-consciousness, ego-alienation and play-acting. The students were uncomfortable and insecure in their performances, but in order to win the approval of teachers, they simulated appropriate performances on the wards. In effect it was 'playing nurse' and not 'being nurse'. However, the greater the success in playing constructive performances, the easier it is to gain the conviction that performances are authentic. The symbolic interactionists would say that this is due to the student's ability to adopt towards himself the favourable responses which his performance in the new role elicits from others. If others regard his performance as trustworthy, competent and legitimate, the student becomes that status which the performances claim for him. So it develops that students fashion performances in front of others which are more in accord with the doctrinal emphasis of the school than with residual elements of their lay imagery of nursing. Rewards for such performances gradually dissipated feelings of hypocrisy or inauthenticity. They were on the way to 'becoming nurse'.

Stage 5—Provisional internalisation

Students had passed through the first four stages by the end of their first year. The next two years were taken up by moving from *provisional internalisation* of institutionally approved perspectives to their *stable internalisation*.

What characterises this stage as 'provisional' is that there exists an inability to be absolutely committed to the new cognitions, percepts and role orientations which guide institutionally approved behaviour. At this time doubts emerge about suitability of the nurse and the practical value of what is taught; the student vacillates between accepting the school's doctrinal emphasis and rejecting it as excessive, misguided or inconsistent.

Progress to stable internalisation is assisted by professional rhetoric and the identification of unambiguous, positive and negative reference models. Professional rhetoric describes nursing as something very different from lay descriptions. Whilst students were disparaging of the rhetoric of their teachers, it served cognitively to structure nursing for them, and provided a scheme by which they could appraise their performance and communicate meanings to significant others. It assisted students to construct a coherent map from their fragmented experiences. At the same time the clinical instructors in the schools represented a positive reference model. These were the people whose rhetoric and professional outlooks the student assimilated in the process of doctrinal conversion. The negative models were the less well educated nurses they met in the clinical settings to which they were assigned. They exemplified very different nursing ideals from the college teachers.

Stage 6—Stable internalisation

The students then reach the final stage of *stable internalisation*. The self-image of the student is now very different from their initial lay imagery of themselves as nurses, and previous ideals and attitudes are suppressed. Once the student moves into professional practice and away from the influences of the school then further revisions and transformations in his identity will occur.

British studies

Like their interactionist American counterparts, those studying student nurses in Britain have identified the importance of the student sub-culture and ways in which they develop strategies for survival. This was exemplified in David Towell's work on psychiatric nurse training where students in the ward shared their own 'social world' (Towell, 1976). Melia (1981) also found that student nurses describe their major experiences in learning to become nurses as taking place in the various clinical settings where they were sent for a few weeks at a time, rather than in their formal classroom teaching. *Situational variables* were important; these are features of the particular situations in which they found themselves and with which they had to cope during their clinical experience.

Shaw et al (1984) argue that major considerations in nurse socialisation are the organisational constraints and the status hierarchy in which students work, and in which they are initially situated at the bottom. McGuire (1969) observed that 'the learner in hospital is never sure whether she is a 'student' or a 'nurse' and suffers from insecurity in both roles' (1969, p. 45). The work of Revans (1974) on the effects of restricted communication and of Menzies (1960) on the kind of defence mechanisms used to manage the anxiety generated in hospital work further reinforce the need to consider the social milieu in which nurses learn nursing. Shaw et al (1984) draw attention to the tension which exists in students between their initial vocational 'mother-surrogate' (Schulman, 1972) orientation to nursing and their rapid concern with authority and hierarchy relationships. Main areas of dissatisfaction were associated with the amount of autonomy granted to students (Heyman et al, 1984). Important to students were the supervisory styles of those in control of them further up the hierarchy and the quality of personal relationships with all grades of staff with whom they worked. Students were concerned about unjustifiable use of authority by others and unfair treatment, especially being made to look foolish or inferior in front of others. An important feature of socialisation for trainees was in coming to terms with the hierarchy in nursing and finding their place within it.

Melia (1981) also emphasised that students are socialised through their experiences of working as nurses. This placed great emphasis on getting the work done, whatever it might be.

Of course the importance attached to getting through the work is not only a major feature for nursing students. As Clarke noted 'a good nurse becomes someone who knows the ropes and pulls her weight' (1978, p. 79). For nursing students, getting through the work is not only important in terms of their relationships with other ward personnel, like nursing auxiliaries, but for 'getting on' with trained staff and on influencing their end of experience ward reports.

While students recognised that what happened in the wards was at odds with classroom teaching, this did not perturb them unduly. Formal teaching provided background knowledge, especially medically oriented facts about disease and its medical treatment. However, learning the ropes, learning nursing, occurred in the clinical areas where the major teachers were not professional nurses at all but nursing auxiliaries i.e., lay assistants. Because students worked with auxiliaries and other students more than with qualified staff i.e. professionals, their training, sometimes likened to an apprenticeship, was seriously deficient. As Melia observed, apprentices are aligned with craftsmen, not with labourers, stay with them for a considerable length of time and become highly proficient. Student nurses on the other hand, hardly have the time to learn a skill before they are moved into a new clinical area. Although 'continuous assessment' was in vogue during Melia's study, students were given little feed-back on how well they were doing and, in the main, were bereft of support. This paucity of contact with qualified nurses meant that, whilst students may acquire a certain amount of skill and proficiency in accomplishing tasks, they were unable to develop any model of nursing beyond this, or to prepare for the role of staff nurse.

The idea of continuity, an important aspect of socialisation mentioned earlier, is here shown to be at odds with the professional socialisation of nurses who are lacking in an anticipatory capacity to step into the professional staff-nurse role. While students could gain and work towards the expectations of their tutors, their meagre contact with ward sisters meant that they were unable to anticipate and prepare, to learn the basis of ward sisters' professional judgements or how they organised care. It was a matter of crossing that bridge when they got to it.

Runciman (1982) has observed the same phenomenon in the transition from staff nurse to ward sister. 'Some sisters remembered that, when they were staff nurses, they had been aware of the status or 'place' of the sister, but they had not understood the duties and responsibilities of the role or how to deal with them. The process of discovering about the range of responsibilities had been slow and sometimes painful . . . 'hit and miss' learning had proved to be inefficient and costly and it seemed that each sister might meet the same difficulty and make the same mistakes as her predecessors. Supposedly reassuring remarks about 'taking a year to get into the job' has done little to lessen feelings of insecurity or to help sisters to cope with other people's altered expectations when status changed suddenly from staff nurse to sister' (Runciman, 1982, p. 145).

While the move from student to staff nurse to sister maintains a degree of situational stability, albeit with role changes, the transition from nursing to health visiting is characterised by marked discontinuity. All Health Visitors must first be Registered Nurses, but to learn health visiting demands leaving behind many of the ways of doing nursing. Dingwall (1977) takes the perspective that studying professional socialisation requires the focus to be on constructing it from the actions of members and of others towards them. This view of profession gives rise to quite a different kind of study of what 'becoming a professional' actually entails, and requires direct observation of the processes involved. It also abandons the idea of socialisation as *enculturation*—the 'passive internalisation of an external normative order in abstraction from any broader social or historical context' (Dingwall, 1977, p. 12). Rather Dingwall adopts a perspective of socialisation as *acculturation*—'a process by which newcomers to a group work to make sense of the surroundings and came to acquire the kinds of knowledge which would enable them to produce conduct which allowed established members of that group to recognise them as competent' (p. 12–13).

Dingwall's observations of Health Visitor students usage of 'profession' in order to establish their activity as profession rather than occupation gave rise to the following list:

A field health visitor is a professional because:

1. She is a certain sort of person, in that:
   1.1 She has certain ambitions and is committed to her occupation.
   1.2 She has certain personal qualities.
   1.3 She dresses in a certain fashion.
   1.4 She carries herself in a certain way.
   1.5 She uses a certain vocabulary of discourse.
   1.6 She uses certain kinds of transport.
2. She has autonomy in her work and knows what is best for her clients. It follows that:
   2.1 No other health visitor will interfere with her clients.
   2.2 No other health visitor will give her orders about her action towards her clients.
   2.3 No other health visitor will give her clients advice which might conflict with hers.
   2.4 She initiates her own contacts.
   2.5 She is self-critical.
   2.6 She enjoys her work and does not require to be stimulated to do it.
   2.6.1 But she does not work to excess at the expense of her own leisure.
3. She is a member of an occupation which:
   3.1 Selects its recruits.
   3.2 Has formal qualification.
   3.3 Is self-governing.
   3.4 Has its own body of knowledge.
   3.5 Has a history.
   3.6 Has research done on it.
4. She has responsibility for supervising other's work:
   4.1 Clinic Attendants.
   4.2 Health Assistants.
5. She is equal to all other professionals but has a discrete area of work. Other professionals include:
   5.1 Social Workers.
   5.2 Doctors.
   5.3 Teachers.
   5.4 University staff.

5.5 Nurses.

5.6 Various therapists.

6. She acts toward others on the assumption that they share this definition of her social location in an empirically identical, for all practical purposes, fashion (Dingwall, 1977, pp. 221–222).

Accomplishing profession

To accomplish health visiting requires demonstrating competent performance in the relevant elements of the list. Dingwall observed that competence did not follow a developmental model in the sense of later success being contingent on mastering earlier components. Rather it was a case of some aspects being more salient at particular times. While aiming for competence, the students adopted a perspective of 'getting through'—a concern with 'passing' rather than some drive for 'excellence'. This was associated with the fact that some students saw health visiting as filling in time until they married and had a familly. Those who already had a family placed health visiting as a secondary concern to family life. Here was no orientation toward health visiting as a rung in a career ladder, except perhaps among the male students. In any case the mere possession of a certificate without any extra distinction is sufficient to guarantee a job at the end of the course. Competence in health visiting, however, is judged on the basis of *total person evaluation* (Psathas, 1968). For health visitors this means being assessed throughout their course—by the end-of-term examinations but also by fieldwork teachers, through case studies, and in individual tutorials with tutors. Competence is a matter not only of knowledge but also of conduct. The latter element is especially precarious for adult students since, because of the completeness of assessment, a judgement of incompetence reflects on the whole person. Dingwall describes how the student learned what was desirable to be judged as competent in the various elements in the list given above. For example, a number of discussions focused on what health visitors should wear to be professional. 'Health visitors were only allowed to dress in the 'professional' manner. Thus one student was admonished for wearing trousers on an institutional visit. 'We have to set an example, Miss Barret.' Several of the students have commented on the disapproval expressed at the clinics where they are now working, when they have worn even 'respectable' trouser suits' (Dingwall, 1977, p. 127). The same kind of learning about what is appropriate for professionals applies to the use of dialect and body position, for example the inappropriateness of elbows on the table. Through their encounters with tutors, other professionals and fieldwork teachers, student health visitors learned 'doing health visitor' and in this way accomplished becoming a professional.

Dingwall's (1977) study is important not only for its theoretical and methodological freshness but also because it raises issues about continuing education and socialisation for roles which follow after initial professional education. Kramer (1974) has coined the term 'reality shock' to describe the powerful experience of nurses discovering that their initial education is in conflict with work world values.

This contrast is extreme for the newly qualified professional. Later in career development are other important features of transition and becoming, such as when professionals move from one role to another, be it from working in hospital to working in other settings or in moving from one step to the next up the career ladder.

Yet there are few studies of socialisation of nurses beyond their formal initial training schemes. Some work is being pursued on cohorts of nurse graduates (Sinclair, 1984) and on particular kinds of nurses, for example the career patterns of sick children's nurses (Hutt, 1983) and, in progress, the career patterns of top nurse managers. What Johnson (1983) has shown is that to plot professional careers through job lists is to miss the important interaction which occurs between professional career and other aspects of the life career, often resulting in compromise decisions. This must be especially so when women are faced with decisions about parenthood and career, but also arises when considerations other than work interests are important for either gender.

PROFESSION AND GENDER

The sociology of profession has recently taken account of the relationship between profession and gender. Simpson and

Simpson (1969) posited a relation between the tendency for semi-professions to be more bureaucratised than full professions and their numerical domination by women rather than men. However, to understand their crucial connection with gender requires an understanding of the historical relationship between professionalisation and patriarchy and this has been taken up by feminist writers such Eva Gamarnikow (1978) and more recently by mainstream sociologists such as Jeff Hearn (1982).

'Patriarchy can be defined as an autonomous system of social relations between men and women in which men are dominant' (Gamarnikow, 1978, p. 99). Rather than being biologically or naturally determined, patriarchy designates social relationships between men and women. As we discovered in Chapter 5, the feminist critique of the family examines male exploitation of women with husbands owning and controlling wives' unpaid labour. All professions throughout history have been male dominated. Nursing and subsequently other health workers were female and were subordinated to medicine in the same way as wives to husbands. This analogy with the family is extended by describing the position of patients as being like that of children. As we saw in Chapter 7 patients come lower down the hierarchy of social relations in health care. Florence Nightingale saw nursing as being entrusted with two functions—hygiene or 'nursing the room', and assisting the doctor. Both can only be practised *after* medical intervention, particularly making a diagnosis. This relationship maintains both a subordinate position to medicine and the division of labour between the two occupations. This was reinforced by the alleged scientific nature of medicine, and the nature of inter-professional relations which reduced the nurse to a non-scientific aide whose authority derived from her relation to medicine. Thus nursing became an occupation *primarily defined by its responsibility for executing medical orders and directives.* As Gamarnikow observes, however, it was believed that the healing process was dependent not only on obedience *per se* but also, more importantly, on the harmonious relations between the two occupations. Any power struggle was to be suppressed. This has its modern counterpart in analysis of 'the Doctor-Nurse Game' (Stein, 1978) described in Chapter 7, whose cardinal rule is avoidance of open disagreement, particularly where nurses wish to offer and doctors to ask for recommendations about patient care.

Nursing became an occupation specifically attractive to middle-class women who had to earn a living. It became a paid job rather than another form of voluntary female Victorian charity. Nursing reformers of the Nightingale era were therefore successful in creating paid jobs for women by, at the same time, not threatening medical control over health care. Nursing was women's work—a good nurse is the same as a good woman. It was *character* that mattered, character linked with the moral attributes and qualities of femininity. Nursing reforms were associated with a training that cultivated feminine character, thereby increasing the difference between men and women. Later came an emphasis on learning tasks to be accomplished—tasks associated with motherhood and other features of running a home. 'Good woman' still equated with 'good nurse', re-emphasising hygiene. In hygiene was rooted any scientific claims of nursing. Future debates addressed issues of whose province hygiene was, because of its close links with menial work. There was a hiving-off of items other than the personal sanitary aspects of patient care to maids and orderlies, while nursing kept for itself those aspects of care more directly related to medical intervention.

The Lady Nurses and Matrons were the power-holders in nursing; they developed an authority structure in hospitals which reproduced a Victorian class and domestic structure (Carpenter, 1977). The care functions of hospitals were carried out by the lower class of female workers but under the moral leadership of upper-class women. Even in psychiatric hospitals, where there were large numbers of male attendants, women without psychiatric training could be in charge. A structure was reinforced which encompassed harsh discipline, total commitment and low pay (Carpenter, 1978).

While nurses evolved a sphere of autonomy they remained subordinate to the medical and male division of labour.

As Runciman (1983) noted in the Records and Rules of the Lady Superintendent of the Royal Infirmary of Edinburgh in 1881: 'No nurse shall be dismissed without the circumstances of the case having been previously referred to the Physician or Surgeon to whose ward she is attached' (p. 22). Matron was head of the female side of the hospital and this situation, while holding certain economic advantages for the health service, could not be called managerial. As Carpenter (1978) reports, the prime practice of nursing was to create and sustain the institution of vocationalism, and its organisation with its authoritarian tendencies crystallised in the voluntary hospitals. Hospitals grew larger and more complex and specialisms in nursing and nurse education emerged. The Matron, in supreme control, became an anachronistic form of management. There were also fewer spinsters to maintain nursing's vocational image. Despite a shortage of labour, there was resistance to employing part-time and married nurses and to raising student nurses' wages. Nevertheless a number of major changes did proceed and reforms were begun.

A new managerial model was proposed in the better interests of staff morale and patient welfare. The idea of a career structure in nursing was formalised in the Salmon Report (Ministry of Health, 1966). Management structures appropriate to industry were directly transposed into nursing and, for the first time, nurse managers were brought into the most senior levels of decision-making. A major effect of the Salmon reorganisation was that men were able to compete on an equal footing for the top posts; indeed their chances of landing top posts were enhanced by their greater geographical mobility. Men are less likely to be tied by their wife's job or to have to care for elderly dependent relatives (see Ch. 6). Women are more likely to have career breaks which jeopardise their chances of establishing credentials by way of continuity or breadth of experience, and are less able to participate in courses which advance career prospects.

Carpenter notes that the Salmon Report was not written in explicit terms favourable to men but that the definition of the new posts in functional rather than female terms and other aspects of the report read as an attack on the effects of female authority. 'In other words nurses have a trained incapacity for management' (Carpenter, 1978, p. 99).

In the study of health visitors, it was only the men and unmarried women who envisaged any career in nursing (Dingwall, 1977). Research for the Briggs Committee on nursing also found that many nurses were not actually seeking promotion (Report of the Committee on Nursing, 1972, para. 526–529).

Careers in nursing, however, currently rest in management. The hierarchical structure and bureaucratic rules legitimate a system of authority relationships between nurses which reflect the very compliant relationships between doctor and nurse which it seeks to counter. The locus of obedience merely shifts from nurse to doctor to nurse to nurse. Despite the attention given to establishing clinical career grades by some members of the profession (DHSS, 1982a) these have not materialised substantially and the thrust to a degree of autonomy, by making patients' nursing problems explicit and different from their medical problems by 'the nursing process', has resulted in a counter-demonstration by medics reasserting their dominance (for example, Bolt, 1983; Mitchell, 1984).

While men remain a minority in nursing, they are able to move quickly up the management ladder and are overrepresented in senior grades. An examination of senior management positions in England shows that 43.8% of District Nursing Officers are men (Health and Social Services Journal, 1982) and that 50.5% of Directors of Nurse Education are men (DHSS, 1980). Men represent only 16.3% of registered nurses in hospitals (DHSS, 1982b). Comparable figures for hospital nursing in Scotland (Gray & Smail, 1982) show that in 1959 12% of those in the grades above ward sister were men. By 1979 this figure had risen to 43% in the administrative grades and 42% among tutors. In the five grades above ward sister in 1959 were 5.1% of all female nurses and 4.5% of all males. By 1979 this had changed to 2.6% of all female nurses and 13% of all males. Overrepresentation of men in higher grades is not confined to nursing. Kadushin (1976) notes that the same trend holds for social work, primary teaching and librarianship. Mackie and Pattullo (1977) provide data about the scarcity of women in all professional groups and the extent of the obstacles in the way of women who want to get to the top, even in professions where their number is very large. Not only is management ideology in the semi-professions largely male oriented, but joining a semi-profession is one route by which men can reach a managerial position. Entering nursing is one way for men to be upwardly socially mobile (Rosen & Jones, 1972).

Hearn (1982) argues that the urge to professionalisation and the development of the semi-professions will eventually lead to domination by men, both in management and in the ranks. He regards professionalisation as merely a shorthand term for a variety of processes by which men move into and increase their influence on the semi-professions. While in the past male domination of nursing was exercised indirectly from outside the profession, now, after changes in both structure and content of nursing, it has begun to be expressed from within.

PROFESSION AND THE FUTURE

What then are the prospects for the future? A number of ideas about profession and professional socialisation have been presented. Yet, given the debates about whether or not nursing and remedial therapy are professions, semi-professions, para-professions or whatever, and whether they *should* be striving for professional status, we are left to ask: Does it really matter? In whose vested interest is it to be labelled profession and what, if any, are its consequences?

More broadly we can consider nursing, physiotherapy and other cohesive groups as occupations, each with a vested interest in defending a set of tasks as providing it with its unique character and providing a claim to its unique existence. Occupations also jostle for social esteem, achieving positions of superiority over some groups, inferiority to others and equality with yet others. The more occupations organise themselves the more they become committed to their occupation, their occupational co-workers and their work (Freidson, 1977). There has been a major increase in the number of nurses who have become members of nursing organisations, particularly the Royal College of Nursing, but also the trade unions with a major interest in health. Johnson (1978) predicts a revolt by female nursing auxiliaries who are asked to do the 'dirty work' but who are increasingly vociferous and organised.

The increased organisation of nursing within the Royal College of Nursing, and as a consequence its louder voice, has resulted in documents like *Towards Standards* (RCN, 1981), and *A Structure for Nursing* (RCN, 1982) being taken seriously by doctors. Scrutator wrote in the British Medical Journal that 'these documents, particularly the one on Standards, go to the heart of relations between the two professions and raise major questions about where the boundary between medicine and nursing should be. Committee members were unequivocal—though with varying levels of politeness—in their criticism of what they interpreted as medically and legally undesirable trespass on doctors' responsibilities' (Scrutator, 1982, p. 1057).

To claim profession would be to claim autonomy and equality with doctors. The notion of equality has some value in the concept 'team', yet, as we identified in Chapter 7, teams remain medically dominated. Even Health Visitors who are the only significant group of nurses who currently have direct access to clients, rather than depending on the selections of the medical profession, are weak members of teams (Dingwall, 1980). The futility of teamwork or equality aspirations with medicine are grounded in the broader social divisions of class and gender as well as in the hospital-centred experience of all health professionals in which medical specialist power in social relations is extreme and which provides all models for subsequent relationships (Davies, 1979).

Fig. 11.2 Unequal status in the primary care team (courtesy of Hexham Courant).

Autonomy in nursing and the remedial professions is well-nigh impossible, since the patients cared for are medically selected. Even midwives, who were at one time independent practitioners, have become medically dominated as childbirth has been medicalised (Donnisson, 1977). Boundaries have been set in the kind of tasks midwives are and are not allowed to do and, more importantly, decision-making about the need for particular interventions has fallen into medical hands and the obstetrician claims ultimate responsibility (Walker, 1978).

A second route to professional progression lies in education. General practitioners, the least specialist and least powerful group of medical staff which was 'near moribund' in the 1950s and 1960s, were forced to organise themselves through the Royal College of General Practitioners *and* to develop schemes of vocational training. All basic nurse education will be carried out in universities in the United States within ten years. Mauksch writes: 'the societal mandate placed on nurses in the US justifies nursing's stance as a profession, and its consequent claim of a place in the university. It is there that it must educate its young, in the manner pursued by all other professions' (1984, p. 57). However, Mauksch is also appealing for graduate professional education rather than first degree level professional education, with first degree work devoted to liberal arts. While the educational route may be powerful, without concomitant changes in the broader social structure and social relationships within health care organisations, it will do little to change the *relative* position of nurses and remedial therapists along the professional continuum.

We have taken a position here, not of championing the professional course nor of decrying the increasingly male-orientated managerialism evident in nursing. What is happening is a part of a broader picture of social change. What happens within and between occupational groups relates to much broader social structural factors.

We have learned something of the processes by which students become professionals, focusing primarily on their practical rather than formal educational experiences. However there are no sociological studies of the knowledge base of professional courses, which are themselves socially organised. The most recently published formal syllabus for mental illness and mental handicap nursing are advocating a basis in 'nursing process' which is reverberating through to nursing practice. Despite current emphasis in community care and prevention in government policy, *all* primary professional education in health care is hospital-centred (Davies, 1979). We now require studies which consider the social organisation of the curriculum and which consider the effects of including in it new subjects, including sociology.

SUMMARY

This chapter has covered some of the ground related to career and profession. The different ways of attempting to define profession and the distinctions made between professions and other occupations were discussed, showing again the influence of sociological perspectives. This applies not only to how professions are characterised but how studies of professions are mounted.

This was shown to be the case, particularly in research about professional socialisation when the focus of study as well as the methods used provide different kinds of information about the process from layman to professional. A major distinction lay in whether socialisation is regarded as enculturation or acculturation.

The third major section was devoted to a discussion of the relationship between profession and gender, and alluded to some feminist writing which describes the nature of relationships which underpin medicine and allied occupations as patriarchal. The rise of managerialism in nursing was described as contradicting the notion of professional autonomy and adding to obedience to doctors, nurses' obedience to other nurses. The increasing dominance of nurse management by men was shown from statistical data and mirrors the trends obvious in similar occupations.

Finally, some issues were raised about the social consequences of striving toward professional status and the inter-professional conflicts which emerge. We pointed out that what happens within professional groups is a manifestation of social change more generally.

REFERENCES

Alaszewski A 1977 Doctors and paramedical workers—the changing pattern of inter-professional relations. Health and Social Services Journal 87: Oct 14, B1–B4

Becker H S 1971 Sociological work: method and substance. Allen Lane, London

Becker H S 1972 A school is a lousy place to learn anything in. In: Geer B (ed) Learning to work. Sage, Beverley Hills, p 89–109

Becker H S, Geer B, Hughes E C, Strauss A L 1961 Boys in white: student culture in medical school. University of Chicago Press, Chicago

Bolt D 1983 Why we are worried about the process. Nursing Times 79: No. 34, 11–12

Bucher R, Strauss A 1961 Professions in process. American Journal of Sociology 66: 325–334

Carpenter M 1977 The new managerialism and professionalism in nursing. In: Stacey M, Reid M, Heath C, Dingwall R (eds) Health and the division of labour. Croom Helm, London, p 165–193

Carpenter M 1978 Managerialism and the division of labour in nursing. In: Dingwall R, McIntosh J (eds) Readings in the sociology of nursing. Churchill Livingstone, Edinburgh, ch 6, p 87–103

Clarke M 1978 Getting through work. In: Dingwall R, McIntosh J (eds) Readings in the sociology of nursing. Churchill Livingstone, Edinburgh, ch 5, p 67–86

Council for the Professions Supplementary to Medicine 1979 PSM education and training. The next decade. Council for the Professions Supplementary to Medicine, London

Davies C 1979 Hospital centred health care: policies and politics in the National Health Service. In: Atkinson P, Dingwall R, Murcott A (eds) Prospects for the national health. Croom Helm, London, p 53–72

Davis F 1975 Professional socialisation as subjective experience: the process of doctrinal conversion among student nurses. In: Cox C, Mead A (eds) A sociology of medical practice. Collier-MacMillan, London, ch 6, p 116–131

Department of Health and Social Security 1972 Management arrangements for the reorganised health service. HMSO, London

Department of Health and Social Security 1980 Directory of schools of nursing, 4th edition. HMSO, London

Department of Health and Social Security 1982a Professional development in clinical nursing—the 1980's. DHSS, London

Department of Health and Social Security 1982b Health and personal social services statistics for England, 1982. HMSO, London

Dingwall R 1976 Accomplishing profession. Sociological Review 24: 331–349

Dingwall R 1977 The social organisation of health visitor training. Croom Helm, London

Dingwall R 1980 Problems of teamwork in primary care. In: Lonsdale S, Webb A, Briggs T L (eds) Teamwork in the personal social services and health care. Croom Helm, London, ch 7, p 111–137

Donnisson J 1977 Midwives and medical men: a history of inter-professional rivalries and women's rights. Heinemann, London

Etzioni A (ed) 1969 The semi-professions and their organisation. The Free Press, New York

Freidson E 1975 Profession of medicine. A study of the sociology of applied knowledge. Dodd, Mead & Co, New York

Friedson E 1977 The futures of professionalism. In: Stacey M, Reid M, Heath C, Dingwall R (eds) Health and the division of labour. Croom Helm, London, p 14–38

Freidson E 1983 The theory of professions: state of the art. In: Dingwall R, Lewis P (eds) The sociology of the professions. Lawyers, doctors and others. MacMillan, London, ch 1, 19–37

Garmarnikow E 1978 Sexual division of labour: the case of nursing. In: Kuhn A, Wolpe A M (eds) Feminism and materialism: women and modes of production. Routledge & Kegan Paul, London, ch 5, p 96–123

Gray A, Smail R 1982 A review of trends in the Scottish hospital nursing labour force 1959–1979. Health Economics Research Unit, Nursing Papers No 1, University of Aberdeen, Aberdeen

Health and Social Services Journal 1982 The Health and Social Services Journal directory of the new NHS. Health and Social Services Journal, London

Hearn J 1982 Notes on patriarchy, professionalisation and the semi-professions. Sociology 16: 184–202

Heyman R, Shaw M P, Harding J 1984 A longitudinal study of changing attitudes to work among nursing trainees in two British general hospitals. Journal of Advanced Nursing 9: 297–305

Horobin G 1983 Professional mystery: the maintenance of charisma in general medical practice. In: Dingwall R, Lewis P (eds) The sociology of the professions. Lawyers, doctors and others. MacMillan, London, ch 4, p 84–105

Hughes E C 1958 Men and their work. Free Press, Glencoe, Illinois

Hughes E C 1961 Education for a profession. The Library Quarterly 31: 336–343

Hutt R 1983 Sick children's nurses. Institute of Manpower Studies, University of Sussex, Brighton

Johnson M 1978 Big fleas have little fleas—nurse professionalisation and nursing auxiliaries. In: Hardie M, Hockey L (eds) Nursing auxiliaries in health care. Croom Helm, London, ch 8, p 103–117

Johnson M 1983 Professional careers and biographies. In: Dingwall R, Lewis P (eds) The sociology of the professions. Lawyers, doctors and others. MacMillan, London, ch 11, p 242–262

Johnson T J 1972 Professions and power. MacMillan, London

Kadushin A 1976 Men in a woman's profession. Social Work 21: 440–447

Kramer M 1974 Reality shock. Why nurses leave nursing. C V Mosby, New York

Macguire J 1969 Threshold to nursing: a review of the literature on recruitment to and withdrawal from nurse training programmes in the UK. Occasional Papers on Social Administration, No 30. Bell, London

Mackie L, Pattullo P 1977 Women at work. Tavistock, London

Mauksch I G 1984 The development of collegiate nursing education in the United States. Nursing Times 80: No. 5, 56–58

Melia K M 1981 Student nurses' accounts of their work and training. Unpublished Phd thesis, University of Edinburgh

Melia K M 1983 Students' views of nursing, 3. Nursing in the dark: students are often left short of information. Nursing Times 79: No. 21, 62–63

Menzies I E P 1960 A case study of the functioning of social systems as a defence against anxiety. A report on a study of the nursing service of a general hospital. Human Relations 13: 95–121

Merton R K, Reader G, Kendall P (eds) 1957 The student physician: introductory studies in the sociology of medical education. Harvard University Press, Cambridge Mass.

Ministry of Health 1966 Report of the committee on senior nursing staff structure. (The Salmon Report). HMSO, London

Mitchell J R A 1984 Is nursing any business of doctors? A simple guide to the 'nursing process'. British Medical Journal 288: 216–219

Moore W E 1970 The professions: roles and rules. Russel Sage Foundation, New York

Olesen V L, Whittaker E W 1968 The silent dialogue: a study in the social psychology of professional socialization. Jossey Bass, San Francisco

Psathas G 1968 The student nurse in the diploma school of nursing. Springer, New York

Reedy B L 1978 The new health practitioners in America—a comparative study. King Edward's Hospital Fund for London, London

Reedy B L E C, Stewart T I, Quick J B 1980 Attachment of a physician's assistant to an English general practice. British Medical Journal 281: 664–666

Report of the Committee on Nursing 1972 (The Briggs Report), Cmnd.5115. HMSO, London

Revans R W 1974 Standards of morale: cause and effect in hospitals. Oxford University Press for the Nuffield Provincial Hospitals Trust, Oxford

Rosen J G, Jones K 1972 The male nurse. New Society 19: 493–494

Roth J A, Ruzek S K, Daniels A K 1973 Current state of the sociology of occupations. The Sociological Quarterly 14: 309–333

Royal College of Nursing 1981 Towards standards: a discussion document. RCN, London

Royal College of Nursing 1982 A structure for nursing. RCN, London

Rueschemeyer D 1983 Professional autonomy and the social control of expertise. In: Dingwall R, Lewis P (eds) The sociology of the professions. Lawyers, doctors and others. MacMillan, London, ch 2, p 38–58

Runciman P 1982 Ward sisters: their problems at work—2. Nursing Times Occasional Papers 78: No. 51, 145–147

Runciman P J 1983 Ward sister at work. Churchill Livingstone, Edinburgh

Schulman S 1972 Mother-surrogate, after a decade. In: Jaco E G (ed) Patients, physicians and illness. A source book in behavioural science and health, 2nd edn. Free Press, New York, ch 16, p 223–229

Schutz A 1964 The well informed citizen. An essay on the social distribution of knowledge. In: Broderson A (ed) Collected Papers, 2. Martinus Nijhoff, The Hague, p 120–134

Scott-Wright M 1973 Nursing and universities. Inaugral lecture. University of Edinburgh, Edinburgh

Scrutator 1982 The week. A personal view of current medicopolitical events. British Medical Journal 285: 1057

Shaw M, Heyman R, Harding J 1984 Competing ideologies: implications for nurse socialisation. In press

Simpson I H 1979 From student to nurse: a longitudinal study of socialization. Cambridge University Press, New York

Simpson R L, Simpson I H 1969 Women and bureaucracy in semi-professions. In: Etzioni A (ed) The semi-professions and their organization. Free Press, New York, ch 5, p 196–265

Sinclair H 1984 The careers of nurse graduates. Nursing Times Occasional Paper 80: 56–59

Stilwell B 1982 The nurse practitioner at work. Nursing Times 78: 1799–1803

Stein L 1978 The doctor-nurse game. In: Dingwall R, McIntosh J (eds) Readings in the sociology of nursing. Churchill Livingstone, Edinburgh, ch 7, p 107–117

Strauss A L 1966 The structure and ideology of American nursing: an interpretation. In: Davis F (ed) The nursing profession: five sociological essays. Wiley, New York, p 60–108

Towell D 1976 Understanding psychiatric nursing—a sociological study of modern nursing practice. Royal College of Nursing, London

Walker J F 1978 Practitioners in their own right: a study of some aspects of the role of midwives. Unpublished MSc thesis, University of Wales, Swansea

Yankauer A, Sullivan J 1982 The new health professionals: three examples. Annual Review of Public Health 3: 249–276

FURTHER READING

Dingwall R, Lewis P (eds) 1983 The sociology of the professions. Lawyers, doctors and others. MacMillan, London

12

Doing sociological research

INTRODUCTION

In the preceding chapters you have learned something of different sociological perspectives and encountered the findings of a number of empirical sociological studies. In order to generate sociological knowledge, sociologists employ a variety of methods ranging from those which are logically similar to the methods of the natural sciences through to reliance on what may be regarded as common-sense interpretations about how society's members produce the society in which they live. There are many text books which give advice about doing sociological research; some are devoted to a particular method like Moser and Kalton's (1971) *Survey Methods in Social Investigation* or Schatzman and Strauss' (1973) *Field Research*, as well as more general texts like Smith's (1975) *Strategies of Social Research*. In addition to these idealised recipes for doing research are accounts of what sociological research is *really* like in texts like Bell and Newby's (1977) *Doing Sociological Research* and its forerunner Hammond's (1964) *Sociologists at Work*. These accounts, rather like Watson's (1968) account of the discovery of DNA, demonstrate that the process of actually doing research, be it in the biological or social sciences, bears little resemblance to text-book prescriptions.

They also demonstrate the range of methods available. In the introduction to their book Bell and Newby (1977) write 'No longer can there be one style of sociology with *one* method that is to be *the* method. Rather there are many (p. 10). They, like ourselves, advocate methodological pluralism, i.e. the use of a variety of methods in sociological research. This chapter describes these methodological divisions and links them with different sociological perspectives.

This position should not come as any surprise since, in Chapter 2, we introduced a range of different perspectives and theoretical positions in sociology. Just as sociologists view society from different perspectives, accept different theoretical assumptions and ask different questions, they also use different methods. There is a close relationship between a sociological perspective and the method used. As we shall demonstrate, each perspective is often committed to using particular research strategies to define, generate, collect and interpret empirical data. Indeed Smith (1975) goes as far as to say 'methods and theory are inescapably connected' (p. 27) irrespective of the degree to which that theory is made explicit. Method here means not merely whether to use interviews or observation but more fundamentally whether to study causes or functions, whether to describe phenomena or explain them, or whether to determine the meaning of a phenomenon or examine the relationship between relevant variables.

Inevitably theory gives rise to a particular definition of the problems to be studied, which influences the selection of method and subsequently the choice of particular techniques of data collection—interviewing, questionnaire, observation and so on. We shall explore some of these considerations later in the chapter using the example of research on suicide, but first, let us consider briefly a difficult and major issue which faces all researchers and sociological researchers in particular: the problem of epistemology.

EPISTEMOLOGY

Epistemology is that branch of philosphy which is concerned with the theory of knowledge. The central concern of epistemology is the question of how we *know* something to be true. It distinguishes between two kinds of knowledge: what we might call *public knowledge* and what we might call *private beliefs*. Public knowledge is that which is generally held to be the case in contrast to private beliefs which is knowledge held by the individual in the sense of *knowing* or having a belief, opinion or faith. Epistemology addresses questions about the means by which we can say or know something or that it is so. It attempts to discriminate between public knowledge and private beliefs, and the process by which we come to have knowledge of the external world. For example, the process of changing beliefs that disease was caused by wicked spirits to the fact that at least some disease is caused by micro-organisms. How do we know something is true? Sociologists face problems in making explicit the procedures they use to acquire sociological knowledge.

By virtue of the subject matter of the discipline, sociologists bring to their studies an awareness that they, like those they study, are social beings. They cannot but hold and impart their own past experience, beliefs and attitudes into the social settings they study. In so doing they interpret social events and create social reality in the context of their own biography and this may be at odds with the social reality of those they have studied. Sociologists, like every other individual, including all other scientists in every discipline, cannot be 'value-free'. This has major implications for how to 'do sociology' and handle sociological evidence. These are epistemological issues and they surface in different ways.

One major development has been the emergence of ethno-methodology. In Chapter 2 we said that ethnomethodologists were principally concerned with studying language as the means whereby society's members, and the ethnomethodologists themselves, gain an understanding of the methods society's members use to accomplish or produce social order. Thus, ethnomethodologists gain an understanding of what people themselves understand and know through language, which is regulated through social processes. Epistemologists have similar concerns. They attempt to understand what sociological concepts like class, status and power mean to the sociologist doing the research as well as to the subjects of the research. Thus an understanding of class held by the sociologist and that held by the subject may be different and gained by different processes. We cannot take for granted that any sociological concept is understood and credited with the same meaning by subjects and researchers. Sociologists, as we indicated in Chapter 5 when discussing the family, will always face problems of this kind since most of the social phenomena they are concerned with will be familiar to them in their own private lives, and their private beliefs will influence their discovery of public knowledge.

A second epistemological concern is the close relationship between some political doctrines and sociology. Some critics regard sociology and sociologists as being politically biased. Marxist sociology is most often criticised, although other perspectives are often tarred with the same brush. Is all sociology politically contaminated? Many establishment figures have this private belief, which they regard as public knowledge. However as far as we know there has been no attempt to describe this relationship empirically. We suspect that the answer would be no, except to the extent that sociologists, like other scientists, bring their own political stance into their work. In this sense all science is influenced by political doctrines. This surfaces in such issues as the linking of heredity and intelligence and debates about the effectiveness of comprehensive schools and grammar schools.

Positivism

Much debate in sociology focuses on doing sociological research. At the centre of this debate is the question about the extent to which sociology should adhere to the positivist tradition of natural science. Over-simplifying, the method of *positivism* is what the natural sciences are supposed to do and is the foundation of statistical theory, exemplified by Karl Popper's defence of quantitative methods in *The Poverty of Historicism* (Popper, 1961). Positivism generally involves the setting up of a hypothesis, for example, that working-class women are less likely to attend for antenatal care than middle-class women, which can be tested by statistical procedures to analyse relationships between variables. Put another way, positivism argues that there is no knowledge without experience of the external world as described by empirical data, for example the proportion of working-class and middle-class women attending for antenatal care. Positivists argue that knowing is based on systematically collected data and not 'unreliable' individual descriptions based on beliefs or opinion about the use of antenatal care by working-class and middle-class women. This basic conception was elaborated by the early sociologists, particularly Comte, who stressed the appropriateness of the positive method for *all* sciences. All scientific knowledge should be acquired in the same manner. Those who subscribe to this position fail to recognise that experimental method is usually impracticable in sociology and that the phenomena studied by sociologists are not uniform, as are those studied by natural scientists. Making a variable like social class measurable is more complex than quantifying natural science variables, such as air pressure or atomic weight. Making variables measurable is called *operationalisation*.

Like that of natural science, the aim of positivism is to reduce explanations of all phenomena to the smallest number of principles or laws. Positivists argue that given enough time and effort, sociologists should be able to uncover the laws which govern and explain social facts. In practice this means providing a sociological theory, at different conceptual levels, (leading eventually to social laws). At the highest conceptual level are abstract postulates which cannot be given precise empirical definition—for example, 'social disadvantage causes ill health'. These postulates give rise to lower-level propositions in the form of hypotheses or predictions which can be tested in the real world—for example, 'there is a higher rate of maternal deaths among lower-class women'. Positivism therefore entails a uniform method of data collection which forces a definite mode of description and classification on the 'reality' being studied.

The principal components of the idealised scientific process advocated by positivism is shown in Figure 12.2. Data are collected about operational variables, and hypotheses would then be upheld or rejected, depending on the findings. Through this process there is a quest for the smallest number of laws which will *explain* how things have worked in the past and *predict* how things will work in the future. At its simplest, if one kind of event has always been observed to have been followed by another event, then all future occurrences of the

Fig. 12.1 Survey method using standardised interviews yielding comparable data (courtesy of Rik Walton).

first event will produce the second. For example, in physics it has been shown that if you keep the pressure of a given gas constant, an increase in temperature will cause a corresponding increase in the volume of the gas. In sociology Janowitz (1956) has listed a number of consequences of social mobility such as 'the greater the social mobility of a family, the greater the instability of the family'.

Positivism therefore depends principally on being able to challenge predictions set up as hypotheses and attempting to falsify them, because, if a prediction fails, then the theoretical proposition giving rise to it must be changed to take account of the findings. Any revision of theoretical concepts and propositions leads to revision of the sociological theory and the whole circular process begins once again. In a perfect and rational world this process is logically defensible.

Unfortunately the world is neither rational or perfect and a strict adherence to the positivists' position can be challenged on a number of grounds. Different views exist about

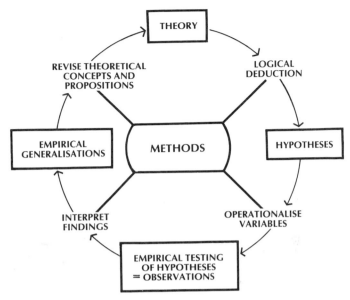

Fig. 12.2 Principal components of an idealised 'scientific' process (modified from Wallace, 1971 In: Bynner & Stribley, 1979).

what are proper tests and grounds for an adequate rejection of hypotheses. We each hold auxiliary beliefs about how phenomena work, which can interfere with positive science and provide justification for *not* rejecting a theory. Scientific practice can be shown to be not very different from the logic employed in magical and religious practices in non-industrialised societies. Evans-Pritchard (1950) showed that the Azande sorcerers were able to deal with what, to an outsider, would be falsifying or non-confirming instances. If one person seeks, through magical means, to injure or kill another, and that person remains in the best of health, explanations as to how this could be so are readily to hand. Something unknown 'went wrong' with the magic on this particular occasion when the oracle was consulted; the ritual incantation was not performed perfectly correctly; or the second person enjoyed access to even stronger magic than the first, and was able to render his efforts ineffective. Giddens (1976) asks 'In what sense, if any, is Western science able to lay any claim to an understanding of the world that is more grounded in 'truth' than that of the Azande?' (p. 138). Perhaps the Azande simply operate with a different overall meaning frame to that which we call science?

There are also criticisms of the logic underpinning positivism. Just because one event has been found to be consequent on another in the past, is that any justification for assuming that this will always be the case? Furthermore, just because one event comes after another it does not necessarily mean that the first *causes* the second or that they are bound together by some other, as yet undiscovered, law. The positivist scientist however can only assume that indeed this is the case and in so doing, is on the way to discovering a chain of events which will ultimately provide causes.

While positivists themselves produce such criticisms as a means of self-reform, sociologists have not been slow to find these arguments grounds for rejecting a positivist or scientistic approach to sociology. Atkinson (1978), whose work on suicide we shall deal with presently, provides a list of assumptions made by positivists together with the kinds of criticisms of positivism made by sociologists (Table 12.1).

These epistemological difficulties have caused a large number of sociologists to reject positivism. This has led Bell and Newby (1977) to question the standards by which sociologists now make decisions about what 'facts' to look at, how to examine them and how to evaluate other people's work. Positivism 'provided the normative standards by which sociological research was both judged and practised . . . it no longer does so, hence sociology's troubles' (p. 21). But, we may ask, is it necessarily a bad thing to have different logical and epistemological bases within sociology giving rise to methodological puralism? Or is it a case of sociology, still a relatively young discipline, feeling pressured to present a sociology adhering to one generally accepted set of canons in order to gain acceptance by the 'academic' community? The basis for such questions lies in the character and stage of development of sociology as a discipline and the extent to which sociological methods are sufficiently cohesive to be shared by members of a 'scientific' community.

Kuhn and normal science

Kuhn's important treatise on physical sciences, *The Structure*

Table 12.1 Summary statement of central assumptions and criticisms of positivism (From Atkinson, 1978)

Positivist Assumptions	Criticisms
Social phenomena have an existence external to the individuals who make up a society or social group and can thus be viewed as objective facts in much the same way as natural facts . . .	Social phenomena are of an essentially different order to natural ones owing to their symbolic nature and the subjective interpretations of social meanings by individuals in a society . . .
hence An observer can identify social facts relatively easily and objectively . . .	*hence* Identifying social phenomena is a very problematic exercise which involves the assumption that an action has a single unchanging meaning for all people, times and situations . . .
hence Numerical and other 'scientific' techniques can be adapted to 'measure' social facts . . .	*hence* Attempts to 'measure' will gloss over the above problems and lead to the imposition of observers' definitions on to a situation where the extent to which these are shared by actors under study is unknown . . .
hence Hypotheses which relate observer-defined variables can be tested . . .	*hence* To construct hypotheses is to assume that the problems listed above are either trivial or have been overcome . . .
hence Social theories can be constructed on the basis of discovered 'relationships' or tested by deducing testable hypotheses from some general theoretical statement . . .	*hence* The bid to explain social phenomena which are seldom adequately described in terms of actor orientations is at best premature and at worst a total misrepresentation of the problem of social reality . . .
hence Sociology can proceed with methodologies based on natural science models.	*hence* Sociology must develop alternative methodologies appropriate for studying subject matter which poses problems not faced by the subject matter of the natural sciences.

of Scientific Revolutions (1962) gave rise to the idea that communities of scientists hold taken-for-granted and unexamined assumptions about what they should study and how it should be studied. They confine their attention to smallscale puzzle-solving within the bounds of their assumptions. Kuhn referred to this shared agreement as a *paradigm* and those sharing it as a *community of scientists*. A shared paradigm produces criteria for judging and testing theories, with limits of acceptable margins of error and with exemplars of how to go about conducting similar research. When scientists operate within a paradigm they gain the support of their colleagues and are approved as doing *normal science*, for example, carrying out everyday routine scientific activity attempting to solve the problems generated by the paradigm within which they are working, 'a strenuous and devoted attempt to force nature into the conceptual boxes supplied by professional education' (Kuhn, 1962, p. 5). Kuhn contends that occasionally the orderly progress of science is disrupted by events which shatter the prevailing norm and, from a number of competing revisionary positions, a new conception of science is produced and a new paradigm emerges to re-establish a new normal science.

This explanation of the development of physical sciences is attractive to many sociologists—partly because its explanation is largely sociological, that is one learns normal science through an educational process which socialises and indoctrinates and a professional training which further eliminates other possible approaches to science, while deviants are excluded and denied a career. It also suggests that, after its positivist critique, sociology has thrown up a number of competing paradigms (or perspectives as we have called them) and it is only a matter of time before sociology settles down to adhere to one of these as its appropriate basis. In this sense sociology may be regarded as *preparadigmatic*. There are a number of criticisms both of Kuhn's original treatise and its appropriate extrapolation to social science (Worsley, 1974; Hawthorn, 1976; Benton, 1977). Perhaps the most powerful is that there never has been a sociology resembling normal science which has broken down, so we cannot be going through a scientific revolution awaiting the emergence of a new dominant paradigm. There are no signs that one school or perspective is ousting the others. Indeed, we could say that British sociology is characterised by a healthy pluralism.

If there is no one acceptable way or agreement that one type of data is 'better' than another then this opens the door for different sociological methods to be applied as appropriate to different aspects of sociological problems. In the next part of this chapter we will deal with three different approaches to the study of suicide as a sociological phenomenon. We have selected this topic partly to reinforce the idea that what may be taken for granted by health professionals is a source of inspiration for sociological study, and what may be seen as a straightforward problem, in definitional terms, for psychiatrists and coroners, is in fact open to different interpretations. We have also selected suicide because it was one of the topics given early sociological treatment, yet it remains of sociological interest.

DURKHEIM AND A STRUCTURALIST TREATMENT OF SUICIDE

Durkheim was a structuralist and a positivist. Like Comte, he treated social facts as things to be regarded independently of the individuals who contribute to them. Durkheim used suicide as a means of showing that such apparently individual acts were more a matter for sociological treatment than the outcome of individual psychology. He was concerned to find the laws which govern suicide, and particularly rates of suicide, within societies. To do this he developed several propositions or hypotheses at different levels of abstraction. The lowest level he could then put to the test against empirical data. These hypotheses are schematically summarised by Maris (1969) and progress from hypotheses at lower levels of generalisation (level III) through to propositions which encompass them, at level II and to a general theoretical premise at level I.

> Having disposed of the extra social factors to his satisfaction, Durkheim proceeds to compound lower-level generalizations of the 'greater than', or ordinal scale variety from his statistics. Some of the more important first level generalizations are listed below, roughly in the order of the appearance in *Suicide* (for the sake of brevity the symbol > is employed to mean 'tend to have a higher suicide rate than').

h1. City dwellers > rural dwellers
h2. The sane > the insane
h3. Adults > children
h4. Older adults > younger adults
h5. In March through August > in September through February
h6. In daytime > in the night
h7. Protestants > Catholics > Jews
h8. Majority groups > minority groups
h9. Upper social classes > lower social classes
h10. The learned > the unlearned
h11. Males > females
h12. The unmarried > the married
h13. The married without children > the married with children
h14. Those in smaller families > those in larger families
h15. Bachelors > widows
h16. Those living in time of peace > those living in time of war
h17. Soldiers > civilians
h18. Elite troops > non-elite troops
h19. Those whose society is experiencing an economic crisis > those
     whose society is not experiencing an economic crisis
h20. Those living in a period of rapid social change > those living in a
     period of slow social change
h21. The rich > the poor
h22. The morally undisciplined > the morally disciplined
h23. Divorcees > non divorcees.

Maris goes on to quote direct from *Suicide* (Durkheim, 1952, p. 208)
what he refers to as Durkheim's second-level hypotheses from which all
those listed above can be deduced:

H1. Suicide varies inversely with the degree of integration of religious
    society.
H2. Suicide varies inversely with the degree of integration of domestic
    society.
H3. Suicide varies inversely with the degree of integration of political
    society.

Finally, on the third level, Durkheim posits a grand hypothesis intended
to subsume all previously mentioned hypotheses. This hypothesis (which
is also a grand empirical generalization if we can assume that the
previous hypotheses were true and that the determination of the
common denominator of them were accurate) states that:

H. Suicide varies inversely with the degree of integration of social
   groups of which the individual forms a part (Maris, 1969, p. 32–33,
   quoted in Atkinson, 1978, p. 12–13).

To repeatedly test and fail to falsify these hypotheses would
provide grounds for their acceptance as laws governing suicidal behaviour. More generally this would uphold the positivist view that it is possible to isolate theories and their
propositions which will ultimately provide an explanation for
human conduct and events. The fact that individuals subjectively experience such events and attribute different meaning
to them could be ignored in the quest for such social laws.
Durkheim was concerned with finding ways of operationalis-

ing the concepts he was working with so that he could measure them and carry out statistical tests of the relationship between them in order to challenge and ultimately strengthen his theoretical exposition of suicide.

To be able to do this it is necessary to accept that suicide, as the dependent variable, like each of the independent variables—integration of religious society, integration of domestic society and integration of political society—is indeed 'thing-like' and sufficiently easy to operationalise and internally consistent to use as a concept. Thus all suicides and all official categorisations of suicide are treated as if they are the same. Durkheim therefore independently defines what suicide *really is*; 'suicide is applied to all cases of death resulting directly or indirectly from a positive or negative act of the victim himself, which he knows will produce this result' (Durkheim, 1952, p. 44). He assumes all official statistics are derived from the uncomplicated application of this definition.

Obviously it was not possible for Durkheim to set up experiments to change the way society functions and examine the consequent suicide rates. What he had to do was to rely on published official statistical data and carry out an analysis of the relationship between them, for example, variable analysis or multivariate analysis, relying on the assumption that if there is a consistent relationship between variables then one is causing the other to happen. This process entailed collecting the suicide rates for different European countries and quantifying measures for his other variables, for instance marriage rates, the amount of divorce, the extent to which a country is Protestant or Catholic or Jewish, whether there is an economic crisis. He posed questions like the extent to which suicide is linked to religious persuasion. To test this he had to identify countries in which a particular religious group predominated, for example Italy, highly Catholic, or Germany, highly Protestant. Even if there were different suicide rates in these two countries it could be a matter of nationality—Italian or German—rather than the predominant religious affiliation. To overcome this problem Durkheim had to seek areas within countries where different religions predominated. In Germany, Bavaria had the fewest suicides and most Catholics and within the provinces of Bavaria there was a direct relationship between suicide rates and the proportion of Protestants and an inverse relationship to the proportion of Catholics. This is diagrammatically expressed:

The more often Durkheim found this kind of relationship, the more certain were his claims that the empirical data indicate a causal link between the variables. Thus, rather than setting out to falsify his hypothesis (Popper's view of the process of scientific enquiry), Durkheim actually relies on accumulating evidence to support his contentions.

His theory, going from lower to higher levels of abstraction as outlined above, was that it was not the fact of being Protestant or Catholic which influenced the individuals committing suicide but that these different religions influenced the degree of integration of communities—protestantism encouraging individualism and catholicism fostering close community ties. This variable he called social integration and is shown as:

It is social integration which is a collective property, a social fact. This same process is worked through for domestic integration:

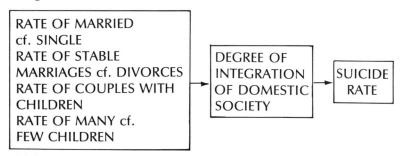

Thus by testing more and more of such relationships Durkheim strengthened his proposition that the cause of one kind of suicide was insufficient societal organisation. He produced a social explanation of suicide which also permitted prediction. He similarly characterised other types of suicide in the same way, but these do not need to concern us here. What is important, however, is the degree of clarity of these major variables or social facts. Acceptance of this theory rests not only on the logic of the relationships between the variables but more so on accepting that suicides and the integration of social groups are adequately conceptualised and measured. There is little point in having appropriate logic applied to inadequately operationalised concepts.

Some of those who followed the Durkheimian approach to suicide while adhering to the positivists' tradition have challenged his interpretation of social integration. For example, Gibbs and Martin (1964) clearly recognised the ambiguities in his treatment of social integration and consequently the lack of a rigorous test of his theory. What Gibbs and Martin did was to attempt a better operationalisation of social integration as the 'stability and durability of relationships' within a population. (As Douglas (1967) notes, they could equally well have chosen the volume or the extent of relationships, for example, frequency of contact, as part of such a definition and no explanation is given for choosing not to do so.) They also decided to focus on status rather than role conflict on the assumption that this is the fundamental determinant of the stability and durability of social relationships within a population. The picture presented by Gibbs and Martin is one of an individual experiencing a role configuration which is so filled with role conflicts that the individual will wish to leave it. If they are unable to do so by other means then they make the ultimate departure by suicide—at least they commit suicide with more frequency than those with less role or status conflict. These reinterpreted variables then form the kind of hypothesis provided here:

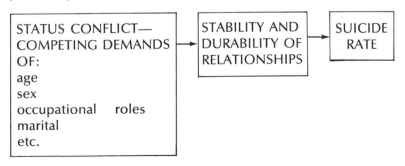

STATUS CONFLICT—COMPETING DEMANDS OF: age sex occupational roles marital etc. → STABILITY AND DURABILITY OF RELATIONSHIPS → SUICIDE RATE

Douglas has pointed up a number of basic flaws in this re-interpretation of social integration which Gibbs and Martin devised because they considered it to be more measurable and hence provide a better test of Durkheim's theory. Gibbs and Martin provide no indication of what actually *causes* this hypothesised relationship, probably because if would ultimately have to be reduced to some kind of collective consciousness or individual personality to produce suicide. Thus, what set out to improve upon Durkheim's work by providing a better empirical test of his theory by better operational definitions of the concepts, in fact provides no test of it at all. Durkheim's theory remains a theory awaiting sound empirical testing.

The meaning of suicide data

The other major and related criticism of Durkheim's work is his interpretation of suicide itself and the use of data from official sources. As Atkinson (1978) points out, published official statistics about suicide are normally given as numbers and tabulated according to a very limited range of variables such as age and sex. Researchers themselves have to work out rates for other groups from other sources of demographic data, and these are not always available in published official statistics.

Often this involves going beyond official statistics back to individual coroners' records of suicides—which provides not only for variability in what is recorded but also in how decisions are made about what to record. Thus suicide data have been derived from official sources which have compiled records in a variety of ways, and because of this they are not equivalent.

We have to deal with this problem ourselves in relation to interpreting official statistics about gestation age as an indicator of late booking of different social classes for antenatal care. Table 12.2 provides figures obtained from Scottish data. We were so impressed by the changes which had taken place in the overall reduction in 'late bookers' that we wrote to the official source, in this case, Information Services Division of the Scottish Health Service Common Services Agency, to check that the figures issued were correct and to ask about their method of collection. It transpires that the 1971 figures

Table 12.2 Percentage of married women making a late antenatal booking (after more than 21 weeks gestation)

Social class	Scotland	
	1971[1]	1981[2]
I Professional	28	11
II Managerial	35	12
III Skilled manual and non-manual	36	12
IV Partly skilled	39	15
V Unskilled	47	18

Sources:
[1] Brotherston Sir J 1976 Inequality: Is it inevitable? In: Carter C O, Peel J (eds) Equalities and inequalities in Health. Academic Press, London, p 85
[2] Information Services Division 1983 Unpublished Tables.

we quoted were based on data collected on about 44 000 women who offered a 'certain' last menstrual period (LMP). Our letter back stated 'I don't think that there was much validation of the data in those earlier days' (Cole, 1984). That is, the LMP was that given by the women themselves and this was combined with date of delivery to produce the calculated gestation date for time of first booking for antenatal care. The 1981 data were based on *married* women, and gestational age at booking was arrived at by calculating backwards from the clinical estimate of gestation at delivery, given in weeks, and subtracting the number of weeks between the date of booking and the date of delivery. This method has been adopted to help eliminate the 'nonsense' gestations which were the result of irregular menstrual cycles and post-pill amenorrhoea. We must conclude therefore that it may be how the statistics are arrived at as much as or rather than changes in behaviour which explains a large reduction in apparently 'late bookers'.

To accept official data also avoids questioning what is to be studied, for example what is meant by suicide and how it is to be studied. This central assumption of agreed definitions made by positivists leaves no room to question whether suicides as perceived in official data are a complete record, or whether official definitions of what constitutes suicide are universally shared. (We can say the same about late booking.) Legal definitions, official categorisations and researchers' theoretical conceptions of suicide do not necessarily coincide.

Probable differences in the definitions underpinning suicide give rise to the important problem of the validity of suicide data as well as their reliability.

In terms of validity we are questioning whether one official definition of death as suicide is necessarily the same as any other, be it official, sociological, theoretical or lay definition, and whether any one is any more correct or relevant. Reliability poses questions about the consistency of such definitions between individuals and cultures and over time and whether there is a 'true rate' to which official rates approximate. In suicide research it is not just a matter of finding the 'error rate' in the statistics. Douglas (1967) adds a further dimension to the problem of official statistics. Picking up Durkheim's notion of social integration, Douglas proposed a possible connection between social integration, rates of concealment and attempted concealment of suicide and the influence this may have on suicide rates. If official rates in part depend upon rates of concealment and if rates of concealment are highest among the more socially integrated, then Durkheimian theory may be more to do with official suicide rates rather than any 'real' rate. This gets us back to the question of what constitutes a 'real' suicide and so the problems of validity and reliability are compounded. Douglas makes the point as follows 'We shall never be very sure about the reliability of the official statistics, and certainly not about their validity, until a great many good studies have been made of the methods used by officials to categorise deaths, their assumptions, their methods of collecting data and tabulating it, and of the 'real' community rates of suicide' (Douglas, 1967, p. 297). This of course raises the question of whether the 'real' rate *is* potentially knowable, but we are then faced with the issue of whose definition of reality should be the focus of such a concern.

Social definitions of suicide

For any research to be done on the subject of suicide a death must be categorised as such and some decision has to be made. One approach to suicide research arising from this problem is to attempt to gain an understanding of how officials actually go about the process of making decisions to categorise a death as suicide rather than as an accident, misadventure, homicide or returning an open verdict. An empirical issue is *how* the categorisations are done and not how well they are done, or how closely they match to any official definition of suicide or ideal conception of how they should be done. This approach involves no longer taking officially generated data at its face value and treating it as 'hard, objective data' about incidents, but attempting to investigate the complexities of the processes and interactions which lead to official categorisations of deaths as suicide. At the same time it involves attempting to 'understand' or 'appreciate' the meanings which those involved attribute to their own actions and to the actions of others—including those of the deceased. In following this approach the definition of suicide becomes not the content of law or that which is written in the coroner's handbook or even that provided by the researcher. Rather it is empirically grounded and evolves from examining the actions of those involved in deciding what constitutes suicide as they go about their everyday work. This interpretation of the issue removes some of the problems of validity and reliability inherent in the criticisms of the positive approach outlined above. It is not, however, without its own problems as we shall see.

ATKINSON AND AN INTERACTIONIST APPROACH TO SUICIDE

Atkinson (1978) examined *how* some deaths get categorised as suicides. In using an interactionist perspective he was concerned with observing and recording at first hand the various social processes which were involved in the work of coroners who have legal responsibility for categorising deaths referred to them. However, categorising deaths involves medical as well as legal concerns and so interaction takes place between two sets of professionals—doctors, on the one hand and, on the other coroners who are usually lawyers (and their clerks who are policemen). This interaction is of continuous importance, especially in the initial stage because, for a death to be referred to a coroner, others must make the decision about whether it is violent, unnatural or 'a sudden death, the cause of which is unknown'. However a death may be sudden but not unexpected; to be referred to a coroner it must be both 'sudden' and 'unnatural'. These quotation marks are used because what constitutes a sudden or an unnatural death is not predefined but itself is socially constructed. Coroners' investigations leading to categorisations of deaths involve a number of different kinds of activities, many carried out by the coroner's officer. These include not only inquests, but examining the scene of death, identification of the deceased, interviews with relatives and other witnesses, arranging and attending post mortems and collecting the evidence together to write reports.

In his initial overtures with coroners while he was setting up his study and before he began his formal data-collection, Atkinson found that officials could see nothing interesting or problematic in what for them was a straightforward activity. They saw categorisation of deaths as an orderly procedure rather than one categorised by ambiguity or uncertainty. This interpretation of their work was one reason Atkinson did not pursue his research using a method well used by those who regard the definition of the problem as unproblematic. That is, he did not resort to questionnaires or interviews asking coroners standardised questions about how they went about their activities because this would have yielded only a generalised account of the 'ordinary' and perhaps some references to what is regarded as 'ordinary' by contrasting this to what coroner's regard as 'extraordinary'. While interviews or questionnaire data would certainly have yielded some pointers, this method would not have been suitable as a means of finding out how decisions are made *in practice* as opposed to in theory. To achieve this understanding demanded a much wider set of data from diverse sources in order to find out the kind of social and interpretative processes involved in the categorisation of deaths. This data certainly included interview material, not of a standardised variety, but interviews which seek to elaborate and clarify observed events. Other forms of data used by Atkinson included analysis of coroners' written reports, newspaper reports of suicides and, most important, first-hand observation of the work of the coroner's officer and inquests.

From the mass of data collected, Atkinson found that coroners must search for specific pieces of evidence to confirm the verdict of suicide and to reject other possible verdicts. The search for 'clues' involved a whole range of sources—the remains, including suicide notes and threats, the mode of dying, location and circumstances of the death and the biography of the deceased person. These 'clues' however are interpreted against and in the light of a variety of taken-for-granted assumptions about what constitutes a 'typical' suicide or a 'typical suicidal biography'. Therefore suicide notes and other 'relics' are not interpreted independently but in conjunction with other 'clues'. Nothing in itself would be sufficient—even what may be regarded as a 'suicide note' must be interpreted by the finders in the context of other 'clues'. Thus clues have to be 'read' (Garfinkel, 1967a) and it is only when they have been 'read' that they can be used as evidence or 'facts'. Thus 'clues' once they are interpreted or considered as 'facts' about the case are then given the status of facts about the case for the purposes of deciding whether it is indeed a suicide. No mode of death is entirely unequivocal although hanging or inhaling exhaust fumes from a car are almost always taken as a definite indicator of suicide. Mode of death suggests what other types of evidence should be sought and directs other activities. An explanatory model of each death is built up and, to be categorised as suicide, no part of it must be inconsistent with the coroner's ideas about what constitutes a typical suicide.

What Atkinson is saying is that coroners hold a view of what constitutes a typical suicide, this is their 'meaning' of suicide. Coroners construct their own common-sense theories of what is suicide and it is this which guides the kind of information sought and its interpretation.

Interactionists' methods

We can see that interactionists and structuralists conceive the problem of suicide very differently. Interactionists seek explanations of how specific groups of individuals interpret and define suicide, in other words how the meaning of suicide is socially constructed. Rather than pursue the studies at a societal or macro-sociological level they carry out much finer-textured analysis at the point where the action takes place in an endeavour to interpret what is happening. Typically data is collected in one or a narrow range of settings to provide a case study, which involves researchers observing and inevitably taking part in what is happening even though they may retain 'observer' status.

This kind of research owes a great deal to anthropologists who studied cultures other than their own. Malinowski (1922) provides three main principles for this type of research: any researcher must espouse scientific values, must live among the people he is studying and must apply a number of techniques for collecting and ordering data and presenting evidence. A distinction is drawn between the data collected, for example the particular question the coroner asks relatives of the deceased at an inquest, and the researchers' *interpretation* of that data, for example that the question reflects the coroner's attempts to reconstruct the deceased person's biography in terms of propensity to commit suicide. Thus interactionist sociology can also be called *interpretative* sociology. It relies on *inference*; for example the inference that a person kneeling in a place of worship is *at prayer* involves assumptions about the social significance of posture, the locale in which the act is taking place and the relationship between locale and religious belief. Problems arise in qualitative social research in connecting observation and interpretation. The purpose of the research is 'to grasp the native's point of view, his relation to life, to realise *his* vision of *his* world' (Malinowski, 1922, p. 25, original italics). The problem therefore is one of knowing that the interpretation provided by the researcher is faithful to the point of view of the subjects of his study, that it *is* their version of their world.

This approach in sociology, while studying our own society, has come to be known as ethnography. The researcher is involved in collecting data at first hand, using participant observation or, more generally, field methods. It relies on making observations as they happen, following these up by informally interviewing informants, collecting written records which are relevant and then turning these into usable data.

In the example quoted of Atkinson's work on suicide this involved him in observing a range of settings, interviewing some of the participants as well as using coroners' records and newspaper cuttings. One of the difficulties, however, is what to observe and what to make of the data. As Atkinson himself said elsewhere about the research strategies adopted by interactionists: 'a funny story here, an apt quote from a 'subject' there, a few extracts from a newspaper or television. Indeed it sometimes seemed that anything one happened to stumble across would do, so long as it seemed relevant in some way to the arguments being presented'. (Atkinson, 1977, p. 42). Collecting data need not be as sloppy as this, but it does raise the problems mentioned earlier of the epistemological status of ethnographic research and how it addresses problems of reliability and validity.

Interactionists criticise positivist structuralists because of the way they operationalise and measure theoretically relevant concepts. Positivists at least indicate before they begin empirical studies what they regard as relevant concepts, how they are operationalised and how they relate theoretically. Interactionists, on the other hand, are likely to set out without an explicit theoretical model to guide their data-collection, and have to generate theory as they go along, interpreting the data they have and creating hypotheses which will provide pointers for new data to be collected. These new data are thus used to test the hypotheses generated. This process of going from data to theory is called *analytical induction*. The term was used by Znaniecki (1934) to *describe* what *actually* happens in doing the research which *begins* with collecting data. More recently it has been used to attempt to specify how it is legitimate to arrive at general propositions by abstracting 'essential features' of observed cases of a phenomenon. This is not the same as 'data dredging' (Fig. 12.3) or 'data snooping', otherwise called innumerative induction from survey research data, which relies on collecting a large number of cases and developing categories and empirical generalisations strictly on the basis of the data to hand. Rather analytic induction involves abstracting out of empirical data and generating categorisations which are then tested against subsequently collected data. It abstracts from a given concrete case the features which are essential to its definition and generalises them to new cases. The stages in this abstract procedure of theory construction are described by Robinson (1951) as:

'1. A rough definition of the phenomenon to be explained is formulated.

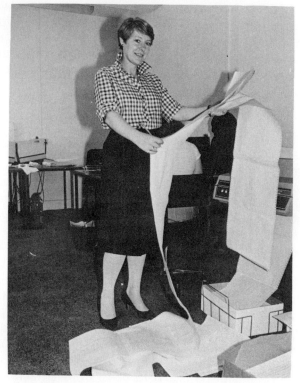

Fig. 12.3 Research yielding large quantities of numerical data may become nothing more than 'data dredging' exercises (courtesy of Nursing Standard).

2. An hypothetical explanation of the phenomenon is formulated.
3. One case is studied in the light of the hypothesis.
4. If the hypothesis does not fit the facts, either the hypothesis is reformulated or the phenomenon to be explained is redefined, so that the case is excluded.
5. Practical certainty may be attained after a small number of cases have been examined, but the discovery by the investigator or any other investigator of a single negative case disproves the explanation and requires a reformulation.
6. This procedure of examining cases, redefining the phenomenon and reformulating the hypothesis is continued until a universal relationship is established, each negative case calling for a redefinition or a reformulation'.

(Robinson, 1951, p. 813).

The procedure calls for successive reformulation of hypotheses. The essential feature of analytical induction is to establish which conditions must be in existence before a phenomenon occurs, leading to the identification of characteristics *all* of which are present when the phenomenon occurs and, when the characteristics are *not* present, the phenomenon does not occur. Through this method *practical* certainty, rather than claims for universality, is achievable. The researcher searches for exceptions, cases in which within the established conditions, the phenomenon does not occur or cases, when, in their absence, it does. These cases would form the focal point for a new examination of the prevailing explanation, with an extension of knowledge. In this way induction always progresses from the basis of observations to generate or test theory.

Lindesmith's (1968) research on opiate addiction provides a clear illustration of the method to produce explanatory propositions. He conducted 70 in-depth interviews with addicts to produce case studies. Lindesmith concluded that the power of the opiate habit is derived basically from the effects which follow the withdrawal of the drug rather than upon any positive effects which its presence in the body produces. Addiction only occurs when opiates are used to alleviate withdrawal distress, after this distress has been properly understood or interpreted by the individual experiencing it, addiction is quickly and permanently established through further use of the drug. If the individual fails to conceive of his distress as withdrawal distress brought about by the absence of opiates, he does not become addicted.

The analytic method followed is best described as setting up a series of critical case studies, leading to successive revisions of the guiding theory. By setting up hypotheses based on findings in earlier cases studied, each one could then be tested against subsequent cases and repeated when any negative case was found. An initial hypothesis was that individuals who do not know what drug they are receiving do not become addicted and that they become addicted when they know what they are getting and have taken it long enough to experience withdrawal distress. This initial hypothesis was destroyed by a negative case. A doctor, who had received morphine for several weeks and was fully aware of the fact, did not become addicted.

Lindesmith had to reformulate and set up a second provisional hypothesis that persons become addicts when they recognise or perceive the significance of withdrawal distress which they are experiencing, and that if they do not recognise withdrawal distress they do not become addicts regardless of other considerations. This hypothesis had to be revised when cases were found in which individuals who had experienced and understood withdrawal distress did not use the drug to alleviate the distress and never became addicts. The revision of this hypothesis involved shifting the emphasis from the individual's recognition of withdrawal distress to his use of the drug to alleviate the distress after this insight had occurred. No negative cases were subsequently found.

Lindesmith was therefore able to conclude that 'this theory furnishes a simple but effective explanation, not only of the manner in which addiction becomes established, but also in the essential features of addiction behaviour, those features which are found in all parts of the world, and which are common sense to all cases' (Lindesmith, 1947, p. 165). Lindesmith's aim was to produce *universal* generalisations which would apply to all cases which could be studied. Finding a single negative case caused either reformulating the hypothesis or redefining the phenomenon of addiction. This is possible because the process is one of building types or classifications out of the data as one goes along, rather than being established *a priori*.

Some would argue that concepts and observations are not so independent, that concepts are not just developed out of observations but neither are they imposed as *a priori* categories. Lachenmeyer writes 'theories are not developed deductively or inductively, but *both* deductively and inductively. There is constant interplay between the observation of realities and the formation of concepts, between research and theorising, between perception and explanation. The genesis of any theory is best described as a reciprocal development of observational sophistication and theoretical precision' (Lachenmeyer, 1971, p. 61). In reality there may be a synthesis of approaches since the researcher is unlikely to arrive at the point of data collection completely without some *a priori* notion of what is *likely* to be the case with hypotheses and concepts tentatively stated.

The researcher is not a *tabula rasa* although Glaser and

Strauss (1967) in their *Discovery of Grounded Theory*, an important text on inductive research, advocate that investigators 'at first, literally ignore the literature of theory and fact on the area under study, in order to assure that the emergence of categories will not be contaminated by concepts more suited to different areas. Similarities and convergencies with the literature may be established after the analytic core of categories has emerged' (p. 37). The question is the extent to which researchers impose concepts on their data and seek data which fit pre-selected concepts.

Those favouring deductive rather than inductive logic have made damaging attacks on logical grounds as well as on the point of keeping one's mind free of prior conceptualisation in such familiar sociological ground as mental illness and social stratification. It would be extremely difficult to conduct a sociological study of the management of dying patients without being influenced by Glaser and Strauss' influential work already described in Chapter 10.

We come therefore to the same kind of issue that confronted us with positivist research—namely the precision of the concepts used and their relationships with theory. Bulmer (1979) contends that 'Interpretative procedures tend to be weak in providing justifications for particular conceptualizations. There is often a shared assumption that the concepts used are fruitful and make sense in the particular analysis being done' (p. 673–674). This assumption leaves aside the whole question of the meaning and inter-subjective validity of concepts, as well as the point at which it can be assumed that concept formation is sufficiently complete to stop seeking new data. We are also left with the problem of the extent to which the interpretative studies carried out by interactionists can be generalised beyond the locales in which they take place.

More seriously still, interactionist studies may be said to be as deterministic as those of positivists because the researcher, albeit using different logic and methods, attempts to define and make causal statements about how it *really* is in the world. Just as the positivists provide a theoretical account of objective reality which is devoid of reference to the meaning of phenomena to the individuals involved so interactionists attempt to understand these meanings but they are filtered and *interpreted* by the researcher. Are interactionists therefore simply providing a different version of reality and is it any better a version than that provided by positivists? Cicourel (1964) contends that the reasoning, interpretations and interactional skills used to produce such explanations are largely unexamined and themselves should be the basis for sociological investigation. Furthermore, since they are likely to resemble those of the subjects they study, the appropriate field for study should be the taken-for-granted and unexamined methods which members—including sociologists—use to produce the shared meanings and collective behaviour which characterise and constitute social life. This is clearly an ethnomethodological viewpoint.

GARFINKEL AND AN ETHNOMETHODOLOGICAL TREATMENT OF SUICIDE

Atkinson's study indicated that coroners had their own common-sense theories about suicide which guided their subsequent actions in categorising deaths. Atkinson wrote:

> 'There appeared to be a convergence between common sense and expert theorising about suicide, and that there were good reasons why the latter was in line with the former. For if coroners regarded evidence, for example, depression or social isolation as strong indicators that a suicide had taken place, it was hardly surprising that statistical analyses based on their decisions would 'discover' such connections. It was still a puzzle as to what the import of this was for their practice of claiming that such correlations supported general explanatory theories . . . . In short, the positivist legacy was still evident in this continued concern to make causal statements about how it *really* is in the world; to replace one kind of determinism with another. . . . At the heart of the final paradigmatic crisis in the research was the problem of what to make of the apparent convergence between common sense and expert theorising about suicide, and in particular whether the implication of this was that the layman's charge against sociology to the effect that it was no more than common sense was, after all, perfectly justified'
>
> (Atkinson, 1977, p. 44).

Ethnomethodologists would of course agree with this to the extent that sociologists must use the same process as anyone else to make sense of a potentially senseless world. Garfinkel called this *practical sociological reasoning* and it is the way that such reasoning takes place that is the heart of their concerns. Related to this are problems of categorisation and description. This applies not only to the status and adequacy of categorisations by researchers as referred to above but to the analysis of how people go about constructing categories in their everyday lives in order to proceed. Ethnomethodologists' concern with suicide therefore stems not from an interest in the subject *per se* (and as such this bears a resemblance to Durkheim's use of suicide merely as a topic by which he pursued methodological interests) but in *describing* the methods used in a practical situation which demands choice and decision making. Similar kinds of situations include jury deliberations of negligence cases and clinic staff selection of patients for out-patient psychiatric treatment (Garfinkel, 1967b). In each of these the central analytic issues are the nature of practical sociological reasoning and reflexivity, concepts which we described in Chapter 2.

Garfinkel (1967a) studied coroners and suicide investigators working for the Los Angeles Suicide Prevention Centre (SPC). The staff of SPC carried out what were referred to as 'psychological autopsies' in which they had to cope with unclassified deaths which were referred to them as equivocal—the same problem as studied by Atkinson. The nature and manner of this practical sociological reasoning is best summed up by Garfinkel in the following way:

> 'SPC inquiries begin with a death that the coroner finds equivocal as to *mode* of death. They use the death as a precedent by means of which various ways of living in society that could have terminated with the death are searched for and read 'in the remains'—in the scraps of this and that, such as the body and its trappings, medicine bottles, notes, bits and pieces of clothing, memorabilia: anything that can be photographed, collected and packaged. Other 'remains' are collected too: rumors, passing remarks, and stories—material in the 'repertoire' of whomever might be consulted through the common work of conversations. These 'whatsoever' bits and pieces that a story or a rule or a proverb might make intelligible are used to formulate a recognizably coherent, standard, typical, cogent, uniform, planful, i.e. a professionally defensible, and thereby for members *recognizably* rational account of how the society worked to produce these remains. This point will be clearer if the reader consults a standard textbook in forensic pathology. In it he will find the inevitable photograph of the victim with a slashed throat. Were the coroner to use that 'sight' to suggest the equivocality of the mode of death he might say something such as this: 'In the case where a body looks like the one in that picture, you are looking at a suicidal death because the wound shows the 'hesitation cuts' that accompany the great wound. One can imagine these cuts are the remains of a procedure whereby the victim first made several preliminary trials of a hesitating sort and then performed the lethal slash.

Other courses of action are imaginable, too, and so cuts that look like hesitation cuts can be produced by other mechanisms. One needs to start with the actual display and imagine how different courses of action could have been organized such that *that* picture would be compatible with it. One might think of the photographed display as a phase-of-the-action. In any actual display is there a course of action with which that phase is uniquely compatible? *That* is the coroner's question'.

(Garfinkel, 1967a, p. 176).

It is by using the concept of reflexivity that Garfinkel provides an understanding of how it was the officials were producing decisions which had to be 'justifiable' and 'reasonable' in the 'circumstances'. He uses the main features of the work of SPC to do so—the organised character of the work that they do and the particular problem of investigating equivocal deaths.

In carrying out their work, Garfinkel showed that the organisational arrangements were taken for granted and not commented upon yet at the same time they were continually being made visible so that others could agree the grounds for actions. The grounds for such activities are not distinct from them but are situationally embedded in the activities to which they relate. This reflexivity is also clearly manifested in the production of clear rational accounts for what were initially referred because they were 'equivocal deaths'. Garfinkel makes the important point that the accounts of a particular death as this or that type of death are constitutive features of the death. The 'remains' and 'relics' which are 'read' in arriving at an account of death which is 'rational for all practical purposes' are not just already there but are all that is there to provide grounds for classifying a death as suicide. In other words the 'relics' which are selected and defined as 'relics' suggest a proposed categorisation, and the proposed categorisation is then checked by reference to the relics. With reference to such procedures coroners and SPC staff

'. . . have to start with *this* much; *this* sight; *this* note; *this* collection of whatever is at hand. And *whatever* is there is good enough in the sense that whatever is there not only *will* do but *does*. One makes whatever is there do. By this is not meant that an SPC investigator is too easily content or that he does not look for more when he should. What is meant rather is that the 'whatever' it is that he has to deal with is what will be used to find out, to make decidable the way that society operated to produce *that* picture, to have come to *that* scene as its end result. In this way the remains on the slab serve not only as a precedent but as a goal of SPC inquiries. *Whatsoever* SPC members are faced with must serve as the precedent by means of which they read the remains in order to see how the society could have operated to have produced what it is that they have 'in the end', 'in the final analysis', and 'in *any* case'. What the inquiry can come to is what the death came to'

(Garfinkel, 1967a, p. 177).

Members of the SPC as in all other imaginable settings are engaged in 'monitoring' descriptions derived from the features of the setting by reference to the features of the same setting. In this way the methods used by members to test hypotheses, rule out alternatives, develop theories and construct categories are the same as those used by sociologists— in other words reflexivity is central to practical sociological reasoning.

Ethnomethodologists' methods

The heading for this section may provide a clue as to why Garfinkel and his colleagues, as far as we can ascertain, provide no clear instructions or programme for how to do ethnomethodological studies or what they might look like. Rather they urge us to examine the studies themselves. Because ethnomethodology sets out with questions about *how* rather than *why* social order is accomplished, and seeks to provide generalised descriptions which go beyond the context in which empirical data were generated, they avoid the position that there could be any recipe for doing ethnomethodology. Researchers have to develop methods of analysis which are the same as those used by the subjects of their study to produce or accomplish the situations being studied through their joint everyday reasoning. They are not seeking to provide an account of reality 'out there' independent to or different from those involved in it.

In order to achieve this kind of analysis Payne et al (1981) point to two basic rules which ethnomethodologists follow. One is to regard the subject matter as 'anthropologically strange'—that is as an anthropologist would study some alien culture. How the ethnomethologist 'sees' the order in the setting he is studying poses questions about his social competence and the whole issue of his reflexivity with his data. Second, social actors in a setting are not regarded as 'rule-

governed dopes' following a set of imposed rules. Rather ethnomethodologists present actors as interpreters of rules.
Rules may apply but they will require extension, adaptation
and modification to suit each unique situation. In this sense
members produce culture rather than are produced by it.

These basic considerations have given rise to two strands
of empirical work. One takes conversational analysis as its
subject matter. This approach rejects the inevitably incom-
plete nature of the data presented in ethnographic studies as
well as their dependence on the competence of the ethnographer for their solution and analytic organisation. They reflect
the researchers' descriptions and interpretations.

Conversational analysis depends on making its data, in its
raw state, publicly available. This depended on the development of tape recorders to provide a faithful, albeit decontex-
tualised, reproduction. Both the data and the procedures by
which ethnomethodologists arrive at some interpretation of
it are made available for scrutiny and evaluation. In order to
carry out the analysis, the ethnomethodologist makes use of
knowledge shared with other members of his culture and dis-
plays this in his efforts to account for this particular collection
of talk. He makes public both his analysis and the uncontaminated, unprocessed data from which it was produced. Conversational analysts do not seek out the exceptional or
extreme. Rather they choose the most 'obvious' social phenomena as a topic. That is, that we can usually talk to each
other effectively and amicably. Conversational analysis seeks
to describe the processes which make possible an apparently
uninteresting sociological phenomenon, for example, everyday conversation. This depends on an analysis of how order
is achieved in verbal interaction and those features which enable an appearance of intelligibility of what is going on among
competent participants.

Recorded talk is potentially the soundest and least contaminated of all data. Moreover, it is data which can be reproduced at the depression of a tape recorder's switch. What
conversational analysts ultimately seek to do is to describe the
context-free structure of talk. They have therefore studied
turn-taking, opening and closing exchanges, topic change and
maintenance, and the design of question and answer sequences. As Atkinson and Drew (1979) say, they are con-

cerned with the '95%' which is common to all settings rather than the '5%' which is context-specific.

The second major ethnomethodological stance is that of ethnomethodological ethnography. Unlike the conversational analysts, they are concerned with the content and substance of conversation, not only its structural features. Payne et al (1981) write 'the ethnomethodological ethnographer starts from the question of how the participants in some event find its character and sustain it, or fail to, as a joint activity. He proceeds by a systematic process of inductive reasoning to specify the actors' models of their everyday social world which can be consulted to generate the observable conduct' (p. 134). This approach is very close to a new ethnographic tradition in anthropology:

> '. . . a society's culture consists of whatever it is one has to know or believe in order to operate in a manner acceptable to its members, and to do so in any role that they accept for any one of themselves . . . culture is not a material phenomenon; it does not consist of things, people, behaviour or emotions. It is rather an organization of these things. It is the forms of things that people have in mind, their models for perceiving, relating and otherwise interpreting them . . . Given such a definition it is impossible to describe a culture properly simply by describing behaviour or social, economic and ceremonial events and arrangements as observed material phenomena. What is required is to construct a theory of the conceptual models which they represent and of which they are artifacts. We test the adequacy of such a theory by our ability to interpret and predict what goes on in a community as measured by how its members, our informants, do so. A further test is our ability ourselves to behave in ways which lead to the kind of responses from the community members which our theory would lead us to expect. Thus tested, the theory is a valid statement of what you have to know in order to operate as a member of the society and is, as such, a valid description of its culture . . . The relation of language to culture is that of part to whole. Theory and method applicable to one must have implications for the other . . .
> (Goodenough, 1964, p. 36–37, quoted in Payne et al, 1981, p. 135).

It is the stress on actors' models as opposed to a researcher's selective interpretation of these models which distinguishes ethnomethodological ethnography from its predecessors.

The explication actors' models depends on the standing of the ethnomethodologist on the margins of the social group being studied. That is the group being studied is regarded as anthropologically strange. Collecting and interpreting data involves a continuous interchange of cultural frames—now taking the perspective of the member and now that of the

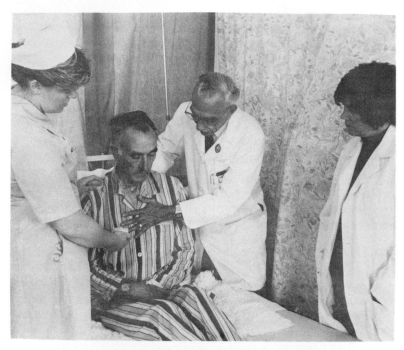

Fig. 12.4 Researchers resort to the ubiquitous white coat beloved of hospital workers while collecting data. They may be in the group but not of the group (courtesy of Rik Walton).

stranger. The reflexivity engendered itself becomes a source of data by enchancing knowledge of the phenomenon being studied through the same intimacy of knowledge of it as the members themselves have. The data presented are more analytic than descriptive, and less a product of the filtering and interpretation by the researcher than in typical ethnographic reports. They also claim to be closer to that used by conversational analysts by presenting *key* conversations or the context in which conversations take place in as complete a form as possible. An example of this kind of research is Phil Strong's (1979) *The Ceremonial Order of the Clinic* which contains a methodological appendix. This includes an account of the identified basis of the social rules adhered to by participants in paediatric clinics. The logic is clearly inductive, going from the data to generate propositions which explain them and which are subsequently tested out with other data.

It can be argued that the ethnomethodologists, by their commitment to explicating as far as possible the relationship between data and its analysis, are being more 'scientific' in their approach than are sociologists using different perspectives and their associated methods of hypothesis testing.

METHODOLOGICAL PLURALISM

In this chapter we have tried to demonstrate the interdependence of methods and sociological perspectives. Indeed, method *is* a perspectival component. Often methods are taught in a prescriptive, cookery-book fashion with recipes requiring certain ingredients processed in a variety of ways to produce the final product. We indicate under *Further reading* texts which accomplish this cookery-book approach. This approach to methods fails to take into account the perspective from which the research is being conducted, the rules of logic being applied and the differential appropriateness of methods for different research questions.

Throughout this chapter we have emphasised the epistemological debates which continue in relation to the positivist traditions of science and the challenges of inductive methods. Indeed Feyerabend (1975) argues that scientists should follow no methodological rules, either inductive or deductive, and that, in reality, scientists frequently change their rules, what they are doing and how they are doing it. For him, there is no point in subscribing to any of the positions we have outlined and he argues *against* method.

This radical position finds little favour with traditional philosophies of science, with prescriptive approaches to how science should be done or with pragmatists attempting to carry out studies. However, debates about the status of sociological knowledge and the methods used to provide it are not confined to the philosophical and sociological communities. In 1982 Sir Keith Joseph, Secretary of State for Education, decreed that no longer did we have a Social *Science* Research Council but an Economic and Social Research Council. The work funded or undertaken by SSRC did not match to *his* normative expectations of science. This raises questions, therefore, for society about the status of knowledge generated by sociology and other forms of social research.

We retain our stance that methodological pluralism is warranted in sociology. Different methods have their place provided one knows what questions to ask. Indeed, we try to practise what we preach. Both of us are currently involved in an evaluation of long-stay accommodation for elderly people. This evaluation uses both traditional experimental and survey methods in the positivist tradition and field methods in the inductivist tradition to provide data relevant to different kinds of questions (Bond, 1984).

We are left in the position of saying that sociology is about studying a social world that is external to the sociologist, but of which he is a part, and which is experienced by him in systematic ways. These ways differ, providing *different* conclusions. However without exception they involve systematic observation, recorded data collection, generating propositions, and testing them to provide confirmation or falsification.

REFERENCES

Atkinson J M 1977 Coroners and the categorisation of deaths as suicides: changes in perspective as features of the research process. In: Bell C, Newby H (eds) Doing sociological research. Allen & Unwin, London, ch 1, p 31–46

Atkinson J M 1978 Discovering suicide: studies in the social organization of sudden death. MacMillan, London

Atkinson J M, Drew P 1979 Order in court: the organization of verbal interaction in judicial settings. MacMillan, London

Bell C, Newby H (eds) 1977 Doing sociological research. Allen & Unwin, London

Benton T 1977 Philosophical foundations of the three sociologies. Routledge & Kegan Paul, London

Bond J 1984 Evaluation of long-stay accommodation for elderly people. In: Bromley D B (ed) Gerontology: social and behavioural perspectives. Croom Helm, London, ch 11, p 88–101

Bulmer M 1979 Concepts in the analysis of qualitative data. Sociological Review 27: 651–677

Bynner J, Stribley K M (eds) 1979 Social research: principles and procedures. Longman & Open University Press, London

Cicourel A V 1964 Method and measurement in sociology. Free Press, New York

Cole S K 1984 Personal communication

Douglas J D 1967 The social meaning of suicide. Princeton University Press, Princeton

Durkheim E 1952 Suicide. Routledge & Kegan Paul, London
Evans-Pritchard E 1950 Witchcraft, oracles and magic among the Azande. Oxford University Press, Oxford
Feyerabend P 1975 Against method: outline of an anarchistic theory of knowledge. New Left Editions, London
Garfinkel H 1967a Practical sociological reasoning: some features in the work of the Los Angeles Suicide Prevention Centre. In: Shneidman E S (ed) Essays in self-destruction. Science Home, New York, ch 8, p 171–187
Garfinkel H 1967b Studies in ethnomethodology. Prentice Hall, Englewood Cliffs, NJ
Gibbs J P, Martin W T 1964 Status integration and suicide. Oregon University Press, Evgene, Oregon
Giddens A 1976 New rules of sociological method: a positive critique of interpretative sociologies. Hutchinson, London
Glaser B G, Strauss A L 1967 The discovery of grounded theory. Strategies for qualitative research. Aldine, New York
Goodenough W H 1964 Cultural anthropology and linguistics. In: Hymes D (ed) Language in culture and society. A reader in linguistics and anthropology. Harper & Row, New York, ch 3, p 36–39
Hammond P E (ed) 1964 Sociologists at work: essays on the craft of social research. Basic Books, New York
Hawthorn G 1976 Enlightenment and despair: a history of sociology. Cambridge University Press, Cambridge
Janowitz M 1956 Some consequences of social mobility in the United States. Transactions of the Third World Congress of Sociology 3: 191–201
Kuhn T S 1962 The structure of scientific revolutions. Chicago University Press, Chicago
Lachenmeyer C W 1971 The language of sociology. Columbia University Press, Columbia
Lindesmith A R 1947 Opiate addiction. Principia Press, New York
Lindesmith A R 1968 Addiction and opiates. Aldine, Chicago
Malinowski B 1922 Argonauts of the Western Pacific: an account of native enterprise and adventure in the archipelagoes of Malanesian New Guinea. Routledge, London
Maris R F W 1969 Social forces in urban suicide. Dorsey Press, Homewood, Illinois
Moser C A, Kalton G 1971 Survey methods in social investigation, 2nd edn. Heinemann, London
Payne G, Dingwall R, Payne J, Carter M 1981 Sociology and social research. Routledge & Kegan Paul, London
Popper K R 1961 The poverty of historicism. Routledge & Kegan Paul, London
Robinson W S 1951 The logical structure of analytical induction. American Sociological Review 16: 812–818
Schatzman L, Strauss A L 1973 Field research. Strategies for a natural sociology. Prentice-Hall, Englewood Cliffs, NJ
Smith H W 1975 Strategies of social research. The methodological imagination. Prentice-Hall, Englewood Cliffs, NJ
Strong P M 1979 The ceremonial order of the clinic. Parents, doctors and medical bureaucracies. Routledge & Kegan Paul, London
Wallace W L 1971 The logic of science in sociology. Aldine-Atherton, Chicago
Watson J D 1968 The double helix: a personal account of the discovery of the structure of DNA. Weidenfeld & Nicholson, London

Worsley P 1974 The state of theory and the status of theory, BSA
   presidential address 1973. Sociology 8: 1–17
Znaniecki F 1934 The method of sociology. Farrar & Rinehart, New York

FURTHER READING

Moser C A, Kalton G 1971 Survey methods in social investigation, 2nd edn.
   Heinemann, London
Schatzman L, Strauss A L 1973 Field research. Strategies for a natural
   sociology. Prentice-Hall, Englewood Cliffs, NJ
Smith H W 1975 Strategies of social research. The methodological
   imagination. Prentice-Hall, Englewood Cliffs, NJ

*A way of looking
Achievements of
    sociology in health care
Using sociology*

13

Appreciating sociology

INTRODUCTION

We have found this a difficult book to write—not just because it has been a time-consuming enterprise which has permeated every corner of our private and professional lives, but because we wanted sociology to be understood by any health professional who happens to read it. At the same time we have tried to avoid trivialising its subject matter. In other words, we realised from the outset that we would need to satisfy the often conflicting perspectives of the professional sociologist and the non-sociologist health professional. Sociology is renowned for its jargon and often incomprehensible language. Many of the critics of this feature of sociology suggest that this is a method of making the subject more mysterious in order to give it an inflated sense of importance. We suspect that there is a lot of truth in this view, but also suggest that it is not something which is peculiar to sociology in particular or even to social science in general. Specialised language is a characteristic of advanced study whether it be about society, the human body or computing. In writing this book we have tried to de-mystify sociology and at the same time show why its language has to be more specific than that used in everyday speech in order that the meaning of its concepts can be more clearly defined.

A WAY OF LOOKING

Sociology is just one way of looking at the world in which we live and act out our daily lives. We saw in Chapter 1 how other social sciences can observe the same phenomenon from different perspectives, providing a variety of insights into the world in which we live. The views of the natural sciences should also not be excluded since, as we hope we have shown, they often take for granted a particular view of society upon which their own particular areas of knowledge and scientific enterprise focus. Thus, for example, the geologist in his quest for oil-bearing rocks takes for granted society's need for oil in particular and for energy in general. It is his own and others' definitions of what society needs which is directing his scientific endeavours.

Sociology, we have argued, is not the monopoly of sociologists. Indeed we have suggested that sociology is for all those who are interested in society or deal with people in their everday lives. The first people to attempt a sociological view of health and illness in Britain were not professional sociologists. In the section devoted to the study of health at the first annual conference of the British Sociological Association in the early 1950s only one of six speakers was a professional sociologist. Of the other five, four were medical doctors and one was a medical administrator (Illsley, 1980). Many of the early patrons of a sociology of health and illness were clinicians and epidemiologists, while the father of medical sociology in Britain, Raymond Illsley, was an ex-economist and town planner interested in class and poverty. Nowadays, some sociologists might argue that the activities of these early pioneers was not sociology at all but social epidemiology. But as we saw in Chapter 1, sociology has many perspectives, and social epidemiology is one of them.

Different ways of looking

In an introductory text about sociology we see it as important not to take sides; but at the same time it is also extremely difficult not to do so. With such a variety of sociological perspectives to choose from any omission will be viewed as favouring a particular perspective or perspectives. Throughout this book we have tried to adopt an eclectic approach to our subject matter. Wherever possible we have provided alternative views of the social world, often juxtaposing the more conservative views of the functionalists with those of the Marxists or ethnomethodologists. We have shown that there is no single correct approach.

A major consequence of choosing any particular perspective is that it asks different questions, uses different methods and very often gets different answers to the other approaches. We illustrated this characteristic of sociology with the example of mental illness in Chapter 2 when introducing different sociological perspectives. In our treatment of different aspects of health care we have drawn attention to contrasting sociological perspectives, identified the kinds of questions asked, described the methods used and reported a variety of answers. We hope that this has been enriching even though, inevitably, it has made the sociology more complex.

These different ways of looking at the social world all involve a critical examination of the world in which we live. Thus like all academics, sociologists examine things critically. However, whereas geologists and meteorologists focus on such topics as the long-term effects of volcanic activity on weather patterns and historians criticise theories about why Napoleon eventually lost his empire, sociologists describe the structures and functions of current everyday life—your life and our lives. Few people will feel threatened by the activities of the geologists, meteorologists or even the historians, since they are discussing events and knowledge which do not impinge directly and obviously on us. The work of the sociologist does. Thus it is not surprising that, for example, industrialists and trade unionists alike feel threatened by sociologists (and in this case epidemiologists) who examine critically the relationships between the activities of the tobacco industry, health and ill health. Being involved in sociological research can threaten people; it can make them feel uncomfortable. This is equally the case where sociologists have attempted to examine their own activities; this is well illustrated by medical sociologists' reaction to Phil Strong's analysis of their work (Strong, 1979)!

So what?

A normal response to the reporting of much sociology is not one of feeling threatened, but one of 'so what?' A number of sociological studies have met with this reaction. However, further research had often identified the initial findings as facts of greater practical and theoretical significance than was obvious at first. In the fifties and sixties, when the rate of unemployment was relatively low, sociological research on the relationship between unemployment and health was treated as insignificant and irrelevant. Admittedly the findings were equivocal. There was little evidence that unemployment caused ill-health, since there were so few unemployed people and ill-health itself was likely to be the cause of some of the unemployment. The dramatic increase in unemployment rates in the late seventies and early eighties makes the earlier research no less equivocal, but the findings are more relevant both theoretically and practically.

Similarly in recent years there has been immense activity by sociologists with ethnomethodological and phenomenological leanings in the study of the language used in interactions between clients and professionals. In their infancy, these studies produced numerous 'obvious' and 'trivial' findings, which were regarded as irrelevant to the practitioners concerned. Yet these same findings are becoming more acceptable to many practitioners who have attempted to change educational practices in order to influence the way in which professionals talk with clients. Indeed, issues in communication have become an increasingly important feature of the curriculum of almost every health professional's initial professional education. One of the problems of much sociological data, is that, because it is about everyday life, it seems obvious when spelt out in a research report. But like hindsight in all aspects of our lives, we may ask 'why did we, as members of society, not see it before?'

As we observed in Chapter 5, when discussing the problems in undertaking studies about the family, we *take for granted* much that happens in our everyday worlds. In the same way as we are often able to see what is happening to others we may often refuse to observe that the same thing may be happening to ourselves. We notice when other people are

Table 13.1 Current research projects listed in *Medical Sociology in Britain*

Research topic	Number of projects
Disability	28
Nursing and related occupations	27
Pregnancy and childbirth	27
General practitioner based studies	23
The elderly	23
Medical and paramedical professions	14
Infant and child health care	14
Health education	13
Women and health	13
Social epidemiology	12
Health care: organisation, policy, planning	11
Historical studies	11
Mental illness	10
Third world	9
Health related beliefs	8
Hospital based studies	7
Death and dying	6
Mental handicap	6
Other studies	12
Practitioner-client communication	(15)*
Provision and use of health services	(15)*
Professional education	(12)*
Ethnic groups	(5)*
Total number of projects	274

Note: * These categories consist entirely of projects classified into one of the preceding categories.

Source: Field D, Clarke B A, Goldie N 1982 *Medical Sociology in Britain. A register of research and teaching*. British Sociological Association, Medical Sociology Group, p 79–131

bad-tempered or tired, but will not readily recognise the symptoms in ourselves. We may recognise immediately the characteristics of marital stress in our friends or colleagues but not in ourselves. Sociology then is one means of sensitising us to facts and issues in our public and private lives, which we would otherwise take for granted.

Although we use and have developed sociology as an academic subject in order critically to examine the world around us, and to sensitise ourselves to things which we take for granted, we also recognise that it is a product of the society in which we live. To survive in the jungle of the educational market-place sociology must present a saleable product. Funding for sociological research will therefore tend to reflect the needs of society in general and of government in particular. These needs are reflected in the current research being undertaken by sociologists concerned with health and illness. The latest Register of research of the Medical Sociology Group (Field et al, 1982) shows not only the extent to which sociology is taught in the various educational establishments for different health professionals, but also the extent to which research activities reflect the interests of society. Table 13.1 shows the number of projects included under various headings in the Register. There are eighteen main categories and four categories which consist entirely of projects catergorised elsewhere. Of course, there is also an 'other' category. To some extent such categorisation will be fairly arbitrary. For example, a study in which one of us is involved concerning the dependency characteristics of the elderly is classified under 'the elderly' but it could equally well have been put in at least three other categories: social epidemiology, disability, and mental illness. Nevertheless, the categories shown provide a useful indication of the interests that sociologists have in health care. It is worth noting that the second largest category consists of research projects about 'nursing and related occupations'. Notice the use of language here. Nursing and related *occupations* compared with the other category, 'medical and paramedical *professions.*' Many projects in other categories are also relevant to health professions.

ACHIEVEMENTS OF SOCIOLOGY IN HEALTH CARE

It is difficult to extol the achievements of sociology, because like the many achievements of natural science and technology such as the motor car or the cardiac monitor, we now take them for granted—in the case of sociological achievements perhaps even more so. At the same time many of its contributions are not tangible and when they are, the time lag between the initial theoretical idea and social change is so great that the change will be embodied in society's rules and expectations. It is now over 25 years since Peter Townsend (1962) published his influential book *The Last Refuge*, which described the institutional environment of residential homes for the elderly (see Ch. 7). Since then there have been improvements in the quality of institutional life. We should not, of course, credit only sociology for pointing out the deficits leading to this kind of change. Sociology is only one of many influences on society. Health professionals themselves, some with more success than others, also make contributions from their particular perspectives.

It would not be appropriate, and even if it were it would be extremely difficult, to catalogue individual sociological studies which have been major influences in shaping society. Rather we should like to identify just some of the themes in this book, which may have sensitised health professionals to look at taken-for-granted phenomena in a different way. In doing so we will attempt to address those themes which are part and parcel of the work of health professionals.

Medical and social models

In Chapter 1 we described two different models of health—the medical model and the social model. We saw in Chapter 4 how the social model helped us to understand the social causes of illness. We also described, in Chapter 8, a social model which helps us to understand an individual's reactions to health or ill-health.

We have argued that the practice of health care is dominated by the medical model, which encapsulates the perspective of the medical profession and those professions related to medicine. The emphasis of the medical model is on illness, disease or ill-health and the need for medical treatment, rather than on health or normality. The medical model also stresses cure not care and we hear phrases like 'preventive medicine' rather than 'promoting health'. In contrast, the social model considers other aspects of health such as care, rehabilitation and health promotion. We have argued that health professionals might find it helpful to consider illness, the causes of illness and patients' responses to their illness from viewpoints other than medical ones.

It is difficult to establish the extent to which the concept of the social model in health has sensitised health professionals to think in a variety of ways. Examination of the curricula of newly developing courses and redrafting of established curricula for health professionals may provide some indication of the extent to which a variety of perspectives on health are being advocated by teachers. Certainly the influence the so-cial model has had on the work of the World Health Organ-isation is not insignificant, as a glance at some of their publications will quickly establish.

Inequalities in health

Both epidemiology and sociology have made major contri-butions to the analysis of inequalities in health, as is evident from the report *Inequalities in Health* (DHSS, 1980; Townsend & Davidson, 1982). An understanding of inequalities in health requires an understanding of social class. We tend to take the concept of social class, like that of the family, for granted and to use it in a variety of ways. In Chapter 3 we emphasised the importance of social class in particular and social stratification in general. Social class has often been used as a panacea to *explain* a variety of human behaviour and this has been the case in understanding health and illness. Many writers have suggested that social class is a *cause* of illness. We disagree. Lower social class is a characteristic of people who are more likely to be ill, not a cause of their ill-health.

Understanding social class and the real causes of inequality in health is a central concern of sociology which should be of interest and value to all health professionals. At an interper-sonal level, studies of social class have helped health pro-fessionals to understand the difficulties they may have in communicating and interacting with patients from different social backgrounds who, as well as having linguistic differ-ences, will probably also have a different perspective on health, ill-health, illness and health care. We have described the scepticism and fatalism of some patients about the ben-efits of measures to prevent ill-health. These data suggest that further efforts need to be made in health education.

A sociological understanding can assist health professionals at all levels to contribute to the reduction of health inequal-ities by adopting a positive approach to the problems faced by disadvantaged clients and patients. This can range from the number of District Nurses and Health Visitors provided in areas according to established need, through to tailoring parenting education to the needs of prospective parents.

Social epidemiology

We have suggested that the social model is helpful in the understanding of the aetiology of illness. In Chapter 4 we focused on two kinds of sociological analysis, both of which inform health professionals about the relationships between a variety of social factors and health. First, we described the relationships between illness and social structure using the tools and methods of social epidemiology. Second, we discussed a model of the origins of health which relates health outcomes to the characteristics and life experiences of the individual.

The importance of both of these analyses can be illustrated in our understanding of prevention. In Chapter 4 we suggest that primary prevention is principally a social activity over which health professionals have little control. However, they still have an important role to play, not only as health professionals, but as individuals, in discouraging smoking, preventing accidents and encouraging sensible eating habits. These aims will probably only be achieved through health education in its various forms. Sociology helps us understand why the mounting of health education programmes can be undermined by other social activities. An understanding of these social processes should equip health professionals to comprehend the difficulties that many of us have in conforming to a life-style which maximises our health status and potential.

The family

In Chapter 5 we used the family as an example of how sociology sensitises us to three aspects of society which we take for granted. Within the context of the notion that the family is the basic unit in health and medical care we discuss three important issues. First, that the way we generally describe the family as a husband and wife with 2.2 children is not particularly useful. The increasing trend toward serial 'marriage', single-parent families and different forms of group living suggests that the family is a more complex social structure than conventional wisdom generally accepts. Second, we observed that the theoretical basis to the study of the family is still in its infancy and does not reflect the real world as documented by epidemiologists and demographers, as well as sociologists. Third, we argue that conventional wisdom about the family is not always a good indicator of the relationship between health and illness, both in the way we promote and maintain health, and in the way the family reacts and copes with illness, particularly chronic illness, in one of its members.

We suggest that the study of the family as the basic unit in health and medical care has assisted health professionals in caring for patients and their families. This interest in the effects of illness on family life and in the effects of the family on illness and health behaviour is likely to become an even more central concern of health professionals as the emphasis on community care for the mentally ill, handicapped and elderly increases and sociology will continue to add to our understanding of the various social mechanisms involved.

Social construction

Central to a sociological understanding is the idea that all human actions are socially constructed. In Chapter 3 we showed that old age is a social category defined by society. The importance of the idea of social construction is illustrated by the way such a social category can impinge on the quality of life of the aged. Thus, for example, different categories of aged receive different benefit entitlements.

At the individual level we saw in Chapter 9 how these social constructions reflect what sociologists call typifications. Throughout our lives we typify in order to know how to react to and with individuals in different social categories. We described how staff typify patients according to their social and work-related characteristics, rather than their medical characteristics, and how patients are treated on the basis of these typifications. Thus sociology helps us to understand how, as individuals, we continually reconstruct the social world around us and how these typifications reflect society's construction of social categories.

The fact that we react to people in social categories challenges the idea that it 'all boils down to personalities'. Individuals within social categories take into account, among other things, the fact that different definitions of the situation will exist, that different roles with specific obligations are being enacted, that different social strata may be involved and that different sets of values are adopted. Because of this we can appreciate that conflicts are a normative feature of social life, present in our interactions with our children, with patients and clients and with other professionals. Seen in this way conflict is inevitable. Similarly, we tend to apportion blame to others for the work they apparently create for us or which they carry out ineptly, for the unreasonable demands they apparently make on us and for the trouble they apparently cause. Taking the perspective of the other is likely to yield a very different picture. Behind these interpretations that all of us tend to make at some point in our social and working lives, lie sociological explanations of why particular states of affairs exist and why they are interpreted in different ways by different people. These explanations transcend personal psychology.

Grasping this point will not provide immediate solutions to our work problems. Indeed it can complicate and raise new problems by asking what are others' views of a particular situation. Unlimited and open visiting of patients in hospital is but one example where this might occur. However, understanding that competing perspectives do exist and that individuals will interpret events from their own social, political and economic stance, may help to make more bearable those forms of social interaction which are stressful and have negative connotations. They may also give rise to more helpful, workable and widely acceptable solutions to problems.

USING SOCIOLOGY

We exemplified some problems of interaction in Chapter 9, specifically in relation to sociological features of the management of pain, and in Chapter 10 related to dying, death and bereavement. Carrying out sociological research and using its findings to gain an understanding of the interpersonal aspects of the work of health professionals may go some way towards providing relevant services to assist those patients or staff who experience such problems to overcome them. As well as heightening awareness that difficulties may exist locally, with

deleterious consequences for patients and staff alike, sociologically derived knowledge can be used at the level of policy
decisions about, for example, whose responsibility it is to
identify bereaved people at risk of social or psychiatric breakdown and to organise services such that supportive interventions are available to those judged as requiring care.
Sociological approaches are also relevant at the micro-level in
assessing forms of interaction between, for example, midwives and women at antenatal clinics, midwives and women
during labour, or midwives and women after the delivery of
a still-birth.

Sociological knowledge may make a number of contributions in circumstances like these. First, in pointing out that
problems of interaction with patients are especially difficult
when competing perspectives exist, when the organisation is
not 'geared up' to deal with them and when the contexts in
which they occur involve highly salient social values. These
have been identified in a number of different settings and are
more than a reflection of idiosyncratic strengths or deficits
among those involved. They demonstrate that particular features of work may require greater attention than given to
them in the past and that their analysis requires an appreciation of their social context.

Second, the findings of sociological research may be used
in policy development at a range of levels as a means of developing appropriate and workable solutions from the variety
of possibilities that might exist. Appropriateness in this sense
will be as much a matter of available skills, talents and resources as of what empirical studies have shown to be
desirable.

Third, sociology may be used in education to encourage
staff to explore their own and others feelings about the subject and to point to processes and facts which may assist in
promoting action learning (Revans, 1976). Group rather than
individual learning should increase the likelihood that possible solutions are acted upon.

Sociological knowledge about particular concerns facing
health professionals may have relevance at any level in the
structure of health care organisations—at regional and district
levels to devise appropriate policies about how resources may
be allocated and services organised; within primary health

care teams to decide the appropriate professional to take responsibility for particular features of care; in hospital wards to agree means by which interactional difficulties may be identified and resolved; by individual professionals to ascertain the nature and extent of family support for patients with different kinds of problems. At an individual level, too, a reading of the sociological literature on specific topics may help to extend awareness and understanding of the concerns currently faced.

In this book we have concentrated largely, but by no means exclusively, on sociology directly generated by and linked to health problems and professions. Health care is a complex institution and is able to benefit from studies in other areas of society. In Chapter 5 we discussed some theoretical issues in the sociology of the family and then in Chapter 6 demonstrated their relevance to health issues; in Chapter 11 the sociology of occupations was helpful in understanding nursing and the remedial professions. The structure of nursing has been influenced by models drawn from industrial organisation and management. An understanding of nursing and some other paramedical work as women's work, and the strong influence of paternalism and capitalism discussed in Chapter 11, has emerged from feminist writers. This topic has recently also become an increasing concern among women doctors.

To gain an understanding of the ways in which individuals, professional groups and organisations are involved in health care work necessitates taking into account other features of our society, as well as the views of *all* those who contribute to it. Throughout this book we have attempted to enrich this understanding by showing the relevance of sociology. We entitled this chapter 'Appreciating sociology'. We trust that you do appreciate it!

REFERENCES

Department of Health and Social Security 1980 Inequalities in health. Report of research working group. DHSS, London
Field D, Clarke B A, Goldie N 1982 Medical sociology in Britain: a register of research and teaching, 4th edition. British Sociological Association, Medical Sociology Group.
Illsley R 1980 Professional or public health? Sociology in health and medicine. The Nuffield Provincial Hospitals Trust, London

Revans R W (ed) 1976 Action learning in hospitals: diagnosis and therapy. McGraw-Hill, London

Strong P M 1979 Sociological imperialism and the profession of medicine: a critical examination of the thesis of medical imperialism. Social Science and Medicine 13A: 199–215

Townsend P 1962 The last refuge. A survey of residential institutions and homes in England and Wales. Routledge & Kegan Paul, London

Townsend P, Davidson N (eds) 1982 Inequalities in health. The Black Report. Penguin Books, Harmondsworth

Glossary

In the text of the glossary, words appearing in italics are themselves defined.

Acculturation. This is the process of contact between *cultures* by which an individual or group is assimilated into the existing culture and which, in turn, modifies the existing culture. The term is used on pages 297–300 to refer to the socialisation process of newcomers to a professional group who conduct themselves in a manner by which established group members recognise them as competent.

Action. Action is distinct from *behaviour* in that it involves meaning or intention.

Ageing. As well as being a genetically programmed process of living organisms, social gerontologists are concerned with ageing as a process linked with the social and demographic structure of human groups; as an aspect of personal status in the life cycle; as a component of stratification in terms of generational membership and as a contemporary social problem raising questions about exploitation, victimisation and stigmatisation. Important are the criteria by which an individual is *labelled* 'elderly'.

Alienation. This describes the estrangement of individuals from themselves and from others. It was originally used by Marx to denote human estrangement rooted in existing *social structures* which denied people their essential human nature. It is now more widely used to denote discontent with society, feelings of moral breakdown in society, feelings of powerlessness and the dehumanisation of large scale organisations.

Attitude. A relatively stable set of beliefs concerning an object and resulting in an evaluation of that object. Attitudes are not necessarily related to behaviour.

Authority. A type of *power* in which people willingly obey commands because they regard the exercise of power as *legitimate*.

Awareness context. In interactionist theory interaction between individuals takes place in awareness contexts—what each knows about the identity of the other and his own identity in the eyes of the other, including what each knows about particular events and situations. This term is referred to on pages 262–266 in relation to dying.

Behaviour. A term used by psychologists to describe observable conduct in response to stimuli. It disregards the subjective aspects of conduct. Sociologists use the term *action* to distinguish meaningful activity from behaviour.

Bourgeoisie. In Marxist theory a description of the middle or ruling classes in capitalist society who are assumed to be interested in preserving capitalism in a struggle with the working class.

Bureaucracy. A concept first defined by Weber to describe a form of administration. His *ideal type* includes a high degree of specialisation and a clearly defined division of labour with tasks distributed as official duties; a hierarchical structure of authority with clearly circumscribed areas of command and responsibility; the establishment of a formal body of rules to govern the operation of the organisation; administration based on written documents; impersonal relationships between organisational members and with clients; recruitment of personnel on the basis of ability; promotion on the basis of seniority or merit; a fixed salary; and the separation of private and official income.

Career. A concept denoting a progression of events which relate to each other. It is often used to describe a sequence of jobs, which may be either structured or unstructured. It may also apply to other sequences of events in the *life career*, such as the patient career.

Career contingencies. Goffman introduced this term to describe points in a *career* at which mechanisms are triggered affecting the course of the career.

Caste. A caste system is a form of *social stratification* in which castes are hierarchically organised and separated from each other by rules of ritual purity.

Class. In Marxist theory class is used to describe two opposing social groups: the *bourgeoisie* and *proletariat*. In Weberian theory a person's class position is the location which he shares with those who are similarly placed in the processes of production, distribution, and exchange.

Class, ascribed. This term describes the position of an individual in terms of the social standing into which he is born and over which he has no control rather than the position he attains by his own achievements.

Clinical uncertainty. It exists when there is a real uncertainty about clinical matters and when information of this kind may be withheld to avoid revealing that uncertainty exists among health professionals.

Community. This term is one of the most elusive and vague used by sociologists. It is now used largely without specific meaning. It may refer to a set of people resident in a geographical area. It may also include elements of a sense of belonging as in 'community spirit'; a self-contained unit in which all of the daily work and non-work activities of a community take place; collections within a particular social structure which are often rural or 'pre-industrial'. Thus notions of 'therapeutic community' or 'care in the community' contain slightly different elements.

Community care. This term refers to the trend of replacing large and often geographically remote institutional facilities with smaller units of residential provision. More recently it has been used to refer to the fact that carers reside in the community.

Concept. In general usage the term mainly means notion or idea. It may be defined as the name for the members of a given class of objects of any sort, or as the name of the class itself. More simply, concept refers to a descriptive property or relation.

Conflict. Social conflict assumes various forms. Competition describes conflict over the control of resources or advantage desired by others where physical violence is not employed. Regulated competition is resolved within a framework of agreed rules. Other conflicts may be more violent and not bound by rules, in which case they are settled by the opposing parties mobilising their *power* resources.

Correlation. It is normal to record a variety of data simultaneously in sociological research. When one datum provides information about the other they are said to be associated or correlated. All measures of correlation indicate the strength of the association between two or more variables. The fact that two variables are correlated does not establish that one is antecedent to or causes the other.

Cultural group. This is the collection of people who share the same *culture*.

Culture. A collective noun which describes the symbolic and learned aspects of human society, including language, custom and convention, and by which human *action* can be distinguished from the *behaviour* of other primates.

Culture of poverty. A term used by Oscar Lewis to describe an impoverished way of life which is remarkably stable and persistent and which is passed down from generation to generation along family lines.

Deduction. A process by which valid conclusions can be logically deduced from valid premises. Rarely are sociological arguments strictly deductive in form, even if they claim to be.

Definition of the situation. The importance of the subjective perspectives of social actors for the objective consequences of social interaction is often summarised in sociology by the notion of defining the situation. One implication of this *concept* is that the 'truth' or 'falsity' of beliefs (definitions of the situation) are not important issues and what matters is the outcome of social interaction.

Design, prospective. A study design in which data are collected as events occur.

Design, retrospective. A study design in which data are collected after the events have occurred.

Deviance, primary. In *labelling theory* primary deviance refers to the act of labelling by another actor, who is accepted by the social group as having the *authority* to do so.

Deviance, secondary. In *labelling theory* secondary deviance refers to the effect the label has on both the people being labelled and other people around them.

Enculturation. The process of *socialisation* as the passive *internalisation* of an existing normative order, in abstraction from any broader social or historical context.

Ethnic group. Conceptual confusion surrounds the distinctiveness of the terms 'ethnic group', *'cultural group'*, 'racial group' and *'caste'*. Sociologists have generally rejected the notion that human groups can be unambiguously defined in terms of their genetic constitution. Social groups are more commonly defined by reference to a shared culture such as language, customs and institutions. A group which claims ethnic distinctiveness is different from one which has had distinctiveness imposed on it by a politically superior group in the context of a political struggle. Ethnicity may, therefore, become the basis for racial separation or for political subordination.

Ethnomethodology. The term literally means 'peoples' methods', invented by Garfinkel to describe a branch of sociology which criticises other perspectives that impose sociological categories on the ordinary person. For ethnomethodologists other perspectives in sociology redescribe what ordinary people do, treating these accounts as deficient. Ethnomethodology aims to study how people ('members') construct their social world and how the orderly nature of that world is achieved. It examines how 'members' work continously to make sense of others. Yet, despite this, the way in which the world is constructed is entirely taken for granted. Ethnomethodology as a sociological perspective is discussed on pages 43–47.

Fact. An observed phenomenon—a thing, an event, a measurement.

Fact, social. Not all facts about human behaviour are necessarily social facts. A *fact* is only social in so far as it exists externally to the individual and exercises constraint over him.

Family. Perhaps the most loosely defined term in the sociologist's vocabulary. *Marriage*, parenthood and residence comprise the three central elements of the family. The important characteristic of these elements is that they are neither necessary or sufficient parts of a definition, but do, in various combinations, delineate a definition of the family. Different ways of conceptualising the family are discussed on pages 110–116.

Family, conjugal. This term is used to define a social group consisting of a man and woman and their dependent offspring. The central element of the conjugal family is parenthood.

Family of marriage. A kinship term which refers to the kin grouping of ego, his or her spouse and their children.

Family of origin. A kinship term which refers to the kin grouping of ego, his or her parent(s) and sibling(s).

Frame. A term coined by Goffman to provide for the analysis of ongoing social actions proceeding within a socially constructed frame. This social framework permits actors to structure interactions, to negotiate, and to attribute meaning to their experience. When actors operate within mutually defined frames this is conducive to a high level of intersubjective communication. Goffman's use of frame is described on pages 218–220.

Function. In *functionalist theory* the consequences of the existence or operation of a unit for other units in a social system is referred to as 'its function'.

Function, latent. In *functionalist theory* a functional relation that is neither intended nor recognised.

Function, manifest. In *functionalist theory* a functional relation having a recognised value.

Functional alternatives. In *functionalist theory* Merton identified the need to get away from the conservative tendency to argue that something is indispensable for the wellbeing of society. There are different and equally successful ways of providing for functions.

Functional autonomy. In *functionalist theory*, the degree to which the parts of a social system are self-sustaining and may survive independently of the system of which originally they were a part.

Functional uncertainty. When uncertainty is imputed into circumstances in which there is no real doubt, for social purposes, this is functional uncertainty.

Health field concept. This concept draws on the *medical* and *social models* of health and illness. Health is attributable to four main elements: human biology, including those aspects of mental and physical health which are a direct consequence of the basic biology of the individual; environment, including all matters related to health which are external to the human body and over which the individual has little or no personal control; lifestyle, including those decisions made by individuals themselves, which have implications for their health; health care organisation which consist of the quantity, quality, arrangement, nature and relationships of people and resources in the provision of health care.

Ideal type. A term used by Weber to make explicit the procedure by which social scientists formulate general abstract concepts such as *bureaucracy* or *career*. Ideal types are thus hypothetical constructs formed by emphasising aspects of behaviour and institutions which are observable. 'Ideal' signifies 'pure' or 'abstract' rather than normative. The precise relationship between ideal types and their empirical referents remains obscure.

Ideology. This is a system of interdependent ideas (beliefs, traditions, principles and myths) held by a social group or society which reflects, rationalises and defends its particular social, moral, religious, political, or economic institutional interests and commitments.

Illness behaviour. A term coined by Mechanic to describe the social factors which influence the ways individuals view signs and symptoms, and the kinds of action engaged in to deal with them.

Impression management. A method of achieving *social mobility* through the manipulation of status symbols and personal attraction.

Indexicality. Ethnomethodologists argue that all actions and utterances are indexical, that is, they depend for their meaning on the context in which they occur. This feature means that actors will normally make sense of actions and utterances of others by referring to their context.

Induction. A process by which the truth of a proposition is made more probable by the accumulation of confirming evidence. It cannot ever be ultimately valid because there is always the possibility of unconfirming evidence.

Institution. A term widely used to describe social practices that are regularly and continuously repeated; are sanctioned and maintained by social *norms*; and which have a major significance in the social structure. The concept has been defined by Berger and Berger as 'a regulatory pattern which is programmed by society and imposed on the conduct of individuals'.

Institution, total. A place of confinement or partial confinement in which all aspects of life are conducted under the control of a single *bureaucratic authority*. Examples of total institutions are prisons, hospitals, army camps and boarding schools.

Institutionalisation. This is the process whereby social practices become sufficiently regular and continuous to be described as *institutions*. This process also permits social practice to modify existing institutions. The term is sometimes used to describe the effects of an institution on social behaviour, so that individuals act out a narrow and repetitive range of behaviour.

Internalisation. This concept refers to the process by which an individual learns and accepts the social *values* and *norms* of conduct relevant to his or her social group or wider society.

Kinship. An anthropological term which describes the social relationships deriving from blood ties (real and supposed) and *marriage*. Kinship is a universal feature of societies and usually plays a significant role in the *socialisation* of individuals and in the maintenance of group solidarity. In complex societies kinship normally forms a fairly small part of the totality of social relations which make up the social system.

Legitimacy. Weber uses the term in his analysis of *power*. Legitimacy means that people accept *authority* as just and that those endowed with authority are given it rightfully. Weber identified three ideological bases of legitimacy: traditional, charismatic and legal-rational, which may confer authority on power holders.

Life career. This concept may be referred to as the life-cycle to describe the development of a person through childhood, adolescence, mid-life, old age and death. However, this does not relate to biological maturation but to transitions through socially constructed categories of age and to variations in social experience of ageing. The length and importance of these stages varies between cultures, and between men and women who have different social experiences during biological ageing.

Marriage. This term describes the relation of one or more men with one or more women which is recognised by custom or law, and which involves certain rights and duties, both in the case of the parties entering the union and in the case of the children born of it.

Maternal deprivation. This term refers to the absence of a stable, continuous and affectionate relationship between a mother and child. In functional theory it is suggested that the absence of such a relationship may lead to an increase in social pathology such as mental illness or delinquency. This theory has important implications for women in society. It implies that women should remain at home to look after young children, a position which has been described as an ideology for keeping women out of the labour force.

Model, medical. The medical model of health assumes that improvements in the health of the population and the quality of health care are attributable to the art and science of medicine.

Model, social. The social model of health emphasises the social rather than the biological contexts in the aetiology of disease and illness and their treatment and care.

Negotiated order. In interactionist theory a concept which regards social phenomena, particularly organisational arrangements, as emerging from ongoing processes of interaction between people. The interaction process involves constant negotiation and renegotiation of the terms of social action, stressing the fluidity and uncertainty of social arrangements.

Neo-natal mortality rate. This is the proportion of deaths in the first four weeks of life.

Norm. Norms are prescriptions serving as common guidelines for *social action*. Human behaviour exhibits certain regularities, which are the product of adhering to common expectations or norms. In this sense human action is 'rule governed'. A social norm is not necessarily actual behaviour and normative behaviour is not simply the most frequently occurring pattern. Since the terms refers to social expectations about 'correct' or 'proper' behaviour, norms imply the presence of *legitimacy*, consent and prescription. Deviation from norms is punished by sanctions. Norms are acquired by *internalisation* and *socialisation*. The concept is central to theories of social order.

Normative. Explanations or theories which assume that the *norms* and *values* of the sociologist hold true.

Organisation. A relatively stable pattern of social relationships of individuals and subgroups within a social system or social group, based upon systems of social roles, norms and shared meanings that provide regularity and predictability in social interaction. The term often refers to specific social groups such as a factory, school or hospital.

Organisation, formal. A highly organised group having explicit objectives, formally stated rules and regulations, and a system of specifically defined roles, each with clearly designated rights and duties.

Organisation, informal. The system of personal relationships that develops spontaneously as individuals interact within a *formal organisation*.

Perinatal mortality rate. This is the proportion of stillbirths and deaths in the first four weeks of life.

Power. This is the ability of an individual or group to carry out its wishes or policies, and to control, manipulate, or influence the behaviour of others, whether they wish to cooperate or not. The agent who possesses power has resources to force his will on others. These resources often stem from social relationships and the individual's position in a group or society. The terms power, authority and influence are sometimes defined as authority terms implying the ability of one person to change the behaviour of another. In this sense power is widely diffused through society rather than being concentrated in a ruling elite.

Power, coercive. A type of *power* in which the holder of power can compel the actions of subordinate individuals or groups by the use or the threat of physical force. This can be acceptable to people if they believe it is administered by appropriate office-holders.

Power, expert. A type of *power* based on the subject's belief that the holder of power possesses superior knowledge and ability.

Power, legitimate. A type of *power* which is the result of an individual's position within a social system or social group. It stems from the *moral authority* of a particular position in the group.

Power, referent. A type of *power* which relates to the prestige of individuals and to some extent relates to the *status* of a person in the social system or social group.

Power, reward. A type of *power* which derives from the exertion of influence by controlling rewards or resources valued by the subject.

Prevention. Three types have been delineated. Primary prevention which involves taking measures in order to prevent disease or injury from occurring. Secondary prevention refers to health care measures which are concerned with identifying and treating ill health. Tertiary prevention is concerned with mitigating the effects of illness and disease which have already occurred.

Profession. In *functionalist theory,* an occupation which may be identified by the following attributes: (1) the use of skills based on theoretical knowledge; (2) education and training in these skills; (3) the competence of professionals ensured by examinations; (4) a code of conduct to ensure professional integrity; (5) performance of a service that is for the public good; (6) a professional association that organises members. These criteria can also be used to measure the degree to which occupations are professionalised.

Proletariat. In Marxist theory this is equivalent to the working class who, in capitalist society, are in conflict with the *bourgeoisie.*

Reflexivity. In *ethnomethodology* this concept refers to the essential interdependence of the circumstances members attribute to social events and their descriptions or accounts of what the events themselves entail. When members take part in a social occasion they use the features of the occasion to make visible to others what is happening and also to make the features themselves come about.

Rites de passage. A term denoting public ceremonies celebrating the transition of an individual or group to a new *status.* Such rites are typically associated with transitions in the *life career,* marked by ceremonies like marriage or retirement parties.

Role. People occupying particular social positions behave in ways according to what is expected of that position rather than their own individual characteristics. Roles are the socially defined attributes and expectations associated with social positions.

Role conflict. This exists when incompatible expectations are held. It can occur at two levels. (1) When an individual perceives a difference between how he thinks he should act out a particular *role* and how he perceives he actually acts out the role. Conflict also occurs when he perceives an incompatability between performing certain prescriptions of one of his roles and carrying out those of another of his role; (2) At a group level conflict occurs when different actors perceive the same role in different ways.

Role making. In interactionist theory, role making is the process of creating and modifying expected behaviour in interaction. Rather than roles being fluid and indeterminate, role making produces consistent patterns of behaviour.

Role taking. In interactionist theory roles are depicted as the outcome of a process of social interaction that is tentative and creative. Individuals imaginatively engage in role-taking new roles and in so doing work out their own roles.

Role set. In functionalist theory the term describes the array of roles and expectations that any individual will confront while taking a particular role.

Roles, multiple. A term which describes the fact that most people are engaged in acting out various roles.

Self-fulfilling prophecy. A false *definition of the situation*, or belief regarding a social situation, which, because one believes it and one acts upon it, it actually manifests itself as a truth, further strengthening the belief.

Sentimental order. In interactionist theory interactions between individuals in social groups produce collective sentiments, which are not internal subjective feelings, but overt observable signs of solidarity between individuals. The *sentimental order* is the level at which these signs are expressed at any one time in response to social circumstances influencing the group. Sentiments are an essential feature of social exchange.

Sick role. A concept originally formulated by Parsons in which illness is regarded as a form of social *deviance* and the ill individual adopts a specific *role*. The sick role is described on pages 211–213.

Social change. Social change is so ubiquitous and varied in form that it has lost importance as a general concept. Its importance as a distinct area for sociological study has its roots in functionalism where the object was to explain the causes and course of changes like the French political and English industrial revolutions, to reveal the 'laws of motion' of society. The theories of Marx and Weber attempted different explanations of large scale social evolution. Attention was subsequently turned to more detailed studies of smaller social units. There is general agreement that change is the normal condition of society everywhere though theoretical disputes as to the nature of change remain.

Social control. This term broadly indicates an aspect of sociology concerned with the maintenance of order and stability. There is broad agreement that this is achieved through a combination of compliance, coercion and commitment to social *values*. In contemporary sociology the concept is primarily encountered in the analysis of *deviant behaviour* where it is an aspect of *labelling theory*. It is agreed that, paradoxically, attempts to increase coercive social control tends to amplify *deviance* rather than reduce it. The implication is that social control depends more on the stability of social groups, community relations and shared values than it does on mere coercion.

Social mobility. This term refers to the movement of individuals between different social strata, usually defined occupationally in western societies. Unlike the situation in *caste* or estate, movement from one *status* to another can be achieved by means which are in the control of the person.

Social stratification. This key concept reflects sociologists' interest in the basic principles of social organisation. The concept refers to social differentiation which produces hierarchical ranks or strata. All members of society will belong to a strata. Within each strata all are equal but strata are superior and inferior relative to each other and these differences are recognised and sanctioned. Different approaches to social stratification are described on pages 50–57.

Social structure. This term refers to the enduring, orderly and patterned relationships between elements of a society. Within sociology there is considerable debate about what these elements should be—people, *roles* or social institutions. Social structure is an abstract theoretical concept and therefore cannot be used as an explanation for any social phenomena.

Socialisation. This term is used to describe the process by which people learn to conform to social *norms* thus making possible an enduring society and the transmission of *culture* between generations. The process has been conceptualised in two ways: (1) socialisation as the *internalisation* of social norms by a process which is self-imposed rather than imposed by means of external regulation. They are thus part of the individual's personality and he therefore feels a need to conform; (2) socialisation may be conceived as an essential element of social interaction on the assumption that people want to enhance their self image by gaining acceptance and status in the eyes of others. Individuals therefore become socialised as they guide their own actions to accord with the expectations of others.

Socialisation, anticipatory. The internalisation of the rights, obligations and expectations of a social *role* preparatory to assuming it.

Sociology, naturalistic. An approach to sociology which questions the assumption that our social surroundings can be subjected to 'scientific' laws as are our physical surroundings. The approach emphasises the distinction between *action* and *behaviour* and the importance of seeing and understanding from the actor's point of view. The approach is theoretical, rather than empirical, and has a different approach to method than that employed in studying the natural sciences.

Sociology, scientistic. An approach to sociology which is grounded in the belief that the logic and methods used in studying natural sciences should be employed also in sociological studies. The approach is empirical rather than theoretical.

Standard mortality ratio. The number of deaths, either total or cause specific, in a given occupational group expressed as a percentage of the number of deaths that would have been expected in that occupational group, if the age-and-sex-specific rates in the general population had obtained.

Status. This term is used in two ways in sociology: (1) status describes the position in a social system as in 'child' or 'grandparent'. Status refers to what the person is whereas the related concept *role* refers to the behaviour expected of people occupying a status; (2) status is used as a synonym for prestige, when social status denotes a position in a publicly recognised hierarchy of social worth. Weber's use of the term status group is described on pages 53–54.

Status passage. In *symbolic interactionism* a term used to describe the process of changing from one *status* to another. Glaser and Strauss in attempting to create a formal theory suggested that properties which would have to be considered in such a change include whether or not the transition is regularised, scheduled, prescribed, desirable, reversible, collective, voluntary, legitimate or disguised.

Stigma. In *labelling theory* the term refers to a relationship of devaluation in which one individual is disqualified from full social acceptance. Stigma is a social attribute which is discrediting for an individual or group. It can be physical (a blemish), documentary (a prison sentence) or contextual (bad company) as well as ascribed or achieved. Its sociological significance lies in the analyses of information management, *deviance* and mechanisms of *social control*.

Sub-culture. This term describes the system of *values, attitudes,* modes of behaviour and life styles of a social group but which is distinct from, but related to the dominant *culture* of a society. While there is a great diversity of subcultures in modern society, the concept has been most used in the study of *ethnic groups*, youth and *deviance*.

Symbolic interactionism. A major sociological perspective deriving from the study of the self-society relationship as a process of symbolic communications between social actors. This perspective is described on pages 37–43.

Theory. In social science the term theory is used loosely and may mean no more than a set of assumptions, *concepts* or relatively abstract inquiry distinguished from empirical research or practical recommendations. More fully developed, a theory is a set of interrelated principles and definitions that serves conceptually to organise selected aspects of the empirical world in a systematic way. The foundation of a theory consists of a set of basic assumptions and axioms from which are derived logically interrelated and empirically verifiable propositions. Although usage varies, the propositions that comprise a theory may be regarded as scientific laws if they have been sufficiently verified to be widely accepted, or as hypotheses if they have still to achieve verification. In either case the propositions which comprise a theory are constantly subject to further empirical testing and revision. Through the process of *deduction* a theory provides specific hypotheses for research and through *induction* research data provide generalisations to be incorporated into and modify theory. The essence of theory is that it attempts to explain a wide variety of empirical phemomena in a parsimonious way.

Theory, action. This is an analysis of *action* which begins with the individual actor. It proceeds in terms of individual actors in typical situations by identifying actors' goals, expectations and *values*; the means of achieving these goals; actors' interpretation of the situation and other elements. Action theory as applied to the analysis of organisations is described on pages 173–175.

Theory, functionalist. A major sociological perspective which emphasises the interdependence of various elements of societies. Functionalism accounts for a social activity by refering to its consequences for the operation of some other social activity, institution, or society as a whole. Functionalism is described on pages 26–32.

Theory, labelling. This theoretical perspective considers sociological explanations of deviance which treats deviance, not as a product of individual psychology or genetic constitutions, but of *social control*. Two important aspects of labelling theory are *primary deviance* and *secondary deviance*. Labelling theory is discussed on pages 193–195.

Theory, middle-range. A term coined by Merton who regarded useful sociological theory as lying between minor working hypotheses and major conceptual schemas.

Theory, systems. In organisational theory a *functionalist* perspective which emphasises explanations of behaviour in terms of the interaction of systems attempting to satisfy their organisational goals.

Trajectory. This term refers to the curve described for an object moving under the action of given forces. In sociology it is used to describe the course and time-scale of events associated with phenomena like dying and pain.

Typification. A major concept in phenomenological sociology used to denote that the great bulk of all knowledge in our life world is typified. That is, it refers not to the individual or unique qualities of things or persons but to their typical features. Typification is the process by which people typify the world about them.

Values. Values are ideas that people hold to be right or wrong. In *functionalist theory*, values are accepted as statements to which each group member assents and is committed and which provide a standard for judging specific acts and goals.

Subject index

Author index